THE CENTURY PSYCHOLOGY SERIES
Richard M. Elliott, *Editor*

Theories of Learning

THE CENTURY PSYCHOLOGY SERIES

EDITED BY

RICHARD M. ELLIOTT, Ph.D., *University of Minnesota*

Theories of Learning

by

ERNEST R. HILGARD
Stanford University

NEW YORK
APPLETON-CENTURY-CROFTS, INC.

Preface

Learning is a central topic within American psychology, and its problems have provided the occasion for hundreds of experimental studies. The science of learning remains in a state of flux, in part because we have not yet reached agreement upon the most appropriate concepts to use in stating our problems and in interpreting our data. This book represents an attempt to provide in one place an introduction to the major theories of learning which are current among psychologists doing research in this important field of study.

The aim is to see theory in relation to experiment. Each of the several theories is therefore illustrated by a selected topic within the field of experimentation. The topic chosen is in each case one actively studied by adherents to the theory. The theory can be judged both by its provocativeness in suggesting experiments, and by its success in dealing systematically with the data which emerge from such experiments.

No one author can be entirely judicious in the treatment of such a wide range of theories as are considered here. My biases have undoubtedly made themselves shown in places where I have thought the exposition to be matter-of-fact. I have approached the task with the desire to be friendly to each of the positions represented, on the assumption that each of them has been proposed by an intelligent and sincere person or group of persons, and that there must be something which each of them can teach us. I have tried not to let this desire to give each a fair hearing prevent pointing out such weaknesses as I have detected in each of the positions. The final chapter exposes my personal preferences, and may be used in part to interpret the blindnesses or excesses which appear in the earlier chapters.

The book has been improved through the careful reading of parts of the manuscript by Paul E. Meehl, Moncrieff H. Smith, Jr., Donald W. Taylor, and John T. Wilson, to whom I wish to express my indebtedness. A special obligation is owing to Richard M. Elliott, editor of the series, who encouraged the project and bettered the product in many ways. The mechanical task of preparing a book is shared by many hands. I wish to acknowledge the typing of Jayne McCracken, the draftsmanship of Ernest R. Wood, and the checking of each reference against the original source by Iris M. Stevenson.

Acknowledgment is made to the following publishers for permission to reproduce figures or quotations: D. Appleton-Century Company, Inc., Cambridge University Press, Columbia University Press, Thomas Y. Crowell Co., Harcourt, Brace & Co., Inc., Harper & Brothers, Henry Holt & Company, Kegan Paul, Trench, Trubner and Company, Longmans, Green & Company, McGraw-Hill Book Company, The Macmillan Company, National Society for the Study of Education, Rinehart & Company, Teachers College, Columbia University, John Wiley & Sons, Inc., Yale University Press. The publishers of the following journals have permitted similar reproductions: *American Journal of Psychology*, *Journal of Experimental Psychology*, *Journal of General Psychology*, *Journal of Psychology*, *Psychological Review*, *University of California Publications in Psychology*. The original source is cited in each case.

E. R. H.

Stanford, California

Contents

Theories of Learning

Chapter 1

THE NATURE OF LEARNING THEORIES

Learning so pervades human activity that any curiosity about the nature of man and his behavior leads sooner or later to inquiry about how his habits are formed, how his skills are acquired, how his preferences and tastes develop, how his knowledge is obtained and put to use. Equally important is how he becomes enslaved by prejudice and bigotry and other learnings which lead to trouble instead of to a satisfactory solution of his problems.

WHY STUDY LEARNING?

Learning is a fact of nature requiring explanation. Scientists are characterized by insatiable curiosity about natural phenomena. The facts of learning, like the facts of growth, reproduction, or heredity, are in need of explanation if we are to understand the organism's relationship to its environment. What happens when an earthworm learns to choose one arm rather than another of a T-maze? When a dog learns to salivate to a ringing bell? When a pigeon learns its way back to its home cage? When a man forgets?

Scientists are characterized also by a faith that answers to such questions can be found through the familiar methods of empirical observation and experimentation. Aroused curiosity, and confidence in possibility of answers to the questions asked, are sufficient occasions for much of the research on learning.

Learning is practically important. We are all learners, and nearly all of us are teachers. Teaching is not limited to schoolrooms. Parents teach their children, hunters teach their dogs, coaches teach athletes, skilled workers teach apprentices, sales managers teach salesmen, physicians teach their patients. The formal teaching agencies—schools and colleges—represent an enormous social investment. Any process which engages as many people for as many hours as teaching does surely deserves the most careful study in order to make the practices as effective and as efficient as possible. The understanding of learning is central to the problems of teaching and of training, in school and out.

Learning theory is crucial to psychologists' system-building. The study of learning does not belong exclusively to psychologists. Physiologists and bio-physicists have a legitimate interest in it; educators, animal trainers, and others faced by the practical problems of the control of learning often have their own approaches to these problems. But the field is one which belongs primarily to psychologists. One reason is historical. Psychology's claim to the field was staked in part by such pioneers as Ebbinghaus (1885),[1] Bryan and Harter (1897, 1899), and Thorndike (1898). Those who have followed in their footsteps have been primarily psychologists. Professional educators have welcomed educational psychology as a foundation science, so that studies in the psychology of learning have gone on concurrently in laboratories of general psychology and laboratories of educational psychology, with much interplay between the pure and applied fields. Under the circumstances, it is very natural for psychologists to feel that the study of learning belongs to them.

In addition to historical reasons, there is another basis on which to account for the psychologist's interest in learning. This is the centrality of the concept of learning in more general systems of psychological theory. A scientist, along with the desire to satisfy his curiosity about the facts of nature, has a predilection for ordering his facts into systems of laws and theories. He is interested not only in verified facts and relationships, but in neat and parsimonious ways of summarizing these facts. Psychologists with a penchant for systems find a theory of learning essential because so much of man's diverse behavior is the result of learning. If the rich diversity of behavior is to be understood in accordance with a few principles, it is evident that some of

---

[1] References cited can be found by author and date in the list at the end of the book.

these principles will have to do with the way in which learning comes about.

Many psychologists make explicit acknowledgment of the centrality of learning in their broader systems. Three examples may be cited.

In his definition of behavior as *molar* rather than as *molecular* (a distinction which lies at the very heart of his system), Tolman [2] lists docility ("teachableness") as the crowning characteristic of such behavior. All molar behavior exhibits docility. Hence learning becomes for Tolman an identifying character of that which he wishes to include as behavior.

Guthrie makes of learning the mark of mind. As he puts it:

The ability to learn, that is, to respond differently to a situation because of past response to the situation, is what distinguishes those living creatures which common sense endows with minds. This is the practical descriptive use of the term "mind." [3]

Hull (1943*a*) in introducing his theory of the behavior sciences, finds it natural to devote the first volume of his series to learning theory. He scarcely distinguishes between a theory of learning and a theory of behavior, so important is learning in his conception of behavior.

Although not all psychologists give this same prominence to learning in their theories, the fact that others do makes it imperative for all to dispose of the problems of learning in one way or another. Hence the systematic aspects of learning theory have special importance to psychologists interested in more general theories.

The different reasons for studying learning lead to different emphases. If one is interested only in immediately practical outcomes, much of what appears to be hair-splitting may be ignored because alternative explanations often arrive at the same suggestions for practice. It is only if one understands the relationship of the theories to larger aspects of system-building that some of the verbal skirmishes can be understood.

[2] Tolman (1932*b*), pages 14-16.
[3] Guthrie (1935), page 3.

THE DEFINITION OF LEARNING

What learning includes. There are many activities which every one will agree count as illustrations of learning: acquiring a vocabulary, memorizing a poem, operating a typewriter. There are other activities, not quite as obviously learned, but which are easily included after a little reflection upon their nature. Among these are the developing of prejudices and preferences and other social attitudes and ideals, including the many skills involved in the social interplay with other persons. Finally there are a number of relatively useless and bizarre learnings, such as tics and mannerisms and autistic gestures.

Such a pointing to illustrations of learning serves very well as a first approximation to a definition. It is, in fact, extremely difficult to write an entirely satisfactory verbal definition. Improving with practice, profiting by experience, seem at first blush to cover the situation, but learning may be neither an improvement nor profitable in its consequences. To describe it as mere change with practice is to confuse learning with growth, fatigue and other such changes. The following definition may be offered provisionally:

Learning is the process by which an activity originates or is changed through training procedures (whether in the laboratory or in the natural environment) as distinguished from changes by factors not attributable to training.[4]

The definition is unsatisfactorily evasive, and partly tautological, in leaving training procedures undefined. The intended meaning can be conveyed only by further discussion.

Maturation versus training. Growth is learning's chief competitor as a modifier of behavior. If a behavior sequence matures through regular stages irrespective of intervening practice, the behavior is said to develop through maturation and not through learning. If the training procedures do not speed up or modify the behavior, such procedures are not causally important, and the changes do not classify as learning. Relatively pure cases like the swimming of tadpoles and the flying of birds can be attributed

---

[4] The definition is modified from an earlier one by Hilgard and Marquis (1940), page 347.

primarily to maturation. Many activities are not as clear-cut, but develop through a complex interplay of maturation and learning. A convenient illustration is the development of language in the child. The child does not learn to talk until old enough, but the language which it learns is that which it hears. In such cases it is an experimental problem to isolate the effects of maturation and of learning. The ambiguity in such cases is one of fact, not of definition.

Work versus training. When activities are repeated in rapid succession, there is often a loss in efficiency commonly attributed to fatigue. Such changes in performance are called work decrements in the experimental laboratory. The units of a work curve are like those of a learning curve: performance plotted against trials or repetitions. Hence the experimental arrangements in obtaining a work curve are essentially those of a training procedure, and at first sight, it appears to be a form of question-begging to define the processes involved by the results obtained. It would be question-begging, however, only if we were to define learning or fatigue as the change in performance. Actually *both* learning and fatigue are *inferences* from the performances, and it is permissible to make such inferences as the obtained performances require or suggest. Work curves tend to show decreasing proficiency with repetition and recovery with rests. Learning curves ordinarily show gains with repetitions and forgetting over rests. These typical differences between learning effects and work effects are evident enough, but the inferences from performance are made on somewhat more complex evidence. It is because of the complexity of these inferences that it is difficult to state a concise definition of learning which will conserve the learning inferences from performance while eliminating the work decrement inferences. The problem is logically the same as distinguishing changes due to maturation and to learning. But again the ambiguity is one of fact, not of definition.

Learning always must remain an inference from performance, and only confusion results if performance and learning are identified. A clear illustration is provided by performance under the influence of drugs or intoxicants. The fact that learned behavior fails when the organism is in such a state does not mean that forgetting has occurred. When the normal state has been restored, the performance may return to normal levels although there has been no intervening training.

Learning and the nervous system. Some definitions of learning avoid the problem of performance by defining learning as a change in the central nervous system. So long as this change in the nervous system remains, temporary changes in state, such as those in fatigue and intoxication, affect performance but not learning. This definition asserts that learning is an inference, but it goes on to make a particular sort of inference about the rôle of the nervous system in learning. In view of the lack of knowledge of what actually does take place inside the organism when learning occurs, it is preferable not to include hypothetical neural processes in the definition of learning. We know that learning takes place. We should therefore be able to define what we are talking about without reference to any speculation whatever. This position does not deny that what we are calling learning may be a function of nervous tissue. It asserts only that it is not necessary to know anything about the neural correlates of learning in order to know that learning occurs.

Learning, problem-solving, and reasoning. After you have learned, there are many things which you are able to do. If you can add and subtract, you can solve many novel problems without learning anything new. Where the solution of problems is relatively mechanical (as in addition and subtraction), the problem may be thought of as merely the exercise or utilization of a learned bit of behavior. When, however, there is greater novelty, more putting of things into relationship, as in reasoning or inventiveness, the process is interesting in its own light, and is not to be described simply as the running off of old habits.

The question has been raised, especially by Maier (1931*a*), as to the appropriateness of including processes like reasoning within the same classification as other kinds of learning. My preference is for including them. Leaving them in does not prejudge their explanation. There may be new factors not found in simpler learning, but there is no assurance that all other kinds of learning follow the same principles. Leaving the doubtful processes in simply asserts that a complete theory of learning must have something to say about reasoning, creative imagination, and inventiveness, in addition to what may be said about memorizing and retaining or about the acquisition of skill.

Definition not a major source of disagreement between theories. While it is extremely difficult to formulate a satisfactory definition of learning so as to include all the activities and processes which we wish to include and eliminate all those which we wish to exclude, the difficulty does not prove to be embarrassing because it is not a source of controversy as between theories. The controversy is over fact and interpretation, not over definition. There are occasional confusions over definition, but such confusions may usually be resolved by resort to pointing, to denotation. For the most part it is satisfactory to continue to mean by learning that which conforms to the usual socially accepted meaning which is part of our common heritage. Where distinctions have to be made with greater precision, they can be made through carefully specified types of inference from experimental situations.

SOME TYPICAL PROBLEMS CONFRONTING LEARNING THEORIES

The preferences of the theorist often lead him to concentrate upon one kind of learning situation to the neglect of the others. His theory is then appropriate to this situation, but becomes somewhat strained in relation to other problems of learning. A comprehensive learning theory ought to answer the questions which an intelligent non-psychologist might ask about the sorts of learning which are met in everyday life. A few such questions will be listed here, and then used later in appraising the theories which different writers present.

1. *What are the limits of learning?* Here is raised the question of the capacity to learn, of individual differences among learners of the same species and of unlike species. There are questions not only of persistent differences in capacity, but of change in capacity with age. Who can learn what? Are the limits set at birth? Do people get more or less alike with practice? These are the sorts of questions which it is natural to raise.

2. *What is the rôle of practice in learning?* The old adage that practice makes perfect has considerable racial wisdom behind it.

Surely one learns to roller skate or to play the piano only by engaging in the activity. But what do we know about practice in detail? Does improvement depend directly on the amount of repetition? If not, what are its conditions? What are the most favorable circumstances of practice? Can repetitive drill be harmful as well as helpful to the learner?

3. *How important are reward, punishment, or other motives in learning?* Everybody knows in a general way that learning can be controlled by rewards and punishments, and that it is easier to learn something which is interesting than something which is dull. But are the consequences of rewards and punishments equal and opposite? Is there a difference between intrinsic and extrinsic motives in their effect upon learning? How do goals and purposes affect the process?

4. *What is the place of understanding and insight?* Some things are learned more readily if we know what we are about. We are better off as travelers if we can understand a time-table or a road map. We are helpless with differential equations unless we understand the symbols and the rules for their manipulation. But we can form vowels satisfactorily without knowing how we place our tongues, and we can read without being aware of our eye movements. Some things we appear to acquire blindly and automatically; some things we struggle hard to understand, and can finally master only as we understand them. Is learning in one case different from what it is in the other?

5. *Does learning one thing help you learn something else?* This is the problem of formal discipline, as it used to be called, or of transfer of training, to use a more familiar contemporary designation. Some transfer of training must occur or there would be no use in developing a foundation for later learning. Nobody denies that it is easier to build a vocabulary in a language after you have a start in it, or that higher mathematics profits from mastery of basic concepts. The question is really one of how much transfer takes place and what its nature is.

6. *What happens when we remember and when we forget?* The ordinary facts of memory are mysterious enough, but in addition to familiar remembering and forgetting our memories may play peculiar tricks on us. Some things we wish to remember are forgotten; some things we would be willing to forget

continue to plague us. In cases of amnesia there are often gaps in memory, with earlier and later events remembered. Then there are the distortions of memory, in which we remember what did not happen, as is so strikingly demonstrated in testimony experiments. What is taking place? What control have we over the processes involved?

These six questions will serve as useful ones to ask of each of the major theories. They suffice to illustrate the kinds of questions which give rise to theories of learning.

BASIC ISSUES ON WHICH THE MAJOR THEORIES DIVIDE

In the chapters which follow there will be paraded a great many theories. Lest the array of theories be too confusing, they have been grouped into two main families.

The two main theories may be designated *association* theories, on the one hand, and *field* theories on the other. Any naming in this way does some violence to the individual theories, but nevertheless the typical American theories of functionalism, connectionism, and behaviorism have a common underlying logic which permits them to be grouped together, and the other theories, stemming chiefly from gestalt psychology, have in turn a contrasting common ground. The theories here classified as association theories have been labelled *reflex arc* theories [5] and *stimulus-response* theories.[6] The field theories group together various varieties of *gestalt, neo-gestalt, organismic,* or *sign-significate* theories.

The distinctions between the families are not always sharp, and there are agreements and disagreements which cut across lines. That is, on some specific issues it would be possible to find association psychologists on opposite sides of the fence, paralleled by field psychologists divided on the same issue. But the total picture does not present such confusion. Although association psychologists do not comprise a single harmonious family, still any one adherent to that position tends to offer explanations more like those of another than like the explanations of any one

[5] Tolman (1934).
[6] Spence (1942*b*).

in the field group. Correspondingly, the members of the field psychology family have in common their opposition to associationist conceptions. It is important to understand this basic cleavage, because there are profound differences in outlook, despite efforts of eclectics and mediators to harmonize the opposing camps.

The differences in systematic outlook may be summarized around five issues: environmentalism-nativism, the part-whole problem, emphasis upon reaction or cognition, the selected physical model, and the problem of historical versus contemporary explanation. These are differences not confined to learning theory, but they lie behind some of the cleavages reflected in learning theory. At the outset it should be stressed that the differences are matters of preference in the interpretation of a much wider range of data than those of learning. They are preferences in the interpretation of natural phenomena in general. Again, it is not that one of the contrasting preferences is exclusively right and the other exclusively wrong. Rather, each group believes that its point of view is scientifically the more fruitful.

1. *Environmentalism versus nativism.* The organism is born with sense organs, muscles and glands, and integrating structures. How its muscles and bones and sense organs and nervous elements function is closely related to their structure. But how they function is rapidly modified by learning. Because the evidence is often somewhat ambiguous, there is room for two interpretations of behavior, one which leans toward natural endowment as explanatory of behavior possibilities, and the other which attributes behavioral outcomes largely to learning.

The preference of associationists past and present has always been for environmentalism, that is, for attributing as much as possible to learning. In the field of perception, for example, the associationist makes much of Stratton's (1896) experiment in which, with experience, he became accustomed to the world as viewed through reversing lenses. The topsy-turvy world came to look all right and to provide cues for ready action. Hence the time-honored question as to how we could see the world right-side up when it is upside down on our retinas is solved by saying that we learn to use what visual cues we have to order our experiences of external reality. Gestalt psychologists (who may be taken as representative of field psychologists for this comparison) have a preference for nativism, in the sense that they account for the interaction of organism and environment largely in terms of the way in which the organism is made. In perception, for example, it is argued that seen motion, third dimension, and other such features attributed by associationists to learning are instead functions of contemporary arrangements, independent of prior experience.[7]

It would be false to carry this distinction to extremes, for associations do not usually accept the extreme environmentalism of a Watson (1925), nor do field psychologists go along with instinct psychologies like McDougall's (1923). However, the preferences are found to hold in intermediate and ambiguous cases, when associationists give "the benefit of the doubt" to learning, gestalt psychologists to the nature of the organism as it interacts dynamically with the environment. These preferences are sufficiently strong to show themselves repeatedly in the controversial writings between association and gestalt psychologists.

2. *The nature of wholes and of parts.* Parts may be thought of as the substances out of which wholes are made. Houses are made of bricks and wood and plaster (or their modern equivalents in glass, metal, and plastics). The whole is composed of all its parts so conceived—no more, no less. Alternatively, a whole may be thought of as a unique pattern or organization of the parts, in which case the whole has properties beyond those of its parts, or is "more" than its parts. Thus a house has an architectural unity which is "more" than the materials of which it is composed. These alternatives—considering wholes according to their composition or according to their organization—represent a second difference in preference between association and field theories.

Association theories tend to consider wholes in terms of their composition. Complex habits are combinations of simpler habits. Complicated skills involve many "bonds" or "conditioned responses." Habit tendencies interact algebraically, so that several tendencies acting at once lead to greater or less vigor of response, depending upon the strengths and the signs of the tendencies. (Some tendencies have negative signs relative to others, that is,

[7] Koffka (1930).

they are in conflict or inhibit each other.) Transfer of training, in one form of association theory, depends upon identical elements in the old and new learning situations. A comparison according to common elements is obviously a comparison according to composition. This preference for describing the whole according to its parts is referred to by critics of association theories as a form of *atomism*, said to be borrowed by associationism from nineteenth century physical science.

Field psychologies have as their most distinctive emphasis the primacy which they give to wholeness characters. That the whole is more than the sum of its parts represents to the field psychologist a basic viewpoint toward nature. Thus the standard illustration of a gestalt, that a melody is more than the tones and intervals of which it is composed, is taken to hold in learning also. Just as a melody is transposable, so something learned on one occasion may by transposition aid in the solution of a new problem. Solving a problem, while having some relationship to the solving of earlier problems, does not consist in the automatic running off of prior habits; even though prior habits may be discovered in the steps toward solution, the attack on the problem has individuality and novelty not describable by the habit components which can be found in it. The wholeness properties must not be lost by a faulty analysis. The field psychologist reverses the associationist approach: the wholes are not to be explained by the parts of which they are composed, but the parts are to be understood as differentiated out from a whole which has logical priority to them.

3. *Reaction and cognition.* The organism interacts with its environment by making sensory discriminations and by engaging in manipulatory, locomotor, and other energy interchanges with it. Some of the organism's interactions are covert, that is, not open to direct observation. Though quiet, the organism may be thinking. Because of the range of activities of interest to the psychologist, some psychologists prefer to lay emphasis on one segment of the organism's conduct, while others choose to emphasize other segments or aspects of its activity. Again there are family resemblances among contemporary associationists which differ from those among contemporary field psychologists.

The preference of the contemporary association theorist for a reaction psychology (laying emphasis upon movements) as over against a cognitive psychology (emphasizing perception-like and idea-like processes) is in part an aftermath of an earlier quarrel over the validity of introspection as a method in psychology. Most of the present day associationists (though not all of them) have been influenced by behaviorism, and share with the behaviorist an abhorrence of the subjective. Hence they prefer to speak of discriminatory reactions rather than of perceptions, avoiding the subjective or introspective connotations of the word perception. Thought processes tend to be interpreted according to their substantive basis in inner speech or other movements. A second root of the contemporary associationist's preference for a reaction-psychology is relatively independent of objections to subjectivity or to cognitive processes as such. It is based on what to the associationist appear to be the facts of the case so far as learning is concerned. That interpretation, stemming from Thorndike and supported by Pavlov and conditioned reflex theory, is that there is in fact a directness of connection between situations and the responses to them, with a minimum of mediation by ideas or idea-surrogates. It is a curious turn of history that the legatees of the doctrine of association of ideas should be the ones with the least use for ideational processes.

The field theorist, like the associationist, does not like to be considered a subjectivist. But unlike the reaction-psychologist he does not have the behaviorist's fear of contamination with subjectivity. He is likely to accept a form of introspection called *phenomenological* as contrasted with the introspections of trained observers. It is phenomenological observation which is used in the description of the difference in appearance between shadows and the surfaces on which they lie, which is used in experiments on seen movement, on the relative constancy of size of familiar objects seen at a distance, and so on. The field psychologist finds such observation important because of the prevalence in perception of organization, of figure-ground, of contours, and so on. While such observations could be translated into the discriminatory responses of reaction psychologists, the field psychologist is likely to believe that something is lost in this translation. Hence even in animal experimentation, in which cognitive processes are not observed, they are inferred by the field psychologist from the observable behavior. It is possible to prefer and to defend the preference for a cognitive psychology, even when all the data are behavioral. On the issue of fact in learning situations, the field theorist lies opposed to the associationist. It is his interpretation of learning experiments that a great deal of what might be called ideation goes on. The word *insight* is one which the gestalt psychologists brought prominently into the literature of learning. For most field psychologists something like insightful learning, be it called learning with understanding or learning under cognitive control, is the characteristic form of learning.

In the distinction between a reaction psychology and a cognitive psychology we have then a choice based both upon a preference as to the appropriate concepts to be used in a scientific psychology, and upon a preferred interpretation of what actually occurs in experiments. The former preference can persist, however experiments turn out. The latter preference, based on what is the case, is subject to change by experiments. If ideational processes are indeed necessary to explain what happens in experiments, the associationist can accept them in his reaction-psychology, although he will prefer to substitute for ideas some movement counterpart of them.

4. *Mechanism versus dynamic equilibrium.* Scientists believe the behavior of organisms to be lawful, at least within limits set by statistical approximations. In favoring some sort of cause-and-effect sequences, psychologists act like any other scientists. There is, however, a range of choice in the selection of the physical model after which we seek to design the laws to be used in psychological explanations. One physical model is provided by machines with rigid parts—with levers, pulleys, gears, motors—machines like typewriters or cash registers. When a key is pushed, the consequence is definitely predictable. The models may vary enormously in complexity, including automatic telephone switchboards and computing bomb-sights, but the principle is the same. A different model is provided by whirlpools, candle flames, and soap bubbles, in which the parts are related to the whole in a less rigid manner. You can scoop a bucketful of water out of a whirlpool without changing it. The whirlpool, candle flame, and soap bubble are illustrations of dynamic equilibria, just as physical

as the machines mentioned earlier, yet suggesting quite different analogies.

The preference of the associationist is for the machine model. The uses made of bonds, reflexes, and other isolatable activities which can be integrated into total habit systems more nearly resemble the model of the machine than of the whirlpool. Like his preference for environmentalism, it is a relative preference only, and the associationist is not bound by a strictly rigid model. Pavlov (1927), in spite of his essentially machine-like conception of conditioned reflexes, had doctrines of cortical action expressed by terms like irradiation and concentration which are not covered by the machine analogy. The same may be said of other associationist writers.

There is no ambiguity about the preference of the field psychologist. He is definitely on the side of the models of dynamic equilibria. Living things, unlike machines, are constantly interchanging their substance with the environment; they remain "the same" only because of a patterning or organization which persists in the midst of change. A single red corpuscle in the blood, as a carrier of oxygen, undergoes rapid change as it courses through the blood vessels. Its hemoglobin remains the "same" not because its molecules are the same after a few hours, but because it has maintained its organization as a separable something throughout the period of observation. There is no contradiction between treating the hemoglobin as so much chemical substance or treating it as a system in equilibrium. But there is a difference in point of view. By adopting the model of dynamic equilibria, the field psychologists warn against any effort to comprehend the totality of behavior in terms of component parts. The whole must always be viewed as a system, to which the parts are subordinate.

5. *Historical versus contemporary causation.* The decision to account for present behavior by its past history, or to explain it according to present circumstances, is not a decision forced by nature. Both approaches are possible; we need not even think that one is, in itself, better science than the other.

Consider a physical analogy. The storage battery fails in your car and the repairman wishes to make a diagnosis. He may take the historical approach. How old is the battery? How many miles have you driven it? Have you done much cold-weather starting, much night driving? Have you had trouble before? On the basis of such evidence he may decide, wisely, that it is time for a new battery. Or he may take the non-historical approach, considering the problem only in its contemporary aspects. He may examine the battery, test it, and decide solely in terms of its present operation whether or not it is worth retaining. Both methods are possible; often they would be used jointly. The historical approach might be more useful if it were a question of the condition of the plates which were not open to inspection. To use the analogy another way, suppose that the battery is in good condition and is now charged. Does it matter whether it was charged during a two weeks' trip you took into the country or whether it was charged in the garage? It does not matter, provided the battery is in the same present condition.

Confronted with a choice between historical and non-historical causation in the formulation of learning theory, the answer of the associationist is clear. He says that in order to account for the present you have to look to the past. What we do now is to act according to our repertory of habits built up in previous experience.

The field theorists believe it more profitable to be concerned with the present. They do not deny the influence of the past, any more than they would deny that a battery could be charged by a ride through the country. Of course you speak English now because you learned English in the past. From a scientific point of view, however, they believe it to be better to study you as the English-speaking person you now are than to concern themselves with what you did as you learned English. Whether or not one agrees with the field theorist, his position is a clear one and defensible as a possible one.

How the difference in preference expresses itself may be illustrated by the manner in which problem-solving is treated. The associationist finds in the solution of a novel problem that the learner assembles his experiences from the past appropriate to the new problem, responding either according to elements common to old and the new situations, or according to aspects of the new situation which are similar to old situations. The field psychologist points out, however, that even with appropriate past experience the organism may not solve the problem if it is presented one way and may solve it if it is presented in another way. Hence the contemporary structuring of the field is said to be more important than previous experience.

These five differences (environmentalism-nativism, part-whole problem, reaction-cognition, mechanism-dynamic equilibrium, and historical-contemporary causation) have been presented in an introductory way to make it clear that what seem to be diametrically opposed points of view may in fact turn out to be differences in preference, each being possible of clear statement, and to a point justifiable. The opposed cases are each made by intelligent men of good will. To what extent a reconciliation or synthesis can be achieved will be considered later.

THE PLAN OF THIS BOOK

The student of learning, conscientiously trying to understand learning phenomena and the laws regulating them, is likely to despair of finding a secure position if opposing points of view are presented as equally plausible, so that the choice between them is made arbitrary. He may fall into a vapid eclecticism, with the general formula, "There's much to be said on all sides."

This is not a necessary outcome of a serious attempt to understand opposing points of view. Science ought to be systematic, not eclectic, but a premature systematic position is likely to be dogmatic and bigoted just as an enduring eclecticism is likely to be superficial and opportunistic. It is possible to have systematization of knowledge as the goal without permitting the desire for system to blind the seeker after it to the truths unearthed by those with views unlike his own.

Throughout the chapters that follow, in presenting one after the other a variety of systematic positions, with illustrative experiments testing their assertions, the effort is made to show that there is something to be learned from each of them. Each has discovered phenomena which move us forward in our knowledge about learning. At the same time, no one has succeeded in providing a system invulnerable to criticism. The construction of a fully satisfactory theory of learning is likely to remain for a long time an uncompleted task.

SUPPLEMENTARY READINGS

GENERAL SOURCES ON THE PSYCHOLOGY OF LEARNING

Hilgard, E. R., and Marquis, D. D. (1940) *Conditioning and learning.*

McGeoch, J. A. (1942) *The psychology of human learning.*

Woodworth, R. S. (1938) *Experimental psychology.* (Chapters 1-9, 29-30.)

THEORETICAL BACKGROUND AND CONTRASTING POINTS OF VIEW TOWARD LEARNING

Heidbreder, E. (1933) *Seven psychologies.*

McConnell, T. R., and others (1942) *The psychology of learning.* *Natl. Soc. Stud. Educ.*, 41st Yearbook, Part II.

Woodworth, R. S. (1931) *Contemporary schools of psychology.*

Chapter 2

THORNDIKE'S CONNECTIONISM

For nearly half a century one learning theory has dominated all others in America, despite numerous attacks upon it and the rise of its many rivals. That influential one is the theory of Edward L. Thorndike, first announced in his *Animal Intelligence* (1898). Its pre-eminence has been aptly expressed by Tolman:

The psychology of animal learning—not to mention that of child learning—has been and still is primarily a matter of agreeing or disagreeing with Thorndike, or trying in minor ways to improve upon him. Gestalt psychologists, conditioned-reflex psychologists, sign-gestalt psychologists—all of us here in America seem to have taken Thorndike, overtly or covertly, as our starting point.[1]

The basis of learning accepted by Thorndike in his earliest writings is association between sense impressions and impulses to action. The association came to be known as a "bond" or a "connection." Because it is these bonds or connections which become strengthened or weakened in the making and breaking of habits, Thorndike's system has sometimes been called a "bond" psychology or simply "connectionism."

CONNECTIONISM BEFORE 1930

There were few changes in Thorndike's theory between 1898 and 1930. During these years Thorndike devoted himself largely to applications of his established theory to problems of educational and social importance. Because of the stability of the con-

[1] Tolman (1938a), page 11.

cepts during these years it is possible to select any one of Thorndike's many publications to serve as a guide to his theory. The major work, from which most of the quotations in what follows have been taken, is the three-volume *Educational Psychology* (1913-1914), which represents the system at the height of its popularity.

The most characteristic form of learning of both lower animals and man is identified by Thorndike as trial-and-error learning, or, as he preferred to call it later, learning by selecting and connecting. The typical experiment is one in which the learner is confronted by a problematic situation in which he has to reach a goal such as escape from a problem-box or attainment of food. He does this by selecting the appropriate response from a number of possible responses. A trial is defined by the length of time (or number of errors) involved in a single reaching of the goal. Thorndike's earliest experiments were of this kind, done chiefly with cats, although some experiments with dogs, fish, and monkeys were included.[2] The typical experiment is that of a hungry cat confined in a box with a concealed mechanism operated by a latch. If the cat correctly manipulates the latch, the door opens, and the cat gains access to the food outside. The first trials are characterized by a great amount of clawing, biting, and dashing about before the latch is moved. The score, as measured in time, is high. On succeeding trials the time scores get lower, but slowly and irregularly. It is this gradualness which suggests that the cat does not really "catch on" to the manner of escape, but learns it instead by the stamping in of correct responses and the stamping out of incorrect ones.

Experiments like this have become so commonplace that the importance of their introduction by Thorndike is easily overlooked. By contrast with the other laboratory situations in which learning was studied, the problem-box situation brought to the fore the problems of motivation, of rewards and of punishments. The typical laboratory experiment on learning before Thorndike was either the memorization-retention experiment of Ebbinghaus or the skill experiment exemplified by the Bryan and Harter studies of learning telegraphy. In both cases

[2] Thorndike (1898) (1911).

motivation remains in the background as one of the contextual features, along with learning capacity and other factors not entering as experimental variables. In his "law of effect" Thorndike brought motivation into the foreground. Trials are defined not by a repetition of a list (Ebbinghaus) or by so many minutes of practice (Bryan and Harter) but by the performance prior to successful goal attainment.

Thorndike saw that in his law of effect he had added an important supplement to the familiar law of habit formation through repetition:

> But practice without zeal—with equal comfort at success and failure —does *not* make perfect, and the nervous system grows *away* from the modes in which it is *exercised with resulting discomfort*. When the law of effect is omitted—when habit-formation is reduced to the supposed effect of mere repetition—two results are almost certain. By the resulting theory, little in human behavior can be explained by the law of habit; and by the resulting practice, unproductive or extremely wasteful forms of drill are encouraged.[3]

The interest in rewards and punishments which grew out of his experiments with animals continued naturally enough as he turned his attention to learning as it occurs in schools. There the arguments over punishment, promotion, school marks and other incentive devices were rife, even though academic psychologists had not yet awakened to the centrality of motivational concepts.

Thorndike's experiments on animals had a very profound influence upon his thinking about human learning. He became convinced, contrary to the then popular beliefs, that animal behavior was little mediated by ideas. Responses were said to be made directly to the situation as sensed. While he did not go so far as to deny ideation among animals, he was convinced that the great bulk of their learning could be explained by the direct binding of acts to situations, unmediated by ideas. A comparison of the learning curves of human subjects with those of animals led him to believe that the same essentially mechanical phenomena disclosed by animal learning are the fundamentals of human learning also. Although always aware of the greater subtlety and

[3] Thorndike (1913*b*), page 22.

range of human learning, he showed a strong preference for understanding more complex human learning in terms of the simpler, and for identifying the simpler forms of human learning with that of animals.

Both theory and practice need emphatic and frequent reminders that man's learning is fundamentally the action of the laws of readiness, exercise, and effect. He is first of all an associative mechanism working to avoid what disturbs the life-processes of the neurones. If we begin by fabricating imaginary powers and faculties, or if we avoid thought by loose and empty terms, or if we stay lost in wonder at the extraordinary versatility and inventiveness of the higher forms of learning, we shall never understand man's progress or control his education.[4]

The systematic position is best understood through the three laws to which he refers: readiness, exercise, and effect. It is in accordance with these laws that animal and human learning takes place.

The law of readiness. The law of readiness is an accessory principle which describes a physiological substratum for the law of effect. It states the circumstances under which man tends to be satisfied or annoyed, to welcome or to reject. There are three such circumstances: [5]

1. When a conduction unit is ready to conduct, conduction by it is satisfying, nothing being done to alter its action.

2. For a conduction unit ready to conduct not to conduct is annoying, and provokes whatever response nature provides in connection with that particular annoying lack.

3. When a conduction unit unready for conduction is forced to conduct, conduction by it is annoying.

Although "conduction units" were referred to in his earlier writings as though he were talking about actual neurones, Thorndike did not, in fact, pay much attention to neuroanatomical details. He talked about neurones to be clear that he was talking about direct impulses to action, and not about "consciousness" or "ideas." It must be remembered that his system antedated behaviorism, even though its emphasis was definitely toward an objective account of behavior. The physiological language was

[4] Thorndike (1913b), page 23.
[5] The wording follows Thorndike (1913a), page 128.

the most available vocabulary for the objectivist prior to the rise of behaviorism. Actually Thorndike's "conduction units" have no precise physiological meaning. It would be difficult, for example, to understand how a physiological unit unready to conduct could be made to conduct.

If for "conduction unit" a term such as "action tendency" is substituted, the psychological meaning of Thorndike's law of readiness becomes clearer. When an action tendency is aroused through preparatory adjustments, sets, attitudes, and the like, fulfillment of the tendency in action is satisfying, non-fulfillment is annoying. Readiness thus means a preparation for action. Thorndike uses the illustrations of an animal running after its prey, getting ready all the while for jumping upon it and seizing it, and of the child seeing an attractive object at a distance getting ready to approach it, seize it, and manipulate it. He says that it is the neurones which prepare prophetically for later actions in the sequence. This somewhat objectionable manner of describing the situation need not detract from the reality of the psychological observation that satisfaction and frustration depend upon what the organism is prepared to do.

There is another kind of readiness familiar to educators. This is illustrated by the use of such a term as "reading readiness" to refer to the child's reaching a maturity level appropriate to the beginning of reading. Thorndike did not use his law of readiness in this way, and it would be historically inaccurate to construe his law of readiness as an anticipation of maturational readiness. There is, of course, a logical relationship between the two kinds of readiness, because interests and motives mature along with capacities. But Thorndike's readiness was a law of preparatory adjustment, not a law about growth.

The earlier law of exercise. The law of exercise refers to the strengthening of connections with practice (Law of Use) and to the weakening of connections or forgetting when practice is discontinued (Law of Disuse). Strengthening is defined by the increase in probability that the response will be made when the situation recurs. This probability may be either a greater probability of occurrence if the situation is repeated immediately, or an equal probability of immediate occurrence persisting longer in time. That is, a stronger connection is in a favored competitive position with other habits, either at the time of its strengthening or if tested after there has been opportunity for forgetting.

The definition of strength by probability of occurrence [6] has a very contemporary ring. It is acceptable in itself to those who might go on to reject the structural basis assigned by Thorndike to changes in strength of connections. Although changes were said to occur in neurones and synapses, even in his earlier writings the precise properties attributed to neurones were cautiously stated and not actually essential to the theory.

The kinds of phenomena falling under the law of exercise are chiefly those of repetitive habits, as in rote memorizing or the acquiring of muscular skills. Learning curves in which performance is plotted against trials represent the quantification of the law of use; forgetting curves give quantitative details for the law of disuse. During the period under discussion, Thorndike accepted uncritically the prevailing principle of learning by doing, even though he had criticized the use of the principle independent of the law of effect. He later altered his position and greatly reduced the emphasis upon the law of exercise.

The earlier law of effect. The law of effect refers to the strengthening or weakening of a connection as a result of its consequences. When a modifiable connection is made and is accompanied by or followed by a satisfying state of affairs, the strength of the connection is increased; if the connection is made and followed by an annoying state of affairs, its strength is decreased.

Two chief objections have been made to the law of effect by its critics. At the height of behaviorism it was objected that satisfaction and annoyance were subjective terms, inappropriate for use in describing animal behavior. But Thorndike was in reality ahead of his critics, for he had early stated what he meant by such states of affairs in what would today be called operational terms:

> By a satisfying state of affairs is meant one which the animal does nothing to avoid, often doing things which maintain or renew it. By an annoying state of affairs is meant one which the animal does nothing to preserve, often doing things which put an end to it.[7]

[6] Thorndike (1913b), page 2.
[7] Thorndike (1913b), page 2.

These definitions are not circular, so far as the law of effect is concerned. That is, the states of affairs characterized as satisfying and as annoying are specified independently of their influence upon modifiable connections. The law of effect then states what may be expected to happen to preceding modifiable connections which are followed by such specified states. The objection that Thorndike was lacking in objectivity in the statement of the law of effect is not a valid one.

The second objection was that the backward effect of a state of affairs on something now past in time is not conceivable. The past is gone, effects can be felt only in the present, or perhaps revealed in the future. The criticism, like the first, is a faulty one. The effect is revealed in the probability of occurrence of the response when the situation next occurs; whether or not such an effect occurs is a matter of observation and experiment, not something to be denied on a priori grounds. In fairness to his critics, it must be said that Thorndike's insistence on a backward influence upon neurones encouraged such objections to the law of effect. Some of his statements were indeed objectionable, but the objectionable statements never did express the essence of the law of effect, which is essentially an empirical matter.

Translated into more familiar words, Thorndike is saying in this law that rewards or successes further the learning of the rewarded behavior, while punishments or failures reduce the tendency to repeat the behavior leading to punishment, failure, or annoyance. So much would be merely a reassertion of common observations. But he went further and insisted that the action of consequences is direct, and need not be mediated by ideas. In this insistence his law of effect anticipates the reinforcement principle adopted in many conditioned response theories. The later changes in theory reduced the importance of annoyers relative to satisfiers, and added some new phenomena, but the central importance of a modified law of effect persists in Thorndike's most recent statements of his position.

Subordinate laws. The major laws of readiness, exercise, and effect were said to have five subsidiary laws applicable to both animal and human learning.[8] Among these occurs one, associative shifting, which is so similar to the non-reinforcement varie-

[8] Thorndike (1913b), pages 23-31.

ties of conditioned response theories that it deserves special mention.

In a short account of Thorndike's views the impression may be given that Thorndike is a more systematic writer than he is. His "system," apart from a few persistent preferences, is a rather loose collection of rules and suggestions. What is called a "law" at any one time is a statement which at the time appeared to Thorndike to have some generality of application. No effort was made to retain internal coherence among the concepts used, or to establish any genuine relationship of coordination or subordination among the laws. The five "subordinate laws" to be discussed are principles which seemed to Thorndike somewhat less important than the major laws of readiness, exercise, and effect. They are not related to the major laws in any clear manner, and in later writings they have been occasionally omitted, occasionally revived.

1. *Multiple response.* The first of the five principles is that of multiple response or varied reaction. In order for a response to be rewarded, it must occur. In a problematic situation the learner tries one thing after another. When the appropriate behavior is stumbled upon, success follows, and learning is possible. Were the organism unable to vary its responses, the correct solution might never be elicited.

2. *Set or attitude.* The second principle is that learning is guided by a total attitude or "set" of the· organism. Responses are determined in part by enduring adjustments characteristic of individuals raised in a given culture. But they are also influenced by more momentary tendencies. The attitude or set determines not only what the person will do, but what will satisfy or annoy him. Thorndike says that a more ambitious golfer will be annoyed by shots which the more modest would cherish. This principle is related to a series of conceptions coming to prominence later in discussions of level of aspiration.

3. *Prepotency of elements.* The third principle states that the learner is able to react selectively to prepotent elements in the situation. That is, man can pick out the essential item and base his responses upon it, neglecting other adventitious features which might confuse a lower animal in a similar situation. This

ability to deal with the relevant parts of situations makes analytical and insightful learning possible.

4. *Response by analogy.* The fourth principle is that of assimilation, or response by analogy. How does man react to novel situations? He responds to a new situation as he would to some situation like it, or he responds to some element in the new situation to which he has a response in his repertory. Responses can always be explained by old acquisitions, together with original tendencies to respond; there is nothing mysterious about responses to novelty.

5. *Associative shifting.* The fifth of these subsidiary laws is called associative shifting. The fundamental notion is that if a response can be kept intact through a series of changes in the stimulating situation, it may finally be given to a totally new stimulus. The stimulating situation is changed first by addition, then by subtraction, until nothing from the original situation remains. Thorndike illustrates by the act of teaching a cat to stand up at command. First a bit of fish is dangled before the cat while you say, "Stand up." After enough trials, by proper arrangement, the fish may be omitted, and the oral signal will alone evoke the response. The most general statement of the principle of associative shifting is that we may "get any response of which a learner is capable associated with any situation to which he is sensitive." [9] This is obviously related to that type of conditioning in which the process is described as substituting a conditioned stimulus for an unconditioned one. Thorndike has noted the similarity, but believes the conditioned response to be a more specialized case under the broader principle of associative shifting. While in his earlier writings associative shifting was but the fifth of the subordinate laws, in later books it has been "promoted," becoming a kind of learning second to that by selecting and connecting.[10]

Controlling the learning situation. There is always some danger of misunderstanding a systematic writer's influence if attention is confined to the more abstract and generalized laws which he proposes, to the neglect of some of the accessory details which give both flavor and body to his teaching. Thorn-

[9] Thorndike (1913*b*), page 15.
[10] Thorndike (1935), pages 191-197.

dike as early as 1913 was giving much more attention to the dynamics of learning than a formal consideration of his laws suggests.

Within the framework of his primary laws, he saw three considerations which affected the teacher's problem in using them in the classroom.[11] These were ease of identification of the bonds to be formed or broken, ease of identification of the states of affairs which should satisfy or annoy, and ease of application of satisfaction and annoyance to the identified states of affairs. The teacher and the learner must know the characteristics of a good performance in order that practice may be appropriately arranged. Errors must be diagnosed so that they will not be repeated. When there is lack of clarity about what is being taught or learned, practice may be strengthening the wrong connections as well as the right ones. At the same time, needed connections may be weakened by disuse. It is especially hard to teach imagination, force, and beauty in literary expression because it is difficult to be specific about the conduct which should be made satisfying at the time it occurs. The importance of specificity runs throughout Thorndike's writings. As we shall see later, this is at once a source of strength in his system, and one of its points of vulnerability.

But Thorndike's advice is not limited to the application of his major laws. He refers also to a number of motivational features not readily deducible from the laws of readiness and effect. Five aids to improvement he lists as the interest series.[12] These he believes to be commonly accepted by educators:

1. Interest in the work
2. Interest in improvement
3. Significance
4. Problem-attitude
5. Attentiveness

To these five he added two more which he felt were open to some dispute. They were the absence of irrelevant emotion and the absence of worry. In his emphasis upon satisfiers and annoyers he is not talking about "crude emotional states," which he believes are to be avoided.

[11] Thorndike (1913b), pages 213-217.
[12] Thorndike (1913b), pages 217-226.

In the case of improvement in skill, the balance turns again toward freedom from all the crude emotional states and even from all the finer excitements, save the intrinsic satisfyingness of success and a firm repudiation of errors which can hardly be called exciting.[13]

Thus to his rather harsh and brittle doctrine of specificity of connections he adds informal considerations which do much to temper it. The active role of the learner, who comes to the learning situation with needs and problems which determine what will be satisfying to him, is recognized implicitly in the commentary on the laws, although it lacks explicit statement in the laws themselves. It is probably these accessory features which have commanded ardent support by Thorndike's followers, while it is the more abstract features which have been the focus of attack by those who have disagreed with him.

The identical elements theory of transfer. Schools are publicly supported in the hope that more general uses will be made of what is learned in school. To some extent all schooling is aimed at a kind of transfer beyond the school. Whether the proper way to achieve this end may turn out to be to teach more formal subject-matter, like mathematics and the classics, or to give more attention to practical subject-matter like manual training and social studies, the problem is a central one for educators.

Thorndike early interested himself in the problem. His theory began to take form in an experimental study done in collaboration with Woodworth [14] and was formally stated in his early *Educational Psychology* (1903). The theory proposes that transfer depends upon the presence of identical elements in the original learning and in the new learning which it facilitates. These may be identities of either substance or procedure. Thus the ability to speak and write well are important in all schoolroom classes and in many tasks of ordinary life. Hence mastery of these skills will serve in different pursuits, and transfer will be effected through what the different situations require in common. The substance of what is required in different situations may be unlike, but there may be procedures in common. The procedures of looking things up in such diverse sources as a dictionary, a

[13] Thorndike (1913b), pages 226-227.
[14] Thorndike and Woodworth (1901).

cookbook, and a chemist's handbook have much in common, despite the unlike contents of the three kinds of book. If an activity is learned more easily because another activity was learned first, it is only because the two activities overlap. Learning is always specific, never general: when it appears to be general, it is only because new situations have much of old situations in them.

Intelligence as measured by tests may be thought of as to some extent a measure of the transfer-capacity of an individual. That is, the test measures the ability to give right answers in relatively novel situations. It is logically sound that Thorndike's theory of intelligence is like his theory of transfer, a matter of specific connections. The more bonds the individual has which can be used, the more intelligent he is.

Thorndike's specificity doctrines of transfer and of intelligence have been highly influential, and have led to a great deal of experimental work. While the problems of the nature of and measurement of intelligence lie outside the scope of this volume, there will be occasion later to consider some of the alternative explanations of transfer.

During the stable period of Thorndike's system there were many changes in psychological climate, but these left him unruffled. The rise of behaviorism and the new importance attributed to the conditioned response affected him but little, because the new enthusiasts were talking a congenial language, even when they included him in their sweeping attacks on everything which preceded them. The attacks by the gestalt psychologists in the '20's were more telling, and he began later to meet some of their criticisms. But it was his own experiments which led him to come before the International Congress of Psychology in New Haven in September, 1929, with the statement, "I was wrong." He there announced two fundamental revisions in his laws of exercise and effect which became the basis for a number of publications dating from 1930.

CONNECTIONISM AFTER 1930

The revisions of his fundamental laws were reported by Thorndike in a number of journal articles and monographs with various collaborators, the main results being gathered in two large volumes under the titles *The fundamentals of learning* (1932*a*) and *The psychology of wants, interests, and attitudes* (1935). The law of exercise was practically renounced as a law of learning, only a trivial amount of strengthening of connections being left as a function of mere repetition. The law of effect remained only half true, the weakening effects of annoying consequences being renounced. For the two central laws there was substituted half the original law of effect.

Disproof of the law of exercise. The type of experiment used to disprove the law of exercise was that in which repetition went on under circumstances in which the law of effect could not be applicable. For example, repeated attempts to draw a line exactly 3 inches long while blind-folded did not lead to improvement, no matter how frequent the repetitions. Practice brings improvement only because it permits other factors to be effective; practice itself does nothing. Thorndike intended that his "repeal" of the law of exercise should be a safeguard against its misuse, not a denial of the importance of controlled practice. The laws of habit strengthening must be those of the conditions under which practice takes place; mere repetition of situations is not enough. If the person is informed each time after his attempt to draw a 3-inch line that his product is too long or too short, he will improve with repetition.[15]

The law of exercise was not, in fact, fully repealed. It is said that repetition of *situations* produces no change in strength of connections, but repetition of *connections* may produce a small advantage for that connection as against competing connections attached to the same situation. The strengthening is almost negligible; for all practical purposes, connections get strengthened by being rewarded, not by just occurring. In one of those curious and optimistically quantitative summaries which Thorndike occasionally makes, he concludes that a single occurrence followed by reward strengthens a connection about six times as much as it would be strengthened by merely occurring.[16]

The truncated law of effect. A number of experiments yielded

---

[15] Trowbridge and Cason (1932). There is indeed more regularizing of performance in his own experiments than Thorndike believed, according to recomputation of his data by Seashore and Bavelas (1941).

[16] Thorndike (1940), page 14.

data showing that the effects of reward and punishment were not equal and opposite, as had been implied in earlier statements of the effects of satisfiers and of annoyers. Instead, under conditions in which symmetrical action was possible, reward appeared to be much more powerful than punishment. This conclusion, if confirmed, is of immense social importance in such fields of application as education and criminology.

One of these experiments was done with chicks.[17] A simple maze gave the chick the choice of three pathways, one of which led to "freedom, food, and company"—that is, to an open compartment where there were other chicks eating. The wrong choices led to confinement for 30 seconds. Statistics were kept on the tendencies to return to the preceding choice if it had led to reward, and to avoid the preceding choice if it led to punishment. Thorndike interpreted his findings as follows: "The results of all comparisons by all methods tell the same story. Rewarding a connection always strengthened it substantially; punishing it weakened it little or not at all." [18]

The corresponding experiment with human subjects consists of a multiple-choice vocabulary test. For example, a Spanish word is given with five English words, one of which is its correct translation. A second and a third word follow, and so on through a list, each word with alternative translations arranged in the same manner. The subject guesses the word which is correct, underlines it, and then hears the experimenter say *Right* ("rewarded" response) or *Wrong* ("punished" response). How will he change his responses the next time through the list? As with the chicks, reward leads to repetition of the rewarded connection, but punishment does not lead to a weakening of the punished connection. In six experiments of this general sort, Thorndike concluded that the announcement of *Wrong* did not weaken connections enough to counterbalance the slight increase in strength gained from just occurring.[19]

Thorndike and his staff went on to collect a series of testimonials about the relative efficacy of rewards and punishments from published biographies and other sources, going back many years.

[17] Thorndike (1932*b*).
[18] Thorndike (1932*b*), page 58.
[19] Thorndike (1932*a*), page 288.

The almost universal evidence of the greater beneficial effect of reward than of punishment gives practical support to the findings of the experiments, which otherwise would be criticized as too far removed from actual life situations.[20]

There were some statistical difficulties in Thorndike's interpretations of his data which caused him to underestimate the significance of punishment. On the whole, however, he probably did a service through calling attention to the asymmetry of the effects of reward and of punishment in some situations.

As in the disproof of the law of exercise, the repeal of the principle of weakening by annoying after-effects is not absolute. It is only direct weakening which is denied. Punishments do, according to Thorndike, affect learning indirectly. Thorndike says that their indirect effect comes chiefly from leading the animal to do something in the presence of the annoyer which makes him less likely to repeat the original connection. But this is not necessarily the case.

An annoyer which is attached to a modifiable connection may cause the animal to feel fear or chagrin, jump back, run away, wince, cry, perform the same act as before but more vigorously, or whatever else is in his repertory as a response to that annoyer in that situation. But there is no evidence that it takes away strength from the physiological basis of the connection in any way comparable to the way in which a satisfying after-effect adds strength to it.[21]

Thorndike has been less successful in his attempts to explain the action of effect than in demonstrating that there are phenomena to which his principles apply. He distinguished between a direct *confirming influence* and the *informative influence* of rewards. Control of behavior according to the information supplied by its consequences implies mediation by ideas of the sort, "If I do this, I get fed, if I do that, I get slapped." Thorndike believes himself to have kept this kind of deliberation at a minimum in his experiments, so that what he has to explain is the direct confirmatory reaction which he says is responsible for the strengthening of responses through reward. This confirming reaction is vaguely described as an "unknown reaction of the neurones" which is aroused by the satisfier and strengthens the connection

[20] Thorndike (1935), pages 135-144; 248-255.
[21] Thorndike (1932a), pages 311-313.

upon which it impinges.[22] The confirming reaction is said to be independent of sensory pleasures, and independent of the intensity of the satisfier. It is highly selective, depending upon aroused drives or "overhead control in the brain." While such an account is far from satisfactory, it at least helps to show where Thorndike stands. He is against mediation by ideas, as an interpretation of effect according to information would imply. At the same time he recognizes the complexity of the reinforcement process, and is not committed to a simple hedonism. The law of effect is no longer a law of affect, as Hollingworth once named it.[23]

Belongingness. In addition to the revisions of the laws of exercise and effect, several new terms entered as Thorndike's system was revised. One of these, *belongingness,* by its recognition of an organizational principle foreign to the structure of Thorndike's theory of specificity and mechanical action, makes concessions to the gestalt psychologists.[24] According to this principle, a connection is more easily learned if the response belongs to the situation, and an after-effect does better if it belongs to the connection it strengthens. Thus a series of sentences may be read, each of the form "John is a butcher. Henry is a carpenter." The association John-butcher is a stronger one following such a reading than the association butcher-Henry, even though the latter connection is based on more nearly contiguous items. The reason is that a subject and predicate belong together in a way in which the end of one sentence and the beginning of another do not. The belongingness of a reward or punishment depends upon its appropriateness in satisfying an aroused motive or want in the learner, and in its logical or informative relationship to the activities rewarded or punished. Thus to be rewarded by having your thirst quenched when you lift a glass of cool water to your lips is reward with belonging. If the same series of movements led sporadically to an electric shock on your ankle, that would be punishment without belonging. While Thorndike states that after-effects are influential without either belongingness or rele-

---

[22] Thorndike (1933c).
[23] Hollingworth (1931).
[24] The point has been made by Brown and Feder (1934). See also Guthrie (1936b).

vance, he points out at the same time that they are more effective when they do belong and when they are relevant.[25]

While the principle of belongingness may be interpreted as something of a concession, the principle of polarity is emphasized as defying gestalt principles.[26] The principle of polarity is that connections act more easily in the direction in which they were formed than in the opposite direction. If you have learned a German-English vocabulary, it is easier to respond to the German word by its English equivalent than to the English word by its German equivalent. If a connection is thought of as a new whole, Thorndike contends, the polarity principle ought not be important. It ought then to be as easy to dissociate parts from the whole in one direction as in another.

Other new terms introduced, such as impressiveness, identifiability, availability, and mental systems, represent informal extensions of notions already latent in the earlier writings.

Discovery of the spread of effect. In 1933 a new kind of experimental evidence was offered in support of the law of effect, evidence described as the *spread of effect*.[27] The experiments purported to show that the influence of a rewarding state of affairs acts not only on the connection to which it belongs but on adjacent connections both before and after the rewarded connection, the effect diminishing with each step that the connection is removed from the rewarded one. The effect acts to strengthen even punished connections in the neighborhood of the rewarded one. The experiments lent support to the automatic and mechanical action of effect. A characteristic experiment was that in which the subject was asked to state a number from one to ten following the announcement of a stimulus word by the experimenter. These announcements by the experimenter (interpreted as "reward" and "punishment," respectively) have conformed either to a prearranged assignment of correct numbers to each word, or to some systematic pattern of "rights" or "wrongs." In either case, the assignment of numbers from the point of view of the subject is arbitrary, and the cue to repeat the number first assigned or to change it comes from what the experimenter says

[25] Thorndike (1935), pages 52-61.
[26] Thorndike (1932a), page 158.
[27] Thorndike (1933a) (1933b).

following each word. The lists are so long that the subject cannot recall on the second trial just what was done on the first one.

After the list was read a number of times in this manner, the responses of the subject were classified to find the number of times the response was repeated. Not only were the rewarded responses repeated more often than the others, but responses called wrong were repeated, if they occurred near to a response called right, beyond chance expectancy. To some extent the phenomena included in the spread of effect come nearest to a "discovery" in the whole of Thorndike's work. Because of the novelty of the phenomena and their systematic relevance, typical experiments in support of and critical of the spread of effect are reviewed below* as illustrative of Thorndike's influence upon experimentation in the field of learning.

EXPERIMENTS ON THE SPREAD OF EFFECT

The spread of effect is the most characteristic feature of contemporary connectionism. It illustrates at once both the relative potency of rewards and punishments and the semi-automatic manner in which effects act upon connections, whether or not they "belong." To the extent that the phenomena of the spread of effect stand upon firm ground, Thorndike's basic conceptions are buttressed against attacks by his critics.

Punishment more effective than Thorndike believed. Thorndike had already changed his mind about the effectiveness of annoyers in weakening connections before the spread of effect experiments were announced. He interpreted his results on the spread of effect as confirming his recently acquired belief in the relative ineffectiveness of punishments in weakening connections. The spread of effect is then, to him, a spread of positive effects, a gradient of reward. Reward is said to strengthen even neighboring punished connections.

In several of his experiments, Thorndike made a faulty assumption about the baseline of chance expectation. He assumed that one alternative in a series of multiple possibilities was as likely to occur as another. That is, if there were four choices, by chance each should occur 25 per cent of the time. If the opportunity is given to repeat the responses, the same one chosen last time should be chosen again in 25 per cent of the cases, if the tendency to respond has been neither strengthened nor weakened during the first occurrence. In practice this chance situation seldom occurs, for whatever predisposition leads to a preference for one of the choices the first time tends to favor that same choice the next time. Suppose there are four alternatives, and the series is presented twice. If there is a 35 per cent agreement on choices between the first and the second time, this does not mean that the gain over chance resulted from repetition. The above-chance preference may have been there on the first trial. This criticism has been made by Stephens (1934) and Hull (1935d), among others, and empirical results show that punishment does in fact lead to fewer repetitions. The result of Thorndike's use of too low a base for chance repetition was automatically to assign too much strengthening to rewards and too little weakening to punishments. The asymmetry could be entirely a statistical artifact.

Tilton, a former associate of Thorndike, repeated the spread of effect experiment with careful controls to determine what the empirical level of repetition would be without the saying of *Right* and *Wrong*, and then proceeded to plot the spread of effect on either side of a rewarded and a punished response.[28] He made a correction also for a serial position effect, that is, for a tendency to repeat the same response to items near the beginning and the end of the list. When correction is made, it is found that the effects of *Right* and *Wrong* are about alike, the announcement of *Wrong* decreasing repetitions about as much as *Right* increases them. A replotting of Tilton's results is shown in Figures 1 and 2.

Tilton's study shows that in the neighborhood of reward there is a tendency for punished responses to be repeated more frequently than remote from reward, but their punishment (being called wrong) suffices even one step from reward to lead to *less* repetition than would occur if the response were neither rewarded nor punished (Figure 1). Similarly, when a response called wrong (punished) occurs in the midst of a series of rewarded responses, the neighboring rewarded responses are re-

[28] The first report is Tilton (1939), but further computations are presented of the same data in Tilton (1945).

peated less frequently than they would have been had they not been in the neighborhood of the punished response. Again, however, their reward (being called right) is enough to lead to their repetition at a *greater* frequency than that represented by the neutral baseline (Figure 2).

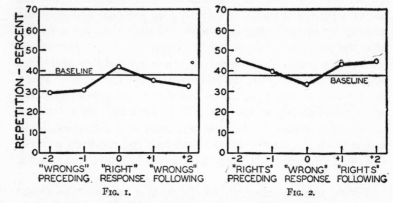

FIGURE 1. GRADIENT OF EFFECT AROUND A "RIGHT" RESPONSE.

Calling a response "Right" increases its repetition, calling a response "Wrong" decreases its repetition, but the decrease is less when the "Wrong" is near to an isolated "Right." Redrawn from Tilton (1945).

FIGURE 2. GRADIENT OF EFFECT AROUND A "WRONG" RESPONSE.

Calling a response "Wrong" decreases its repetition, calling a response "Right" increases its repetition, but the increase is less when the "Right" is near to an isolated "Wrong." Redrawn from Tilton (1945).

Because Tilton used the conventional method of obtaining spread of effect, repeating lists over and over again, and allowing right responses and wrong responses to appear with any degree of separation, he had to make a rather elaborate analysis in order to exhibit just what was in fact happening within his experiment. Martens (1946) introduced a corrective by arranging the experimental situation so that each position before and after reward has an equal opportunity to be represented in the final spread of effect pattern. This she did by limiting the training and testing to one trial each on each list. That is, on one trial through a list of words the subject arbitrarily assigned numbers and was informed each time whether the number was right or wrong. The experimenter was able to assign the word *Right* to prearranged positions, all other positions being assigned the word *Wrong*. Then a single additional trial was used to determine the extent to which the subject would repeat the numbers called *Right* and repeat or change the numbers called *Wrong*. The statistical handling and interpretation of the effects of *Right* and *Wrong* are greatly simplified, for according to the prearranged pattern there are an equal number of opportunities to give the same response or a different response to each of several positions before and after the rewarded connection. The control situation consisted in the subject's assigning numbers as in a free association experiment, with the list repeated twice, no announcements of *Right* or of *Wrong* being used.[29] Her results in this modified situation supported Tilton's, so far as the effect of a rewarded response imbedded in the midst of punished responses is concerned. That is, the effect of *Wrong*, even adjacent to the rewarded connection is greater than whatever influence can be attributed to the spread of the effect of *Right*. The direct effects of both *Right* and of *Wrong* are greater than any spread from one to the other.

Stephens (1941), like Tilton, a former student of Thorndike, has made an interesting mediating suggestion that "symbolic" reward strengthens weak connections more than "symbolic" punishment weakens them, but symbolic punishment weakens strong connections more than symbolic reward strengthens them. According to this view, it was because Thorndike tended to work mostly with weak connections, that he got the results he did. Stephens' experiment was done by using statements such as appear on attitude scales to determine certain convictions held strongly by the subjects, others held less strongly. Then a law of effect experiment was arranged, in which multiple-choice answers were permitted to selected statements, and the subject was informed which choice was correct. The method of information was the ingenious one of using chemically prepared paper

---

[29] The "empirical chance" or "neutral" level of repetition depends upon the instructions within the control period. Martens' method, which sought "natural" associates between words and numbers, as in the free association experiment, led to a higher baseline of repetition than Wallach and Henle's (1941) method, which may have mildly discouraged repetitions. This is a matter calling for further study. The interpretation of the relative efficacy of reward and punishment depends on the assumed baseline, and if there is arbitrariness about the baseline there must be arbitrariness in the interpretation of positive and negative effects.

so that the correct response came out in color when it was marked by the instrument provided. This permitted the experiment to be done with groups. When the experiment was then repeated, it was possible to see which tendency was the greater, to repeat the response answered correctly or to change from the response answered incorrectly. The change was found to be correlated with the conviction represented by the answer. The better established replies were more influenced by punishment, the less well-established by reward.

There is a difficulty of interpretation in this experiment which may help to account for uncertainty in other experiments about the relative influence of reward and of punishment. There is a logical difference between responding in the intelligent direction to *Right* and to *Wrong*. The intelligent response to *Right* is to do again what was last done. This makes possible immediate rehearsal; the task is clear. The intelligent response to *Wrong* is to do something different, but what to do is less clear. It is necessary both to remember what not to do and to form some sort of hypothesis as to what to do. Under time pressure this vagueness might well produce an asymmetry between responses following *Right* and *Wrong*. In the case of poorly established convictions, it may be harder to remember what was said that was called *Right* than in the case of well-established convictions to remember what was said that was called *Wrong*. If that were true, Stephens' results would follow. Anything which makes it easier to make the necessary discriminations in one case than in another will effect the relative potency (statistically) of saying *Right* or *Wrong*. In other words, the situation is not nearly as mechanical and stupid as it appears; in fact, the results can be best understood on the assumption that the individual is doing his best to act intelligently under somewhat confusing circumstances.

The theory of discrete connections probably faulty. The spread of effect as Thorndike describes it presupposes a series of stimulus-response connections with no other organization among them than succession in time. What is strengthened (or weakened) is the tendency for a stimulus to be followed by the response which accompanied it the last time. Other experimenters have given evidence that additional principles of organization do apply, and the automatic spread of the influence of reward to neighboring connections is either incorrect or a gross oversimplification.

Zirkle (1946a) by changing the order of stimulus words on successive trials showed that what was repeated was a neighboring response, not a stimulus-response connection. That is, a tendency to repeat the response "five" given originally to the word "youthful" two steps removed from reward, was found on the next trial to be given to "supports" as the stimulus word in the corresponding position. There was no increase in the tendency to say "five" after "youthful," unless it appeared in its old place. Under the usual arrangements of the experiment on spread of effect, it would be impossible to distinguish between strengthening a response or a connection, but under the special circumstances of Zirkle's experiment it is clear that response is the more important beneficiary of the reward.

This suggestion by Zirkle that it is the response rather than the connection which enters prominently into spread of effect data receives further support from the experiments of Jenkins and Sheffield (1946). They show that guessing habits are important in the usual spread of effect experiments. Guessing habits refer to patterns of response, not to isolated stimulus-response preferences. They found that if a rewarded response was repeated, other responses following it were also repeated; if a rewarded response was not repeated, other responses in its neighborhood were not repeated beyond chance levels. Hence the *repetition* of a rewarded response appears to be more important than the fact of reward. The major effect of reward is to lead to repetition of the correct response; once this success is achieved, the repetition of responses after the reward depends upon guessing habits.

There are thus seen to be organizational factors in the spread of effect not described simply by remoteness of connections from rewards.

Is "reward" the basis for the enhancement effect? The presumption is made in Thorndike's experiments that the repetition of the response called *Right* is directly rewarding. That this may not be the case is shown in the experiments of Wallach and Henle (1941, 1942). The subject believed himself to be in an experiment on extra-sensory perception, so that as he went through a list he was trying to assign the number which had been assigned by someone else for that particular trial. Hence a response called *Right* on one trial might be incorrect on the next trial. There was thus no intent to learn the *Right* responses, and in fact the hearing of the word *Right* did nothing to improve the repetition of either the rewarded response or its near neigh-

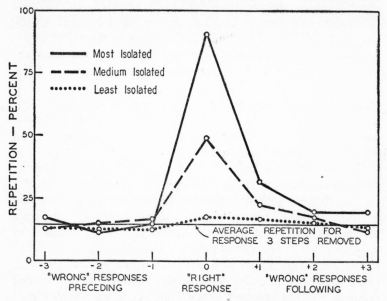

FIGURE 3. GRADIENT OF EFFECT AROUND "RIGHT" RESPONSES WITH THREE DEGREES OF ISOLATION.

All isolated responses called "Right," all neighboring items called "Wrong." The differences among the three curves depend upon the differences in degree of isolation of the items called "Right." The most isolated item, a nonsense syllable in red capital letters; the medium isolated item, a word in black capital letters; the least isolated item, a word printed like all other items, in black lower-case letters, isolated only by being called "Right" in the midst of words called "Wrong." Plotted from Zirkle (1946b).

bors. It appears that what the subject is trying to do is more important than one would suppose from Thorndike's insistence on the automaticity of the effect of reward.

Another of Zirkle's experiments [30] bears importantly on the question of what causes the repetition of the response called

[30] Zirkle (1946b).

Right. Influenced by the possibility that something like a figure-ground relationship may be effective in these situations, Zirkle arranged to have three degrees of isolation of the response called *Right.* It was his conjecture that with greater isolation there would be greater repetition of this response, and perhaps of its near neighbors also. The degrees of isolation were obtained by inserting within a list of black lower-case words as the words to be called *Right* (a) a nonsense syllable in red capital letters, the

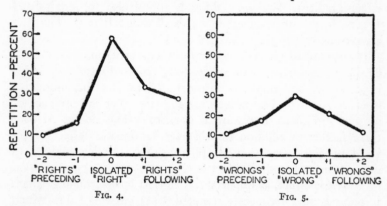

FIG. 4.   FIG. 5.

FIGURE 4. GRADIENT OF EFFECT AROUND ISOLATED "RIGHT" ITEM IN THE MIDST OF OTHER "RIGHT" ITEMS.

Isolated item the nonsense polysyllable "lsjbcz quentbm" in the midst of ordinary nonsense syllables, responses to all of which were called "Right." Plotted from Zirkle (1946*b*).

FIGURE 5. GRADIENT OF EFFECT AROUND ISOLATED "WRONG" ITEM IN THE MIDST OF OTHER "WRONG" ITEMS.

Isolated item the capitalized word *WITHDRAW* in the midst of lower-case words, responses to all of which were called "Wrong." Note the tendency to repeat which is nearly as great as in the case of responses called "Right," Figure 4. Plotted from Zirkle (1946*b*).

highest degree of isolation, (b) a word in black capital letters, the next degree of isolation, and (c) a word printed the same as all the other words, in black lower-case letters, but isolated solely by being called *Right* in the midst of consecutive words called *Wrong.* The results are plotted from Zirkle's data in Figure 3. His prediction was fully confirmed. Not only was the most iso-lated response most regularly repeated, but its repetition was fol-lowed by the enhanced repetition of the words immediately following. Because the spread of effect was not demonstrated for the words immediately preceding, it is possible that guessing habits to which Jenkins and Sheffield have called attention may have been responsible for the greater repetition of the responses to words immediately after the most isolated rewarded words.

That isolation is indeed a potent factor is shown by further findings of Zirkle that an isolated word called *Right*, in the midst of other words all called *Right* generates a typical spread of effect gradient. The same thing is found also for an isolated *Wrong* in the midst of other words all called *Wrong*. The data are plotted in Figures 4 and 5.[31]

Is a spread of effect demonstrable? The experiments just cited all show a gradient around successfully repeated responses, which is in essence the empirical spread of effect. But the alternative interpretations to Thorndike's are so many, that the presence of a "pure" gradient of reward is open to serious doubt. At least three factors in addition to whatever "automatic" effect of reward remains have been identified: (1) set or instructions, in determining what the subject is trying to do,[32] (2) an isolation or emphasis effect, as important as reward in determining which response is most frequently repeated,[33] (3) guessing habits which result in systematic repetitions beyond a focal response which is itself repeated for the reasons already mentioned.[34] These three factors are in addition to several systematic statistical errors which are found in many earlier studies. These errors include the following three: (1) the use of faulty estimates of "empirical" chance frequency of repetitions,[35] (2) including crowded responses in determining responses before and after a reward, thus

[31] The experiments of Muenzinger and Dove (1937) should be cited in this connection. In one series the rewarded response was learned in advance, thus guaranteeing its repetition. The gradient of repetitions about it might conform both to Zirkle's isolation effect and to the Jenkins and Sheffield guessing sequence.

[32] Wallach and Henle (1941). It is true that Thorndike allows for "overhead controls" in his interpretation of the confirmatory reaction, but little is ever made of it by him.

[33] Zirkle (1946b). The possible rôle of emphasis was earlier suggested by Tolman, Hall, and Bretnall (1932). The isolation effect came to Zirkle's attention through the work of von Restorff (1933).

[34] Jenkins and Sheffield (1946). The suggestion was earlier made by Tolman (1936), but he did not follow it up.

[35] Pointed out by Stephens (1934), Hull (1935d), Tilton (1939).

confusing the gradient of preceding responses with the gradient of following responses,[36] (3) repeating the lists many times, so that as *Right* responses accumulate the *Wrong* responses which remain are predominantly those which are stereotyped and resistant to change. Because late in practice these are necessarily near to *Right* responses, it will appear statistically (and spuriously) that *Wrong* responses near to *Right* ones are excessively repeated *because* of their proximity to *Rights*.[37]

It is evident that more experiments are needed to determine just what is happening to determine the gradients which are found. It is too early to say that there is no residual gradient of reward after corrections are made for the statistical difficulties in earlier experiments and for the additional factors now known to offer complications to Thorndike's earlier explanations of what occurred.

There is an important experiment with rats which appeared to support the spread of effect, that of Jenkins (1943). A maze consisting essentially of a series of diamond-shaped sections permitted the rat to continue to progress through the maze whether it turned right or left at each choice point. Food was presented at one of the common points in the middle portion of the maze. If the spread of effect holds, it would be predicted that the rat would vary his behavior less on succeeding trials at those choice points near the reward, both before and after it. The results supported this conjecture. One difficulty arises in this experiment, however, and that is a preference both before and after the successful choice point for a turn corresponding to that which led to food. That is, both anticipatory and perseverative responses occur, tending to result in a spurious spread-of-effect curve. The animal instead of strengthening separate responses before and after the reward is instead generalizing the response made near the reward. The experiment demonstrates the difficulty of getting entirely satisfactory evidence on the spread of effect.

Importance of definitive experiments on the spread of effect. The assumption of intelligent behavior (however accounted for) can explain the direct effects of symbolic rewards and punish-

[36] Pointed out especially by Tilton (1939) (1945).
[37] To the best of my knowledge, this criticism, although fairly obvious, has not previously been reported.

ments. If an intelligent subject is told that what he has just done is wrong, he can try something else; if told that what he did is right, he can try to remember what he did and repeat it at the next opportunity. It is the phenomena of the spread of effect which make difficult an interpretation on the assumption of intelligent adjustment, and strengthen Thorndike's position on the automatic and relatively mechanical influence of rewards and of punishments. For those who stand in opposition to Thorndike's views, the spread of effect presents a challenge which they cannot overlook. They must either show that the phenomena do not exist, or they must somehow incorporate the phenomena into their theories. For Thorndike, the spread of effect is the last line of defense. If it fails, there is little of theoretical interest left in what were once the dominant laws of learning.

ESTIMATE OF THORNDIKE'S POSITION

Before proceeding to an appraisal of the contemporary significance of Thorndike's position, his answers to the standard problems of learning will be summarized. By attempting such a summary for each writer it will be simpler to keep perspective on their similarities and differences.

Thorndike's position on typical problems of learning. Thorndike's answers are briefly summarized according to the six typical problems discussed in the first chapter.

1. *Capacity.* Learning capacity depends upon the number of bonds and their availability. The differences between bright and dull are quantitative rather than qualitative, although intelligence has dimensions of altitude as well as of breadth.[38] The theory of intelligence is consonant with the identical elements theory of transfer.

2. *Practice.* Repetition of situations does not in itself modify connections. Repetition of connections leads to a negligible increase in strength, unless the connections are rewarded. Practice is important because it permits rewards to act upon connections.

3. *Motivation.* Reward acts directly on neighboring connections to strengthen them; punishment has no corresponding direct weakening effect. Punishment may work indirectly, however,

[38] Thorndike and others (1927).

through making the learner do something else which may confront him with a reward. "Ideas" need not intervene; connections may be strengthened directly, without awareness.

4. *Understanding.* The rôle of understanding is minimized, not because it is undemonstrable, but because it grows out of earlier habits. The best way to get understanding is to build a body of connections appropriate to that understanding. When situations are understood at once it is a matter of transfer or assimilation, that is, there are enough elements in common with old situations to permit old habits to act acceptably.

5. *Transfer.* The theory of identical elements is espoused. Reaction to new situations benefits by the identity of these new situations, in part, with old situations, and also by a principle of analogy described as assimilation.

6. *Forgetting.* The original law of disuse assumed forgetting to take place without practice in accordance with the empirical findings of studies such as those of Ebbinghaus. Later books have not dealt with the problem in any detail; the law of disuse is not mentioned, but some decay with no practice is still implied.

The flavor of Thorndike's theory has all along been that of the automatic strengthening of specific connections—directly, without intervening ideas or conscious influences. While not an avowed behaviorist, and willing occasionally to use subjective terms, the emphasis is certainly behavioral. It would be unfair to leave the discussion of Thorndike without referring again to his insistence on measurement, and through that insistence his contribution to the improvement of the learning of skills in the schools. There is an energetic empiricism about Thorndike's experimenting and theorizing which may compensate for its lack of systematic elegance.

The specificity doctrine a source both of strength and of weakness. Thorndike gave great impetus to what has sometimes been called the scientific movement in education—the movement which suggests that educational practices be regulated according to verified outcomes of specific practices. His tremendous drive led to enormous output in fields as varied as handwriting scales, dictionary-writing, methods in arithmetic, spelling, intelligence tests, and vocational guidance. But the secret of his output is not only energy: the output stems also from his matter-of-fact conception of science, that in order to do something about anything you have to know specifically what you are about.

The specificity doctrine helps you to roll up your sleeves and get to work. Consider, for example, all the complications involved in the teaching of reading. What is it that the child is to be taught? Philology? Grammar? Semantics? It takes a Thorndike to give the simple answer: "Words." With that answer he proceeded to count the frequency with which each word occurs in English, by tabulating millions of printed words from all manner of sources. He then arrived at the most common words. These are the words which must surely be understood. He made available lists and dictionaries to facilitate teaching according to the most needed words. A specificity theory like Thorndike's tells the educator where to look and how to measure in a baffling field like schoolroom practices.

The specificity doctrine is also a source of weakness, and it has been the target of the most severe attacks upon Thorndike. The illustration above shows the kinds of criticisms which Thorndike invites. Is language no more than words? Are the most frequent words really what we wish to teach? Perhaps we need to think of language as a means of expression, as logic in action, and must therefore equip the child with the minimum set of tools necessary for adequate communication. That this approach is a possible one has been shown by the development of Basic English, wherein the central vocabulary of 850 words overlaps only in part with Thorndike's most frequent words.[39] The approach of Basic English takes into account the organized character of language as an instrument of meaning. Thorndike, true to association tradition, tends to think of language as a collection of words, which he sets out to treat quantitatively.

In Thorndike the analytical emphasis of all association theory also pervades the conception of rewards and punishments, and weakens somewhat the analysis of these phenomena. The notion that the law of effect works mechanically on all connections in the neighborhood of the rewarded one makes of reward some-

[39] E.g., Richards (1943). The basic list of 850 words includes words in the seventh thousand of Thorndike's count, such as *advertisement* and *sneeze*.

thing extrinsic to the activity in question, something pinned on adventitiously. In his effort to show that it *may* work this way, and occasionally does, Thorndike has played up a scientific curiosity out of all proportion to its social importance. Actually more important are the internal relationships between success and what the individual is trying to do, goals which satisfy aroused motives or needs. Again, texts may be cited in proof of the fact that Thorndike knows all this—he early quoted the "interest series" as we have shown, and later added the notion of "belongingness" —but that does not alter the conclusion that his scientific preoccupations led him away from the internal relations of effort and success to the external relationship of any satisfying state of affairs strengthening any connection which happened to be near it.

Perhaps more heat has been generated over Thorndike's subordination of insight and understanding to drill and habit than over any other aspect of his writings. While ho thought insight very rare in animals—perhaps rarer than it actually is—he did not deny insight in man. It is only that he was not awed by it, and thought it best understood by the same associative laws applying in other situations. Just as erroneous inferences are made because of habitual associations which throw the learner off his course, so the insights of the genius are made by appropriate habitual associations and analogies. He has this to say of reaction to novel situations:

There is no arbitrary *hocus pocus* whereby man's nature acts in an unpredictable spasm when he is confronted with a new situation. His habits do not then retire to some convenient distance while some new and mysterious entities direct his behavior. On the contrary, nowhere are the bonds acquired with old situations more surely revealed in action than when a new situation appears.[40]

Although this comment is true enough, Thorndike's failure to give real concern to the way in which past habits are utilized in problem solution, to consider what arrangement makes a problem hard, what easy, when the same essential bonds are involved, is a genuine limitation. The difference is a real one for school practice. It is possible to teach number combinations first (establish

[40] Thorndike (1913*b*), page 29.

the "bonds"), then expect some glimmer of understanding later, or it is possible to achieve some understanding of what numbers are for, to comprehend the situation as a problem, and then to learn the combinations in this context. In the end you come out at the same place, knowing the tables and knowing how to use them, but it is not a foregone conclusion that the one method of teaching will be more efficient than the other, either for knowing precisely what has been taught or for being able to apply it in new situations. Thorndike's preoccupation with bonds has insured that we turn to others, not Thorndike's followers, for a more careful appraisal of the role of meaning and understanding.

SUPPLEMENTARY READINGS

BOOKS

Thorndike has been a prolific writer. His bibliography published in the *Teachers College Record*, 1939-1940, 41, 699-725, contains 441 items from 1898 to May, 1940.

The following books are representative of his contributions on learning:

Thorndike, E. L. (1911) *Animal intelligence.*
Thorndike, E. L. (1913) *The psychology of learning (Educational psychology,* Vol. II)
Thorndike, E. L. (1922) *The psychology of arithmetic.*
Thorndike, E. L. and others (1928) *Adult learning.*
Thorndike, E. L. (1932) *The fundamentals of learning.*
Thorndike, E. L. (1935) *The psychology of wants, interests, and attitudes.*

SHORTER INTRODUCTIONS

Gates, A. I. (1942) Connectionism: Present concepts and interpretations. *Natl Soc. Stud. Educ.,* 41st Yearbook, Part II, 141-164.
Rock, R. T., Jr. (1940) Thorndike's contributions to the psychology of learning. *Teach. Coll. Rec.,* 41, 751-761.
Sandiford, P. (1942) Connectionism: Its origins and major features. *Natl. Soc. Stud. Educ.,* 41st Yearbook, Part II, 97-140.
Thorndike, E. L. (1940) The ABC of human behavior. Chap 2 in *Human nature and the social order,* 5-20.

CRITICAL REVIEWS

Brown, J. F., and Feder, D. D. (1934) Thorndike's theory of learning as gestalt psychology. *Psychol. Bull.,* 31, 426-437.

Cason, H. (1932) Review of Thorndike's *Human learning*. *J. abn. (soc.) Psychol.*, 27, 214-222.

Hull, C. L. (1935) Special review of Thorndike's *The fundamentals of learning*. *Psychol. Bull.*, 32, 807-823.

McGeoch, J. A. (1933) Review of Thorndike's *The fundamentals of learning*. *J. gen. Psychol.*, 8, 285-296.

Tolman, E. C. (1936) Connectionism; wants, interests, and attitudes. *Character and Pers.*, 4, 245-253.

REPRESENTATIVE EXPERIMENTS

A scientific theory can best be judged by its consequences in experimentation. This requires an appraisal of the kinds of experiments to which the theory leads and a review of the interpretations offered for the obtained data. A preferred theory ought to lead to cogent experiments and to suggest convincing interpretations.

Following this and succeeding chapters there will be short lists of experiments, useful in estimating the theories in this way. Many other references would be equally satisfactory for this purpose.

Lorge, I. (1936) Irrelevant rewards in animal learning. *J. comp. Psychol.*, 21, 105-128.

Rock, R. T., Jr. (1935) The influence upon learning of the quantitative variation of after-effects. *Teach. Coll. Contr. Educ.*, No. 650, 78 pp.

Thorndike, E. L. (1908) The effect of practice in the case of a purely intellectual function. *Amer. J. Psychol.*, 19, 374-384.

Thorndike, E. L. (1910) Practice in the case of addition. *Amer. J. Psychol.*, 21, 483-486.

Thorndike, E. L. (1924) Mental discipline in high school studies. *J. educ. Psychol.*, 15, 1-22; 83-98.

Thorndike, E. L. (1927) The influence of primacy. *J. exp. Psychol.*, 10, 18-29.

Thorndike, E. L. (1932) Reward and punishment in animal learning. *Comp. Psychol. Monogr.*, 8, No. 39, 65 pp.

Thorndike, E. L. (1933) An experimental study of rewards. *Teach. Coll. Contr. Educ.*, No. 580, 72 pp.

Thorndike, E. L., and Lorge, I. (1935) The influence of relevance and belonging. *J. exp. Psychol.*, 18, 574-584.

Thorndike, E. L., and Rock, R. T., Jr. (1934) Learning without awareness of what is being learned or intent to learn it. *J. exp. Psychol.*, 17, 1-19.

Chapter 3

GUTHRIE'S CONTIGUOUS CONDITIONING

In some respects, Edwin R. Guthrie's system is very much like Thorndike's. It is a stimulus-response association psychology, objective and practical. But in other respects the systems are very different. It is such similarities and differences which define the problems of contemporary learning theory.

Thorndike accepts two kinds of learning, selecting and connecting (under the law of effect), and associative shifting. For him, associative shifting was originally the fifth of some subsidiary principles, and by far the major burden has been carried by selecting and connecting. For Guthrie, on the contrary, a conception very like associative shifting is made the cornerstone of his system, and learning of the trial-and-error sort is derivative and secondary. Guthrie does not accept the law of effect in Thorndike's sense, and this is the basic cleavage between their systems.

THE BACKGROUND OF BEHAVIORISM AND OF CONDITIONING

Guthrie is a contemporary behaviorist who lays much stress upon conditioning as the characteristic form of learning. Before turning to his own theories it may prove helpful to consider the background against which they have emerged.

Watson's behaviorism. Behaviorism as a "school" of psychology is usually thought of as originating with Watson (1913), who became its most vigorous spokesmen. There were other varieties of behaviorism, however, and Guthrie was led to his position by way of Singer (1911), with whom he had studied. The behaviorists have in common the conviction that a science of psychology must be based upon a study of that which is overtly observable: physical stimuli, the muscular movements and glandular secretions which they arouse, and the environmental products which ensue. The behaviorists differ somewhat among themselves as to what may be inferred in addition to what is measured, but they all exclude self-observation (introspection) as a legitimate scientific method. Partly as a protection against an indirect use of introspection, the behaviorists have tended to prefer experimentation on animals and infants.

Watson's *Behavior: An introduction to comparative psychology* (1914) was the first book to follow the announcement of his new position. In it occurred his attempted refutation of Thorndike's law of effect, and the substitution of the laws of frequency and recency. He believed that animal learning, as in the maze or problem-box, could be explained according to what the animal had most often been led to do in the situation, with the most recent act favored in recall. Because the successful act was both most frequent and most recent, its recurrence could be explained without recourse to an added principle of effect. This denial of effect was part of his program of getting rid of the residual subjectivity which he felt was implied in Thorndike's concepts of satisfiers and annoyers. While the frequency-recency theory did not survive its criticisms,[1] it serves to point up Watson's desire to find objective laws to substitute for those with even a tinge of subjective flavor.

The behaviorist knows that other events intervene between measured stimuli and the responses to them. In order to preserve a systematically coherent position, these intervening events are posited to be much like the observed ones, that is, *implicit* or *covert* stimulus-response sequences. In his early studies on the control of the maze habit, Watson (1907) had attributed great importance to kinesthetic stimuli as integrators of the habits involved. Because kinesthetic stimuli are aroused as a result of the organism's movements they fit well into a behavioral or re-action psychology. Even the unobserved processes inferred to be going on between stimuli and responses are said to be com-

[1] Peterson (1922); Gengerelli (1928).

prised of movements and movement-produced stimuli. This emphasis upon kinesthesis as the integrator of animal learning served Watson well when he became puzzled about human thought processes. He decided that thought was merely implicit speech, that is, talking to oneself. Sensitive enough instruments, he conjectured, would detect tongue movements or other movement accompaniments of thinking. He was thus able to hold to his consistent behaviorist position without denying that thinking goes on.

It was somewhat later that Watson discovered that the conditioned reflex of Pavlov and Bekhterev might serve as a useful paradigm for learning.[2] Because it grew out of the objective tradition within Russian physiology, it fitted his temper and he adopted it enthusiastically. In Watson's later writings the conditioned reflex was central to learning, as the unit out of which habits are built.

Watson's general textbook *Psychology from the standpoint of a behaviorist* appeared in 1919. It was soon followed by other books written from an avowedly behavioristic standpoint. Among these was Smith and Guthrie's book, *General psychology in terms of behavior* (1921). Like Watson's book, it treated all of psychology from a behavioral viewpoint, and made use of conditioning principles. It, too, laid great stress upon movement-produced stimuli. Hence there is a family relationship between the two books, although they differ greatly in expository style. Watson laid far more stress upon the details of physiology and anatomy, and upon appropriate methods for the behavioral study of psychological relationships. Smith and Guthrie showed less concern for experimental and neurophysiological detail, but instead gave a plausible interpretation of ordinary experience as described consistently from the new standpoint. Guthrie's contemporary writings preserve the flavor of the Smith and Guthrie book. Despite their similarities, Guthrie's point of view must be considered as something other than a working out of Watson's position.[3]

The conditioned reflex or conditioned response. The condi-

[2] Watson (1916).
[3] It is suggested in the next chapter that Hull's position, rather than Guthrie's, is more logically the descendant of Watson's.

tioned reflex principle is conceptually so simple as to make an attractive prototype for learning. Certain stimuli lead regularly to reflex responses. A light flashed into the eye causes pupillary constriction, a tap on the patellar tendon leads to a knee jerk, chemicals on the tongue produce salivation. Such natural reflexes are called *unconditioned reflexes* and the stimuli which produce them are called *unconditioned stimuli*. If a second stimulus, not originally leading to the response, is frequently presented slightly before or accompanying the unconditioned stimulus, it presently comes to elicit the response. Such a stimulus is called a *conditioned stimulus* and the learned response is called a *conditioned reflex*. Because of the desire to extend the principle to responses not obviously reflex, later writers have usually preferred the less specific word "response" to the word "reflex," so that the movements involved are called conditioned and unconditioned responses, whether or not they conform to the definition of a reflex.

The study of conditioned salivary responses in dogs was carried out systematically by Pavlov [4] over many years, and he discovered most of the relationships which later studies have more fully explored. The translations of his terms have become common in the literature of learning.

The appearance or strengthening of a conditioned response is said to take place through *reinforcement*. Reinforcement refers primarily to the experimental arrangement of following the conditioned stimulus by the unconditioned stimulus, although the word is sometimes used to refer to the process of strengthening which is implied. When the conditioned stimulus is presented alone, unaccompanied by the unconditioned stimulus, it is said to be *non-reinforced*. Under repeated non-reinforcement there is a tendency for the conditioned response to weaken or even to disappear completely. This is referred to as *experimental extinction*, or, more simply, *extinction*. By extinction may be meant either the experimental arrangement of non-reinforcement, or the weakening process itself. Extinction is not, in fact, a destruction of the conditioned response, for when the animal is returned to the laboratory after a rest following extinction, the conditioned response is usually found to have reappeared. This return of response strength after extinction, without intervening reinforce-

4 Pavlov (1927) (1928).

ment, is called *spontaneous recovery*. The simple history of a conditioned response is then its strengthening through reinforcement, its weakening through extinction, and its recovery with rest.

Two additional concepts are extremely important in the extension of conditioning principles. These are *generalization* and *discrimination*. A new conditioned stimulus, not previously reinforced, may elicit a conditioned response the first time it is presented. The probability that it will do so is increased if it is similar to the conditioned stimulus which has been reinforced. Thus if a conditioned stimulus is obtained to one tone, another tone, at a slightly different frequency, will also produce a conditioned response, with lesser magnitude the further the separation of the tones. This process whereby a novel stimulus produces a response learned to another similar stimulus is known as *generalization*. If the two stimuli are sufficiently distinguishable, the organism can be taught to respond to one of them and to cease responding to the other. This is done by the method of contrasts. That is, one of the stimuli is regularly reinforced, the other regularly non-reinforced. The selective extinction which results is known as *conditioned discrimination*, because the organism has learned to react differentially to the two stimuli which at first evoked more nearly the same response. Discrimination may be between patterns of stimuli as well as between single stimuli.[5]

In choosing to use what has been learned from conditioned response experiments, Watson and Guthrie selected somewhat different alternatives. Watson used the Pavlov experiment as the epitome of learning, made of the conditioned reflex the unit of habit, and built his system on that foundation. Guthrie, unlike Watson, starts with a principle of conditioning or of associative learning which is not dependent strictly upon the Pavlov kind of experiment. To Guthrie, Pavlov's experiment is a highly artificial one, useful for the relationships it exhibits, but itself requiring explanation according to more general principles. For Watson the conditioning experiment provided the answers he sought as to how learning takes place; for Guthrie the conditioning experiment raises as many questions as it answers.

[5] A glossary of terms used in conditioning experiments may be found in Hilgard and Marquis (1940), pages 341-353.

CONTIGUITY OF CUE AND RESPONSE: THE ONE LAW OF ASSOCIATION

The lowest common denominator of learning. Guthrie's one law of learning, from which all else about learning is made comprehensible, is stated by Guthrie as follows: "A combination of stimuli which has accompanied a movement will on its recurrence tend to be followed by that movement." [6]

There is an elegant simplicity about the statement, which avoids mention of drives, of successive repetitions, of rewards or of punishments. Stimuli and movements in combination: that is all. This one principle serves as the basis for a very ingenious and intriguing theory of learning.

A second statement is needed to complete the basic postulate about learning: "A stimulus pattern gains its full associative strength on the occasion of its first pairing with a response." [7]

This somewhat paradoxical statement, in view of undeniable improvement with practice, is a very necessary adjunct to the theory, because it makes possible a number of derivative statements about learning and forgetting. It can be thought of as a kind of recency principle, for if learning occurs completely in one trial, that which was last done in the presence of a stimulus combination will be that which will be done when the stimulus combination next recurs.

How can Guthrie demonstrate that more complicated forms of learning conform to these simple principles? As in the case of other sophisticated theorists, he does not proceed by denying familiar forms of learning. His problem is that of showing that learning as we know it can, in fact, be shown not to contradict these basic principles. He does not deny that there is learning which may be described as insightful or purposive or problem-solving. It is Guthrie's task to show that each of these forms requires no new principles of explanation beyond the primary law of association by contiguity.

Why strict contiguity of measured stimulus and response is not essential. One of the standard experiments in the literature

[6] Guthrie (1935), page 26.
[7] Guthrie (1942), page 30.

of conditioning is that showing the importance of the time interval between the conditioned stimulus and unconditioned response. The empirical results suggest a gradient, with a most favorable interval with less favorable intervals on either side of it.[8]

Guthrie is able to hold out for strict simultaneity of cue and response in the face of these data by proposing that the true cue being conditioned is not the stimulus as measured. An external stimulus may give rise to movements of the organism. These movements in turn produce stimuli. When associations appear to be made between stimuli and responses separated in time, it is because these intervening movements fill in the gap. The true association is between simultaneous events.

There is a strong preference for movement-produced stimuli as the true conditioners in Guthrie's system. They permit the integration of habits within a wide range of environmental change in stimulation, because these stimuli are carried around by the organism. It appears that some of this preference dates from the early emphasis of Watson (1907) on kinesthesis as the basis of control of the maze habit, a position no longer tenable.[9] Such covert movement-produced stimuli provide ever-present alibis for conduct which cannot be inferred from external stimulus-response relationships.

Why repetition brings improvement. The reason that practice brings improvement is that improvement, and other forms of success, refer to activities, to outcomes of learnings, rather than to movements. Guthrie believes that his interest in movements, and the prediction of movements, is almost unique among learning theorists; others, he says, are interested in goal achievements, end results of one sort or another. One difference between him and Thorndike is that Thorndike is concerned with scores on tasks, with items learned, pages typed, or correct responses attained. Guthrie is concerned only with the movements of the organism, regardless of whether they lead to error or success.

A skill, such as getting the ball into the basket in a game of basketball, is not one act but many. It does not depend upon a

---

[8] Hilgard and Marquis (1940), pages 158-173; Reynolds (1945a), Kimble (1947).
[9] Honzik (1936) found kinesthesis to be one of the least useful of several sensory controls of the maze habit.

single muscular movement, but upon a number of movements made under a number of different circumstances. Any one movement may be learned in any one trial, but to learn all the movements demanded by the complicated skill calls for practice in all the different situations: while near the basket and far away, on one side and on the other, with and without a guard nearby. Practice is necessary, but it acts, not in accordance with a law of frequency, but according to the simple principle of the attachment of cues to movements. The more varied the movements called for in a given act of skill, and the more varied the cues which must become assimilated to these movements, the more practice is required. There is no mystery about the length of time it takes to learn to operate a typewriter: there are so many keys in so many combinations, calling for the attachment of a great many cues to a great many responses. It is concomitantly necessary to get rid of the faulty associations which lead to what, from a product point of view, is an error. This is done by having the correct behavior occur to the cue which previously gave rise to the faulty behavior. When finally all the cues lead to acceptable behavior, the task is mastered. The apparent contradiction of single-trial learning with actual experience of painstaking fumbling before success is achieved is resolved when the skilled task is seen to be composed of a large number of habits.

Associative inhibition, forgetting, and the breaking of habits. The fact of extinction is one of the findings of conditioning experiments that is in need of explanation. Because cues should remain faithful to their responses, Guthrie cannot agree to extinction as a decay due to mere non-reinforced repetition. According to him, extinction always occurs as associative inhibition, that is, through the learning of an incompatible response. His is an interference theory, and hence requires no new principles, because the original learning and the interfering learning follow the same rules.

Forgetting is explained in the same way. If there were no interference with old learning there would be no forgetting. It has been shown, for example, that conditioned responses, even though in some respects they appear fragile, are actually quite resistant to forgetting.[10] The long-lasting character of these con-

[10] E.g., Hilgard and Campbell (1936); Wendt (1937).

ditioned responses is to be understood because they represent learning highly specific to a situation not confronted in daily life. If the learners lived in the laboratory, their responses would be subject to more interferences. Guthrie's position is but an extreme form of the retroactive inhibition theory of forgetting, to be discussed in greater detail later.

If it is desired to break up a habit (that is, to accelerate its forgetting), it is only necessary to cause other movements to occur in the presence of the cues to the habit. The problem of locating the cues and substituting other behavior often takes time, because many cues may lead to the undesirable habit.

> Drinking or smoking after years of practice are action systems which can be started by thousands of reminders. . . . I had once a caller to whom I was explaining that the apple I had just finished was a splendid device for avoiding a smoke. The caller pointed out that I was at that moment smoking. The habit of lighting a cigarette was so attached to the finish of eating that smoking had started automatically.[11]

Guthrie suggests three ways in which activities are commonly weakened:

1. The first method is to introduce the stimulus which you wish to have disregarded, but only in such faint degree that it will not call out its response. This is the method of training a horse to the saddle by starting with a light blanket, and gradually working up to full equipment, at no time permitting the horse to become so startled that it plunges or struggles.

2. The second method is to repeat the signal until the original response is fatigued, and then continuing it, so that new responses are learned to the signal. The "broncho-busting" of the western ranches followed essentially this technique.

3. The third method is to present the stimulus when other features in the situation inhibit the undesirable response. One illustration given by Guthrie is that of training a dog not to catch and eat chickens by tying a dead chicken about its neck. As it struggles to get rid of the corpse it develops an avoidance response to chickens at close quarters. Another example, illustrating undesirable learning, is the disobedience learned by the child

---

[11] Guthrie (1935), page 139.

whose mother calls him when he is too occupied with what he is doing to obey.

SOME DERIVATIVE APPLICATIONS

In his two books *Psychology of learning* (1935) and *The psychology of human conflict* (1938), Guthrie gives many applications of his theory of learning to the control of practical learning situations, and in the handling of personality problems. There are no formal additions to the basic principle of learning, although there are some derivatives which, once accounted for, play an important role in further discussions. Among these are the explanation of the action of rewards, without making use of a principle like effect, and the use of anticipatory responses as substitutes for ideas and intentions.

Motives and rewards. Motivation for Guthrie is not a principle of learning; it enters learning only because it determines the presence and vigor of movements which may enter into associative connection. It is the movements which occur that get associated; if a hungry cat acts differently from a well-fed cat, her movements may be different and hence her learning different. She learns what she does.

While Guthrie believes as everyone else does that rewards influence outcomes, his rejection of the law of effect and of the principle of reinforcement in conditioning [12] is based on the position that there is nothing new added to associative learning by reward except a mechanical arrangement. This mechanical arrangement, which places reward at the end of a series of acts, removes the organism from the stimuli acting just prior to the reward. Hence, being removed from the stimuli, the behavior to these stimuli is preserved intact. Instead of behavior being strengthened by reward, reward preserves it from disintegration. It was just as strong before the reward occurred, but, if there had been no reward, behavior in the same situation would have changed. The act leading to the reward, being the last act in the situation, is the one favored when the situation next repeats itself.

[12] The principle of reinforcement, as used by Hull, is very similar to the law of effect, and implies more than the experimental arrangements within simple conditioning.

Guthrie describes the results of punishment as he does those of reward, neglecting to consider the differences between the reward and punishment situations. To say that the child does what he last did in the punished situation is not to account for the efficacy of the punishment but for its lack of efficacy. It is all right, in the case of reward, to do what you last did; if, when you have been punished, you do what you last did, you are simply in for more punishment. Guthrie's anecdotal writing permits him to gloss over a special problem such as that created by punishment. He has ways of talking about it, if it should be forced to his attention,[13] but these ways lack the clarity and neatness of the associative description he prefers.

Anticipatory responses; intentions. Conduct is organized into sequences in which people make plans and carry them out, or at least start to carry them out. Guthrie is aware of this and devotes a chapter to learning with and without intention.[14]

He and Smith had earlier followed the lead of Sherrington and Woodworth in considering sequences of behavior as composed of precurrent or preparatory responses and consummatory responses.[15] Such acts appear from the outside to be intentional, for the earlier adjustments clearly are in readiness for the consequences which are to follow. These anticipatory responses or readiness reactions are said to be conditioned to maintaining stimuli.

The typical case is that of the hungry rat running down an alleyway to food at the end. The activity is maintained by the internal stimuli aroused by food deprivation to which running and eating behavior have been conditioned in the past. That is, the rat found food at some other time after running while hungry. These internal stimuli, plus the stimuli from the runway (if it has been previously a path to food) maintain the running of the animal against competing responses, such as stopping to explore. Anticipatory salivation or chewing movements give directional character to the behavior. All this food-anticipation is

[13] Avoidance of punishment can be treated within Guthrie's system by way of anticipatory responses and readinesses, as discussed in the next section. However, Guthrie usually writes as though the learner does again what was last done in the presence of the punishment.

[14] Guthrie (1935), pages 202-211.

[15] Smith and Guthrie (1921); Sherrington (1906); Woodworth (1918).

fulfilled if there is food at the end of the maze. Because the stimuli of hunger and anticipation are now removed, and the animal is out of the maze, all the learning is intact for a new trial at a later time. This is about as complex a description as Guthrie ever indulges in, and the details are not taken as seriously as Hull, for example, takes them. But the paradigm provides a way of talking about human intentions and purposes also.

The essence of an intention is a body of maintaining stimuli which may or may not include sources of unrest like thirst or hunger but always includes action tendencies conditioned during a past experience—a readiness to speak, a readiness to go, a readiness to read, and in each case a readiness not only for the act but also for the previously rehearsed consequences of the act. These readinesses are not complete acts but they consist in tensions of the muscles that will take part in the complete act.[16]

This statement goes a long way toward the point of view which those with very different theories of learning accept. The only feature which keeps it within the bounds of Guthrie's theory is that all the readinesses, including the readiness for the "previously rehearsed consequences of the act," are said to consist in tensions in the muscles. This assumption, characteristic of the behaviorist position, remains in the realm of conjecture rather than of demonstration.

The control of the learning process. It is part of the charm of Guthrie's writing that it is closely in touch with life, and provides amusing but cogent suggestions for meeting the problems of animal training, child-rearing, and pedagogy. This practicality is not a necessary characteristic of the system, for if one seriously attempted to provide evidence for the theory he would be buried in the midst of the precise movement correlates of measurable stimuli, and the muscular tension accompaniments of preparatory adjustments. But the system is not intended to be taken seriously in that sense. As long as a convenient way of talking about things can be found without seeming to contradict the system, quantitative precision is not essential. It is Guthrie's conviction that scientific laws to be useful must be approximately true, but they must also be stated coarsely enough to be teachable to freshmen.[17]

[16] Guthrie (1935), pages 205-206.
[17] Guthrie (1936a).

Most of the practical advice which Guthrie gives is good advice, and he succeeds in making it appear to flow from the theory. Consider the following example:

The mother of a ten-year-old girl complained to a psychologist that for two years her daughter had annoyed her by a habit of tossing coat and hat on the floor as she entered the house. On a hundred occasions the mother had insisted that the girl pick up the clothing and hang it in its place. These wild ways were changed only after the mother, on advice, began to insist not that the girl pick up the fallen garments from the floor, but that she put them on, return to the street, and re-enter the house, this time removing the coat and hanging it properly.[18]

Why was this advice given? Behavior is in response to stimuli. Hanging up the coat was in response to her mother's pleading and the sight of the coat on the floor. In order to attach the desired behavior to its proper cues, it was necessary to go outside and come into the house, so that entering the house became the cue for hanging up the coat.

The following statements represent the kind of suggestions which recur in his writings:

1. If you wish to encourage a particular kind of behavior or discourage another, discover the cues leading to the behavior in question. In the one case, arrange the situation so that the desired behavior occurs when those cues are present; in the other case, arrange it so that the undesired behavior does not occur in the presence of the cues. This is all that is involved in the skillful use of reward and punishment. A student does not learn what was in a lecture or a book. He learns only what the lecture or book caused him to do.[19]

2. Use as many stimulus supports for desired behavior as possible, because any ordinary behavior is a complex of movements to a complex of stimuli. The more stimuli there are associated with the desired behavior, the less likely that distracting stimuli and competing behavior will upset the desirable behavior. There would be fewer lines confused in amateur theatricals if there were more dress rehearsals, since the cues from the stage and the actors are part of the situation to which the actor responds. An-

18 Guthrie (1935), page 21.
19 Guthrie (1942), page 55.

other way of putting this is to rule that we should practice in the precise form later to be demanded of us.

EXPERIMENTS ON THE PUZZLE-BOX

One of the serious lacks in the previous history of Guthrie's proposals has been the failure to set convincing experiments. Such an experiment has recently been fully reported [20] and now provides a much more tangible ground on which to come to grips with both the strengths and the weaknesses of Guthrie's position.

It is fitting that Guthrie and Horton should have chosen as a characteristic experiment the behavior of the cat in escaping from a puzzle-box, because this situation has already been the occasion for both experiment and theory. Thorndike's classical experiment has already been cited (page 20). This gave the send-off to Thorndike's theory by convincing him that little of the cat's behavior was mediated by ideas, and much of it controlled by the influence of rewards. Adams' (1929) repetition of Thorndike's work gave much more evidence for ideas. These two experiments represent extremes of theory in addition to providing detailed descriptions of behavior as background for the Guthrie and Horton experiment.

Adams' repetition and supplementation of Thorndike's work. Adams (1929) repeated Thorndike's experiment as faithfully as possible, noting details of the cat's behavior instead of relying solely on time curves. He also designed some other experiments, of which the following is typical.

A piece of liver is suspended from the top of a wire cage, so that the liver rests on the floor inside the cage, loosely held by the thread. A hungry cat in the room with the cage but outside it, sees the liver and walks over to the cage. It hesitates for a time and its head moves up and down as though it is studying the string. Then it jumps on top of the cage, catches the string in its mouth, raises the liver by joint use of mouth and paw, and leaps down with the stick at the end of the string in its mouth. The liver is pulled to the top of the cage, but is unfortunately torn off. In another trial the cat is successful in obtaining the liver by pawing the stick, taking it in its mouth and jumping down

[20] Guthrie and Horton (1946).

again. This time the liver was more securely fastened, and the response is successful.

Adams argues that this kind of behavior is very different from the random slashing about described by Thorndike, and appears by analogy to be controlled by ideas. If the cat has used its past behavior and habits, it has used them in a new situation in a remarkably appropriate manner.

The Guthrie and Horton experiment. Because of their wish to record details of movement rather than to score achievement in some other manner, a special problem box was designed which permitted the cat to be fully observed during the period prior to solution, and its exact posture to be recorded photographically at the moment it activated the release. The release mechanism was a small pole set in the midst of the floor of a glass-covered cage with exit door in the front. The animal entered through a starting box and tunnel at the rear. If it touched the pole in any manner at all, the front door was opened and the animal could escape into the room. A camera was operated as the door was opening, so that a photograph of the animal was obtained at the moment of release, while it was still in contact with the pole.

In each of three preliminary trials the animal entered the box through the tunnel and made its way out the front door, which was left ajar, to find a bit of salmon on the table top in front of the box. The first of the regular trials followed. During the regular trials the experimenters kept notes of the animal's behavior as it entered the box through the tunnel at the rear, and the camera recorded the exact time and position when it struck the release mechanism.

The results are remarkable for the amount of repetitiousness in each cat's successive releases. A cat which bites the pole may do so time after time; one which has escaped by backing into the pole may back almost endlessly in its efforts to escape by the same movement. Others use front paws or hind paws, or roll against the pole. The cat, in full agreement with the theory, learns the method of escape in the first trial and then repeats what is essentially the same solution time after time. Some cats have several modes of escape which they use at different times, or they have one type of escape for a long time and then shift to another. These exceptions to the principle of doing what was done the last time are accounted for on the basis of a different entrance, which changes the stimulating conditions; the result of accidental distractions; or, having been in the box a long time and failing to operate the release by a familiar method, some new method may supersede the familiar one. The fact that the last

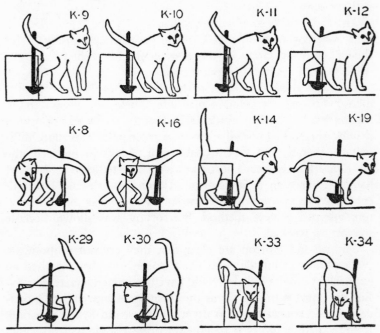

FIGURE 6. ALTERNATIVE STEREOTYPED RESPONSES OF A SINGLE CAT ESCAPING FROM THE PUZZLE BOX BY TOUCHING THE POLE.

Responses K-9 through K-12 illustrate one type of response used frequently by cat K. The remaining pairs of pictures show four other response types used by the same cat. Reproduced from tracings of photographs taken automatically at the time of release. From Guthrie and Horton (1946).

movement—the movement at the time of release—is the most stereotyped, is in agreement with the principle that such an act will remain intact because nothing can interfere with it, the cat leaving the situation as soon as he strikes the release mechanism. The fact that the food reward is inconsequential is shown by the cat's often failing to eat the fish or to lick the milk provided for it.

Guthrie and Horton say that they have seen in the behavior of their cats all that Adams and Thorndike report. But they have also seen a degree of stereotypy which points strongly to the tendency for behavior to repeat itself under similar conditions. Some of the tracings of photographs of Guthrie and Horton's cats are shown in Figure 6.

This behavior is so convincing that it has to be acknowledged. It is coherent with all that Guthrie has been proposing in his theory. That is surely as much as could be wished for by a theorist from a series of experiments.

Why did these cats learn so much more easily than Thorndike's? The answer given is plausible. These cats always found the release mechanism available in exactly the same form, and readily operable. Thorndike's release mechanism was more difficult to operate, and was probably not always in precisely the same position. Hence Thorndike's cats had to learn a series of habits rather than a single habit. When Guthrie and Horton's cats failed to operate the mechanism by a familiar method they, too, adopted a new method. Stereotypy was shown because stereotypy worked.

Guthrie and Horton are clear that they are not proposing a test of the cat's intelligence. They could easily have devised an experiment in which there would have been much less stereotypy. But the point is that as far as the learning of movements is concerned, the animal tends to do what it last did in the situation. If the situation forces it to do something else, it will do something else. Cats do not jump at the place where a bird was previously caught if there is no bird there, though they may lie in wait at the same spot.

The experiments are accepted by the authors as fully justifying the theory which Guthrie has all along expounded:

It has been our conclusion from our observation of this series of experiments that the prediction of what any animal would do at any moment is most securely based on a record of what the animal was observed to do *in that situation at its last occurrence*. This is obviously prediction in terms of association.[21]

Some objections to the Guthrie and Horton experiments as representative of animal learning. The experiments of Guthrie

[21] Guthrie and Horton (1946), page 42.

and Horton are appropriate ones for showing that, under limiting conditions, learned responses may show a high degree of
stereotypy. To go beyond this and assume that these experiments
provide the typical case for animal learning is misleading.

According to the authors themselves, varied behavior super-
venes if the response of the animal does not release it from the
box fairly quickly. The stereotypy appears to result in part at
least because the problem is an easy one. It may be mastered in
a single trial, and the later trials are then merely the repeated
performances of a learned act. There is little remarkable about
easy learning taking place promptly, or about its being repeated
when there is nothing to block it and reward to sustain it.

A problem may be easy without being clear. That this easy
problem was at the same time baffling to the cat is evidenced by
the difficulty which the cats found in using the pole when it was
displaced by a few inches from its original position.

A baffling situation further engenders stereotypy. This has
been pointed out frequently since G. V. Hamilton's early observations.[22] This matter is discussed later (pages 302-308).

The two features of the Guthrie and Horton situation which
may be supposed to have given rise to stereotyped responses are
that the task is (1) easy, in the sense of being promptly solved,
and (2) baffling, in the sense of the response being unclearly
related to its consequences. The most economical response in a
confusing but short-term situation is to do what was successful
the last time. If a door which is stuck opens promptly when you
happen to raise up on the knob, the tendency will be great to
repeat that behavior the next time, without inquiring into the
physics of the situation. Maybe it would also open if you pushed
down, but there is no need to try the alternative if the problem-
solution comes quickly. Stereotypy is something to be recognized
and reckoned with, but it may represent but a very special case
of learned behavior.

The quoted statement that every prediction made on the basis
of a past occurrence is a prediction in terms of association is
open to question. To prophesy that a man who owns and wears
only blue ties will wear a blue tie tomorrow is an actuarial prediction pure and simple, with no learning theory in it, like the

[22] Hamilton (1916)

prediction of an insurance company that a given percentage of people will die at a given age. The only assumption is a certain uniformity of events when taken *en masse*—an assumption scarcely attributable to associationism.

To account for learning, rather than for the repetition of learned acts, one has to account not for uniformity but for change. Upon learning in this sense the Guthrie and Horton experiments throw little light. Most of the change in behavior took place in the neglected early trials in which the cats learned to find their way out of the box through the glass door. There was, to be sure, the supplementary learning to use the pole to open the door. This constituted at once a baffling but an easy problem, which led to stereotypy. A harder but clearer problem, like the string-pulling problems studied by Adams, would be solved by fewer animals, but those which solved them could use the solutions in novel situations. Thus the chosen learning situation has a great deal to do with what aspects of behavior will be revealed. The problem-box of Guthrie and Horton, which at first blush appears to lay bare the primitive nature of learning, may in fact be a fairly confused and specialized situation poorly designed to show the behavior of the cat as it would solve a problem which, while harder for it, was more appropriate to it in clarity of cue-response relationships.

ESTIMATE OF GUTHRIE'S POSITION

Guthrie's position on typical problems of learning. By way of comparative summary, how Guthrie stands on the several representative problems of learning will be briefly stated.

1. *Capacity.* Problems of capacity are ignored, so far as formal treatment is concerned. Presumably any response which the organism can make can become associated with any stimulus to which he has a response—a generalization about the possibility of learning which is reminiscent of what Thorndike says about associative shifting. If pressed, Guthrie could find a basis for difference in capacity both in the differentiation of movement and in the discrimination among proprioceptive cues. All animals are not equally versatile and equally equipped with receptors.

2. *Practice.* Practice assimilates and alienates cues, until a whole

family of stimulus combinations comes to evoke a whole family of responses which lead to the outcome socially described as successful performance. Because skill represents a population of habits, learning appears to accumulate with repetition, although basically each individual habit is learned at full strength in a single repetition.

3. *Motivation.* Motivation affects learning indirectly through what it causes the animal to do. Reward is a secondary or derivative principle, not a primary one as in Thorndike's system. Reward works because it removes the animal from the stimulating situation in which the "correct" response has been made. It does not strengthen the "correct" response, but prevents its weakening because no new response can become attached to the cues which led to the correct response. Thus there is a relative strengthening, because responses to other cues get alienated. Punishment is inadequately handled by the categorical statement that the learner does what he did last time as a consequence of punishment.

4. *Understanding.* Concepts like "insight" are handled in a derisive manner, although it is recognized that learning with foresight of its consequences may occur. The tendency is to talk down such learning, however, just as Thorndike does, and to emphasize the stupid, mechanical, and repetitive nature of most human as well as animal learning. Such learning with intention and foresight as does occur is explained on the basis of conditioned anticipatory or readiness reactions, based upon past experience and hence not contradicting association principles.

5. *Transfer.* Learning transfers to new situations because of common elements within the old and new. In this the position is rather like Thorndike's. Stress is laid, however, on the identity being carried by way of common responses evoked, the proprioceptive stimuli being sufficiently similar from responses to a variety of stimuli to evoke common conditioned responses. The emphasis upon movement-produced stimuli thus represents Guthrie's supplementation to Thorndike.

Because of his principle of responses being conditioned to all adventitious contiguous stimuli, Guthrie expects rather little transfer, and is, in fact, rather extreme about it. The only way to be sure to get desired behavior in a new situation is to practice in that new situation as well. To be able to perform in a variety of situations, you have to practice in a variety of situations.

6. *Forgetting.* Learning is said to be permanent unless interfered with by new learning. Hence all forgetting is due to the learning of new responses which replace the old responses.

By contrast with Thorndike, Guthrie is an avowed behaviorist, who makes it a matter of some importance to get rid of subjective terms, to refer, for example, to inner speech instead of to thinking. The emphasis upon movement-produced stimuli is part of this older behaviorist tradition which Guthrie carries into the present. While an orthodox behaviorist in these respects, his is an informal behaviorism, with little of the brittleness of earlier Watsonianism.

The theory an ingenious oversimplification. The uncertainty which exists in practically all learning experimentation makes the fact minded psychologist suspicious of a finished system at this stage of our knowledge. One of the sources of doubt about the scientific validity of Guthrie's system lies in its assured answers to the problems of learning—answers which have remained the same through all the controversies over matters of experimental fact which have raged since the system was first announced. Favorite experiments, cited in earlier statements, have been disproven without any modifications appearing in later versions of the theory. This means that the theory is not very sensitive to experimental data.

The lack of close affiliation with experimentation is evident also in the few experiments which the theory has suggested to those who have come under its influence. It is not that kind of theory. Even the Guthrie and Horton experiments, which fill a much needed gap, are essentially descriptive. The data are presented raw, without any of the attempts at quantification familiar in contemporary scientific writing. There is no way of telling whether or not there is a consistent reduction in time scores when the animal uses a familiar mode of response, whether longer times are taken when a secondary mode is used, and so on. Even this best support of the theory is but an illustration of it, and not something which contributes in a satisfactorily critical way to precise knowledge about learning and its conditions.

Criticism of Guthrie's position is rendered somewhat difficult by the nature of the task which he sets himself. It is not quite clear whether he believes his system to have any responsibility with respect to details.

The principle of association or conditioning is not an explanation of any instance of behavior. It is merely a tool by which explanation is furthered. A tool is not true or false; it is useful or useless.[23]

The paradox of the theory lies in the kind of sophistication implied in this statement, combined with a casualness which baffles the critic. It is not unfair to ask of the position that it substantiate its claims, which are, indeed, far-reaching, and are competitive with the claims of others.

Of the opposing points of view to which he objects, Guthrie generously admits that their phenomena and the terms used to describe them are correct and useful for certain purposes.[24] What he says in essence is that what they do is all right for limited purposes, but it is not very helpful so far as understanding ordinary learning is concerned. When he attempts to show why they are not helpful he resorts to superficial criticisms and just occasionally to ridicule. All other writers are said to be concerned with outcomes, in the form of success or goal achievement. Under their theories, he says, the teacher must be a mere passive element in the situation, and cannot be told how to influence the outcome.[25] This *non sequitur* indicates a failure to take opposing claims seriously. Insight, if not predicted on the basis of past experience, must be in the category of luck, and hence lie outside of science.[26] While many of Guthrie's observations are astute, a cavalier handling of serious alternatives to his own gives the impression of immutability inappropriate in a growing science.

It is a curious thing that a theory which stresses observable minutiae (chiefly proprioceptive stimuli precisely coincident with specific muscular response) should gain its support chiefly from the grossest of observations, primarily anecdotal. This is both the basis of its appeal, and the warning sign of its weakness. Its appeal

[23] Guthrie (1935), page 232.
[24] Guthrie (1942), page 57. The positions referred to are those of gestalt psychology, Lewin and Tolman.
[25] Guthrie (1942), page 57.
[26] Guthrie (1935), page 25.

lies in the ability to comprehend, that is, to have something appropriate to say about, the ordinary learning activities of everyday life, including the symptoms found in the psychological clinic. This complicated material is talked about in dramatically simple terms, and there is little doubt that Guthrie is without a peer in this respect.

Close examination shows, however, that this appeal of practicality and simplicity is gained by the avoiding of responsibility for the very detail upon which the system logically rests, that is, the detail of precise stimulus and response relationships, and the precise movements out of which behavior is composed. The failure to take seriously the problem of what actually happens if a person does what he did last time in the presence of punishment, the failure to pay any attention to the double gradient of Thorndike's spread of effect (which refutes the theory that reward works by taking the organism out of the situation), the failure to deal with the problems of stimulus organization, so that there is some basis for predicting how much of the same pattern is needed to elicit a previously learned response, the failure to show in any detail how new responses arise out of attempts to elicit at once two or more old responses—these are but a few of Guthrie's failures to take responsibility for the detailed working out of the principles which he enunciates so confidently.

On the positive side, it is clear that Guthrie has made some genuine contributions, preeminently through pointing out the large element of repetitiveness and stereotypy in behavior. This emphasis sensitizes others to neglected aspects of response. The advice which he gives about learning is generally good advice, for Guthrie is a wise person. But the advice is seldom critically related to the theory, and could as well be derived from the theories of his opponents.

Perhaps some of those who have come under Guthrie's influence may go on to extend his theory, with responsibility for detail. The Guthrie and Horton experiments show that a critical experimental program is possible. Guthrie's personal preference for anecdotal evidence is not necessarily a consequence of his theory. At the present time, the theory as stated is grossly oversimplified, but this does not mean that with appropriate amendments based on careful experimentation it might not become a serious rival of other carefully worked out theories.

SUPPLEMENTARY READINGS

BOOKS

Guthrie, E. R. (1935) *The psychology of learning.*
Guthrie, E. R. (1938) *The psychology of human conflict.*

SHORTER INTRODUCTIONS

Guthrie, E. R. (1930) Conditioning as a principle of learning. *Psychol. Rev.,* 37, 412-428.
Guthrie, E. R. (1942) Conditioning: A theory of learning in terms of stimulus, response and association. *Natl. Soc. Stud. Educ.,* 41st Yearbook, Part II, 17-60.
Spence, K. W. (1942) Theoretical interpretations of learning. In F. A. Moss, edit., *Comparative psychology* (Revised edition), 280-329. (Guthrie's theory is treated on pages 298-307.)

CRITICAL REVIEWS

Carmichael, L. (1936) Review of Guthrie's *The psychology of learning. J. gen. Psychol.,* 14, 490-492.
Hilgard, E. R. (1935) Review of Guthrie's *The psychology of learning. Psychol. Bull.,* 32, 306-309.
Sears, R. R. (1939) Review of Guthrie's *The psychology of human conflict. Psychol. Bull.,* 36, 829-830.

REPRESENTATIVE EXPERIMENTS

Carter, L. F. (1936) Maze learning with a differential proprioceptive cue. *J. exp. Psychol.,* 19, 758-762.
Carter, L. F. (1941) Intensity of conditioned stimulus and rate of conditioning. *J. exp. Psychol.,* 28, 481-490.
Guthrie, E. R. (1933) Association as a function of time interval. *Psychol. Rev.,* 40, 355-367.
Guthrie, E. R., and Horton, G. P. (1946) *Cats in a puzzle box.*
Miller, J. (1939) The rate of conditioning of human subjects to single and multiple stimuli. *J. gen. Psychol.,* 20, 399-408.
Seward, J. P. (1942) An experimental study of Guthrie's theory of reinforcement. *J. exp. Psychol.,* 30, 247-256.
Smith, S., and Fitch, E. E. (1935) Skill and proprioceptor pattern. *J. genet. Psychol.,* 46, 303-310.
Voeks, V. (1945) What fixes the correct response? *Psychol. Rev.,* 52, 49-51.
Voeks, V. (1948) Postremity, recency, and frequency as bases for prediction in the maze situation. *J. exp. Psychol.* (To appear.)
Yacorzynski, G. K., and Guthrie, E. R. (1937) A comparative study of involuntary and voluntary conditioned responses. *J. gen. Psychol.,* 16, 235-257.

Chapter 4

HULL'S SYSTEMATIC BEHAVIOR THEORY

Clark L. Hull, greatly impressed by the appearance of the translation of Pavlov's *Conditioned reflexes* (1927), shortly began a series of theoretical and experimental studies which are models of system-making. Because the system is developed more formally than Guthrie's it may more properly be considered a fulfilment of the behavioristic program as proposed by Watson. Hull's theory is strictly a behaviorism, avowedly mechanistic and studiously avoiding reference to consciousness; its central concept is habit, and it derives most of its information about habit from conditioned responses; complex learning is derived step by step from what is known about more elementary forms of learning. In other respects Hull's system is very different from Watson's. Hull takes the detailed findings of conditioning experiments seriously in their quantitative aspects while Watson was chiefly interested in the paradigm which conditioned responses provided; something like Thorndike's law of effect lies at the very heart of Hull's system, while Watson rejected the law of effect; for Watson's policy of denials and negations, Hull substitutes a positive program of trying to explain purposes, insights, and other phenomena difficult for a behaviorism to encompass.

AN INFORMAL VERSION

Because of his preoccupation with scientific system-making, Hull has not cared to present a version of his theory which would present its substance in easily accessible form, sacrificing precision for the sake of a wider audience. This lack is filled in part by the introductory chapters of the book *Social learning and imitation* by Miller and Dollard (1941), which is written in an expository style more like that of Guthrie than of Hull, although it is based on concepts expounded by Hull in Yale seminars. They have achieved the sort of statement of Hull's theory which Guthrie might have written had he believed in it. Miller and Dollard are not disciples of Hull, strictly speaking, and they have made contributions of their own. As an introductory statement, however, their point of view may be taken as representing in substance that to which Hull subscribes.

Drive, cue, response, reward. The theory is introduced by an anecdotal experiment.[1] The subject is a six-year-old child who likes candy and is hungry for it. While she is out of the room a piece of her favorite candy is hidden under the edge of the center book in the lower shelf of a bookcase of several shelves. She is brought into the room, told there is candy hidden under one of the books, and asked if she wants to try to find it. She does, so she proceeds to look for the candy, after she is told that she must replace each book after looking under it, and that she may eat the candy when she finds it. She finds the candy after spending 210 seconds and examining 37 books. The next time she goes right to the lower shelf, and it takes her only 87 seconds and she looks under only 12 books. The next time she finds the candy under the second book examined, and it has taken her only 11 seconds. The next time she doesn't do so well. She starts at the other end of the shelf and works back. The authors speculate that she either was just lucky the time before, or introduced some other notion as a result of her previous experience with hiding games, such as, "He'll probably change the place now that I know it." Thereafter she continues to do better until on the ninth and tenth trials she goes right to the correct book and gets the candy.

Her behavior has changed markedly. Instead of requiring 210 seconds and stopping, asking questions, turning away, looking under magazines, searching in other parts of the room, picking up wrong books, and making other useless responses, she now goes directly to the right book and gets the candy in two seconds. She has learned.[2]

[1] Miller and Dollard (1941), pages 13-16.
[2] Miller and Dollard (1941), page 16.

According to Miller and Dollard there are four factors in learning: drive, cue, response, and reward.[3] Even this preliminary listing of the four factors is enough to point out a difference in substance between the theories of Guthrie and Hull. According to Guthrie, association occurs whenever cue and response are together, but according to Hull (and Miller and Dollard) the association between the cue and response is regulated by their relationship to drive and reward.

A *drive* is a strong stimulus which impels to action. Some drives are primary or innate, such as pain, thirst, hunger, or sex. Some are secondary or acquired, such as anxiety, fear, special appetites, the desire for money or social approval. Without drives the organism does not behave and hence does not learn. The experimenters had to be sure that the little girl wanted candy enough to participate in the game which they had arranged. Her drives were a complex of hunger, a cultivated appetite for candy, and secondary drives related to social participation and social approval.

Responses are elicited by *cues*. Cues determine "when he will respond, where he will respond, and which response he will make." The cue value of a stimulus depends on its distinctiveness, the drive value on its strength. Thus stimuli may serve either as goads to action, as signposts along the way, or as both of these at once. The child was given a great many cues. She was told that the candy was under a book, and that she would be permitted to eat it when she found it. The room and its contents suggested to her all sorts of things which might be picked up. If the book under which the candy was hidden were not in some way distinctive—in size, in color, in position—she could never have solved the problem.

Drive impels the individual to *respond* to certain cues. Only if the response occurs can it be rewarded and learned, and one of the tasks of training is so to arrange the situation that the desired response will occur. The little girl was impelled to begin picking up books by her appetite for candy and her knowledge that candy was to be found under a book. The instructions shortened the period of fumbling, compared, for example, with instructions only that the candy was somewhere in the room. The instruc-

[3] Miller and Dollard (1941), pages 16-36.

tions started her picking up books, so that the correct book had a reasonable chance of being picked up and rewarded.

Responses made to cues in the presence of drives will be learned if they are *rewarded*. If they are not rewarded, the tendency to repeat them will be weakened. Rewards produce reduction in drives; drive-reduction is, in fact, what makes them rewarding. That is why it is rewarding to be relieved from pain, to drink when thirsty, to eat when hungry. Drive-reduction, while theoretically essential to reward, is not always evident, especially in the case of secondary drives such as anxiety or desire to conform socially. For practical purposes rewarding situations can be identified by the fact that they do serve as rewards, that is, they strengthen stimulus-response connections. The dynamics of the drive-reduction situation need not be understood in each case. Just as there are secondary drives, so there are secondary or derived rewards. Money is the clearest illustration. Money is a reward because it is a route to many primary rewards. In the case of the little girl, it is not necessary for her to eat the candy in order to be rewarded by it. A poker chip might have served as well, provided it kept her at the task. We know that the candy was rewarding because she learned while seeking it.

It is said that the action of rewards is automatic. That is, in agreement with Thorndike, rewards act directly to strengthen cue-response connections, and do not require statements or thoughts about reward. Such statements do occur. The child may think about the candy she is looking for, or wonder how many pieces she is going to be allowed to eat; she may realize how happy her father is because she is doing well, and how much she likes to please her father. But all this knowledge about rewards has to be learned, so say Miller and Dollard, through the automatic action of rewards somewhere in the past.

Other principles from conditioning experiments. In common with Hull, Miller and Dollard believe conditioned response experiments to be a useful source of supplementary learning principles. They discuss six such principles: extinction, spontaneous recovery, generalization, discrimination, gradients in the effect of reward, anticipatory response.[4]

What Miller and Dollard call *gradients in the effects of reward*

[4] Miller and Dollard (1941), pages 37-53.

is what Hull calls the *gradient of reinforcement* (earlier, the goal gradient), and what Thorndike calls the *spread of effect*. All agree that cue-response sequences are strengthened in the neighborhood of reward, the nearer to the reward the greater the strengthening. This is the crux of the difference between the theory and that of Guthrie.

The principle of *anticipatory response* is something which the theories of Guthrie and Hull have in common. Anticipatory responses, in a behaviorist's system, carry a great load, being used to account for expectations, purposes, ideas, and other such psychological activities usually thought of as peculiarly subjective.

Miller and Dollard have succeeded better than anyone else to date in giving, in informal exposition and homely illustration, the gist of a theory substantially in agreement with Hull's principles. But the formal character of Hull's thinking is of equal importance with its substance, and any fully adequate exposition cannot avoid coming to grips with its details.

THE POSTULATES

The structure of the system which Hull accepts requires him to propose a short list of postulates (or laws) as the basic principles of the theory. Because the effort is made to keep the list short, the postulates must have sufficient generality to be used in the development of numerous theorems. If the whole structure is to be rigorous, great care must be taken in definition. Only then can inferences be made and tested quantitatively. In order to achieve such clarity and precision, meticulous exposition is needed. This Hull has provided in his books. The whole *Principles of Behavior* (1943) is an elucidation of sixteen postulates. Because it is our purpose to show what Hull is trying to do, rather than to repeat in detail how he does it, some liberties will be taken in paraphrasing his postulates and in assigning titles to them.[5] Precision will be sacrificed in order to point up the topical relevance of each of the postulates, thus making it somewhat easier to grasp the system as a whole.

[5] The citation is in each case given to the page in Hull (1943a) on which the full statement can be found. In Hull's book the postulates are without titles.

The external cues which guide behavior. The general plan of Hull's system is straightforward. The complete behavioral event begins with stimulation provided by the external world and ends by a response, also part of the interplay with the environment. Everything else lies within the organism as influencing in one way or another the prediction as to what response will occur, if any, following the onset of the stimuli. The set of intervening processes, which are scientific constructs rather than observables, are anchored, as Hull says, at both ends—at the stimulus-end and at the response-end.

The postulates begin with the representation of the stimulus in afferent neural processes. The first two postulates may be paraphrased as follows:

Postulate 1. *Afferent neural impulses and the perseverative stimulus trace.*

Stimuli impinging upon a receptor give rise to afferent neural impulses which rise quickly to a maximum intensity and then diminish gradually. After the termination of the stimulus, the activity of the afferent nervous impulse continues in the central nervous tissue for some seconds.[6]

Postulate 2. *Afferent neural interaction.*

Afferent neural impulses interact with other concurrent afferent neural impulses in a manner to change each into something partially different. The manner of change varies with every impulse or combination of impulses.[7]

The first postulate is required to allow for the persistence in time of the results of stimulation. One consequence is to permit

---

[6] Modified from Hull (1943a), page 47. As an indication of details omitted in paraphrasing, the postulate is quoted in full here:

"When a stimulus energy (S) impinges on a suitable receptor organ, an afferent neural impulse (s) is generated and is propagated along connected fibrous branches of nerve cells in the general direction of the effector organs, via the brain. During the continued action of the stimulus energy (S), this afferent impulse (s), after a short latency, rises quickly to a maximum of intensity, following which it gradually falls to a relatively low value as a simple decay function of the maximum. After the termination of the action of the stimulus energy (S) on the receptor, the afferent impulse (s) continues its activity in the central nervous tissue for some seconds, gradually diminishing to zero as a simple decay function of its value at the time the stimulus energy (S) ceases to act."

[7] Modified from Hull (1943a), page 47.

events inside the nervous system to form associations on the basis of simultaneous occurrence, even though according to external measurements the events might be separated in time. This is the counterpart of the use made by Guthrie of movement-produced stimuli, except that Guthrie permits movements to fill the time gap, while Hull assumes that the impulses themselves persist, possibly independent of movement. A related consequence is to permit afferent processes initiated at different times to modify each other before they lead to action. If the first process did not persist until the second occurred, there could be no interaction.

The postulate of afferent neural interaction permits Hull to derive the properties of patterned stimuli—the essence of the gestalt perception problem. He has been severely criticized for concealing within this postulate the acceptance of all that is really crucial in the derivations from it.[8] Hull believes that through this postulate he has achieved a rapprochement with gestalt psychology which represents a good sign of the maturing of psychological science.[9]

The postulate is objectionable, we may grant, not for its content, but for its lack of denotative specificity. It says, in effect, that every combination of afferent impulses is unique, and then from that starting point appears to derive the fact that combinations of stimuli may act differently from the separate stimuli of which they are composed. The resolution of Humphrey's arpeggio paradox [10] amounts to the assertion that the reason the subject reacted differently to the tone alone and to the tone in the arpeggio was that in the latter case the neural pattern was different! The reply merely restates the question, and a truism takes on the character of a discovery. The best that can be said for the postulate of neural interaction is that it represents an honest recognition that the problem of patterning in perception is a genuine one. The postulate does not solve the problem; it takes the problem from the field of perception and buries it in the nervous system.

To what extent are these first two postulates *molar* rather than

---

[8] Leeper (1944), Skinner (1944), Meehl (1945). Hull has defended his position, Hull (1945a).

[9] Hull (1942), page 77.

[10] Humphrey (1928), Hull (1943a), pages 372-374.

molecular? Hull claims to have taken over the concept of molar behavior from Tolman (1932*b*), yet Tolman would prefer to make his inferences from behavior, without assuming neurophysiological details. Hull's reply would have to be that the distinction between molar and molecular is a relative one after all. The molecular description of afferent neural interaction would have to tell where and how the afferent impulses interact. To the extent that Hull's postulates are based on processes inferred from behavior and not intended to be verified as neurology, they are molar; to the extent that there is a serious effort to describe the verifiable neurophysiology underlying learning, they would have to be classified as molecular.

Responses to need; reinforcement and habit strength. Among the non-observables which affect responses to stimuli are the drives which operate and the habits which have been built up in the past on the basis of such drives. The next two postulates explicate the manner of habit strengthening through reinforcement, and are in some respects the basic postulates.

Postulate 3. *Innate responses to need.*

Organisms at birth possess a hierarchy of need-terminating responses which are aroused under conditions of stimulation and drive. The responses activated by a given need are not a random selection of the organism's responses, but are those more likely to terminate the need.[11]

Postulate 4. *Reinforcement and habit strength.*

Habit strength increases when receptor and effector activities occur in close temporal contiguity, provided their approximately contiguous occurrence is associated with primary or secondary reinforcement.[12]

The third postulate is preparatory to the need-reduction theory of primary reinforcement. The innate relationship between need and responses leading to its reduction is conjectured on the basis of naturalistic observation: the reaction to pain is withdrawal of the injured part; the hungry infant is likely to show lip movements; hunger or sexual tensions lead an animal to locomotion because the satisfaction of these drives requires commerce

---

[11] Modified from Hull (1943*a*), page 66.
[12] Modified from Hull (1943*a*), page 178. The postulate is quoted in full in footnote 25 of this chapter.

with food or with an animal of the opposite sex. A hungry animal is less likely to choose sleep as the response to hunger than some other response. Out of all possible reactions, those are selected which have some chance of meeting the need.

The status of drive in the system is that of a non-observable construct or an intervening variable. This means only that drive has to be inferred from something else (such as hours of food deprivation) rather than directly measured. Hull's willingness to depart from observables (or potentially observables) represents an advance over more primitive behaviorisms.

Primary reinforcement, in the fourth postulate, is identified with diminution of need. Secondary reinforcement is mediated by a stimulus which has been closely and consistently associated with the need reduction. The action of reward is that given in the anecdote from Miller and Dollard. The child will learn to select the book if her hunger is relieved by eating the chocolate, or by the sight of the chocolate, since that sight has so often been associated with hunger reduction.

The postulate as formally stated further specifies the manner of summation of increments of habit strength upon repetition of reinforcement, and sets the upper limit of habit strength in terms of three variables:

1. The magnitude of need reduction involved in reinforcement
2. The delay between response and reinforcement
3. The interval between conditioned stimulus and response, or, in the case of a delayed conditioned response, the time of action of the conditioned stimulus before the response begins

The upper limit tends to be a maximum when need reduction is great, delay between response and reinforcement is short, and there is little separation between conditioned stimulus and reaction. Optimal values may lie within arrangements that depart slightly from maximum need reduction and from strict contiguity of reaction and reinforcement or contiguity of stimulus and reaction. Probably the optimal time relationships are for the reaction to follow the conditioned stimulus by a short interval of time, and for the reinforcement likewise to follow the reaction. The most favorable relationships are those of immediate succession rather than of simultaneity.

Habit strength is to be measured in a unit called a *hab* (short for habit), one *hab* being 1/100 of the upper limit of habit strength as set by the maximum obtainable under optimal conditions.

This fourth postulate is the heart of the learning theory. In it are summarized the basic conditions under which learning takes place, the fundamental operation of rewards, the effects of repetition, and the gradients of reinforcement. It will be necessary to return to it.

Stimulus equivalence. Learning is never completely specific to the situation in which it originally arose, and all theories require some principle of stimulus equivalence. Hull takes over the concept of generalization from Pavlov.

Postulate 5. *Generalization.*

The effective habit strength aroused by a stimulus other than the one originally entering into conditioning depends upon the remoteness of the second stimulus from the first on a continuum in units of discrimination thresholds (just noticeable differences).[13]

The more similar one stimulus is to another, the more nearly it can substitute for the other in arousing conditioned responses. Hence there may be described a *gradient of generalization*.[14] Hull recognizes, of course, that only limited families of stimuli can be ordered in simple psychophysical continua. There are various forms of logical or mediated similarity to which this postulate cannot apply directly. Such secondary generalizations will defy any kind of quantitative ordering. Hull is aware of the possibility of mediation by way of intermediate responses, a favorite explanation of Guthrie's, but Hull believes such mediation to be so specialized and contingent as not to belong in the postulate system.

Drives as activators of response. Needs or drives enter twice into the determination of behavior, once in habit formation, again in the utilization of that habit in performance. When an organism

[13] Modified from Hull (1943*a*), page 199.
[14] Important papers showing attempts to derive the form of the gradient of generalization, and to apply it to problems of stimulus equivalence and discrimination, are those of Spence (1937) and Hull (1939*a*). Whether or not a universal form of gradient is to be expected has been discussed by Razran (1938) and Spence (1939). See also Hull (1947).

is quiet or asleep, it has not lost its habits of running about; the habits are there to be activated by aroused drives. The next two postulates deal with this state of affairs.

Postulate 6. *Drive stimulus.*

Associated with every drive is a characteristic drive stimulus whose intensity increases with strength of drive.[15]

Postulate 7. *Reaction potentiality aroused by drives.*

Habit strength is sensitized into reaction potentiality by the primary drives active at a given time.[16]

Because there is a stimulus pattern characteristic of its drives, the organism can discriminate between patterns, and learn, for example, to turn one way when hungry, another way when thirsty.[17] This differentiating rôle of drive supplements its reinforcing or activating rôles.

According to the seventh postulate, readiness to respond on the basis of habit strength awaits drive. Hull believes the relationship to be some sort of multiplicative one, so that reaction potential is a kind of product between drive and habit strength. Reaction remains potential and not overt at this point—remains a kind of readiness to move and act and respond—because response evocation is contingent upon the resistances which the reaction potential may encounter.

The unit of measurement of reaction potential is the *wat* (a contraction honoring the name of Watson). *Habs* become *wats* when acted upon by drives (measured in a unit called the *mote*, derived from motivation). The maximum of reaction potentiality is 100 *wats;* the maximum strength of drive is 100 *motes.*

The distinction between learning and performance recognized in the difference between *habs* and *wats* is an important one. It emphasizes that habit strength is revealed in action only under appropriate conditions.

Barriers to response. One of the reasons that reaction potential does not always lead to response evocation is that opposing inhibitions may be encountered. Three postulates deal with inhibition.

[15] Modified from Hull (1943*a*), page 253.
[16] Modified from Hull (1943*a*), page 253.
[17] Hull (1933), Leeper (1935*a*), Kendler (1946).

Postulate 8. *Reactive inhibition.*

The evocation of any reaction generates reactive inhibition. Reactive inhibition is spontaneously dissipated in time.[18]

Postulate 9. *Conditioned inhibition.*

Stimuli associated with the cessation of a response become conditioned inhibitors.[19]

Postulate 10. *Oscillation of inhibition.*

The inhibitory potential associated with every reaction potential oscillates in amount from instant to instant.[20]

According to the eighth postulate, experimental extinction—the decrease with repetition of a non-reinforced response—becomes but a special case of the tendency of all responses, through the fact of occurrence, to develop a barrier to their own repetition. This inhibition subsides with the passage of time. In conditioning terminology this consequence has been called spontaneous recovery.

The unit of inhibitory potential is the *pav* (honoring the name of Pavlov). It may be defined by the *wat*, since one *pav* can inhibit one *wat*.

According to the ninth postulate, stimuli which occur at the time reactive inhibition is being generated become capable through conditioning of eliciting this inhibition, that is, of reducing the effective reaction potential of concurrent conditioned responses. This conditioned inhibition acts like any other habit, and is not dissipated in time like reactive inhibition.

Finally, the prevention of response (or its reduction) through reactive and conditioned inhibition is further modified through the waxing and waning of the inhibitory potential. The concept of oscillation arose out of the observation that organisms vary from moment to moment in their ability to perform well-established habits. In memorizing nonsense syllables, a syllable correctly anticipated on one trial may be missed on the next trial. The tenth postulate assigns the oscillation to inhibition. In the earlier book (1940) the reaction threshold was made to oscillate;

[18] Modified from Hull (1943a), page 300.
[19] Modified from Hull (1943a), page 300.
[20] Modified from Hull (1943a), page 319.

in *Principles of behavior* the threshold remains constant but the reaction potential is made to oscillate by attaching to it a fluctuating inhibitory appendage. The choice of what is to vary is largely a matter of convenience at this stage of system-making. This mode of dealing with behavioral fluctuations is very ingenious, and has led to useful deductions.

Response evocation. We have now moved through the chain of events and inferences between the stimulus and the moment of response. If the momentary effective reaction potential (the resultant of reaction potential and the fluctuating inhibitory potential) is of sufficient strength to bring response above threshold, a response will appear, with quantitative characteristics which depend upon how much above threshold the momentary effective reaction potential is. The remaining postulates describe the threshold, and consider the units of response measurement.[21]

Postulate 11. *Reaction threshold.*

The momentary effective reaction potential must exceed the reaction threshold before a stimulus will evoke a given reaction.

Postulate 12. *Probability of reaction above the threshold.*

The probability of response in striated muscle is a normal (ogival) function of the extent to which the effective reaction potential exceeds the reaction threshold.

Postulate 13. *Latency.*

The more the effective reaction potential exceeds the reaction threshold, the shorter the latency of response in striate muscle.

Postulate 14. *Resistance to extinction.*

The greater the effective reaction potential, the more unreinforced responses of striate muscle may occur before extinction.

Postulate 15. *Amplitude of response.*

The amplitude of responses mediated by the autonomic nervous system increases directly with the strength of the effective reaction potential.

Postulate 16. *Incompatible responses.*

When reaction potentials to two or more incompatible responses occur in an organism at the same time, only the reaction whose effective reaction potential is greatest will be evoked.

[21] Postulates 11 through 16 are all to be found on page 344 in Hull (1943a).

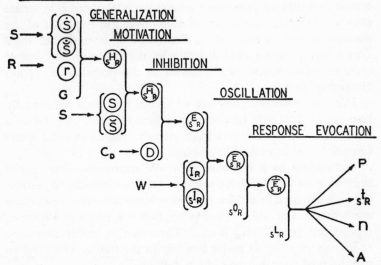

FIGURE 7. DIAGRAM SUMMARIZING THE MAJOR SYMBOLIC CONSTRUCTS IN HULL'S SYSTEM OF BEHAVIOR.

Š, the physical stimulus energy

R, the organism's reaction

š, the neural result of the stimulus

š̃, the neural interaction arising from two or more stimulus components

r, the efferent impulse leading to reaction

G, occurrence of reinforcing state of affairs

$_sH_R$, habit strength

S, evocation stimulus on same stimulus continuum as Š.

s, the neural result of S

š, neural interaction

$_s\bar{H}_R$, the generalized habit strength

C_D, the objectively observable phenomena determining the drive

D, the physiological strength of the drive

$_sE_R$, the reaction potential

W, work involved in evoked reaction

I_R, reactive inhibition

$_s\bar{I}_R$, conditioned inhibition

$_s\bar{E}_R$, effective reaction potential

$_sO_R$, oscillation

$_s\dot{\bar{E}}_R$, momentary effective reaction potential

$_sL_R$, reaction threshold

p, probability of response evocation

$_st_R$, latency of reaction evocation

n, number of unreinforced reactions to extinction

A, amplitude of reaction

After Hull (1943a), page 383.

It is to be noted that the units of measurement implied in postulates twelve to fifteen are physical units, obtained by counting, timing, or measuring. It is from these physical response units that you have to work back through a process of inference to units in *wats* or *habs*. The distinction between striate muscle reactions and responses mediated by the autonomic nervous system is a matter of laboratory convenience. Responses in striate muscle also have a dimension of amplitude, and responses of the autonomic system also have a dimension of latency, but these dimensions are not included; just why the arbitrary selection of units of measurement was included in the postulate set is not altogether clear.[22]

The final postulate gives one additional condition occasionally responsible for lack of correlation between effective reaction potential and response evocation, namely, the mechanical interference by an incompatible response.

The system as a chain of symbolic constructs. The special symbols used by Hull have not thus far been introduced because they are required as a convenient shorthand only when equations are written. The chief defining symbols are given in Figure 7, reproduced from Hull's book.[23] There are six major processes, represented by the six major brackets in the figure. The diagram may be read from left to right as follows:

1. *Reinforcement.* Habit strength ($_SH_R$) is the result of a reinforcement of stimulus-response connections in accordance with their proximity to need reduction. (Postulates 3-4)

2. *Generalization.* Generalized habit strength ($_S\bar{H}_R$) depends both upon direct reinforcement and upon generalization from other reinforcements. (Postulate 5)

3. *Motivation.* Reaction potential ($_SE_R$) depends upon the interaction of habit strength and drive. (Postulates 6 and 7)

4. *Inhibition.* Effective reaction potential ($_S\bar{E}_R$) is reaction potential as reduced by reactive inhibition and conditioned inhibition. (Postulates 8 and 9)

5. *Oscillation.* Momentary effective reaction potential ($_S\hat{E}_R$) is effective reaction potential as modified from instant to instant by the oscillating inhibitory factor associated with it. (Postulate 10)

6. *Response evocation.* Responses are evoked if the momentary effective reaction potential is above the threshold of reaction. Such

---

[22] It is tacitly assumed that the measures are highly correlated, and can be interchanged through transforming equations. This is not actually the case, as shown by the correlations presented in Hilgard and Marquis (1940), page 138, Lumsdaine (1941), Humphreys (1943a). There are more sources of variability than can be accounted for by assigning all oscillation to one underlying process.

[23] Hull (1943a), page 383.

responses may be measured according to the probability of reaction, latency of reaction, resistance to extinction, or amplitude. (Postulates 11-16)

The system is a single chain of symbolic constructs, tied to the physical world at both ends. It is anchored to antecedent observable events in the physical environment and the organism, and, on the consequent side, to observable and measurable reactions. This anchorage makes possible the systematic manipulation of the logical constructs in mediating valid deductions. A system may be rooted in empirical fact even though its variables are constructs and not observables.[24]

The gradient of reinforcement and the goal gradient. Among the principles within Hull's system that of the *gradient of reinforcement* is central. It is a part of Postulate 4, the discussion of which was curtailed above in order that an overall view of the pattern of the sixteen postulates could be presented with greater conciseness.

Postulate 4 covers more detailed topics than those suggested in its short paraphrasing.[25] It includes (1) the principle of primary and secondary reinforcement as related to need reduction, (2) the summation of increments of habit strength as a result of re-

[24] For further discussion of the logic of this kind of system, see Bergmann and Spence (1941), Spence (1944), MacCorquodale and Meehl (1947).

[25] Postulate 4, because of the number of topics covered and because of its centrality in the system, is here given in full:

"Whenever an effector activity $(r \rightarrow R)$ and a receptor activity $(S \rightarrow s)$ occur in close temporal contiguity (sCr), and this sCr is closely and consistency associated with the diminution of a need (G) or with a stimulus which has been closely and consistently associated with the diminution of a need $(\dot{G})$, there will result an increment to a tendency $(\triangle sH_R)$ for that afferent impulse on later occasions to evoke that reaction. The increments from successive reinforcements summate in a manner which yields a combined habit strength (sH_R) which is a simple positive growth function of the number of reinforcement (N). The upper limit (m) of this curve of learning is the product of (1) a positive growth function of the magnitude of need reduction which is involved in primary, or which is associated with secondary, reinforcement; (2) a negative growth function of the delay (t) in reinforcement; and (3) (a) a negative growth function of the degree of asynchronism (t') of $\dot{S}$ and R when both are of brief duration, or (b), in case the action of $\dot{S}$ is prolonged so as to overlap the beginning of R, a negative growth function of the duration (t'') of the continuous action of $\dot{S}$ on the receptor when R begins." (Hull, 1943a, page 178.)

peated reinforcements, and (3) the upper limit of growth of habit strength as determined by three variable relationships. The first of these relationships is that of the amount of need reduction produced by the reinforcement. The second is the interval of time separating the reaction to be strengthened and the reinforcement. The third is the length of time between the conditioned stimulus and the reaction. It is the temporal gradients in the last two or these three relationships which are here the subject of discussion. Hull refers to two intervals of separation, not ordinarily distinguished in conditioning experiments.

Because in classical conditioning the unconditioned reaction defines the reinforcement, the usual time gradients in classical conditioning are gradients of stimulus-response separation, called by Hull stimulus-response asynchronism. It is assumed that in classical conditioning the interval between reaction and reinforcement is constant.[26] Experiments selected by Hull as representative [27] indicate that a certain short interval (a fraction of a second) provides the point of *optimal stimulus asynchronism*. If the stimuli occur closer together or farther apart (in either order) less conditioning results. The gradients are steep, and the form of the gradient is established by events occurring within a few seconds of stimulus-response separation.[28] This gradient of asynchronism is not to be confused either with the gradient of reinforcement or the goal gradient, to be described below.

The measurement of the gradient of reinforcement depends upon experiments of the instrumental conditioning type, in which an act such as pushing a lever or running down an alley leads to the goal object and reinforcement. Delay may be introduced between the act to be rewarded and the goal-object which provides the reinforcing state of affairs. Thus the delivery of the pellet of food which is the reward for lever-pressing may be

[26] Because the time intervals in classical conditioning are usually short, the change in response-reinforcement interval which comes when an anticipatory conditioned response develops is ignored by Hull. In trace or delayed conditioned responses this would be a source of confusion in determining the relative efficacy of different degrees of stimulus-response asynchronism.

[27] Wolfle (1930) (1932), Kappauf and Schlosberg (1937).

[28] It is this stimulus-response interval with which Guthrie (1933) is concerned. He believes that the gradient appears empirically only because we do not measure the underlying processes which are themselves contiguous.

postponed for an arbitrary number of seconds in order to study the effect upon rat learning of such a delay. The gradient of reinforcement is derived from such delayed reinforcement experiments, as distinguished from the stimulus-response separation experiments of classical conditioning. Hull believes, on the basis of a delayed reinforcement experiment done with rats in the lever-pressing box,[29] that the basic gradient of reinforcement is fairly short, in the case of the rat, "possibly no more than thirty seconds and very probably less than sixty seconds." [30]

Other experiments on the effect of delayed reward, such as those of Wolfe (1934) show that in a simple alley maze, the reward is effective for learning with much longer delays, at least as long as twenty minutes, the longest delay tested. A gradient is shown here, also, with the longer intervals less effective for learning than the shorter ones. Such a gradient Hull calls a *goal gradient* to distinguish it from the shorter gradient of reinforcement. Hull conjectures that the longer goal gradients are generated from primary reinforcement gradients via secondary reinforcement. A maze provides many cues which, through association with reward, may themselves become secondary reinforcing agents. Through a chain of overlapping gradients of reinforcement, a longer goal gradient results.[31]

While the goal gradient is not therefore the primary one it was earlier considered to be, it is a derivative or intermediate principle, which, once established, again serves its former purposes in the explanation of more complex learning. The original application was to the maze. The principle mediated the deduction that responses nearer to the goal would be more strongly conditioned than those farther removed, so that short paths would be preferred to longer ones, blinds near the goal would be eliminated more readily than blinds farther away, longer blinds would be more readily eliminated than shorter ones, and so on.[32] The goal gradient principle was later applied to field-force problems as

[29] Perin (1943*a*, 1943*b*).
[30] Hull (1943*a*), page 142.
[31] The conjecture is developed by Spence (1947).
[32] Hull (1932). For an introductory exposition, see Hilgard and Marquis (1940), pages 216-221. For the history of the problem of the goal gradient, and its later revisions, see Hull (1943*a*), pages 159-160.

studied by Lewin.[33] For example, in experiments involving the circumventing of barriers between the learner and a visible goal, Hull proposed that the reaction to the perceived goal-object should behave in accordance with the goal gradient. That is, the nearer the learner came to the goal, the stronger should be its response-evoking power. Thus Hull, by way of the goal gradient, came to conclusions similar to those described by Lewin as goal-attraction in relation to distance.

The habit-family hierarchy. A second derived principle is that of the habit-family hierarchy. This is not included among the postulates of *Principles of behavior* because, like the goal gradient, it is a principle at intermediate level, being itself derived from more basic principles. It carries great weight, however, in the deduction of further behavioral phenomena.

Because there are multiple routes between a starting point and a goal, the organism learns alternative ways of moving from a common starting point to a common goal-position where it finds need satisfaction. These alternatives constitute a habit-family because of an inferred integrating mechanism. The integration into a family is by way of a common *fractional anticipatory goal reaction*, present as each alternative is active. The fractional anticipatory goal reaction provides a stimulus (s_G) to which all overt responses are conditioned. Through the differential action of the gradient of reinforcement, some responses are less strongly conditioned to s_G than others. The starting responses of longer routes, for example, are more remote from reinforcement than the starting responses of shorter routes. Hence the latter are more strongly reinforced, and more strongly conditioned to s_G. As a consequence, the alternative behavior patterns are arranged in a preferred order. The less favored routes are chosen only when the more favored are blocked. It is this set of alternative habits, integrated by a common goal-stimulus, and arranged in preferential order, that constitutes a habit-family hierarchy.

It is further deduced by Hull that if one member of a habit-family hierarchy is reinforced in a new situation, all other members of the family share at once in the tendency to be evoked

[33] Hull (1938). The problems were such as proposed by Lewin (1933a) (1935).

as reactions in that situation.[34] This makes possible the explanation of response equivalences and other appropriate reactions in novel or problematic situations, such as those found in insight and reasoning experiments.

The principle was first applied to maze learning,[35] serving chiefly to explain the tendency for the rat to enter goal-pointing blinds, even though such entrances had never been reinforced in the maze situation. Goal-orientation was taken to represent an inappropriate transfer of spatial habits acquired in free space. Another application was in relation to the detour experiments.[36] The difficulty of turning away from a perceived goal beyond a barrier depends on the presence of habit-family hierarchies as well as upon goal-gradients. In the usual experience of free space, the favored path is the straight line between the learner and the goal. The next-favored starting response is that making least angle with the goal. The greater the angle, the less favored is the starting response in that family of habits built up in previous experience. Hence, when blocked, the learner prefers a path which, say, goes off at a right angle to one which requires that he turn his back on the goal. In some objective situations he may come to choose a longer path to a shorter one, if the habit-family hierarchy proves to be misleading.

A deductive theory. A modern deductive scientific system proposes to make its predictions according to theorems which can be derived step-by-step from basic postulates or laws. Because these predictions are stated in a form which can be subjected to precise test in the laboratory, the system is empirical as well as rational. The alternative is to be empirical only, that is, descriptive of what happens under controlled conditions, arriving inductively at generalizations which summarize the data. Such a descriptive, inductive science is sometimes called *positivistic*, to contrast it with the *hypothetical-deductive* kind of system which Hull adopts.[37]

The formal steps in the exposition of a deductive system like

[34] Formal deduction is given by Hull (1937), page 27.
[35] Hull (1934a).
[36] Hull (1938).
[37] Descriptive positivism or extreme empiricism is to be distinguished from *logical positivism*, which is congenial to the hypothetical-deductive approach. See, for example, Carnap (1936) (1937), Spence (1944).

Hull's are as follows: (1) definition of terms, (2) statements of fundamental postulates or laws, (3) derivation of theorems following by necessity from these laws, (4) indirect verification or refutation of the postulates by experimental tests of the theorems,[38] (5) correction of the postulates found to be faulty. The logical interaction among postulates, theorems, and experimental results keeps the system provisional and self-correcting. In the end that system will survive which, with the minimum number of postulates, can deduce the largest number of facts without internal contradiction.

Because of the nature of the task which Hull has set himself, the written reports of his work are becoming increasingly forbidding. There are inevitably many abstract symbols and complex mathematical equations in a system of this kind. To criticize Hull for these features of his system would be like criticizing a physicist for making his theories difficult. Criticism must be differently directed. But the fact remains that the book by Hull and his collaborators entitled *Mathematico-deductive theory of rote learning* (1940) is the most difficult ever written by psychologists. The later volume, *Principles of behavior* (1943), was originally planned to be called a "primer" of behavior, and is intended to be at a much less difficult level. The complexities which persist in it are of the sort which any serious student of behavior must be prepared to master.

EXPERIMENTS ON ROTE MEMORIZATION

The foregoing digest of Hull's postulational system suffers because of its failure to show how at each step Hull has been concerned to keep the postulates moored to relationships found in experiments through the testing of theorems deduced with the aid of these postulates. In order to remedy this defect to some extent, the following material will lay emphasis upon the experimental consequences which may be verified in the laboratory, as shown in the experiments on rote memorization found within the earlier book.[39] Although its system of postulates differs

[38] Some postulates may be tested by direct experiment, but the logic of the system permits indirect test by way of multivariable predictions.
[39] Hull, Hovland, Ross, Hall, Perkins, and Fitch (1940).

slightly from that just presented, the point of view has not been altered radically, and the material serves somewhat more satisfactorily to illustrate the interrelationship between data and theory.

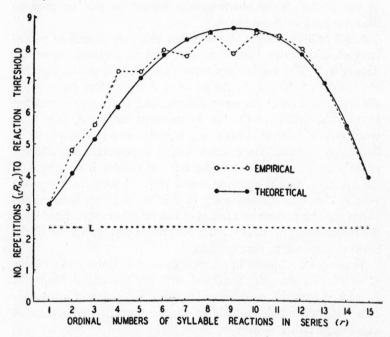

FIGURE 8. SERIAL POSITION EFFECT IN THE MEMORIZATION OF A LIST OF 15 NONSENSE SYLLABLES.

The reaction threshold is defined as the mean of the trial on which the first successful repetition occurs and that on which the last failure occurs, prior to mastery. The horizontal broken line represents the threshold value (L) on the assumption of no inhibition. Only the first and last syllables are relatively free of intra-serial inhibitions, and so may be learned with repetitions only slightly greater than threshold values. The theoretical curve is made to pass through the empirical values at trials 1, 8, and 15. Reproduced from Hull and others (1940), page 106.

The book covers three main bodies of factual material: (1) serial position effects, having to do with relative ease of learning and other factors associated with the ordinal position of a nonsense syllable in a list being memorized, (2) reminiscence and forgetting, relating the initial rise in the curve of retention to other factors such as distributed practice, serial position, and length of list, and (3) reaction thresholds and the course of memorization. A guide to these topics, in relation to the theorems and postulates made use of, may be found in an earlier review of the book.[40] Some characteristic deductions will be used to illustrate each of these topics.

Serial position effects. A somewhat elaborate system of postulates about reactive inhibition is needed to improve an earlier deduction.[41] The earlier argument succeeded in predicting that the middle of the list should be more difficult than the ends. It did not predict that the most difficult item is actually somewhat beyond the middle of the list. In the new deduction, each nonsense syllable is treated both as a stimulus and as a response, as before. A stimulus trace (now called a perseverating afferent neural trace) continues after the exposed syllable is no longer in the aperture. At any moment traces from all previously exposed syllables, back to the beginning of the list, make up the stimulus complex. The pattern of excitation and inhibition summated over the traces acting while a syllable is exposed determines the likelihood of response to that syllable.

The success achieved in the new deduction is shown in Figure 8, which compares the empirical with the theoretical results. It is evident that the new formula places the point of maximum difficulty beyond the middle of the list, and fits the results of experiment rather well.

It is not the fit of theoretical curve and empirical curve which determines the systematic elegance of the deduction, because as good or better fit might be obtained by ordinary curve-fitting methods, without any theory about the parameters (or constants) in the curve. In this case, however, the curve is a rational one. That is, the parameters have meaning in the theory, and the form of the curve follows from the nature of the processes taking place. The values of the constants are finally determined by fitting the rational curve to the empirical data.

Only one of the derived constants shows on the figure. That is L, the reaction threshold, computed to be 2.32 trials for this list of fifteen items. The reaction threshold is the number of

---

[40] Hilgard (1940).
[41] Hull (1935a).

repetitions needed to bring each syllable to the threshold of recall *if there had been no interfering inhibition*. The piling up of inhibitions causes the items in the middle of the list to be most difficult to learn. The threshold is defined empirically for each syllable as the number of repetitions midway between the first success and the last failure. The computed theoretical value of *L* lies just below the empirical value for the first syllable, as might reasonably have been expected.

The curve was fitted by the use of simultaneous equations with three constants, the constants being computed so that the curve would pass through the obtained (empirical) values for syllables 1, 8, and 15. The three constants which emerge from the computation are $\triangle K$, *F*, and *L*. The meaning of *L*, the reaction threshold, has already been given. $\triangle K$ is the amount of inhibition generated by each repetition of each syllable. It applies directly to the trace of the exposed syllable, but spreads at reduced values to the other trace segments acting at the time. *F* is the factor of reduction whereby the inhibition associated with several component stimulus-trace segments is decreased from the segment representing the exposed syllable to those segments representing syllables more remote in point of origin. Because *L*, $\triangle K$, and *F* are theoretical constructs given systematic meaning, they have a different status from the parameters of just any curve which might be fitted to the points of Figure 8.

The real test of the rational significance of *L*, $\triangle K$ and *F* comes as they are applied to the form of the serial position curve for a list of different length. With length as the only altered variable, subjects of comparable ability, learning comparable materials, ought to have the same values of *L*, $\triangle K$ and *F* in the new situation. Unfortunately the values do not show much consistency from situation to situation, and to that extent the deduction is not completely satisfactory.

Reminiscence and forgetting. The postulate that inhibition is dissipated more rapidly than excitation is reasonable in view of spontaneous recovery following the extinction of conditioned responses. On the assumption that what is retained will depend on the algebraic interaction of excitation and inhibition, it can be predicted that there will be a rise in the curve of retention before the usual forgetting is shown, as in Figure 9.

The thatched portion of the curve shows the initial rise (reminiscence), resulting from the combination of the two theoretical curves. The experimental data predicted are those such as Ward (1937) obtained, Figure 10.

How is integration achieved between the postulates and their consequences for serial position effects, and the new postulates and

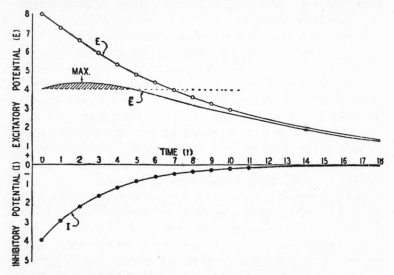

FIGURE 9. PREDICTION OF REMINISCENCE EFFECT AS A CONSEQUENCE OF THE DIFFERENTIAL DECAY OF EXCITATORY AND INHIBITORY POTENTIALS.

The top curve represents the course of decay of excitatory potentials (E). The bottom curve represents the decrease in inhibitory potential (I). Because the rate of decay of I is more rapid than that of E, the combined curve of effective excitatory potential (Ė) rises before it falls. The shaded portion represents the "reminiscence" effect. Reproduced from Hull and others (1940), page 121.

the consequences for changes in time? It is characteristic of an integrated system that it becomes applicable to situations to which a number of its principles are appropriate at once. These new situations often look superficially quite unlike the situations from which the principles were originally drawn. Among the theorems and corollaries mediated by the principles just discussed are a number having to do with massed and distributed practice, difficulty of learning associated with length of list, and the like. For example, it is predicted that the relative disadvantage suffered by syllables in the middle of the list should be greater with massed than with distributed practice. This happens because such disadvantage is said to be due to the accumulation of inhibition, and under massing such inhibitions cannot dissipate as they can

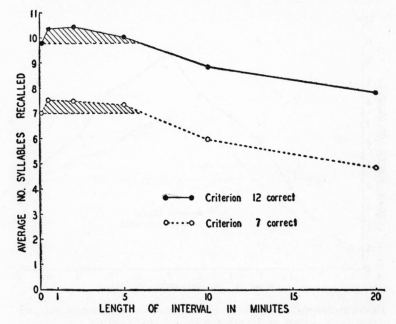

FIGURE 10. REMINISCENCE EFFECT IN THE RECALL OF NONSENSE SYLLABLES.

The cross-hatched portions show that within the first five minutes after memorization of nonsense syllables recall is somewhat greater than immediately after memorization. It is these data which are predicted in Figure 9. Based on the results of Ward (1937) as reproduced by Hull and others (1940), page 263.

under distribution of trials. Confirmatory results are shown in Figure 11, based on data from Hovland (1938).[42]

[42] While the Ward-Hovland data are consistent with the conjectures presented in the text, the whole matter of the relationship between reminiscence and serial position effects is reopened by experiments of Melton and Stone (1942). They found pronounced serial position effects in the memorization of adjectives, but failed to find the expected reminiscence effects over short time-intervals.

The curve of memorization. The constants which enter the curve of memorization overlap those of the serial position curve. Here is illustrated one of the tests of a good system, almost completely lacking in psychology: the recurrence of a theoretical-experimental constant in a new context.

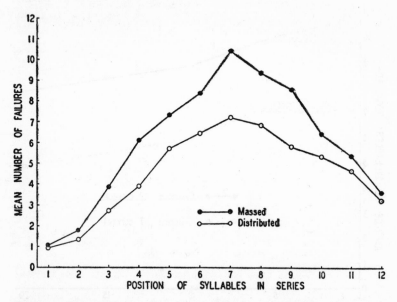

FIGURE 11. SERIAL POSITION EFFECTS IN THE LEARNING OF NONSENSE SYLLABLE LISTS BY MASSED AND DISTRIBUTED PRACTICE.

While the middle portions of the list are more difficult in both cases, the relative difficulty is greater under massed practice. This is predicted on the grounds that this difficulty is a matter of inhibitory potential, some of which is dissipated between trials in distributed practice. Based on the results of Hovland (1938) as reproduced by Hull and others (1940), page 186.

The curve of acquisition depends upon the cumulative effects of $\triangle E$, the increment of excitation due to each repetition, in addition to the effects of $\triangle K$ and L, which are already familiar. A further constant σ_L is needed to represent the oscillation of the threshold. (It will be recalled that oscillation is assigned to inhibitory potential in the later system; here it is the threshold which oscillates.) While actually all these constants need not be used at once in mediating deductions about the course of memorization, a coherent treatment, using all of them, is logically possible.

One prediction is that the form of the curve of acquisition *for all syllables which required the same number of trials to reach mastery,* will be in the form of an ogive. The fact of oscillation of the threshold from moment to moment in a chance manner would result in such a curve if the underlying excitatory strength

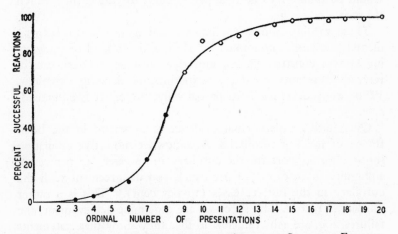

FIGURE 12. EMPIRICAL LEARNING CURVE FOR NONSENSE SYLLABLES EQUALLY DIFFICULT TO MASTER.

From a number of sessions in which nonsense syllables were memorized, data were chosen for those syllables for which final mastery was preceded by eight failures. The curve represents the percent of successful responses per trial for 163 such syllables. According to the prediction, a curve plotted in this manner should be in the form of an ogive. Reproduced from Hull and others (1940), page 162.

were increasing linearly with repetition. Syllables requiring the same number of trials to master are pooled for this purpose because they are presumed to be about equally difficult. The prediction is that the approach to the threshold and the post-threshold portions of the curve should take ogival form. In Figure 12 are shown empirical results for syllables requiring 8 trials to mastery. The form of the curve is roughly ogival. This is one of the better fits; in general the fit is not considered satisfactory [43]

[43] Hull and others (1940), page 164.

and in the new system the postulates have been somewhat modified.

The empirical fact of response oscillation first noted in the memorization situation by Hull (1917) is of considerable interest. It is a useful illustration of the manner in which the treatment of data can be influenced by theory. The empirical "learning curve" of Figure 12 is just as empirical as any; yet this form of plotting would be unlikely to be used were it not for the theory which led to it.

These exhibits suffice to indicate the nature of the experimental predictions attempted by Hull, and the kind of integrating system constructed. An important feature is systematically relevant constants, rooted in experimental defining situations. While the success has been partial only, the effort is commendable.

Quantitative experimental evidence is presented in the book for 71 of the 110 corollaries. A somewhat subjective tabulation shows clear support for the corollary in 39 cases (55 per cent), ambiguity in 20 cases (28 per cent), and disagreement with the corollary in the rest, 12 cases (17 per cent).[44] This is a rather substantial record. The successes are a genuine achievement; the failures, too, are achievements, in that they show that statements have been made clear enough so that data can disprove them.

ESTIMATE OF HULL'S POSITION

Hull's position on typical problems of learning. Because he has been willing to face the problems of learning posed by others as well as those which he set himself, it is possible to assign Hull a position on the representative problems chosen as the basis for comparing the different points of view.

1. *Capacity.* A volume on individual differences is promised as the second of the books in the series of which *Principles of behavior* is the first. One account of material to appear in this volume has been published.[45] Individual differences in capacity are to be explained according to differences in the constants of the type discussed above (e.g., $\triangle E$, $\triangle K$, L, etc.). It is not clear

[44] Hilgard (1940).
[45] Hull (1945b).

whether or not learning will modify these constants. That is, of course, the basic problem of the relationship between learning and relatively persistent individual differences.

2. *Practice.* Mere contiguous repetition does nothing except to produce reactive inhibition; all improvement depends upon reinforcement. Hull is in this respect in agreement with Thorndike, and opposed to Guthrie.

3. *Motivation.* Because need-reduction is used to explain the reinforcing effect of rewards, it is used also to explain the reinforcing effects of punishment. This it does by finding *escape* from punishment essential if punishment is to be reinforcing. This assimilation of punishment to reward is accepted, and need-reduction is used to explain the reinforcing effects of both reward and punishment. Food reward relieves hunger-tension; escape from shock reduces shock-tension. Any more complicated relationships involving anxiety, avoidance, expectation, and the like, may be derived from the simpler principles of reinforcement. Drive is complexly related to learning; it serves in reinforcement, in activating habit strength into performance, and in providing differential internal stimuli.

4. *Understanding.* Hull has dealt with the problem of directing ideas and with novel problem-solving in several papers.[46] The main thread running through the papers is that the organism's own responses furnish stimuli which are the surrogates for ideas. Responses which provide such stimuli are called "pure stimulus acts" because their function is that of furnishing stimuli. These responses are often in the nature of fractional anticipatory goal responses, and the stimuli from them help to marshal the habits appropriate to the problematic situation. Ideas thus have the substantive quality which Guthrie also assigns them. Two general principles emerge as important, both depending upon the presence of fractional anticipatory responses and discriminations among the stimuli which these responses arouse. These are the principle of the goal gradient and the principle of the habit-family hierarchy, as previously described.

5. *Transfer.* There are two aspects of transfer: equivalence of stimuli and equivalence of responses. Hull explains equivalence of stimuli either on the basis of generalization or via intermediate

[46] Hull (1930, 1931, 1935c, 1938).

reactions. Alternative responses are explained on the basis of the habit-family hierarchy, so that if a favored response fails, another response, lower in the hierarchy, is called forth. All responses in the hierarchy have in the past led to the same goal.

6. *Forgetting.* In the volume on rote learning the decay of excitation is postulated by Hull as occurring according to a kind of law of disuse. This position is reaffirmed in the later book.[47] That forgetting should occur lawfully does not preclude the possibility that the lawfulness is engendered by the cumulative interferences of ordinary life outside the laboratory. But Hull has not said so. Reminiscence effects—increases over lapse of time—are explained on the basis of recovery from inhibition.

When reviewed according to the conventional problems of learning, Hull's theory introduces few new conceptions not found in Thorndike or Guthrie. His originality consists rather in the rigorous systematic and quantitative approach he makes to the problems. It is according to his systematic successes and failures that he is to be judged.

Is reinforcement theory sound? Hull's system is built around a conception of scientific method, and the system could still hang together even though many of its details were changed. But the theory of reinforcement is in a somewhat unique status. It is so central that if it is not valid the whole system collapses.

In some respects the theory of reinforcement is on firm ground. There are instances in which rewards clearly involve need reduction. The hungry animal eats and is no longer hungry; the dog steps on a thorn, withdraws its paw, and is no longer in pain. It is plausible enough that we learn to do the things which make us more comfortable, which bring an end to annoyance, which terminate our restlessness and leave us (for the moment) at peace. One or another form of this theory has prevailed ever since man began to reflect upon the whys and wherefors of his behavior. The historically familiar doctrine is that of hedonism, that is, the belief that man seeks pleasure and avoids pain. To

[47] Hull (1943*a*), page 296. The decay of habit strength with the passage of time is carried forward from the earlier book, Hull and others (1940). Although the principle is included in Corollary XX of the 1943 system, it implies a postulate which is missing from the 1943 set.

some extent the hedonistic theory must be true; to some extent, consequently, the need-reduction theory must be true, because it is an objective restatement of the theory. But the sufficiency of the theory is not so easily settled, for the theory makes of need-reduction the only and essential principle of primary increase in habit strength.

The evidence actually does not go very far beyond the commonsense level. *The identification of reinforcement with need-reduction is an hypothesis, not something convincingly demonstrated.* Evidence from experiments is indirect at best. There is the experiment of Finan (1940a) which showed that an equal number of reinforcements produced more learning in rats longer deprived of food, as measured by resistance to extinction after hunger conditions were equated. But there are alternative interpretations, such as higher attention-value (or its equivalent in intensity of response) when the animals were hungrier. Two hypotheses oppose that of need-reduction: (1) learning takes place because of contiguity of stimulus and response, and what action need-reduction may have is derivative and not essential (Pavlov, Guthrie); (2) learning takes place cognitively, and the need-reduction principle applies to performance but not to learning (Tolman).

Hull believes Pavlov and Guthrie are mistaken in their failure to recognize the essentiality of need-reduction as the basis for reinforcement in simple conditioning. He goes to some pains to show that Pavlov's dog was really learning on the basis of reward even in the classical Pavlovian experiment. The dog salivated to the bell after salivating to the food because the bell-salivation combination occurred in the neighborhood of the need-reduction following eating by a hungry dog.[48] In assimilating Pavlov's experiment to the need-reduction theory, Hull is rejecting Skinner's (1938) distinction between two kinds of conditioning.

The problem of need-reduction is somewhat more difficult in the case of learning by punishment, but Hull adopts the solution that when you learn by punishment the reinforcement is not the punishment but the escape from punishment.[49] To end the pun-

[48] Hull (1943a), pages 76-79.
[49] The typical experimental illustration is that of Mowrer (1940). See also Mowrer and Lamoreaux (1942).

ishment is rewarding. In some sense all reward is escape from "punishment"—escape from hunger pangs, escape from a parched throat, escape from anxiety. There are some difficulties with this identification of punishment with reward, which are best brought forward in the differences between *escape* and *avoidance*.[50] Escape is rewarding, and like any other reward, strengthens the behavior which terminates the aroused state. But many punishments lead to doing something quite different from the behavior just prior to the punishment. If an animal runs down an alley, meets a charged grid, and leaps ahead from it to safety, the leap is associated with need-reduction (pain alleviation) so that, by strict reinforcement theory, the next time the animal should do what it last did, only perhaps more intensely. It should run down the alley faster, touch the grid and make a jump ahead to safety. (This, by the way, should be Guthrie's prediction also, since leaping from the grid prevented any unlearning of the last bit of behavior to the grid.) Rats do not do this. They slow up in the alley, and try not to approach the grid. That is the difference between escape and avoidance behavior.

This criticism of reinforcement theory, and other critical evidence which might be directed against it, are deflected by an important supplementary conception—secondary reinforcement. The principle of secondary reinforcement is that any stimulus which has been associated with need-reduction may itself serve as a reinforcing agent. Thus secondary reinforcement depends upon stimulation, rather than upon the termination of stimulation (that is, upon need-reduction), and the relationship to aroused need is therefore remote. Any reinforcing situation which does not conform to the circumstances of primary reinforcement can readily be assigned to secondary reinforcement. While there are rules which ought to be followed in deciding whether reinforcement is primary or secondary, these are extremely difficult to make precise, especially in the case of complex organisms with a rich background of experience. The presence of language in man provides such a rich set of secondary reinforcement mechanisms that most effective rewards beyond early infancy are secondary. Even a response which appears to be fragmentary and detached, like a conditioned knee-jerk, may in man be compli-

[50] Hilgard and Marquis (1940), pages 56-62.

cated by previous experience with stumbling and recovery of balance, with pain-avoidance sequences, and the like. It is never quite clear, in such a case, just what the reinforcing situation is.

Even the experiment which Hull has adapted from Skinner as the source of most of his quantitative statements—lever pressing by a rat-in-a-box—is a very complicated segment of behavior. Hull sometimes forgets this, and writes as though he were down to bedrock when using this experiment as a reference source. It is convenient to have a reference experiment around which quantitative results are built, but the quantitative laws *in their quantitative aspects* are those of the rat-in-a-box, not the laws of either physiology or behavior. As one example, the assumption that the primary reinforcement gradient extends about 30 or 40 seconds, on the basis of Perin's (1943*b*) experiments, is almost certainly limited to the rat-in-a-box. The dangers in building laws of behavior around artificial quantities should be evident enough in view of the history of the delayed reaction experiment. In Hunter's (1913) apparatus, rats could delay for 10 seconds, in Honzik's (1931) for 45 seconds, in McCord's (1939) for 360 seconds. While it might be supposed that the shorter delays are physiologically more primitive, the situation is better understood from the opposite point of view: the shorter delays were found when the problem set the animal was more difficult and when its solution involved more intermediate steps. To assume that Perin's situation is free from the possibilities of secondary reinforcement of inhibiting sort, so that it yields the "true" limits of delay, is gratuitous. Most of the rats were reported to wait quietly after pressing the lever during the period of delay before the food was delivered. They were in the food compartment, at the food receptacle, both rich as secondary reinforcing agents. But what was rewarded was this quiet waiting; it is significant that with the longer delays some rats, instead of learning to press the lever, just learned to wait quietly, so that their results could not be used in the computations. May not the conditioned inhibition under these circumstances have interfered with the learning of the lever-problem and shortened the period of delay over which learning could be demonstrated?

The notion that gradients of running speed and the like in more difficult mazes are complicated by processes other than a simple gradient of reinforcement is, of course, acceptable.[51] There is good justification for using the term *goal gradient* for the performance gradients in more complicated situations, and *gradient of reinforcement* for the more direct situations such as Perin's. The objection is being raised to the assumption that Perin's work sets the limits *in seconds*, to gradients of reinforcements. Probably no single experiment will do this.[52]

The eventual status of reinforcement theory will depend upon systematic inferences from a variety of experiments. For the moment it may suffice to point out that for both Thorndike and Hull, reinforcement theory is at the very center of their conception of learning. They are not too severely challenged by Guthrie, for to some extent he is offering but an alternative theory of reinforcement. The most threatening series of experiments are those on latent learning, to be considered later.

The problem of measurement. Habit strength, drive, reaction potential, inhibition, are all scaled values with units assigned to differences in intensity, yet none is directly measurable.

Is this scientifically permissible? The answer is *Yes*, not because of some ultramodern conception of science, but because there is no alternative. The logical problem can be illustrated simply by three illustrations:

a. Because the area of a rectangle is known to be the product of its length by its breadth, its area is *measured by inference* when its length and breadth are measured. Its area is not directly measured, and is subject to errors of measurement of both length and breadth, but the *objectivity* of the measurement of area is not questioned. The subjective errors to which its indirect measurement are liable are of the same sort found in direct measurement.

b. The relationship between the period of a pendulum (T), its length (l), and the acceleration of gravity (g) is expressed by the equation $T = 2\pi\sqrt{\dfrac{l}{g}}$. If the period of the pendulum and its

---

[51] Hilgard and Marquis (1940), pages 169-170.

[52] Since this was first written, comments on Perin's experiments have appeared by Voeks (1945) and by Spence (1947). Voeks interprets the results independent of reinforcement, applying Guthrie's theory. Spence concludes that Perin's gradient is too long, rather than too short,—if there is really any primary reinforcement gradient at all.

length are known, the gravitational constant (g) can be *measured by inference* in exactly the same manner as area in the example above. The subjective difference that you "see" the area measured and do not "see" the acceleration of gravity is of no consequence. The gravitational constant is also an *objective* measurement, provided the assumptions leading to the equation are met.

c. One of Hull's equations shows for a given set of data that habit strength ($_sH_R$) in habs is related to the amplitude of galvanometer deflection (A) in millimeters by the equation: [53]

$$A = .141 \times {_sH_R} + 3.1$$

For every value of A in millimeters it is possible to assign a value of $_sH_R$ in habs. *If the systematic assumptions hold, the measurement in habs is fully as objective as the measurement in millimeters.* But, it may be said, the measurements in millimeters hold even if the systematic assumptions do not hold. Therefore they are on a sounder factual basis. Measurements in millimeters have, in fact, *no meaning whatever* psychologically unless some assumptions hold. More millimeters may not even mean more of any correlated psychological variable. You can translate back and forth from habs to millimeters as readily as you can get from millimeters to any other psychological variable.[54]

There is a sense in which anchorage to facts has meaning. Within our systematization of ideas and within our arrangements for obtaining data there is much which is arbitrary. We may choose our definitions and our postulates with great freedom. But there are at the same time coercive features in the nature of the world and organisms which place limits upon speculation. It is to keep speculation within the tolerance limits allowed by natural relationships that we experiment and record agreement and disagreement with our theories. We have no assurance that by doing so we are discovering nature's own laws. Natural laws are not there to be discovered; they have to be invented to fit certain

[53] Hovland (1937); Hull (1943*a*), page 121.

[54] Hull has by no means solved the problem of units of measurement in learning. One *hab* is not equal to another, because it represents 1/100 of a maximum which differs for every learner. The units have been criticized by Meehl (1945) and by Lashley and Wade (1946). Despite the cogency of these criticisms, it may be said that Hull has succeeded in indicating the possibility of measurement of inferred psychological processes.

aspects of nature. Two sets of laws may both fit nature. We can occasionally be sure that we have asserted propositions which do *not* fit reality; we can never be sure that those which fit now are ultimately to remain as "nature's laws."

Some current weaknesses. Reviewers of Hull's book have differed violently in their appraisal of it. Many of the weaknesses in detail will prove self-corrective, just as earlier demonstrated weaknesses led to revisions of theories previously suggested. The following critical points appear worth repeating:

1. The hypothesis of afferent neural interaction, while a useful step toward the recognition of the problems of perception, is somewhat question-begging in a system of this sort. It commits the fallacy of assigning a neural name to a psychological problem. It is at too high a level of organization to fit symmetrically into a postulate system designedly selected to represent the simplest behavior mechanisms. We need the laws of interaction as surely as we need other psychological laws. Hull has usefully called attention to this need. The objection is only to the systematic use which he has made of the postulate.

2. The neglect of the experiments on latent learning, severely critical of the reinforcement principle, is a serious omission. It is permissible to choose illustrations for a systematic book like Hull's from a limited sphere of experimentation, and there is no obligation to be encyclopedic. But no system can afford to ignore the places where it fits least well. Ultimately it is such places which matter most to the survival of the system.

3. The neglect of experiments on intermittent reinforcement avoids other challenges to the doctrine that habit strength increases step by step with each reinforcement. These experiments, originated by Pavlov, have in common the feature of demonstrating that the strengthening of conditioned responses is not a simple function of the number of reinforcements.[55] Reinforcement on a fraction of the trials may lead to more conditioning and to greater resistance to extinction than reinforcement every

---

[55] The first experiments on partial or intermittent reinforcement were those of Pavlov (1927), pages 384-386. Later experiments include those of Brogden (1939), Brunswik (1939), Cole (1939), Denny (1946), Finger (1942a, 1942b), Humphreys (1939a, 1940, 1943b), Mowrer and Jones (1945), and Skinner (1938).

trial. The problems are admitted by Hull in a passing reference in the text.[56]

4. The failure to make a more complete analysis of the punishment situation, both logically and experimentally, leaves punishment subsumed under reward, as affecting learning through a common mechanism, need-reduction. Punishment arranged as need-reduction is only one of the possible arrangements of punishment in a learning situation, and not the usual one.

The method of system-construction a genuine service to psychology as science. Whatever its deficiencies in detail, the system which Hull proposes has set a model for other theorists to emulate. While it is legitimate to ask that he face the difficulties before the system, there is every reason to expect him to do so eventually. It is understandable that in getting under way he wished to state his principles as clearly as he could, selecting experimental illustrations which made it as plausible as possible. An excess of debate would have made a difficult book even more difficult. His system is fluid enough to stand a good deal of tampering. It is a healthy sign that its assumptions are so fully exposed that they can be attacked.

It is my belief that as psychology matures, its systematic books will look very much like Hull's. The formal character of the system is what one expects of science. The present set of postulates will probably not survive very long. That, however, does not mean that they will not have been of service in advancing our knowledge of learning.

SUPPLEMENTARY READINGS

BOOKS

Hull, C. L., Hovland, C. I., Ross, R. T., Hall, M., Perkins, D. T., and Fitch, F. B. (1940) *Mathematico-deductive theory of rote learning.*

Hull, C. L. (1943) *Principles of behavior.*

[56] Hull (1943*a*), page 337. In a seminar memorandum, Hull proposed an explanation which has been tested experimentally by Mowrer and Jones (1945). It is conjectured that reinforcement may strengthen a sequence of responses as well as a single response, and this response sequence must be considered a unit in both reinforcement and extinction. In a somewhat related explanation, Denny (1946) draws upon secondary reinforcement as an important factor. The matter is complex, and these explanations do not dispose of it.

SHORTER INTRODUCTIONS

Hilgard, E. R. and Marquis, D. G. (1940) *Conditioning and learning*. Hull's earlier derivations of serial learning and maze learning are epitomized on pages 207-226; his interpretation of problem-solving on pages 236-243.

Hull, C. L. (1942) Conditioning: Outline of a systematic theory of learning. *Natl. Soc. Stud. Educ.*, 41st Yearbook, Part II, 61-95.

Spence, K. W. (1942) Theoretical interpretations of learning. In F. A. Moss, edit., *Comparative psychology* (Revised edition), 280-329. Hull's theory is treated on pages 311-324.

CRITICAL REVIEWS

Hilgard, E. R. (1940) Review of *Mathematico-deductive theory of rote learning:* The psychological system. *Psychol. Bull.*, 37, 808-815.

Kantor, J. R. (1941) Review of *Mathematico-deductive theory of rote learning. Amer. J. Psychol.*, 54, 300-304.

Koch, S. (1944) Review of Hull's *Principles of behavior. Psychol. Bull.*, 41, 269-286.

Leeper, R. (1944) Dr. Hull's *Principles of behavior. J. genet. Psychol.*, 65, 3-52.

Marhenke, P. (1940) Review of *Mathematico-deductive theory of rote learning:* The logical system. *Psychol. Bull.*, 37, 815-817.

Ritchie, B. F. (1944) Hull's treatment of learning. *Psychol. Bull.*, 41, 640-652.

Skinner, B. F. (1944) Review of Hull's *Principles of behavior. Amer. J. Psychol.*, 57, 276-281.

Welch, L. (1945) An examination of Dr. Leeper's review of Hull's *Principles of behavior. J. genet. Psychol.*, 67, 3-15.

REPRESENTATIVE EXPERIMENTS

Ellson, D. G. (1938) Quantitative studies of the interaction of simple habits. I. Recovery from specific and generalized effects of extinction. *J. exp. Psychol.*, 23, 330-358.

Grice, G. R. (1942) An experimental study of the gradient of reinforcement in maze learning. *J. exp. Psychol.*, 30, 475-489.

Hovland, C. I. (1939) Experimental studies in rote-learning theory. IV. Comparison of reminiscence in serial and paired associate learning. *J. exp. Psychol.*, 24, 466-484.

Hull, C. L. (1934) The rat's speed-of-locomotion gradient in the approach to food. *J. comp. Psychol.*, 17, 393-422.

Hull, C. L. (1935) The influence of caffeine and other factors on certain phenomena of rote learning. *J. gen. Psychol.*, 13, 249-274.

Hull, C. L. (1939) Simple trial-and-error learning—an empirical investigation. *J. comp. Psychol.*, 27, 233-258.

Miller, N. E. (1935) A reply to "Sign-Gestalt or conditioned reflex?" *Psychol. Rev.*, 42, 280-292.

Mowrer, O. H. (1940) Anxiety-reduction and learning. *J. exp. Psychol.*, 27, 497-516.

Perin, C. T. (1942) Behavior potentiality as a joint function of the amount of training and the degree of hunger at the time of extinction. *J. exp. Psychol.*, 30, 93-113.

Rouse, R. O. (1943) The oscillation function in compound trial-and-error learning. *J. comp. Psychol.*, 35, 177-186.

Spence, K. W. (1942) The basis of solution by chimpanzees of the intermediate size problem. *J. exp. Psychol.*, 31, 257-271.

Woodbury, C. B. (1943) The learning of stimulus patterns by dogs. *J. comp. Psychol.*, 35, 29-40.

Chapter 5

SKINNER'S DESCRIPTIVE BEHAVIORISM

In a series of papers beginning in 1930, B. F. Skinner has proposed a system of behavior coordinated with observations of animal performance in a type of experiment which he invented. The experiments and theories are summarized in his *The behavior of organisms* (1938). As an avowed behaviorism making use of conditioning principles his system is to be understood in relation to the theories of Guthrie and Hull; as a stimulus-response psychology it belongs to the family of theories branching off in one way or another from that of Thorndike. Before returning to a comparison with related theories, it will be instructive to examine the more distinctive features of Skinner's proposals and the experiments to which they have led.

RESPONDENT AND OPERANT BEHAVIOR

The greatest break with conventional stimulus-response psychology within Skinner's system is the distinction between respondent and operant behavior. Conventional stimulus-response psychology enforced the dictum "no stimulus, no response" by assuming the presence of stimuli when none were identifiable. Although it was often convenient to talk about "random" or "spontaneous" responses, it was not doubted that stimuli were present to elicit them, if the experimenter only had means of detecting them. Skinner finds this method of forcing facts both undesirable and unnecessary. He proposes that two classes of response be distingushed, a class of *elicited* responses and a class of *emitted* responses.

Respondent and operant distinguished. Responses which are elicited by known stimuli are classified as *respondents*. Pupillary constriction to light and the knee jerk to a blow on the patellar tendon serve as convenient illustrations. There is a second class of responses, not correlated with any known stimuli. These emitted responses are designated *operants*, to distinguish them from respondents. While the conventional treatment of such responses is to consider them as respondents with unknown stimuli, Skinner holds the conviction that the stimulus conditions, if any, are irrelevant to the understanding of operant behavior. Because operant behavior is not elicited by recognized stimuli, its strength cannot be measured according to the static laws of the reflex, which are all stated as functions of stimuli. Instead, rate of response is used as a measure of strength.

An operant may, and usually does, acquire a relation to prior stimulation. In that case it becomes a *discriminated operant;* the stimulus becomes an occasion for the operant behavior, but is not an eliciting stimulus as in the case of a true reflex. Skinner extends the term reflex to cover the operant, although this is somewhat awkward since several of the laws of the reflex do not apply. A simple illustration of an operant coordinated with a stimulus would be a reaction-time experiment as commonly conducted in the psychological laboratory. The correlation between stimulus and response may easily be changed, as by instructions to lift the finger from the key instead of pressing down. The relationship of latency of response to changes in stimulus intensity is very different in the case of a discriminated operant than for an elicited response, say the lid reflex to sound—a respondent. Such a comparison between a discriminated operant and a respondent has been made by Peak (1933), in comparing the characteristics of voluntary and reflex eyelid responses to sounds differing in loudness.

Most human behavior is operant in character. The behavior of eating a meal, driving a car, writing a letter, shows but little of respondent character. The emphasis which Skinner places upon operant behavior is an important one, for there is no doubt that the stimulus-response formula has been carelessly overworked.

Two types of conditioning. Related to the two types of response there are said to be two types of conditioning.

The conditioning of respondent behavior is assigned to Type
S, because reinforcement is correlated with stimuli. The conditioned stimulus (*e.g.*, a tone) is presented together with the
unconditioned stimulus (*e.g.*, food) and thus comes to elicit the
response (*e.g.*, salivation). Pavlov's classical conditioning experiment is said to be of Type S. Its two laws are the Law of Conditioning of Type S, and the Law of Extinction of Type S.[1] The
law of conditioning makes such conditioning depend upon the
approximate simultaneity of stimuli. The evidence for the existence of Type S conditioning is actually quite slim, because much
that seems by experimental arrangement to conform to classical
conditioning is better understood as a consequence of factors
other than contiguity of stimulus and response. Hull has denied
the existence of conditioning of Type S; Skinner admits that it
does not appear experimentally in pure form.[2] Pavlov's experiment is a particularly bad example to use as an illustration of
Type S because of the prominence of eating behavior following
the presentation of conditioned and unconditioned stimuli. But
Skinner does not attribute much importance to Type S in any
case. Whether or not there is such conditioning would not matter too much to his system.

Type R he believes to be much the more important. This is
the conditioning of operant behavior, and the letter R is used to
call attention to the important term in the correlation with reinforcement. In this case it is a *response* which is correlated with
reinforcement. The experimental example which he uses throughout is lever-pressing. This response may be strengthened by following it with food and eating. It is not the *sight* of the lever
which is important; it is the *pressing* of the lever. The conditioned response does not resemble the reinforcing response; its
relationship to the reinforcing stimulus is that it causes it to
appear. In operant conditioning, conditioning of Type R, reinforcement cannot follow unless the conditioned response appears. The two laws of Type R are not unlike those of Type S,
including a law of conditioning and a law of extinction. The law
of conditioning of Type R may be compared to Thorndike's law
of effect and Hull's principle of reinforcement: *If the occurrence*

[1] Skinner (1938), pages 18-19.
[2] Skinner (1938), page 238.

of an operant is followed by presentation of a reinforcing stimulus, the strength is increased.[3] Note that the reinforcing situation is defined by its stimulus; this Hull does only for secondary reinforcement. What gets strengthened is not a stimulus-response connection, because the operant requires no stimulus; this statement is unlike Thorndike and Hull.

This dependence upon the posterior reinforcing stimulus gives the term operant its significance . . . The operant . . . becomes significant for behavior and takes on an identifiable form when it acts upon the environment in such a way that a reinforcing stimulus is produced.[4]

The mechanical arrangement under which Type R conditioning is usually demonstrated is that suggested by the quotation, a situation in which the response of the organism produces the reinforcing agent. This is what has been called instrumental conditioning to distinguish it from the arrangements of classical conditioning.[5]

One suggestion offered quite tentatively by Skinner[6] is that conditioning of Type S may be limited to autonomic responses, Type R to skeletal behavior. The crucial question is whether Type S occurs at all; if it does, it may well be limited to autonomic responses. That Type R occurs is evident, and most skeletal responses, including those obtained under the arrangements of classical conditioning, can easily be shown to conform to the pattern of discriminated operants. The fact that probability of response evocation, as Hull calls it, is such a convenient measure of conditioning in these situations is enough to suggest that it is *operants* and not *respondents* being dealt with. It is significant that Hull's postulate which proposes to use probability as a measure of response is limited to skeletal responses, although he makes no reference to Skinner's conjecture. Actual experiments in which autonomic conditioning takes place (salivation, galvanic response) are full of indirect accompaniments of Type R. When the circumstances seem almost ideal for demonstrating Type S conditioning, as in attempts to condition pupillary con-

[3] Skinner (1938), page 21.
[4] Skinner (1938), page 22.
[5] Hilgard and Marquis (1940), pages 51-74.
[6] Skinner (1938), page 112.

striction by presenting a tone along with a light, it is extremely difficult to obtain any conditioning at all. The few cases which have found conditioning are in doubt, and one of the more plausible of these [7] is full of Type R circumstances.

CHANGES IN REFLEX STRENGTH

In order to get at the quantitative relationships within operant conditioning, Skinner designed a special apparatus suitable for use with white rats. It consists essentially of a darkened sound-resisting box in which the rat is placed. There is a small brass lever within the compartment which, if pressed, delivers a pellet of food. The lever is connected with a recording system which keeps a graphical account of the number of lever pressings plotted against the length of time that the rat is in the box. By a carefully controlled handling of the animals, remarkably consistent and "lawful" results can be obtained. Changes can be introduced so that food is not delivered every time the lever is depressed. The consequences of doing this and of making other changes in the situation have been systematically reported.

The evident consequence of reinforcement of an operant like lever-pressing is to increase the rate with which the operant is emitted. This change is described as a change in *reflex strength*.[8] But reflex strength is, in fact, a derivative of a more fundamental change which reinforcement has brought about—the establishment of an increased reservoir of responses remaining to be emitted.

The reflex reserve. Reinforcement determines the total number of operant responses which will be emitted, if time enough is allowed for them to appear. This total number represents the *reflex reserve* to be drained according to the rate of responding. The rate of responding is in fact determined by the size of the reserve, so that with a greater reserve there is a higher rate of responding, provided nothing happens to change the proportionality between reserve and reflex strength. Reflex strength (momentary rate of responding) is thus a secondary consequence of reinforcement.

[7] Hudgins (1933).

[8] The word "reflex" is used with a special meaning differing from the use within reflex physiology. This usage will be discussed later.

It would be a mistake to suppose that momentary rate of response measures the consequences of reinforcement, because rate can change without a change in reserve. While rate ordinarily increases as the reserve increases, this implies a constant proportionality between rate and reserve. This proportionality may be changed by changes in the state of the organism, so that rate will be affected while reserve remains the same. The factors which change the proportionality are facilitation, inhibition, emotion, and drive. They are not to be confused with learning, which changes the reserve.

A single reinforcement may create an appreciable reflex reserve. After receiving food following a single response to the lever, a rat may respond 50 or more times, yielding a typical extinction curve.[9] The reserve increases slowly with additional reinforcements so that after 100 to 250 additional reinforcements under standard conditions of the experiment, the reserve does not exceed 200 responses. An extinction curve following a single reinforcement and one following 250 reinforcements are reproduced in Figure 13.

The curves are cumulative ones, not to be confused with learning curves as usually plotted. As the curve levels off it means that responses have stopped; as the curve is constructed it is not possible for it to fall.

The notion of a reserve of responses to be emitted is a fascinating one, and it is somewhat illuminating to search for parallels in human behavior. The "stimulus-hunger" described in infants by Ribble [10] may be illustrative. She finds that infants have a daily quota of *sucking* per day, say two hours of such activity—not two hours of *feeding*. If their food requirements are met in less sucking-time, they suck their fingers, pacifiers, or other objects. It is not altogether far-fetched to consider sucking as an operant which has been reinforced by feeding so as to create a reflex reserve which can be exhausted only by sucking.[11]

Clinical observations with human adults furnish other parallels.

[9] Skinner (1938), pages 85-90.
[10] Ribble (1943), pages 31-32.
[11] The possibility exists that this "reserve" is innate rather than acquired, although it is difficult to untangle the interaction between drive and learning. Immature or premature infants are said by Ribble to need a longer period of daily oral exercise than normal ones.

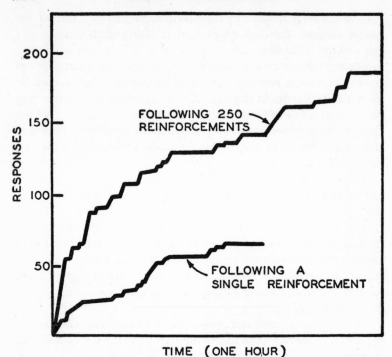

FIGURE 13. EXTINCTION OF LEVER-PRESSING BY RATS FOLLOWING A SINGLE
REINFORCEMENT AND FOLLOWING 250 REINFORCEMENTS.

Although several times as many responses are emitted after 250 reinforcements as after a single reinforcement, it is evident that the total number of
responses in the "reserve" does not increase in direct proportion to the
number of reinforcements. Data from Skinner (1933) and F. S. Keller and
A. Kerr (unpublished data), replotted from Skinner (1938), pages 87 and
91. Both curves have been moved back so that time is here shown as from
the first response.

A similarity may be detected to the Freudian conception of
libido as a dynamic reservoir of repressed (therefore learned)
activities, seeking expression in one form or another. The external
situation is an occasion for libidinal expression, rather than a
strictly eliciting stimulus complex. Skinner touches on related
clinical manifestations in trying to clarify the difference between
drive and reserve.[12] He states that in certain forms of neuras-
thenia, where the motivation does not seem to be at fault, the

[12] Skinner (1938), pages 376-377.

reserve may be empty. The opposite case of a full reserve, he says, raises the question of sublimation, and seems to answer the objection that sublimating behavior is incapable of satisfying a drive. The effect is not a change in the drive but an emptying of the reserve. These fragmentary suggestions are important hints as to possible extensions of the concept of reflex reserve to ordinary behavior.

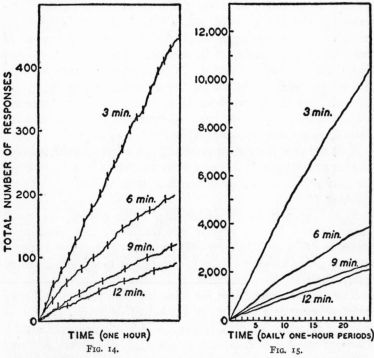

FIG. 14.   FIG. 15.

FIGURE 14. RESPONSES WITHIN ONE SESSION OF PERIODIC REINFORCEMENT.
    A pellet was delivered every 3, 6, 9, and 12 minutes, respectively. The more frequent the reinforcement, the more rapid the rate of responding, although each rate is relatively uniform. After Skinner (1938), as reproduced by Hilgard and Marquis (1940), page 151.

FIGURE 15. RESPONSES WITHIN REPEATED SESSIONS OF PERIODIC REINFORCEMENT.
    Responses of the same rats whose records are given in Figure 14 are here accumulated for successive daily sessions. The uniformity of rate persists throughout. When expressed as number of responses per reinforcement this rate is described as the "extinction ratio." After Skinner (1938), as reproduced by Hilgard and Marquis (1940), page 151.

Reserve not a simple function of reinforcement. There are special procedures by which much larger reflex reserves can be built up. These have in common that they depend upon reinforcement of but a fraction of the responses. Two arrangements have been described by Skinner. One of these, known as *periodic reconditioning*, consists in reinforcing responses at standard intervals of time, all intervening responses going unreinforced. A pellet may be delivered every 3, 6, 9 or 12 minutes (that is, reinforcing the first response which occurs after the elapsed interval). This arrangement, which delivers a standard amount of reinforcement per hour, results in very uniform rates of responding, the rate being proportional to the amount of reinforcement. Under standard conditions of experimentation and drive, for example, Skinner found about 18 to 20 responses per reinforcement, over a considerable range of intervals. The uniformity of rates of responding is illustrated in Figures 14 and 15.

This uniform number of responses per reinforcement is called the *extinction ratio*. In addition to its theoretical interest, it serves conveniently as a measure of learning under different conditions of drive.

Following periodic reconditioning, reflex reserves are much larger than following regular reinforcement. The situation is stated in this way: *The most efficient means of building a reserve with a given number of reinforcements is to administer them periodically.*[13]

The second arrangement for achieving high reserves is that of *reinforcement at a fixed ratio.* Instead of delivering a pellet of food at standard intervals of time, a pellet is delivered after a standard number of responses. In one study they were delivered after 16, 24, 32, 48, 64, 96, or 192 responses. Under these circumstances very high rates of responding are achieved, as shown in Figure 16.

The extinction ratio has appeared to change from the order of 20:1 under periodic reconditioning to 200:1 under reinforcement at a fixed ratio. Because the conditions of drive have not changed, this requires special analysis, lest the concept of extinction ratio be invalidated.

There are three aspects of Figure 16 which require explana-

[13] Skinner (1938), page 137.

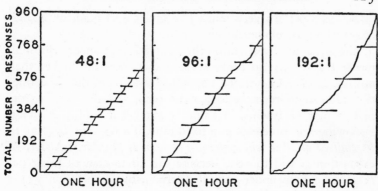

FIGURE 16. RESPONSES WITH REINFORCEMENT AT A FIXED RATIO.
Responses from individual rats reinforced every 48, 96, and 192 responses, as indicated by the horizontal lines. Under these circumstances very high rates of responding develop, the highest rate being found with the lowest frequency of reinforcement. After Skinner (1938), as reproduced by Hilgard and Marquis (1940), page 152.

tion: (1) the very high rates of responding, (2) the delay after each reinforcement, and (3) the acceleration between reinforcements. The interpretation of the high rate of responding offered by Skinner is that each lever-pressing in the early part of a run acts as a discriminatory stimulus with reinforcing properties—as a secondary reinforcing agent. The responses are made, in common language, not "because they produce food, but because they bring the production of food nearer." [14] The delay after each reinforcement has a twofold explanation. First, there is a negative factor associated with reinforcements which are separated in time. It is as though the rat discriminates the time relationships and says to himself: "I've just been fed; there's no use working since nothing will be forthcoming for a while." Second, the reserve has been weakened by the "strain" imposed upon it by the preceding run (the metaphor is Skinner's).[15] The positive acceleration after the delay is attributed to the decrease in the negative factor associated with reinforcement, the recovery from the strain on the reflex reserve, and the increase in the secondary reinforcing factor as the next reinforcement is approached, or, better, as the preceding one is left farther behind. The conse-

[14] Skinner (1938), page 300.
[15] Skinner (1938), pages 297-298.

quence is a pattern very much like Hull's goal gradient, a similarity which is acknowledged.

The meaning of a strain on the reserve is that under reinforcement at a fixed ratio responses occur at rates far higher than normal. Enormous rates of responding are found during extinction after reinforcement at a fixed ratio, and the limit of the reserve may be reached in 10 or 15 minutes instead of an hour. Following reinforcement at a fixed ratio, *if a response is going to be emitted at all it will come out as soon as possible.*[16] A state of exhaustion is said to arise because the circumstances bring out responses which under normal discriminative stimulation would have remained in the reserve for some time.

These somewhat complicated facts and interpretations are of great interest for learning theory. They bear importantly upon the interpretation of reinforcement. *Whatever the interpretation of reinforcement, it is not permissible to assume that habit strength corresponds in any direct manner to the number of primary reinforcements.* Something else always enters to change the situation drastically from a one-to-one correspondence between strength and reinforcement: the number of non-reinforcements, the pattern of distribution of reinforcements and non-reinforcements, the number of previous conditionings and extinctions, and so on. This has already been pointed out as one of the serious difficulties with which Hull's theory is confronted. A second point is important: *a single primary reinforcement has its consequences for learning enormously increased by secondary reinforcement derived from it.* A single pellet of food may under appropriate arrangements reinforce the emission of 20 or 200 responses. The increased range of effectiveness is said to be due to secondary reinforcement by discriminatory stimuli. The consequences for behavior of such stimuli is quantitatively so much greater than the consequences of primary reinforcement that some encouragement is given thereby to those who accept conceptions of learning which deëmphasize primary reinforcement. Surely the facts of everyday life show long sequences of behavior which are very infrequently reinforced. Occasional satisfaction sustains activity in the face of many failures. Intermittent reinforcement is much more common than regular reinforcement.

[16] Skinner (1938), page 295.

and the ordinary adaptive economy of the organism functions in situations not unlike periodic reconditioning.

Drive. According to Skinner, drive is a *state* hypothesized to account for variability in reflex strength. The food drive is typical. It may be controlled experimentally through the operations of "feeding and fasting" and its consequences may be measured by the same sorts of behavior used to measure conditioning. It is a mistake to treat drive as a stimulus. This faulty practice arose from a ready identification of the hunger drive with the stimuli arising from stomach contractions (correlated with hunger pangs). Actually the hunger drive can remain at high levels after preliminary eating which removes hunger pangs, and in the case of other drives the associated internal stimuli are even more difficult to define, if indeed they can be found at all. Drives act like drugs and other internal states to affect behavior without regulating behavior as stimuli do.

Any momentary sample of behavior is not indicative of the relative contributions of conditioning, drive, and emotion. It is necessary to distinguish the separate effects of drive, conditioning, and emotion by the lawful changes in behavior correlated with them.

A change in drive directly affects the strength of a reflex, but it is not supposed to change the size of the reflex reserve.[17] In that respect it differs from reinforcement, which changes both the strength and the reserve. This means that if drive is reduced by feeding a rat before an extinction series, it may be expected to respond at a lower rate because of the reduced drive, but it will continue to respond until it has emitted as many responses as a hungry rat. "Failure to receive a pellet means as much to a slightly hungry rat as to a very hungry one." [18] The more food an animal has received in the prefeeding, the slower will responses be emitted in the early part of the extinction period, but the prefed animals tend to catch up by the end of an hour's run.

[17] The relationships are complex. Under benzedrine the responses in the reserve appear to be multiplied, so that, contrary to the generalization about the relationship between drive and reserve, a "state" may occasionally change the reserve (Skinner, 1938, pages 415-416). Further experiments in progress may change the interpretation of the relationship between drive and reserve.

[18] Skinner (1938), page 390.

The effect on conditioning of change of drive is different from the effect on extinction. It may be supposed that a hungrier rat will yield a higher rate of conditioning than a less hungry rat. The most convenient method for investigating this is periodic reinforcement following prefeeding. When rats otherwise fed under standard conditions are prefed 0, 2, 4, or 6 grams of food, the extinction ratio falls in essentially linear fashion. In one summary of such data the extinction ratio for the rats not prefed was about 15:1 and it fell progressively to a ratio of about 7:1 with drive reduced by prefeeding.[19] The change in rate of responding corresponds to the change in rate with extinction. But the effect on the *reserve* is different. Different drives were said not to change the reserve within extinction. However, with higher drives the reconditioning effect of a single reinforcement increases, so that the reserve is replenished more quickly.[20] This apparently gives added support to Hull's conjecture that reinforcement is a function of drive.

Emotion and punishment. Just as drives are inappropriately classified as stimuli, so, according to Skinner, emotions are often unwisely classified as responses. Weeping at a bruised shin is said to be emotional, but weeping to a cinder in the eye is not. This way of treating emotion is rejected in favor of considering it to be a state, in many ways like drive. The state will be inferred from the strength of the reflexes which it affects.

The effects of punishment are often emotional by this definition. Punishment might act dynamically as negative conditioning, as though reinforcement were being subtracted, but in fact it does not serve in this way. If at the beginning of extinction the rat is slapped on its feet when it presses the lever, its rate of responding is depressed, but it eventually recovers. The reflex reserve has not been reduced by the punishment, as it should be if the punishment were negative conditioning.[21] Such a temporary effect upon strength but not upon reserve is defined as emotional. It is an effect upon the relation between reserve and rate, not upon the reserve itself. There is here some support for Thorndike's belief that punishments do not act opposite to re-

[19] Skinner (1938), page 392.
[20] Skinner (1938), page 402.
[21] Skinner (1938), page 154.

wards, and, by inference, a rejection of Hull's assimilation of punishment to reward.[22]

Because of the importance of the problem of punishment, Estes' (1944) study, carrying further Skinner's earlier explorations, will be reviewed later as an experimental illustration of Skinner's system.

DISCRIMINATION AND DIFFERENTIATION

In situations which require more than a change in rate of responding, two features stand out. One is the discrimination between stimuli, so that a given response may be made to one of a pair of stimuli and not to the other member of the pair. A second feature is differentiation of response, so that response is altered or adjusted appropriately to the situation. The complexities of behavior can be understood according to discriminations and differentiations arranged into appropriate chains or patterns.

Discrimination of stimuli. The standard lever-pressing experiment may serve the purposes of discriminatory conditioning if the lever-pressing delivers a pellet of food in the presence of a positive, supporting stimulus (e.g., a 3 c.p. light) and fails to deliver it in the absence of this discriminatory stimulus. The rat learns to respond only when the light is on, but the light does not actually elicit the response. The relationship is one which may be called a *pseudo-reflex*, because the discriminatory stimulus has a relationship to the operant which has some of the properties of a reflex, such as latency. The difference between a discriminatory stimulus being an occasion for a response and eliciting it is clarified by an example. I reach for a pencil lying on the desk, but I reach only when the pencil is there. Therefore the pencil has something to do with my reaching. If it were dark, and there were no pencil there, I might grope for it because the discriminatory stimuli would be lacking. The pencil does not elicit reaching in the light any more than in the dark. It is only the occasion for reaching.[23]

When the food is delivered only in the presence of the light, the situation is a sort of controlled periodic reconditioning, for

[22] Skinner (1938), page 242.
[23] Skinner (1938), page 178.

lever pressing is reinforced only part of the time. Eventually response occurs almost exclusively when the light is on, so that nearly every response is reinforced. The reflex reserve which is built up at this stage is not that of periodic reconditioning, but that of ordinary every-trial reinforcement. There are two operants with the same form of response, one with the light on, one with the light off; they are selectively reinforced and extinguished. There is an interaction called *induction* by Skinner which corresponds to Hull's generalization; whatever happens to one operant affects the other to some extent. There is a common reserve, because the form of response is independent of the discriminative stimuli which happen to be active at reinforcement. It is true that responses occur more frequently to the complex of stimuli which accompanied reinforcement, but such stimulus complexes serve merely as a sort of "patterned filter" through which the reserve is expressed in response.

The following statements are offered to clarify this somewhat complex situation: [24]

1. Responses accumulated in the presence of the positive stimulus are available in the presence of the negative stimulus. This is the principle of inductive conditioning or generalization.

2. Responses emitted in the presence of the negative stimulus are subtracted from the reserve available under the positive stimulus. This is the principle of inductive extinction.

3. Selective reinforcement and extinction increase the number of responses available chiefly in the presence of the positive stimulus. This is the positive half of the principle of discrimination.

4. Responses acquired in the presence of the positive stimulus may become less readily available under the negative stimulus. This is the negative half of the principle of discrimination—the breakdown of induction.

The discrimination experiment is always complicated by an additional fact of importance. The positive stimulus which acts as the occasion for the response and for the reinforcement becomes itself a secondary reinforcing agent. This has already been considered in relation to reinforcement at a fixed ratio.

Skinner believes that his arrangement for obtaining discrimina-

[24] Skinner (1938), page 229.

tion is superior to that usually used, in which a choice of responses confronts the animal. His rats may either respond to the lever or not respond. They do not have to choose between two levers, or between a right and a left turn. He believes the discrimination box to be a "crude instrument" for studying the nature of the process,[25] and finds Tolman's (1938a) dependence upon choice-point behavior to be a severe limitation.[26] The objection is that in the choice situation no measure of strength is obtained—only a measure of relative strength.

Differentiation of a response. Among a number of novel and useful distinctions made by Skinner is that between discrimination of stimuli and differentiation of response. In operant conditioning reinforcement can be made contingent on either (a) the properties of accompanying stimuli (when the result is a discrimination), or (b) the properties of the response (when the result is a differentiation).

The rat may be taught, for example, to press the lever with a given force, or to hold it down for a given duration, in order for the pellet to be delivered. The basic rule of operant conditioning applies, that the response must occur before it can be reinforced. Extreme forms or values may be obtained by successive approximations. Operant responses are emitted with an original range of form or intensity (Hull's response oscillation). If only the more extreme values are reinforced, the whole distribution shifts, so that higher and higher values may be obtained. The training method of successive approximations permits the finally learned behavior to be very different from that originally emitted.

Animal trainers are well versed in this method. As a sort of *tour de force* I have trained a rat to execute an elaborate series of responses suggested by recent work on anthropoid apes. The behavior consists of pulling a string to obtain a marble from a rack, picking the marble up with the fore-paws, carrying it to a tube projecting two inches above the floor of the cage, and dropping it inside. Every step in the process had to be worked out through a series of approximations, since the component responses were not in the original repertoire of the rat.[27]

[25] Skinner (1938), page 231.
[26] Skinner (1938), page 437.
[27] Skinner (1938), pages 339-340.

Response novelty is one of the features rather badly accounted for in most stimulus-response systems. Thorndike's law of assimilation, Guthrie's principle of compromise movements, and Skinner's successive approximations are all attempts to deal with the problem. The concept of emitted behavior has advantages over that of elicited behavior. It has always been embarrassing for theories of the conditioning type to try to find original stimuli to produce the responses called for in singing a song or in writing a poem. Such stimuli are unnecessary for emitted behavior.

THE REFLEX AS THE NATURAL UNIT OF BEHAVIOR

In the foregoing account of some of the kinds of data which Skinner collects and of the concepts used in describing them, his more general theory has been implied rather than made explicit. Skinner is definitely interested in supporting a scientific theory of a specific kind. He favors what he calls a purely descriptive system, and a frankly analytical one. How he goes about system-making is best illustrated in his discussion of the *reflex* and its laws.

Skinner believes that a purely descriptive system in order to be scientific and not a mere "botanizing" of behavior, must choose an appropriate natural unit of behavior. A real unit will not be an artificial part taken improperly out of context, nor will it be something too complex to enter into orderly relations as a descriptive unit. The level of specification found to be necessary is not something a priori, but is the level found in experience "marked by the orderliness of dynamic changes." [28] Skinner believes that his system has a merit not possessed by other stimulus-response systems—the discovery of this appropriate unit: the reflex, as he defines this term.

The reflex behavioral, not neuroanatomical. By a reflex Skinner means a lawful correlation between a class of stimuli and a class of responses. The reflex is not to be identified with the spinal reflex, which is defined topographically; its reference is solely to behavior and not to anatomy or neurology. The definition rests on a dynamic relationship. What is a stimulus, what

[28] Skinner (1938), page 40.

is a response, what is a reflex can be defined only according to the lawful experimental consequences when the reflex unit is isolated.

The reflex as an analytical unit is actually obtained in *practice*. The unit is a fact, and its validity and the validity of the laws describing its changes do not depend upon the correctness of analytical assumptions or the possibility of a later synthesis of more complex behavior.[29]

The laws of the reflex. There are static laws, dynamic laws, and laws of interaction.

The static laws refer to the quantitative properties of representative reflexes. They are reminiscent of the laws of spinal reflexes: the law of threshold, the law of latency, the law of magnitude of response as a function of intensity, the law of after-discharge, and the law of temporal summation.[30]

The dynamic laws include "classical examples," which means, presumably, that they too derive from the study of spinal reflexes: the law of refractory phase, the law of reflex fatigue, the law of facilitation, the law of inhibition. In addition there are other examples, logically similar but differing in the nature of the operations affecting reflex strength: the laws of conditioning, extinction, drive, and emotion.[31] These have already been considered.

The laws of interaction give an answer to the part-whole problem. They are: the law of compatibility, the law of prepotency, the law of algebraic summation, the law of blending, the law of spatial summation, the law of chaining, and the law of induction.[32]

There is a family resemblance between the topics covered in Skinner's laws and in Hull's postulates (1943*a*), although as they are given by Skinner the laws are defining principles, and are not stated so as to be used to deduce behavior. Skinner's laws are unlikely to be found false, because they are worded in such a form that they are true at the level of general observation. They provide a framework for further specification and quantification.

[29] Skinner (1938), page 29.
[30] Skinner (1938), pages 12-14.
[31] Skinner (1938), pages 14-19.
[32] Skinner (1938), pages 29-33.

They enter exposition quite differently from Hull's postulates. Actually, there is little reference to the laws as the data from experiments are discussed.

How laws of this kind define the system and set experiments might be illustrated by a parallel example from plant growth. Preliminary observation would soon establish the fact that growth varies with the amount of water in the soil, the range of temperature, and the amount of sunlight. Before beginning further experimental work it would be possible to set up a series of growth laws: a law of moisture, a law of temperature, a law of illumination, together with some presumptive laws of their interaction. For example, it is plausible that with more moisture in the soil the plant could thrive at somewhat higher room temperatures. An experimental program might easily be motivated by these laws. One can imagine the greenhouse with thermostats, moisture controls, shades, and sunlamps. The laws of growth could be worked out according to these and similar variables without any regard for the physiology of cells or for the chemistry of growth hormones. The observations would, in fact, be governed largely by the descriptive system implied in the laws, but the aim is not to prove or disprove these laws. This is essentially what Skinner has proposed and what he has succeeded in doing. There is this difference, that the isolation of a reflex to be studied and the selection of units of measurement is a more perplexing problem than defining plant growth.

Skinner's theory in relation to other stimulus-response theories. From the standpoint of Thorndike's distinction between associative shifting and learning under the law of effect, Guthrie, Hull, and Skinner fall in three different relationships to Thorndike. Guthrie accepts contiguous conditioning only, which corresponds to Thorndike's associative shifting and Skinner's Type S conditioning. Hull's is a reinforcement theory, related to Thorndike's law of effect and to Skinner's Type R conditioning. Hull rejects the principle of contiguous conditioning, or associative shifting, independent of reinforcement. That leaves Skinner most like Thorndike, from this standpoint, both accepting two types of learning which are not quite reconcilable. Skinner, like Thorndike, believes the reinforcement (or operant) type of learning to be the more important.

Because both of their systems represent quantifications of data based on a common typical experiment (rat lever-pressing), it is most natural to compare the positions of Skinner and Hull. They both are well aware of the scientific models which they have adopted, and they believe these models to be unlike. Hull favors the hypothetical-deductive method, while Skinner prefers a descriptive system without hypothetical predictions. Skinner believes that Hull's method is merely a technique of verification, and does not provide a system at all. He objects to hypothesis as a form of prophecy, and prefers a straight descriptive account of what is found in experiments. It is because of this preference that his system has been referred to in the title of this chapter as a descriptive behaviorism. It might have been called equally well a positivistic behaviorism.

Skinner occasionally refers to the difference in scientific model between his system and Hull's. Hull has chosen Newtonian mechanics for a model, with its fundamental laws of motion and everything else derived as theorems from them. For his model Skinner prefers something like physical chemistry.[33] Just what he means by this is not altogether clear but one or two points may be made. For one thing, physical chemistry is concerned with a great deal of empirical material: boiling points, melting points, energy interchanges. These are not highly predictable from basic postulates. Physical chemistry is also concerned with a search for natural units of description, whether the atom or electron or what not, which will make relationships lawful. Field physics has not rendered obsolete the notion of chemical elements represented in the periodic table, even though one element can now be transmuted into another. Perhaps Skinner in the choice of this model refers to the analytic assumptions and to the importance of descriptive material, by contrast with the almost purely mathematical approach of Newton.

In his review of Hull's *Principles of behavior*, Skinner (1944) detects a vacillation in Hull's theory between "laws" and "postulates." A functional relationship which can be directly studied is, according to Skinner, a "law" and not a "postulate." Many of Hull's later postulates are of this sort, and Hull himself does not distinguish between a principle, a postulate, and a law. Skin-

[33] Skinner (1938), page 434.

ner believes that Hull's theory is moving somewhat in the direction of his own.

Examination of Skinner's work shows that its positivistic descriptions are not without inference. Such conceptions as drive,
emotion, reflex reserve (especially a strained reserve) have much
the rôle of intervening variables in the systems of Tolman and
Hull.

It may well be that the scientific logics of Skinner and of Hull,
when put to work, come out more nearly alike than when talked
about abstractly. In any case, Skinner's denial of hypotheses must
not be permitted to lead to the belief that his is an ultra-empiri-
cism, which measures just anything for the sake of measuring it.
His system is better described as a variety of functionalism, in
which the basic dimensions are carefully explored before the
precise experiments are done to fill in the gaps of knowledge.
Related functionalisms are to be discussed in the next chapter.

THE CONSEQUENCES OF PUNISHMENT AS ILLUSTRA-
TIVE OF EXPERIMENTS WITH OPERANT
BEHAVIOR

Some of the suggestions about the action of punishment which
Skinner had earlier made were more extensively studied by Estes
(1944) under his direction. Estes' work serves as a convenient
example of the experimental approach to a problem by an inves-
tigator adopting Skinner's general point of view. Estes chose a
more conventional terminology than Skinner, avoiding words
like "operant" or "reflex" or "emitted," but the experiments
could have been described in Skinner's words. It is of some
interest that Estes found the more usual vocabulary satisfactorily
precise for his purposes.

On the assumption that punishment does have effects, the two
chief possibilities are that it weakens the habit or that it merely
suppresses response. If the habit is weakened, punishment acts
as a negative reinforcement, or as an agent hastening extinction.
If the response is merely suppressed, the response has not been
eliminated from the organism's repertory, or, as Skinner would
put it, the reflex reserve is not reduced. Skinner's preliminary
experiments favored the latter alternative, that punishment sup-

presses the rate of responding without eliminating responses from the total of responses to appear in extinction. Estes points out that the alternatives are genuine ones in the light of clinical experience. It is familiar that behavior may be repressed, and not overtly expressed, although the tendencies continue to exist at considerable strength.

Punishment does not act as a negative reinforcement. In agreement with Skinner (and the later Thorndike), Estes finds that punishment does not lead to a reduction in the total number of responses given during extinction, even though there is suppression of response following the punishment. Some characteristic findings are shown in Figure 17.

On the basis of additional experiments in the series, Estes concludes that the total number of elicitations of the response necessary for extinction may be reduced somewhat by punishment, but the time required for complete extinction of the response will not be affected by the punishment. More generally, the conclusion is reached that a response cannot be eliminated from an organism's repertory by the action of punishment alone.

Punishment more importantly associated with stimuli than with responses. If punishment were a reinforcing agent similar to reward, it would act on responses, in accordance with Skinner's principle of Type R conditioning. That its more significant correlation is with discriminative stimuli is pointed out by Estes on the basis of several kinds of evidence.

In one experiment [34] the animals of the experimental group were shocked at intervals of approximately thirty seconds, care being taken not to shock them during or immediately after a response to the lever. Recovery from the effects of punishment follows the same course (i.e., the same mathematical function fits the course) as the course following punishment of the response itself. It is argued therefore that the effect must be due to the contiguity of the disturbing stimuli with stimuli in the box which normally act as occasions for lever pressing.

This conjecture was tested in another experiment [35] in which the rat was left in the box for an adaptation period following

[34] Estes (1944), Experiment I.
[35] Estes (1944), Experiment J.

punishment. During this time the lever was withdrawn, so that response to it was impossible. The effects of the short period of severe punishment were almost completely dispelled, confirming

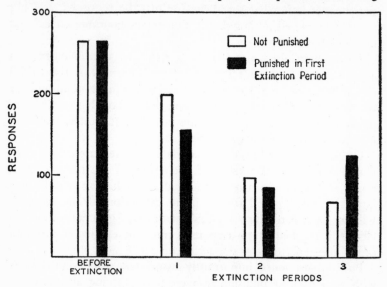

FIGURE 17. EVIDENCE THAT PUNISHMENT DEPRESSES RATE OF RESPONDING WITHOUT DECREASING THE RESERVE.

Responses of two groups of 8 rats each are compared. While the groups were not alike in their response frequency prior to extinction, their rates have been equated, and other comparisons are based upon this adjustment. Within the first extinction period one group of rats received an average of 9 punishments (electric shocks while pressing the lever). This punishment reduced the number of responses on the first day, and perhaps on the second, but by the third day there was a compensatory increase in the number of responses so that the total responses of the group punished on the first day and of the group not punished are the same over the three days of extinction. Data from Estes (1944), Experiment A, corrected for differences prior to extinction.

the interpretation that punishment was related to the stimulating situation rather than specifically to the response.

Periodically administered punishment more effective than punishment at every occurrence. If punishment is delivered every time the response is made, the rate of responding is seriously depressed. While it is not depressed as much if punishment is given only occasionally, the effects of punishment persist longer in the latter case.[36] This is shown in two experiments, in one of which the test is made by simple extinction, the other in which the extinction follows an adaptation period. The results are most

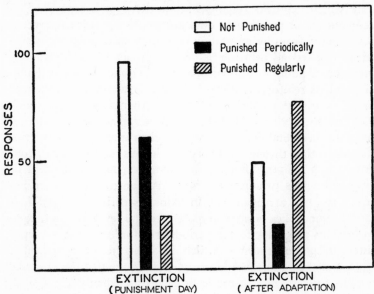

FIGURE 18. EVIDENCE THAT PERIODIC PUNISHMENT IS MORE EFFECTIVE THAN REGULAR PUNISHMENT.

The mean numbers of responses of three groups are shown, a control group extinguished in the usual manner, a group punished for responding whenever response occurred, and a group punished periodically, for responses occurring within every fourth minute of the 40-minute extinction period. Following the experimental day there were two adaptation days, when the animals were placed in the boxes with the levers retracted. The results for extinction are for the first day with the exposed lever, after these adaptation days. The adaptation period has almost completely eradicated the results of regular punishment, but the consequences of periodic punishment persist. Each group consisted of 6 rats. Data from Estes (1944), Experiment K, corrected for differences prior to extinction.

striking following adaptation. Adaptation does not bring recovery after periodic punishment as it does after every-trial punishment. The results are shown in Figure 18.

[36] Estes (1944), Experiments E and K. The average number of punishments received by the rats turns out to be about the same for both groups. Although many responses go unpunished in the periodic situation, responding is at a higher rate than for rats punished whenever they respond.

The explanation given by Estes is not altogether satisfying. He accepts a twofold theory of the effect of punishment. One principle, already referred to, is that punishment creates an emotional state which depresses responses while the state is aroused. This consequence of punishment does not lower the reflex reserve. It is recovered from by adaptation or during subsequent extinction trials. The second principle is one congruent with Hull's interpretation of punishment, that is, an interpretation of the cessation of shock as reinforcing. Estes believes the withdrawal responses to be positively conditioned by the termination of the shock delivered by the lever. He believes, further, that such withdrawal responses are conditioned more strongly through periodic reinforcement than through ordinary continuous reinforcement, consistent with Skinner's findings for conditioning in general. This explanation fails to adjust the interpretation to a difference between the two arrangements. In Skinner's periodic reconditioning, the rat makes positive responses to the lever between reinforcements and prior to the periodic reinforcement. It is a consistent response tendency which is strengthened periodically. The parallel case for punishment would require that the rat make withdrawal responses to the lever each time when not punished, if periodic punishment were to be effective. While it may be true that such responses were made between times of punishment, no evidence is presented and such evidence as we have shows more positive responses to the lever within periodic punishment than within continuous punishment. A fully adequate interpretation of punishment has not yet been given.

Punishment in the practical control of behavior. Estes suggests several practical implications of his study.

The main finding is that a response cannot be eliminated from the organism's repertory more rapidly with the aid of punishment than without it. Permanent weakening comes about only by non-reinforced elicitation—and this weakening process may be prevented if punishment suppresses the response. This is in line with clinical findings about forms of aggressive or hostile responses which have come under parental or other social punishment. They are not eliminated until they can be brought to free expression, when the behavior can be appropriately redirected.

Another disadvantage of punishment lies in the concomitant

emotional state which is aroused. This state will suppress other responses than the one punished. The lack of specificity of its target is a weakness of punishment.

On the positive side, there are several "rules" which serve to show when and how punishment may be useful:

1. Punishment may be used to hold a response at low strength. Under these circumstances, punishment has to continue indefinitely, as it does not eliminate the response. The continuing punishment is equally or more effective if administered occasionally than if it is given every time the objectionable behavior occurs.

2. It is possible to take advantage of the period of suppressed response following punishment in order to strengthen some other response by reinforcement.

3. It is important that punishment be given in the presence of the discriminative cues for the response. Delayed punishment is likely to prove ineffective because it is given at a time when the discriminative stimuli leading to the undesired conduct are absent.

The series of experiments by Estes, with their interpretations, show how, within the experimental and theoretical framework of Skinner's system, it is possible to experiment upon problems genuinely relevant to the practical control of learning situations. The difficulty remains of finding appropriate ways to test the implications in a social context.

ESTIMATE OF SKINNER'S SYSTEM

Skinner's position on typical problems of learning. Because of his caution about extrapolating beyond the data presented in his investigations, it is not quite clear just what position might be taken in some instances on problems which do not fit directly into the conceptual scheme. In what follows it has occasionally been necessary to make assumptions coherent with other portions of the system, even though direct references are missing.

1. *Capacity*. In a descriptive system, it is to be expected that the laws will contain empirical constants differing for various species and for different members of each species. The eating rate, for example, cannot be expected to remain the same for young and for old animals, and for animals unlike in their food preferences. Because *lawfulness* rather than *laws* is what the sys-

tem insists upon, differences in capacity are not of central importance. There is no suggestion that at higher capacity levels the laws are essentially any different; verbal behavior in man, for example, is said to conform to the general principles of operant behavior.

2. *Practice.* Something like a simple law of exercise is accepted for Type *S* conditioning, while for Type *R* conditioning depends upon repeated reinforcement. The laws of extinction are also laws of exercise, but exercise in the absence of reinforcement. The building of a reflex reserve is not a simple consequence of the number of reinforcements, but depends upon the arrangements of reinforcement, as in periodic reconditioning or reinforcement at a fixed ratio.

3. *Motivation.* In agreement with Thorndike, reward is found to increase reflex strength, while punishment has no corresponding weakening influence. The treatment of punishment is more sophisticated than that by Guthrie or Hull. While there are several ways in which punishment enters, one is to create the state called emotion, which reduces rate of responding without weakening the reflex reserve. Drive and emotion are both treated as states of the organism—not as stimuli or as responses.

4. *Understanding.* The problem of understanding is essentially irrelevant to the discussion within the framework of Skinner's system. Most behavior which would ordinarily be called voluntary is subsumed under the discriminated operant. Because of the correlation between responses and their consequences, it would not be hard to impose a cognitive interpretation upon operant behavior, but Skinner does not do so. The secondary reinforcing character of discriminating stimuli is close to what Tolman calls sign learning.

5. *Transfer.* Skinner prefers to use the term induction for what is commonly called generalization in conditioning literature. Such induction is presumably the basis for transfer, although Skinner has little to say about it.

6. *Forgetting.* There is no special theory of forgetting proposed, although the distinction between extinction and true forgetting is maintained. The suggestion is that both conditioning and extinction are long remembered. Spontaneous recovery does

not mean that extinction is forgotten, for successive extinctions show the results of earlier ones.

The reflex no longer a satisfactory unit. When he first committed himself to the reflex as his unit (Skinner, 1931), he referred to the correlation between a class of stimuli and a class of responses. If this correlation was lawful, he believed the term reflex to be appropriate. A case could be made for his position, but the consequence was no more than to discover as his unit what Thorndike had earlier named the "connection" or "bond." Thorndike, too, accepted the correlation between situations and responses as the basis for his unit.

When Skinner developed the notion of emitted behavior, his earlier unit was no longer appropriate. The discriminated operant, which is the basis of experiment and theory in the newer writings, is at one place referred to as a *pseudo-reflex*.[37] He points out that it would be a great mistake to suppose that the correlation established between a discriminated stimulus and an operant followed the laws of the reflex. Thus the systematic correlation between stimuli and responses, a legitimate extension of the historical term reflex, is no longer appropriate in dealing with operants. The terms which enter a reflex relationship should be those of stimulus and response. Skinner's concern has appropriately shifted to mere lawfulness of behavior, not lawfulness in stimulus-response relationships. Anyone else starting from his present conception of behavior would find the concept of the reflex more troublesome than helpful.

Present insulation from other systematic viewpoints. Skinner has not yet presented his system in a form to make it fully accessible to others, because he has avoided the transformations which would show its relevance to what others are doing and thinking. There are only the barest of references to other systematic writers, and analogies and extrapolations are left almost entirely to the reader. In spite of the difficulties in the way of a comparative exposition, the position has been included because of suggestions within it that are likely in the future to become influential in the development of learning theory.

The most striking contribution is the emphasis upon operant behavior as emitted, in contrast to respondent behavior as elicited.

[37] Skinner (1938), pages 236-239.

If the notion of operant behavior can be defended and extended, it may do much to break down the rigid stimulus-response conceptions which have too long been dominant in American psychology. The related concept of a reflex reserve is one new to learning theory, and needs demonstration over wider segments of behavior.

Extension to human learning. While a science of behavior does not succeed or fail by its applicability to human problems, the human animal is a learner *par excellence*, and a comparative psychology of learning is ultimately to be judged by the success with which it includes human learning within its scheme. In his book, Skinner has avoided more than the most casual references to human behavior. This does not mean that he is uninterested, and he has, in fact, promised a volume on verbal behavior.[38] From the fragmentary publication which he has already done in this field, one can say only that he believes words to be emitted according to the same rules as lever-pressing in rats, that language usage is determined by social reinforcements, and that a quantitative theory of verbal behavior is possible along the same lines as those charted in his book on rat experiments.

The applying of statistical measures to words reveals lawfulness, as shown by the work of Zipf (1935). Skinner has contributed several studies of the dynamics of speech through word counts, including words "read into" chance groupings of speech sounds,[39] and associations as found in the Kent-Rosanoff lists and subsequent modifications.[40] In a study of alliteration in Shakespeare's sonnets, he showed that alliteration does not occur any more than would be expected by chance, if Shakespeare's words had been drawn out of a hat.[41] This is illustrative of other studies of sound patterning.[42] These studies are mentioned only to prevent a distorted view of Skinner's goals arising because the earlier discussion was limited to experiments with rats.

There are elements of originality in Skinner's system which commend it to the careful student. Its extensions in the future may importantly modify the emphases within psychology.

[38] Skinner (1945), page 271.
[39] Skinner (1936c).
[40] Skinner (1937), Cook and Skinner (1939).
[41] Skinner (1939).
[42] E.g., Skinner (1941).

SUPPLEMENTARY READINGS

BOOKS

Skinner, B. F. (1938) *The behavior of organisms.*

SHORTER INTRODUCTIONS

Skinner, B. F. (1935) The generic nature of the concepts of stimulus and response. *J. gen. Psychol.,* 12, 40-65.

Skinner, B. F. (1935) Two types of conditioned reflex and a pseudo type. *J. gen. Psychol.,* 12, 66-77.

CRITICAL REVIEWS

Finan, J. L. (1940) Review of Skinner's *The behavior of organisms. J. gen. Psychol.,* 22, 441-447.

Hilgard, E. R. (1939) Review of Skinner's *The behavior of organisms. Psychol. Bull.,* 36, 121-125.

Krechevsky, I. (1939) Review of Skinner's *The behavior of organisms. J. abn. (soc.) Psychol.,* 34, 404-407.

REPRESENTATIVE EXPERIMENTS

Estes, W. K. and Skinner, B. F. (1941) Some quantitative properties of anxiety. *J. exp. Psychol.,* 29, 390-400.

Heron, W. T. and Skinner, B. F. (1937) Changes in hunger during starvation. *Psychol. Rec.,* 1, 51-60.

Heron, W. T. and Skinner, B. F. (1940) The rate of extinction in maze-bright and maze-dull rats. *Psychol. Rec.,* 4, 11-18.

Keller, F. S. (1941) Light-aversion in the white rat. *Psychol. Rec.,* 4, 235-250.

Skinner, B. F. (1932) Drive and reflex strength. *J. gen. Psychol.,* 6, 22-37; 38-48.

Skinner, B. F. (1933) 'Resistance to extinction' in the process of conditioning. *J. gen. Psychol.,* 9, 420-429.

Skinner, B. F. (1936) The reinforcing effect of a differentiating stimulus. *J. gen. Psychol.,* 14, 263-278.

Skinner, B. F. (1936) The effect on the amount of conditioning of an interval of time before reinforcement. *J. gen. Psychol.,* 14, 279-295.

Skinner, B. F. (1936) The verbal summator and a method for the studying of latent speech. *J. Psychol.,* 2, 71-107.

Skinner, B. F. (1941) A quantitative estimate of certain types of sound-patterning in poetry. *Amer. J. Psychol.,* 54, 64-79.

Skinner, B. F. and Heron, W. T. (1937) Effects of caffeine and benzedrine upon conditioning and extinction. *Psychol. Rec.,* 1, 340-346.

Wentink, E. (1938) The effects of certain drugs and hormones upon conditioning. *J. exp. Psychol.,* 22, 150-163.

Chapter 6

CURRENT FUNCTIONALISM

The developments within American psychology out of which behaviorism grew have flourished alongside it and continue to be well represented in contemporary psychology. These related developments are varieties of *functionalism*, a word originally applied to the somewhat loosely formulated point of view identified with Angell, Carr, and their students at the University of Chicago. The term is equally applicable to the position represented by Woodworth at Columbia, often separately designated as *dynamic psychology*. The two viewpoints are so much alike that there is little reason to preserve the distinction. Both Chicago functionalism and Columbia dynamic psychology are stimulus-response psychologies which preceded and did not capitulate to behaviorism. Although they belong within the same broad family of association theories to which Thorndike, Guthrie, Hull, and Skinner have been assigned, they represent a form of association theory which is in some respects more nearly continuous with the views of preexperimental associationists—of men like Hartley, Brown, Hamilton, the Mills, Spencer, and Bain.

Unlike nineteenth century associationism, the emphasis of contemporary functionalism is out-and-out experimental. The functionalist group is composed largely of those psychologists who have followed Ebbinghaus' lead in translating the problems of learning and retention into experimentable form.

THE CARR-ROBINSON LAWS OF ASSOCIATION

Harvey A. Carr was the successor to James R. Angell at the University of Chicago. Edward S. Robinson had studied with both Angell and Carr, and had spent the early years of his teaching career on the staff at Chicago. Their common viewpoint regarding the laws of association came to expression at about the same time, in an article by Carr entitled *The laws of association* (1931) and in a small book by Robinson called *Association theory today* (1932*a*). Both admitted that contemporary functionalism was historically continuous with earlier association psychology; both insisted that the present form of associationism could be defended as a quantitative experimentalism. What was needed, they said, was more laws to express the functional relationships between the variables found important in learning experiments. While they do not come out with exactly the same laws, their point of view is so similar that one may be taken as representative of their common point of view. What follows is based upon Robinson's statement of the position.

The items entering into association. Robinson defends a frankly analytical point of view toward the problem of association. "The ideal of associational analysis is to segregate, from any complicated psychological event, as many associated items as possible and to state as fully as possible the conditions accounting for their association."[1]

In order to stay within the realm of psychological activities he prefers to speak of *instigating* and *instigated* items and acts, rather than of stimulus and response. His list of instigators and instigatable processes turns out as follows:

Instigating Processes	*Instigatable Processes*
1. Sensory processes	1. Perceptions
2. Sensations	2. Ideas
3. Complete perceptual acts	3. Feelings
4. Ideational processes	4. General sets
5. Affective activities	5. Muscular movements
6. Determining tendencies	6. Glandular secretings
7. Inhibition	7. Inhibition

Omitted as instigators are stimuli, muscular and postural adjustments, and glandular secretions. This is in line with the desire to keep the association between psychological processes. Psychological processes may eventuate in physical processes like movements

---

[1] Robinson (1932*a*), page 27.

and secretions, but they always originate in an aroused condition of the organism. The refusal to admit the stimulus is somewhat arbitrary, for the direction from physical process to psychological process can be handled just as well as the direction from psychological process to physical process. But Robinson believes that movements belong to the organism in a way that external stimuli do not.

If one were to characterize Robinson's lists of items entering into associative connection it would be to comment primarily on its breadth. Robinson reacted strongly against the strictures of behaviorism; he used to tell his classes at Yale that he didn't like a psychology which said: "You mustn't say this, and you mustn't say that." He knew that it was not quite clear to speak of ideational processes, but he felt it better to talk about ideational processes than to disguise ignorance by translating them (whatever they were) into something equally unknown, such as implicit speech.

Principles of association may be formulated as laws of associative formation (learning) or as laws of associative revival (recall or recognition). Principles such as contiguity and frequency apply to associative formation; a principle like recency applies to associative revival. It is possible to prefer one or the other of these types of principle, or to use both after the precedent of Thomas Brown. Those who limit their principles to associative revival tend to use Sir William Hamilton's term *redintegration*. A contemporary example may be found in the writings of Hollingworth. But Robinson makes his choice in favor of the principles of associative formations: "The strength of any associative connection is a function of the conditions of contiguity, frequency, vividness, and so on, obtaining at the time the association was formed." [2]

The law of contiguity. In later associationist writings of the preexperimental period a distinction first made by Thomas Brown (1820) came to be generally accepted. This is the distinction between *primary* or *qualitative* laws (usually stated as the laws of similarity, contrast, and contiguity) and *secondary* or *quantitative* laws (frequency, vividness, emotional congruity, mental set, etc.). The primary laws were said to represent the basic con-

[2] Robinson (1932a), page 66.

ditions for associative formation or associative revival, while the secondary laws determined which of many possible associates was formed or recalled. Both Carr and Robinson reject this distinction, and treat all associative laws as quantitative.

Contiguity is usually considered the most important law of association, and it is the one which has survived the others in conditioning theories like that of Guthrie. Robinson's statement of the law is:

> The fact that two psychological processes occur together in time or in immediate succession increases the probability that an associative connection between them will develop—that one process will become the associative instigator of the other.[3]

To make of this a quantitative law all that is necessary is to express quantitatively the relationship between a pair of continuous variables—time-interval and degree of association. This is the same sort of relationship implied in all the other laws.

To express associative strength as a function of time interval is not the only alternative. Another possibility, rejected by Robinson, is that of reducing all contiguous association to simultaneity or immediate succession. In order to accept this alternative it is necessary to fill the experimentally measured time interval with implied associative mediators, so that the association is "really" between touching events.

> Why should not the burden of proof be assumed by those who insist that there is always a mediator, even when they are unable to demonstrate it, rather than by those who admit no mediation of this sort unless there is positive evidence of its existence?[4]

This illustrates a point of disagreement between Robinson and Guthrie, whose views have already been discussed. It shows a certain reluctance on Robinson's part to make inferences beyond the data systematically gathered in experiments.

The law of assimilation. This law has two complementary expressions:

> Whenever an associative connection is so established that an activity, A, becomes capable of instigating an activity, B, activities other

---

[3] Robinson (1932a), page 72.
[4] Robinson (1932a), page 77.

than A also undergo an increase or decrease in their capacity to instigate B.[5]

Whenever an associative connection is so established that an activity, A, becomes capable of instigating an activity, B, that same A will vary in its capacity for instigating certain activities other than B.[6]

These two statements are Robinson's revisions of Thorndike's law.[7] The law substitutes for the law of similarity, which is rejected on the grounds that similarity refers to a logical relationship, whereas psychological similarity has to be defined circularly, according to things reacted to *as* similar. Reacting to things *as* similar is exactly what the law of assimilation is about.

The law of assimilation carries a great deal of responsibility in Robinson's theory. It accounts, in general, for phenomena of transfer of training, whereby one learning modifies another. It covers what conditioned response writers call generalization, what gestalt writers call transposition. And, finally, it provides for the novelties in behavior which have led other writers to lay emphasis upon insight.

To say that it accounts for these aspects of behavior is somewhat misleading. As best it sets a framework within which the associationist can work experimentally on problems of originality. It cannot be denied that associationists have been more interested in the problem of how past habits are marshalled for the meeting of present situations than in discovering any genuine novelty in the attack on problems.

The law of assimilation points a moral for anyone attempting to debate the merits of one system against another. The moral is this: Reputable theorists do not permit gaps in their systems which make the system subject to easy demolition by those who disagree with it. Even though the writers within their tradition may have neglected important problems, there will always be found a way of talking about the data which others have collected in their study of these problems. The opposing systematist may deny the facts for a while, or consider them to be too trivial to be taken seriously, but ultimately *all the systems accept all the facts*. The law of assimilation lets Carr and Robinson include

[5] Robinson (1932a), page 86.
[6] Robinson (1932a), page 92.
[7] Thorndike (1913b), page 28.

many of the facts of gestalt psychology of learning, though they and their students might have shown little interest in discovering these facts.

The law of frequency. The general principle that practice makes perfect is limited by the fact that exercise also brings fatigue, and that other things happen within repetitions, such as changes in motivation.

While the practice curve is the usual expression of the relationship between frequency and associative strength, Robinson believes that a more general law can be derived from studies of relative frequency. By relative frequency he means the conditions

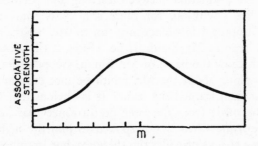

FIGURE 19. HYPOTHETICAL LAW OF RELATIVE FREQUENCY.

The curve is intended to show that associative strength increases as relative frequency increases up to some optimal value. Beyond this the overcrowding of repetitions results in less rapid increase in associative strength. After Robinson (1932*a*), page 103.

such as are used in experiments on the distribution of practice. Too concentrated practice usually shows deleterious effects, while too widely spaced practice permits forgetting between trials. There is presumably some optimum distribution between these extremes. The general law is not stated by Robinson, but is illustrated by the figure reproduced as Figure 19.

Robinson's law put into words would read somewhat as follows:

When other conditions of presentation favor increase in associative strength, the associative strength achieved in a given time increases with the frequency of presentation of the associated items up to an optimum frequency, then decreases as the frequency of presentation is increased above that optimum.

That both increases with frequency and decreases with frequency ought to be expected appears obvious to Robinson because both learning curves and work curves are plotted on the
same coordinates.

One of the weaknesses of the frequency principle as discussed
by Robinson—a weakness in his other laws as well—is that associative strength is defined by performance. He fails to note that
psychological reality is always an inference from the data of
experiment. To accept plotted data as psychological reality is
a convenient empiricism, but it is the empiricism of actuarial
statistics, and not that of systematic science.

Perhaps the distinction between learning and performance requires further discussion, for there still exists some confusion
about it.[8] Suppose I introduce my son to Mr. Smith, and I ask
him to say hello to Mr. Smith. If he refuses, am I to assume that
he does not know the name of Mr. Smith? Suppose the next day
he begins talking about the Mr. Smith he met the night before.
Has he just then learned the name? It is obvious that the inference can be made from the later performance that he actually
learned the name when it was spoken to him the night before.
Performance always provides the evidence, but learning is always
inferred. Under many circumstances there is such a close correspondence between performance and learning that one can be
used as a measure of the other, but the distinction is a necessary
one, especially when work decrements, the influence of drugs,
and related factors distort the simple correspondence between
learning and performance. We shall return to this problem later,
when latent learning is under discussion.

The law of intensity. Robinson does not state a law, but he
believes that the relationships are subject to experimentation and
lawful formulation. The law would have to take into account
relative intensities of instigating and instigatable activities. As far
as affective intensity is concerned, intense unpleasantness may act
oppositely to intense pleasantness. It may be noted in passing
that Thorndike's law of effect is subsumed under the law of
intensity. In this practice Robinson is following Carr's earlier
identification of the principle of effect with the sensory conse-

[8] McGeoch (1942), pages 597-599.

quences of an act.[9] Carr, as we shall see (page 157) adopted a motivational scheme not unlike that of Woodworth (1918) and Smith and Guthrie (1921) in which drives arouse behavior until an incentive relieves the drive state through consummatory response. Robinson's neglect of motivation is therefore not a necessary part of contemporary association.

Other laws. Both Carr and Robinson believe that new laws should be stated as additional variables prove to be important in experiments. Among the further laws proposed by Robinson are the *law of duration*, the *law of context*, the *law of acquaintance*, the *law of composition* and the *law of individual differences*. Several of these make grudging acceptance of considerations brought to prominence by the gestalt psychologists. The law of context allows of some influence of the whole on the part, but does not concede the centrality of field structure as proposed by gestalt psychologists. The law of composition, which admits that some things are easier for the organism to learn than others, is a reply to Köhler's [10] charge that associationists pay no attention to the natural propensities of the organism. The law of individual differences recognizes the facts brought to light by standardized tests of intelligence and other measures of associative capacities.

With these laws, Robinson rests his case. He states that it is his firm conviction that the facility of associative fixation is a function of all the variables enumerated. If that be true, there are "laws" of these factors, whether or not our knowledge of them is definite.

The difference between Robinson's position and that of the associationist writers already considered lies in his catholicity about the terms entering associative connection and in the kinds of variables considered. The contrast is sharpest with Guthrie, who seeks to reduce the number of associative laws to one single law of contiguity while Robinson enlarges the number. Guthrie also limits associations to stimuli and movements, while Robinson has a long list of instigators and instigatable activities. There is a logical similarity between Robinson's methodological pragmatism and Skinner's descriptive behaviorism, but the development of

---

[9] Carr (1925), pages 93-95.
[10] Köhler (1929), page 294.

the two systems is so different that understanding one of them helps little in the understanding of the other.

One hint as to the difference between the systems of Robinson and Skinner, in view of their agreement that laws should be empirical ones expressing the relationships between variables known to be significant, lies in their preoccupation with limited, but unlike, experimental situations. It is clear in Robinson's book that he has in mind the memorization and retention experiment as the characteristic experiment on associative learning. Occasional references to conditioning, to skills, and to problem-solving are subdued in preoccupation with the kinds of associative fixation and reinstatement found in the nonsense syllable experiment. Because of this preoccupation, motivation and reinforcement are not important problems to Robinson. Skinner, on the other hand, accounting for the lever-pressing activity of his rats, is little concerned about many of the problems which bother Robinson, but is necessarily concerned about the problems of motivation and reinforcement. The memory drum runs on, presenting one item after another, whether or not the subject responds, but nothing happens in Skinner's box unless the rat first pushes the lever. There is a circular relationship between theory and experiment. The theory predisposes to the selection of a given kind of experiment, but once the experiment is selected it helps to mold the extensions of the theory. One task which faces the eclectic is to discover whether or not some of the theories can be harmonized because their differences are a result of focussing on different aspects of the large field of learning.

The McGeoch-Melton dimensional principle. The general spirit of the Carr-Robinson laws of association has been extended to an interpretation of learning according to the *dimensions* of learning situations or of learning processes by McGeoch and Melton. McGeoch had studied with both Carr and Robinson at Chicago, and Melton first studied with McGeoch at Washington University and later with Robinson at Yale. Both McGeoch and Melton are therefore in direct line of descent from the earlier Chicago functionalism.

The old problem of the attributes of sensation had been solved by Boring (1933a) by renaming them dimensions, and by giving criteria whereby the dimensions could be functionally (or operationally) defined. The problem of how many dimensions there are becomes a matter of demonstration. There are as many dimensions as there are consistent and distinguishable quantitative functions which can be reproduced under defined laboratory conditions. McGeoch (1936), adopting a similar logic, proposed what he called the *vertical dimensions of mind*, referring essentially to levels of complexity found in learning experiments. Melton (1941*a*) supported and developed the proposal that the most fruitful way in which to experiment upon learning was to discover and to explore the dimensions of variation.

To Carr and Robinson the variables considered were chiefly those affecting a single process of associative learning or of associative strength. At least these were the variables which were summarized in their laws of association.[11] Neither Melton nor McGeoch show any desire to propose a new set of laws of association. They accept as equally cogent other dimensions of variation not easily formulated as laws of association. The two chief classes of variation are those dependent upon experimental arrangement, which might be called *situational dimensions*, and those which depend upon the psychological functions involved, which might be called *process dimensions*.

The situational dimensions call attention to the fact that what is found out about learning is likely to be different in one experimental arrangement than in another. A very different problem is presented to the learner by a path through a maze, the rotating target of a pursuitmeter, a list of syllables on a memory drum, a reflex to be attached by conditioning to a new stimulus, and a mathematical problem to be solved by reasoning.

The process dimensions are correlated in a coarse way with the situational dimensions, but are distinguishable. They include such considerations as the amount of discovery required before the correct response is made (a distinction between *rote learning* and *problem-solving*), the involvement of motor or ideational responses (as between *motor skills* and *verbal memory*), and the

[11] Both Carr and Robinson anticipated the dimensional principle, not limiting themselves to the framework of "laws" of association. Illustrations are given by Carr's experiments on teaching and learning (Carr, 1930), in which the amount and position of "guidance" was a major variable. Robinson proposed that the amount of "understanding" could become a variable (Robinson, 1932*b*, page 96).

relevancy of motivating conditions (*incidental learning* as against *intentional learning*).

Experiments have to be classified according to more than one dimension. Thus rote learning and reasoning experiments are alike on the dimensions verbal-nonverbal, but unlike with respect to the amount of discovery involved in the adequate response. It is important to recognize that the classification is not according to fixed types, but always according to scales which have intermediate values. Learning is not blind on the one hand and insightful on the other; there are degrees of understanding involved from a minimum at one extreme to a maximum at the other, with most cases falling between these extremes.

The dimensional position is further characterized as a *relativity* attitude as against a *constancy* attitude.[12] According to the relativity attitude there is no "true" curve of learning or of forgetting; there are only predictable results which are found to hold when the appropriate conditions are specified. These results under specified conditions are the generalizations to which studies of learning lead.

THE FUNCTIONALIST'S TREATMENT OF MOTIVATION

The adaptive act according to Carr. The lack of dynamic flavor to the laws of association proposed by Carr and by Robinson is out of keeping with functionalism's primary emphasis upon the adjustive problems of an organism actively adapting itself to the exigencies of its environment. That this is a consequence of too much attention to the memorization experiment in the formulation of these laws, rather than to anything inherent in the system, is evident upon examination of Carr's fuller treatment of the problems of learning in his textbook.[13] The treatment is begun in two consecutive chapters, the first on some principles of organic behavior, the second on perceptual-motor learning.

The principle is accepted that all behavior is initiated by stimuli, so that the point of view is similar to other stimulus-response psychologies, with the difference that responses may be

[12] Carr (1933).
[13] Carr (1925).

ideational as well as motor. It is activities with which Carr is concerned, not movements. An adaptive açt is described as involving a motivating stimulus, a sensory situation, and a response that alters that situation in a way which satisfies the motivating conditions. The external object by which the organism satisfies its motives is called the incentive, or the immediate objective or goal of the response. (The more remote goal, such as maintaining the life of the organism by preventing starvation, does not enter directly into the control of the act.) More specifically, a motive is described as a relatively persistent stimulus that dominates the behavior of an individual until he reacts in such a manner that he is no longer affected by it. This makes of a motive what Smith and Guthrie call a maintaining stimulus. The adaptive act is organized to obtain certain sensory consequences (i.e., the termination of the motivating stimuli) and the act can be interpreted as completed only when the consequences are attained. The interpretation of the end phase as a sensory change became Carr's way of talking about the empirical law of effect.[14] It is this interpretation which permitted Robinson to subsume effect under his Law of Intensity. But the whole adjustment process is to be understood as organized around genuine motivating needs.

A problem is said to be created out of four circumstances under which there is a lack of adjustment between an organism's needs, its immediate environment, and its reactive equipment.

1. The environmental means of satisfying motives may be lacking, and these objects must be discovered or created. Practically every organism is confronted with the problem of finding food.

2. Environmental obstructions are encountered and these obstructions must be circumvented in some fashion. For example, man builds bridges, drains swamps, and tunnels mountains as a means of satisfying his various motives.

3. An organism may lack the requisite motor ability to react to a situation. For example, the human infant is incapable of satisfying its needs under the most favorable environmental circumstances.

4. A conflict between two mutually exclusive tendencies also constitutes a problematical situation. An organism may possess several antagonistic modes of responding to the same object, such as curiosity and fear in the presence of a novel situation.[15]

[14] Carr (1938).
[15] Carr (1925), page 87.

The problem is solved by means of a "variable, persistent, and analytical motor attack" in which the organism tries out various possibilities which have worked for it in the past. Because of reacting according to similarities between present and earlier situations, its attempts are not random and aimless. Variability of attack is itself controlled by the effect of the organism's movements upon the sensory situation. Biting at a wire mesh or attempting to dig through a cement floor results in sensory consequences which are not conducive to continuing the activity. This is Carr's alternative to Thorndike's "stamping out" and to Guthrie's "extinction" of such responses.

This discussion shows that problem-solving behavior is treated by the functionalist in much the same manner as by other contemporary psychologists within the association family. Motivation is recognized as maintaining action, and as defining the terminal stage of an activity sequence. Problem-solving behavior, energized under the motivating stimulus, makes use of past experience by responding to the similarities between present and former situations.

Woodworth's dynamic psychology. Robert S. Woodworth early associated himself with Sherrington, the physiologist, and the pattern of receptor-connector-effector relationship became natural to him as he thought about psychological problems. His friendship and collaboration with Thorndike in his first years at Columbia identified him to some extent with the connectionist psychology, so that Gates,[16] a leading defender of Thorndike's psychology, accepts both Woodworth and Thorndike as exponents of a common position. Despite these affiliations with the physiology of the reflex arc and with Thorndike's connectionism, Woodworth has never kept his psychological thinking within the boundaries of one theoretical position. In his own words, he has held to the "middle of the road," and he has been receptive all along to new ideas. The tolerance of his position squares it better with functionalism than with the stricter positions of either connectionism or behaviorism. This does not mean that Woodworth has been merely an onlooker and mediator. He has shown theoretical interests throughout his writings, but his views have never coalesced into a rigid system.

[16] Gates (1942).

In a small book entitled *Dynamic psychology* (1918) Woodworth gave expression to his own theories of motivated action in relation to learning. It was this book which gave currency to the term "drive" as alternative to "instinct." Woodworth set the stage for the prominence which drives and motives were presently to have within psychology.

The cycle between aroused activity and quiescence is discussed according to *preparatory* and *consummatory* reactions, Woodworth crediting Sherrington [17] with the distinction. Consummatory reactions are those which satisfy basic drives or needs, activities such as eating or escaping from danger. They are directly of value to the organism. Their objective mark is that they terminate a series of acts, leading either to rest or to the turning by the organism to something else. A preparatory reaction is only indirectly or mediately of value to the organism, its value resting on the fact that it leads to or makes possible a consummatory reaction. The objective mark of the preparatory reaction is said to be that it occurs as a preliminary stage leading to the consummatory reaction.

Preparatory reactions are of two kinds. One kind represents alert attention, "a condition of readiness for a yet undetermined stimulus that may arouse further response." Another is the kind of preparatory adjustment evoked only "when the mechanism for a consummatory reaction has been aroused and is in activity." The latter sort of reaction is goal-directed, and evokes seeking behavior, as when a hunting dog, having lost a trail, explores about in order to get back on it.

A new conception introduced is that of ongoing activity as itself a drive—activity once under way leading to its own completion. Even if the original drive under which the activity started has ceased to operate, the activity, if incomplete, may continue. The distinction between drive and mechanism breaks down when it is asserted that the mechanism (i.e., the reaction under way) may become its own drive. Allport later (1937) proposed that motives may become *functionally autonomous*, that is, completely divorced from their primal sources in basic needs of the organism. Activity leading to further activity, and functional autonomy, are very similar conceptions. Both are related to the

[17] Sherrington (1906).

problem of secondary reinforcement. If stimuli associated with reinforcement themselves come to have reinforcing power, it may be that a system of derived rewards may be built up which will continue to have motivating power without recourse to the satisfaction of any basic need. The increasing importance attaching to secondary reinforcement in theories like Hull's and Skinner's shows Woodworth's perspicacity in being the first to recognize that the distinction between drive and mechanism becomes less sharp as activity gets under way.

Another facet to Woodworth's motivational theory is the abiding interest which he has shown in the concept of "set," dating from his early experiments on imageless thought. It was the new emphasis brought about by the imageless thought controversy which in the first decade of this century provided functionalism's supplementation to traditional association psychology. Although Angell and Woodworth were on opposite sides of the fence on some issues concerned with the introspective contents of thought, they were in agreement on the dynamic consequences of predisposing sets and intentions.[18]

The sets and intentions emphasized by the students of imageless thought, and the preparatory reactions oriented toward consummatory responses are concepts with a similar dynamic loading. They are both directional, they are both inferred from the manner in which behavior sequences are organized. In a later development of his conception of set, Woodworth introduces what he calls the *situation-set* and the *goal-set* (1937). The situation-set refers to adjustments to environmental objects; the goal-set refers to the inner "steer" which gives unity to a series of varied but goal-directed activities.

The important suggestion in the concept of situation-set is that the environment must be brought into the psychological account in a manner not suggested by the usual stimulus-response psychology. Guthrie, for example, makes much of the fact that he is interested in movements, not in outcomes. Woodworth takes the opposite position. Movements are, to Woodworth, less important than the information about the environment to which these movements lead. The rat in the maze learns spatial relationships, not running habits; in the problem-box the cat dis-

[18] Woodworth (1906); Angell (1906).

covers the door-opening character of the button, not a sequence of manipulatory movements. As Woodworth puts it: "The character of goodness attaches for the animal not to his movements in manipulating the button, but to the button as an object." [19]

It is to Woodworth's credit that his long history of espousing stimulus-response concepts did not so fix his thinking that he was unable to go outside this systematic framework as he felt it necessary. The conception of situation-set presents a kind of bridge to ways of looking at psychology that have been carried out more fully by others, notably by Tolman and Brunswik. Through the years, Woodworth's use of "set" and related concepts has prevented his falling into a static or merely descriptive system.

EXPERIMENTS ON RETROACTIVE INHIBITION AS ILLUSTRATIVE OF CURRENT FUNCTIONALISM

There is a story sometimes told of David Starr Jordan, Stanford's first president, which, even though apocryphal, is appropriate here. He was an authority on fishes. As the new university got under way, he began to call the students by name. He soon found, however, that every time he learned the name of a student he forgot the name of a fish. Hence, the story goes, he no longer attempted to learn the names of the students.

The interference with the recall of something previously learned as caused by the learning of something new is called *retroactive inhibition*. First studied by Müller and Pilzecker (1900), it has been a favorite topic of study by those following in the Ebbinghaus tradition. Robinson (1920) did his doctoral dissertation on it. McGeoch and Melton and their collaborators have published numerous research reports concerned with it.[20] Retroactive inhibition is thus an appropriate topic to examine as one of the chief experimental interests of the functionalists.

The similarity factor. Among the variables affecting the de-

---

[19] Woodworth (1937).

[20] A review of the experimental literature and theories can be found in McGeoch (1942), pages 458-507. See also Britt (1935) and Swenson (1941). Representative studies appearing since these reviews include Thune and Underwood (1943), Underwood (1945), Irion (1946), Minami and Dallenbach (1946), Osgood (1946), Postman and Alper (1946).

gree of retroactive inhibition is the similarity between the material first learned (Material A) and the material (Material B) interpolated between the learning and recall of Material A, which reduces the retention of Material A. Reflecting upon the problem, Robinson [21] proposed a theoretical analysis, which he proceeded to test experimentally. Several other experimenters have extended the test of his theory [22] so that it serves conveniently to illustrate how the theory relates itself to experimental fact.

Characteristically, Robinson proposes that similarity of materials is not an absolute, but is something which can be scaled from identity at one end of the scale to extreme unlikeness at the other end. This mode of thought, as we have seen, is characteristic of all of Robinson's laws. Similarity is one "dimension" along which materials can be scaled.

With this dimension in mind, Robinson argued that the interpolation of identical material (Material B the same as Material A) would simply provide additional practice on Material A, hence lead to increased retention on the test trials during which retroactive inhibition is usually shown. Because retroactive inhibition with dissimilar materials was already an established fact, the natural conjecture on the assumption of continuous variation is that the amount of retroactive inhibition would increase gradually as dissimilarity was increased. Now, asks Robinson, what is likely to happen at the other end of the scale, as the original material (Material A) and the interpolated material (Material B) become extremely unlike? Presumably retroactive inhibition represents some sort of interference based on similarity between the original and interpolated activity. If there is very little similarity there should be very little retroactive inhibition. Putting all these considerations together, it is reasonable to expect a maximum of retroactive inhibition at some intermediate point of similarity between Materials A and B. Robinson formulated the whole generalization in words as follows: "As similarity between interpolation and original memorization is reduced from near identity, retention falls away to a minimum and then rises again, but with decreasing similarity it never reaches the level obtaining with

[21] Robinson (1927). A somewhat similar suggestion had been made by Skaggs (1925).

[22] E.g., Harden (1929), Dreis (1933), Kennelly (1941), Osgood (1946).

maximum similarity." [23] He expressed this graphically by the figure reproduced as Figure 20.

His own experimental test of the generalization was very simple. By the memory span method he studied the recall of the first four of a series of eight consonants as this recall was interfered with by the last four of the consonants. That is, the first four were considered to be Material *A*, the last four Material *B*, and the similarity and dissimilarity of Materials *A* and *B* were con-

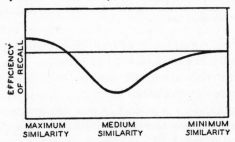

FIGURE 20. SIMILARITY AS A FACTOR IN RETROACTIVE INHIBITION.

The curve is intended to show that retroactive inhibition bears a quantitative relationship to the degree of similarity between the interpolated activity and the material originally memorized. With maximum similarity, the interpolated activity provides positive transfer, hence increases the efficiency of recall. Maximum interference with recall is predicted to fall at some intermediate value of similarity. After Robinson (1927), page 299.

trolled. Similarity was defined as partial identity. Maximum similarity meant that the second four consonants were like the first four; maximum dissimilarity meant that all the last four differed from the first four. The arrangements and results are shown in the accompanying table.

The results confirmed the hypothesis only partially. As seen in the table (p. 164), retroactive inhibition, shown by decreasing retention of the original material, increased as the interpolated material became increasingly dissimilar. This was part of the conjecture. But the decrease in the amount of retroaction (increase in recall) with maximum unlikeness was not found. In fact, with the materials totally dissimilar, retroactive inhibition was at a maximum.

[23] Robinson (1927).

ROBINSON'S TEST OF THE SIMILARITY FACTOR IN RETROACTIVE INHIBITION

Degree of Similarity	Example of Original Material *	Example of Interpolated Material	Per Cent Recall of Original Material
Identical	d-q-k-w	d-q-k-w	100
3 common elements	d-q-k-w	d-q-k-x	97
2 common elements	d-q-k-w	d-q-l-x	90
1 common element	d-q-k-w	d-r-l-x	83
Unlike	d-q-k-w	f-r-l-x	81

* Schematic only. Original lists not reported.

The fault rests not so much with the theory as with the definition of similarity as partial identity of materials. At extreme unlikeness of materials there still remain similarities in process. Where there are not similarities in process, retroactive inhibition is indeed reduced. This is evident in that one extreme of unlikeness—rest—produces less retroactive inhibition than the learning of interpolated materials of any sort. Even the general activities which go on in waking hours produce more interference than those which go on during sleep. Other experiments, following Robinson's lead, are well summarized by McGeoch.[24]

The experiment usefully illustrates Robinson's point of view both directly and indirectly. It shows directly his interest in converting qualitative distinctions—e.g., similarity—into functional variables which can be subjected to test. He succeeded in opening up a field of experimentation which a number of other workers have entered.

But indirectly the experiment also shows how the associationist habit of thought intrudes into what is otherwise a simple, straightforward and matter-of-fact experiment. In spite of Robinson's sophistication in regard to the concept of similarity, it seemed most natural for experimental purposes to define similarity as percentage of common parts. This is exactly the predilection to which gestalt psychologists object so vehemently: the tendency to derive properties of a whole according to its composition. Psychological similarities between learning activities are not coordinate with the number of common parts in the materials

[24] McGeoch (1942), pages 461-466. Typical experiments on the interfering effects of general activity as contrasted with sleep or quiescence are those of Jenkins and Dallenbach (1924), Van Ormer (1932), Newman (1939), Minami and Dallenbach (1946).

comprising the learning task. The associationist knows this, but the point is that he does not take it seriously until he is forced to. He knows well enough that the words BREAD and LOAF are psychologically more similar than BREAD and BEAD, although the latter pair have more letters in common. Yet in the design of experiments he tends to fall back upon description in terms of parts.

It is not essential that an associationist ignore these other kinds of similarity. Robinson himself, in fact, has given a trenchant criticism of careless uses of similarity,[25] and because of this criticism in his formal writings rejects the law of similarity by substituting a law of assimilation. But the associationist habit of thought is so pervasive that the whole tends most naturally to be characterized by the parts which make it up. Even when similarities of meaning are introduced (synonyms) the assumption is made that lists are essentially collections of items.[26]

This does not mean that experiments done under these conditions are not good experiments. They are among the best controlled and most revealing experiments we have. But theory enters into them in two ways. In the first place, it encourages experimentation by showing where experiments are needed and by proposing convenient modes of attack. In the second place, it tends to limit the experiments because of certain assumptions which are taken for granted. Fortunately, the experiments are to some extent self-corrective. The definition of similarity, for example, gets increasingly psychological as the experimental results fail to confirm a reasonable hypothesis because the earlier experiments were designed on a faulty conception of similarity.

Retroactive inhibition as negative transfer. Improvement in a function because of practice on something else is defined as transfer; therefore, by definition, retroactive inhibition is a form of negative transfer. This follows because practice on something else has interfered with an earlier acquired function.

But the transfer theory of retroactive inhibition is something more than a defining label. It sets what McGeoch calls competition-of-response theories against the original perseveration theory

[25] Robinson (1932a), pages 84-85.
[26] E.g., McGeoch and McDonald (1931). For evidence of increasing concern over arrangement as well as composition, see Irion (1946) and Osgood (1946).

of Müller and Pilzecker, and within transfer theories there are a number of possibilities.

The perseveration theory assumed that following learning there was a time required for that which was learned to become set or consolidated. If new learning intervened too promptly this process of perseveration was disrupted. Thus the deleterious effect of interpolation could be accounted for as preventing the consolidation of the earlier learning. The obvious test of the hypothesis is a study of the most damaging time of interpolation. If interpolation shortly after learning is more detrimental than interpolation shortly before recall (the total elapsed time being the same in the two cases), then evidence would be in favor of perseveration. The results are not consistent enough to support or refute the perseveration theory.[27]

As a practicable attack on the problems of the locus of interference in retroactive inhibition, it is possible to look for disrupting intrusions in which items from Material A crop up in the learning of Material B, and in which items from Material B crop up in the relearning or recalling of Material A. To the extent that such items are found, at least one factor in retroactive inhibition has been located.

A number of experimenters have studied the intrusions between original and interpolated lists. Because our purpose is not to summarize the literature but to characterize the interaction between experiment and theory, the study by Melton and Irwin (1940) suffices as an illustration.

Following the characteristic pattern of exploration along a dimension of continuous change, they decided to see what the limiting conditions were for the amount of retroactive inhibition when the degree of learning of the interpolated material was permitted to vary from a few trials to very many trials, relative to the trials devoted to the learning of the original material. There was reason to believe that retroactive inhibition might be at a maximum when the degrees of learning of original and interpolated material were similar, and that the amount of retroactive inhibition might be less as the interpolated material was overlearned.

[27] This is the conclusion reached by both Britt (1935) and Swenson (1941), but the matter is still open. See also Postman and Alper (1946).

The experiment was meticulously controlled, and its methodology is reported in great detail. It will well repay study by anyone planning experimental work in memorization or retention, or by anyone wishing to have a firsthand knowledge of how experiments talked about in books like this are actually done.

The results showed a greater amount of retroactive inhibition with moderate increases in the degree of interpolated learning, and some decrease in retroactive inhibition with the maximum amount of interpolated learning. Some of the results are given below.

INFLUENCE OF DEGREE OF INTERPOLATED LEARNING ON THE AMOUNT OF RETROACTIVE INHIBITION (Melton and Irwin, 1940)
Test on Original List After 30 Minutes

Degree of Interpolated Learning	Items Correctly Recalled *	Trials Required for Relearning †
Rest (control)	5.58	12.5
5 trials	2.04	13.6
10 trials	1.33	14.6
20 trials	0.92	14.9
40 trials	1.54	12.3

* First relearning trial, Cycle II.
† Relearning to one perfect trial, Cycle II.

The table may be read as follows. Recall following interpolated learning gets less and less with interpolation of 5, 10, and 20 trials but somewhat more is recalled after an interpolation of 40 trials than after 10 or 20 trials. There is still considerable retroactive inhibition as measured by recall after the 40 trial interpolation. Relearning also takes longer after interpolation, getting progressively longer for 5, 10, and 20 trials of interpolation. Following 40 trials on the interpolated learning, however, there is no longer any evidence of retroactive inhibition as measured by relearning. Recall and relearning scores agree in showing less retroactive inhibition following the largest amount of interpolated learning than following the next largest, but there is sufficient difference between the amount of inhibition shown by recall and by relearning after the 40 interpolated trials to suggest that retroactive inhibition is somewhat transitory.

It might be inferred from the previous discussion that a fol-

lower of the Robinson type of association theory would stop
with the graphical presentation of the empirical relationships
shown in the table. Actually he goes on to answer as best he
can the questions which his data raise.

Melton and Irwin begin their theoretical discussion with an
insistence on the importance of a dimensional analysis of retroactive inhibition.

Studies involving the systematic variation of the formal, meaningful, or process similarities of the two learning activities, of the degrees
of learning of the original and interpolated activities, etc., contribute
to the completion of this analysis of the conditions of retroactive
inhibition. Clearly, this dimensional analysis is essential to the formulation and validation of a theory of retroactive inhibition.[28]

But, in spite of this creed, they do not wait for all this evidence, for they are as eager as anyone else to get directly at what
they call "the behavior correlates" of the measured loss in retention. They are interested in the locus, the direction, and the
essential nature of the inhibition.

One way of getting at the problem directly is to study the
number of intrusions from one list to another as a factor in the
interferences. Thus in the relearning trials in which retroactive
inhibition is demonstrated there are some intrusions from the
interpolated list. This confusion of the two lists accounts in part
for the amount of retroactive inhibition. Careful analysis showed
somewhat more intrusions from interpolated lists practiced 5 and
10 trials than from those practiced more trials. Apparently with
greater degree of learning the interpolated list was more nearly
a unit, and its items did not crop up in another context. Melton
and Irwin summarized these relationships in the diagram reproduced as Figure 21. It is significant that a residual factor (Factor
X) is actually of more importance than the overt intrusions.

What is the nature of Factor X? They believe it to be a sort
of unlearning of the original list which goes on while the interpolated list is being learned. The intrusions which came from the
original list into the interpolated list develop associative inhibitions which in a sense disrupt the original learning. The theory
has been examined and extended by Underwood (1945) who

[28] Melton and Irwin (1940), page 193.

points out that failure of response may also be evidence for interference, but at a stage in which the faulty associate is recognized
as wrong and is not spoken aloud.

It appears not unlikely that some more dynamic theory may be
needed to account for the facts of retroactive inhibition—some
theory more like that of the gestalt psychologists. The promi-

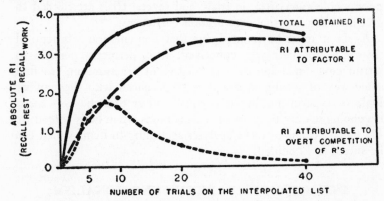

FIGURE 21. THE TWO-FACTOR THEORY OF RETROACTIVE INHIBITION.

The uppermost curve represents the empirical amount of retroactive inhibition (RI) as measured by recall. The material of original and interpolated learning consisted of lists of 18 nonsense syllables of low association value. The amount of retroactive inhibition was found to vary with the
degree of learning of the interpolated material. The broken curves below
represent the two factors to which the RI is to be attributed. The overt
competition (the first factor) is estimated from the measured intrusions of
items from the interpolated list in the attempted recall of the original list.
The residual curve represents Factor X (the second factor), which is
inferred to be an "unlearning" of the original list while the interpolated
list is being learned. From Melton and Irwin (1940), as reproduced by
McGeoch (1942), page 499.

nence of Factor X shows that the search in terms of specific
associates to specific items does not carry far enough. It is quite
possible that degree of organization may be the important variable. Such a theory would take a form somewhat as follows.
Processes with a low degree of internal organization are more
susceptible to retroactive inhibition than processes with a high
degree of internal organization; and processes with a given degree
of organization are interfered with more by interpolated processes with a low degree of organization than by processes with

a high degree of organization.[29] On the assumption that degree of learning is correlated with degree of organization, the Melton and Irwin results would be predicted. But number of trials is not the only measure of internal organization, and the test of such a theory would go beyond the systematic arrangement of the Melton and Irwin experiment. A list of 18 nonsense syllables is a poor whole even after 40 trials, and several trials are needed to give a list any internal organization whatever.

Again it must be pointed out that contemporary functional theory is not narrowly conceived. It is perfectly possible to introduce a dimension such as "degree of organization," to find some way of scaling it, and then to go ahead with the familiar logic of experiment. But it is equally clear that the association psychologist only turns to such dimensions when he is forced to. He much prefers to make analyses according to items which can be sorted and counted.

ESTIMATE OF CURRENT FUNCTIONALISM

Current functionalism is not a unified theory like those earlier discussed. What bonds of unity there are lie in a tolerant acceptance of a wide range of psychological phenomena and a conviction that the task before psychology is to subject the many variables to quantitative study. Such a methodological unity permits wide diversity in content.

The functionalist position on the typical problems of learning. Within such an unstructured system there is no one clear answer to most problems of learning. The answer to be expected is that "it all depends on conditions." In practice the situation is not quite as free as this implies, for gradually there accumulate more commonly accepted generalizations.

1. *Capacity*. Robinson recognized individual and species differences in his laws of individual differences and of composition. It was in line with functional developments for McGeoch to include in his book a chapter on learning as a function of age, sex, and test intelligence. McGeoch believes that the increase of

[29] The gestalt approach to retroactive inhibition may be found exemplified in von Restorf (1933) and Newman (1939). Köhler's interpretations are given in Köhler (1940).

learning ability with age is best accounted for on the basis of two hypotheses: first, organic maturation, second, changing psychological conditions (transfer, motivation, personality traits).

2. *Practice.* The law of frequency is to Robinson a law of relative frequency, which therefore recognizes the losses in score when practice is overcrowded along with the gains when trials are more appropriately spaced. There is a tendency to emphasize the form of the learning curve, and to seek the conditions under which one form rather than another is to be found. There is, however, no diatribe against·a law of exercise.

3. *Motivation.* Woodworth's dynamic psychology places motivation at its core. Carr accepts in principle the preparatory-consummatory sequence, assigning motivation the role of a continuing stimulus to be terminated by the goal-response. The concept of "set" enters into the more conventional experiments on memorization and skill as a motivational supplement to the more familiar laws of association. It is the preoccupation of the functionalist with such tasks as the learning of rote verbal series which has tended to place motivation in the background rather than the foreground of theories such as Robinson's.

4. *Understanding.* While the associationist recognizes that meaningful material is more readily learned than nonsense material, degree of meaning is but one of the dimensions upon which materials can be scaled. Hence he does not believe problem-solving or insight to require interpretations beyond ordinary associative learning. The organism uses what it has learned as appropriately as it can in a new situation. If the problem cannot be solved by analogy, the behavior has to be varied until the initial solution occurs. Insight is perhaps an extreme case of transfer of training.[30]

5. *Transfer.* Following Thorndike, transfer falls chiefly undeɪ the law of assimilation. That is, transfer depends upon degree of likeness between the new situation and the old. Woodworth reinterprets the theory of identical elements to mean only that transfer is always of concrete performances.

What the theory of identical elements demands is that transfer should be of concrete performances, whether simple or complex

[30] McGeoch (1942), page 528.

makes no difference to the theory [31] . . . Perhaps anything that can be learned can be transferred. But does not everything that can be learned have the concrete character of an act or way of acting? [32]

6. *Forgetting.* The favorite theory of forgetting is that of retroactive inhibition, but the functionalist does not insist that this is the whole story. There may be some forgetting according to passive decay through disuse, and there may be forgetting through repression, as pointed out by Freud.[33]

Functionalism as an experimentalism. The survival of association psychology in its functional experimental forms shows that a radically empirical psychology need not be a behaviorism. It is possible to cast problems in quantitative and experimentable form without being at all narrow in the kinds of reference which the variables make to reality. Within functionalism there is an indifference to the question whether "sets" and "meanings" and the like are "mental" or "physical," so long as they can be brought under control for purposes of study.

Functionalism is empiricist rather than systematic. It eschews inference for established experimental relationships between demonstrable variables. Its laws are quantitative, directly descriptive of data. There is a healthy respect for data, and there is a commendable urge to state issues specifically in a form subject to test. The relativism brings with it a freedom from bigotry. Before his untimely death, Robinson had turned to social problems, with the conviction that the same methods would work there. So long as people were forced to think in terms of specifics he believed that they could often reach agreement, even though on larger issues they were swayed by prejudice and preconceptions.[34]

The disadvantage of an extreme empiricism and relativism lies in its lack of articulating principles to cut across empirical laws. What results is a collection of many "laws," without hierarchical structure. There is no economical multidimensional apparatus for fitting together the various two-dimensional functional relationships, each of which is necessarily cast in the form: "other things being equal." If the dimensional program of the Chicago func-

[31] Woodworth (1938), page 177.
[32] Woodworth (1938), page 207.
[33] Robinson (1932b), pages 113-118.
[34] The point of view is represented in Robinson (1935).

tionalists were fulfilled we should have a large handbook of data, with each of the several laws illustrated by a number of graphs showing the variations of associative strength under specific conditions. Empirical multidimensionality would be achieved through experimental designs testing several variables at once, but unless some simplifying steps were taken, the possible combinations and permutations of conditions would mount fabulously. Dimensional analysis puts data in order for exposition and for verification, but in itself does not connect the data into an economical scientific system. Such a system has to be rational as well as empirical.

That there is actually some tendency to leave the relationships in a "raw" empirical state is illustrated by one of the systematic programs carried out by Carr and his students on the relationship between guidance and learning. After the extensive series of experiments the matter is left in the unsatisfactory state suggested by the following quotations:

> The comparative data, taken at their face value, indicate that the verbal methods are most effective. Owing to the varied conditions of the several experiments, however, it is unwise to make any generalizations as to the relative effectiveness of the various methods used . . .
>
> We may call attention to the fact that all of these methods and devices are actually employed in teaching the proper form in various acts of skill, such as swimming, dancing, golf, tennis, football and track athletics. . . . Are these methods valuable? . . . I shall make no attempt to answer these questions on the basis of our experimental data. A considerable experience has taught me the futility of making predictions as to what will happen in situations which apparently very closely resemble those that have been investigated. . . .
>
> I am raising these questions and recounting the results of these experiments in order to impress the reader with the fact that the problem of the best and most effective ways of teaching is a very real, genuine, and exceedingly complicated problem, one that confronts each one of us nearly every day of our lives, one that we know very little about, and one that is capable of scientific investigation.[35]

Is this all that is to result from ten years of experimentation on a problem? Merely to show that the problem is one capable of study?

Those who accept the functional point of view do not always

[35] Carr (1930).

stop with empirical relationships left in the form of summarized data. As illustrated by the experiments on retroactive inhibition, they go on to a consideration of what lies beneath their data, and make the necessary inferences to harmonize the results from several experiments. There has been the tendency, however, to bring the theories in late, as a kind of talking about the results which have been achieved. The theories have seldom entered the experiments in the critical manner suggested by the deductive logic of a system such as Hull's. What is lacking is intervening variables, or some substitute for them, which in the end could be represented by constants interchangeable from one situation to another. The younger functionalists will undoubtedly amend the scientific logic of their teachers in order to add these rational considerations to the extreme empiricism which they were taught.

Functionalism as an eclecticism. As long as competent and informed men disagree about the data and principles of learning there will be a place for mediators, for those who try to resolve disagreements not by taking sides but by finding a common ground which preserves what is useful in the contentions of all parties to the ongoing controversies. To the extent that such mediators borrow selectively from the views of others they are known as eclectics.

Functionalism is in some respects an eclectic position. It is eclectic on the problem of introspection versus behavioral description, by accepting both in the account of psychological activity. A favorite illustration is that less attention is required to details as a skill is mastered. Knowledge about the representation of details in awareness requires an introspective report, while the mastery of the skill may be studied by observation of the overt movements. Functionalism is eclectic on the problem of blind versus intelligent learning, accepting a continuum between these extremes, according to the dimensional analysis of McGeoch and Melton. Any point of view which is pragmatic and pluralistic can easily incorporate concepts from alien systems; hence functionalism is well suited to play the mediating role. What Woodworth has called "broad and rather unsystematic functionalism" he believes to be the characteristic American tradition.[36]

[36] Woodworth (1943), page 29.

Functionalism is, however, an eclecticism with a bias—the bias of associationism in favor of analytic units, historical causation, environmentalism. The bias is more evident in Chicago functionalism than in that of Woodworth, who has shown himself friendlier to less associationistic concepts. New data may be accepted but forced back into older concepts not fully appropriate. Thus some of the novelty of the observations made in insight experiments is lost when insight is treated as merely another illustration of the familiar transfer of training experiment. Similarly, what goes on in the reasoning process is not fully encompassed by treating reasoning as trial-and-error learning merely a little farther out on the dimension of explicit-implicit response. Those who disagree with the associationist position object to the functionalist's incorporating of new experimental findings without accepting the theoretical implications of these findings. This is a problem with which the eclectic always has to wrestle: how much can be taken over without incorporating its systematic context? The functionalist has not been greatly concerned about the inner consistency of his borrowings because he is less concerned than others about the inner consistency of his own concepts. What consistency there has been is provided by the framework of associationism within which the functionalist works.

Whatever the systematic limitations may be, it must be recognized that great energy for experimental study has been released within the functionalist group. The books of Woodworth (1938) and McGeoch (1942) amply attest to this. Out of the large number of research investigations on memory and skill, done largely within this group, there has come a rich body of data and factual relationships with which anyone interested in learning must be familiar.

SUPPLEMENTARY READINGS

BOOKS

McGeoch, J. A. (1942) *The psychology of human learning.*
Robinson, E. S. (1932) *Association theory today.*
Woodworth, R. S. (1918) *Dynamic psychology.*
Woodworth, R. S. (1938) *Experimental psychology.*

SHORTER INTRODUCTIONS

Carr, H. A. (1931) The laws of association. *Psychol. Rev.*, 38, 212-228.

Heidbreder, E. (1933) *Seven psychologies.* (Chapter 6, Functionalism and the University of Chicago; Chapter 8, Dynamic psychology and Columbia University.)

Melton, A. W. (1941) Learning. In Monroe, W. S. (Editor) *Encyclopedia of educational research.*

Woodworth (1930) Dynamic psychology. In Murchison, C. (Editor) *Psychologies of 1930.*

CRITICAL REVIEWS

Boring, E. G. (1933) Review of Robinson's *Association theory today. Psychol. Bull.*, 30, 451-455.

Köhler, W. (1943) Review of McGeoch's *The psychology of human learning. Amer. J. Psychol.*, 56, 455-460.

McGeoch, J. A. (1932) Review of Robinson's *Association theory today. J. gen. Psychol.*, 7, 231-237.

REPRESENTATIVE EXPERIMENTS

Bills, A. G., and Stauffacher, J. C. (1937) The influence of voluntarily induced tension on rational problem solving. *J. Psychol.*, 4, 261-271.

Bruce, R. W. (1933) Conditions of transfer of training. *J. exp. Psychol.*, 16, 343-361.

Cook, T. W. (1941) Mirror position and negative transfer. *J. exp. Psychol.*, 29, 155-160.

Courts, F. A. (1939) Relations between experimentally induced muscular tension and memorization. *J. exp. Psychol.*, 25, 235-256.

Luh, C. W. (1922) The conditions of retention. *Psychol. Monogr.*, 31, No. 142, 87 pp.

McGeoch, J. A. (1932) The comparative retention values of a maze habit, of nonsense syllables, and of rational learning. *J. exp. Psychol.*, 15, 662-680.

Robinson, E. S., and Brown, M. A. (1926) Effect of serial position upon memorization. *Amer. J. Psychol.*, 37, 538-552.

Robinson, E. S., and Heron, W. T. (1922) Results of variations in length of memorized material. *J. exp. Psychol.*, 5, 428-448.

Stroud, J. B. (1932) Effect of complexity of material upon the form of learning curves. *Amer. J. Psychol.*, 44, 721-731.

Van Ormer, E. B. (1932) Retention after intervals of sleep and of waking. *Arch. Psychol.*, N. Y., 21, No. 137, 49 pp.

Waters, R. H. (1928) The influence of tuition on ideational learning. *J. gen. Psychol.*, 1, 534-547.

Woodworth, R. S., and Sells, S. B. (1935) An atmosphere effect in formal syllogistic reasoning. *J. exp. Psychol.*, 18, 451-460.

Chapter 7

GESTALT THEORY

During the first quarter of the century in America the quarrels within academic psychology lay chiefly inside the framework of association psychology. Structuralism, functionalism, and behaviorism were all members of the association family. A few dissident voices, such as Freud and McDougall, got little hearing. This complacency was disturbed by the new gestalt doctrine which influenced American learning theories chiefly through the appearance in English of Wolfgang Köhler's *Mentality of apes* (1925) and Kurt Koffka's *Growth of the mind* (1924). The theory had been developing in Germany since it was first announced by Max Wertheimer in 1912, but these books, and the visits of Köhler and Koffka to America about the time of their publication, brought the new theory vividly to the attention of American psychologists.

Koffka's book had an important effect upon American learning theory because of its detailed criticism of trial-and-error learning as conceived by Thorndike—an attack at the very heart of the currently popular theory. The vigorous attack upon Thorndike (and upon behaviorism, although Thorndike was not, strictly speaking, a member of the school) was supported by Köhler's well-known experiments on apes, described in detail in his book which appeared close to Koffka's. Köhler's book brought the notion of insightful learning into the foreground, as an alternative to trial-and-error. He showed how apes could obtain rewards without going through the laborious processes of stamping out incorrect responses and stamping in correct ones, as implied in Thorndike's theories and as displayed in the learning curves of

177

Thorndike's cats. Apes could use sticks and boxes as tools, they could turn away from the end of the activity toward a means to the end.

Köhler's experiments with apes were done in the years 1913-1917, on the island of Tenerife off the coast of Africa. His book about these experiments [1] appeared in English a few years later and immediately was widely read and quoted. Two main series of experiments interested the American psychological public in the problems of insight. These were the box-problems and the stick-problems.

In the single-box situation, a lure, such as a banana, is attached to the top of the chimpanzee's cage. The lure is out of reach, but can be obtained by climbing upon and jumping from a box which is available in the cage. The problem is a difficult one for the chimpanzee. Only Sultan (Köhler's most intelligent ape) solved it without assistance, though six others mastered the problem after first being helped either by having the box placed beneath the food or by watching others using the box. The problem was not solved by direct imitation of others. What watching others use the box did was to lead the observer to attempt to use the box as a leaping platform, but sometimes without making any effort whatsoever to bring it near the lure. When the problem was mastered, a chimpanzee alone in a cage with box and banana would turn away from the goal in order to seek the box and to move it into position. This "detour" character of insightful behavior is, according to Köhler, one of its important features.

The box-stacking problem, requiring that a second box be placed upon the first before the banana can be reached, is much more difficult. It requires both the incorporation of the second box into the pattern of solution, and a mastery of the gravitational problem of building a stable two-box structure. While the emphasis in secondary accounts of Köhler's work is usually upon the intelligence which his apes displayed, he himself is at pains to account for the amount of apparent stupidity. In the box-stacking experiment, for example, he believes that the apes have shown insight into the relationship of "one-box-upon-another," but not into the nature of a stable two-box structure. Such physi-

[1] Köhler (1917).

cal stability as was achieved in later structures was essentially a matter of trial-and-error.

The stick problems required the use of one or more sticks as tools with which to rake in food out of reach beyond the bars of the cage. The beginning of insight occurs as the stick is brought into play, although often unsuccessfully, as when it is thrown at the banana and lost. Once it has been used successfully, it is sought after by the chimpanzee and used promptly. The most dramatic of the stick-using experiments was in a problem mastered by Sultan, in which eventually two sticks were joined together after the manner of a jointed fishing pole in order to obtain a banana which could not be reached with either stick alone. The process was a slow one, and the first placing of the sticks together appeared to be more or less accidental. Once having seen the sticks in this relationship, however, Sultan was able to "get the idea" and to repeat the insertion of one stick into the end of the other over and over again.

While the attack by Köhler and Koffka was chiefly upon Thorndike, it came at a time when American psychology was in the grips of a confident but somewhat sterile behaviorism. It is hard to see at this distance why such a commonsense and familiar notion as insight in learning should have created such a stir. But at the time Watsonian behaviorism had, in fact, won support for a fairly "hardboiled" view of learning, according to which the organism was played upon by the pushes and pulls of the environment and reacted in ways essentially stupid. Lloyd Morgan's canon which had seriously undercut the attributing of higher mental processes to animals had fairly well succeeded via behaviorism in excising them from man also. Therefore the restoration to sanity represented by the insight experiments gave new hope to teachers and others who saw thinking and understanding returned to respectability. Insight was not a new discovery—it was a return to a conception laymen had never abandoned. Nobody uninfluenced by peculiar doctrines would ever have denied insight as a fact—yet it took Köhler to restore it as a fact in American psychology. It was, in some respects, time for a change, and Köhler's experiments dramatized release from the negatives of Thorndikian and Watsonian thinking.

That the more enthusiastic reception for the new learning

theories should have come first from the educators is not surprising.[2] There had already been a rift growing between Thorndike and the more progressive group within education, who, under Dewey's leadership, had made much more than he of the capacity of the individual for setting and solving his own problems. The new insight doctrine fitted nicely their slogan of freeing intelligence for creative activity.

Animal psychologists like Yerkes, who had never espoused behaviorism, welcomed the new movement as a natural development. Yerkes himself had done experiments on insightful learning independent of gestalt influences,[3] and the intelligence demonstrated by Köhler's apes did not surprise him. Curiously enough, insightful learning in sub-human animals was less threatening to theorists than learning by understanding in man, chiefly because it was still the rather rare and unusual behavior among animals. Rats still learned mazes, it was thought, without insight. So the animal experimenters added insight experiments to their list, and continued both old and new experiments. But if the insight doctrine were to be accepted in human learning, the field would be wide open for destroying all the familiar laws of learning as they applied to man. It is not surprising that those who were at the time concerned more largely with human learning, such as Thorndike, Robinson, and Guthrie, should all have been cool to the insight concept.

The visible opposition between Köhler and Thorndike was over insight and trial-and-error, that is, over intelligent learning as contrasted with blind fumbling. But the opposition between gestalt psychology and association psychology goes much deeper. In order to understand this opposition, it will be necessary to examine the gestalt views in greater detail.

There are a number of variants within the gestalt movement, and among those strongly influenced by gestalt conceptions. Köhler and Koffka were closest to Wertheimer, the official founder of the school. This chapter is devoted to their treatment of learning. Lewin, while originally from Berlin and definitely within the ranks, broke enough new ground so that a separate

---

[2] It was an educator-psychologist, R. M. Ogden, who translated Koffka (1924).

[3] E.g., Yerkes (1916).

chapter is devoted to his position. All four of these men, originally German, eventually settled in America, where three of them (Koffka, Lewin and Wertheimer) have since died. They are the leaders of what is historically gestalt psychology.

The fullest and most systematic treatment of the problems of learning from the gestalt viewpoint is found in Koffka's *Principles of gestalt psychology* (1935). It was written after a period of acclimatization to America, and so meshes somewhat better than earlier writings with the concerns of American psychologists. Most of the direct references will be made to this source.

THE LAWS OF ORGANIZATION

Gestalt psychology had its start and has achieved its greatest success in the field of perception. Its demonstrations of the rôle of background and organization upon phenomenally perceived processes are so convincing that only an unusually stubborn opponent will discredit the achievement. The primary attack upon association theory was an attack on the "bundle hypothesis" sensation theory—the theory that a percept is made up of sensation-like elements, bound together by association.

When the gestalt psychologists turned later to the problems of learning, the equipment brought to the study of learning was that which had succeeded in the field of perception, and the arguments previously used against the sensation were turned against the reflex. In spite of the attention which Köhler's ape experiments received, gestalt psychologists can be fairly said to have been only moderately interested in learning. This does not mean that their few experiments are without significance; it means only that they have considered the problems of learning secondary to the problems of perception. Perhaps in America the shoe is on the other foot, and in preoccupation with learning we have too long neglected the relationship between the two fields.[4]

The starting point for Koffka's treatment of learning is the assumption that the laws of organization in perception are applicable to learning. This applicability is enhanced because of the

[4] The point has been made by Leeper (1935b).

prominence in learning given in his theory to the initial adjustment, to the discovery of the correct response in the first place. Since this discovery depends upon the structuring of the field as it is open to the observation of the learner, the ease or difficulty of the problem is largely a matter of perception. In some sense, Köhler's apes were presented with perceptual problems; if they literally "saw" the situation correctly, they had "insight."

The application of the laws of organization to learning problems is done too casually by Koffka to be very convincing, but if he had been more systematic about it, the development of the argument might have gone along the following lines. There would be a guiding principle (the Law of Prägnanz) and four laws of organization subordinate to it, the laws of similarity, proximity, closure, and good continuation.

The law of Prägnanz. The law of *Prägnanz* [5] suggests the direction of events. Psychological organization tends to move in a given direction rather than another, always toward the state of *Prägnanz*, toward the "good" gestalt. The organization will be as "good" as prevailing conditions allow. A "good" gestalt has such properties as regularity, simplicity, stability, and so on.

Because of the dynamic properties of "fields," the conditions of equilibrium are necessarily important. In physics, processes which terminate in stationary distributions are characterized by certain maxima and minima, as by a minimum of energy capable of doing work. This minimum for the whole sometimes requires a part to absorb a maximum of energy. The law of *Prägnanz* is a law of equilibrium like these principles of the maximum or minimum in physics. It ought to correspond to them in reality, since it is the phenomenal representation of physiological processes which obey physical laws. In effect, however, it is used as an analogy. When organization moves toward a minimum, it is characterized phenomenally by the simplicity of uniformity; when it moves toward a maximum, it is characterized by the simplicity of perfect articulation. [6] "We might say, sacrificing a great deal of the precision of the physical proposition, that in

---

[5] The German word is inadequately translated as "pregnancy." It has the meaning of "*knapp, und doch vielsagend*" (compact but significant).
[6] Koffka (1935), pages 171-174.

psychological organization either as much or as little will happen as the prevailing conditions permit." [7]

Learning situations are problematical situations. They therefore give rise to tensions and to disequilibria. Some such principle as the Law of *Prägnanz* becomes appropriate to them, although Koffka does not develop the point, except by way of the other laws, each of which, in its own way, is an illustration of the more general principle.

1. *The law of similarity.* The law of similarity or of equality is the counterpart of association's law of similarity. This and the other laws all derive from Wertheimer (1923). He used it as a principle determining the formation of groups in perception, such as groups of lines or dots. Similar items (e.g., alike in form or color) or similar transitions (e.g., alike in the steps separating them) tend to form groups in perception. The law is applied by Koffka to the selection of a memory trace by a process active at the time of recall. That trace will be selected by an excitatory process which possesses the same wholeness character. The meaning of trace selection will be considered later. The meaning is conveyed sufficiently by the process of recognition, where a face present now recalls the same one as seen earlier and results in the feeling of familiarity.

2. *The law of proximity.* Perceptual groups are favored according to the nearness of the parts. Thus if several parallel lines are spaced unevenly on a page, those nearer together will tend to form groups against a background of empty space. Such a patterning holds also within audition, as in the grouping of successive clicks. Then the proximity is a temporal one. As it applies to memory, the law of proximity becomes a law of recency. Old impressions are less well recognized and recalled than new ones because the recent trace is nearer in time to the present active process. [8]

3. *The law of closure.* Closed areas are more stable than unclosed ones, and therefore more readily form figures in perception. As applied to learning, closure is an alternative to the law of effect. The direction of behavior is toward an end-situation

[7] Koffka (1935), page 108.
[8] Koffka (1935), page 464.

which brings closure with it. It is in this manner that rewards influence learning.

So long as activity is incomplete, every new situation created by it is still to the animal a transitional situation; whereas when the animal has attained his goal, he has arrived at a situation which is to him an end-situation.[9]

In a problematic situation the whole is seen as incomplete and a tension is set up toward completion. This strain to complete is an aid to learning, and to achieve closure is satisfying. This is the meaning of the above quotation, and shows how closure is an alternative to effect.

4. *The law of good continuation*. This is the last of Wertheimer's principles taken over by Koffka, although Wertheimer had several more. Organization in perception tends to occur in such a manner that a straight line will continue as a straight line, a circle as a circle, and so on. Closure and continuation are aspects of articulate organization. Organization applies to learning as well as to perception.

How perceptual problems are carried over into learning may be illustrated by an experiment of von Restorff (1933). She showed that in the recall of nonsense material, part of the difficulty lies in the homogeneity of the material. If lists of paired associates are constructed so that one pair is of very heterogeneous material, this pair will be retained much better than the pairs of items representing materials more frequently repeated. The interpretation is that the heterogeneous items stand out like a figure on the ground, exactly as in perception.

THE SPECIAL PROBLEMS OF LEARNING

The general point of view of gestalt psychology is expressed in the statement that the laws of organization apply equally to perception and to learning. There are, however, special problems within learning to which Koffka devotes considerable discussion. Because of his anti-empiricist position, he has to find some way of dealing with the evident influence of earlier experiences on present performance. The problem is best approached via mem-

[9] Koffka (1924), page 102. From *The growth of the mind* by K. Koffka, Kegan Paul, Trench, Trubner & Co., Ltd., London, 1924.

ory, in which the past is represented somehow in the present. A second problem concerns the gradual transformation which takes place as skills of the trial-and-error sort are mastered. Finally, of course, there is the problem of restructuring the present field, as implied in insightful learning and in productive thinking.

The rôle of past experience: the trace theory. Because modification by and through experience is part of the very definition of learning, the gestalt attitude toward experience is important.

The gestalt preference is distinctly for conceiving psychological processes as the function of the present field, and the influence of past experience is refuted in situation after situation in which to others it seems to be important. Examples include the perceptual constancies—whereby a man looks man-size at a distance, a red coat looks equally red in sunshine and shadow. The illusions of movement and perception of third dimension are also included. Koffka, in spite of a vigorous objection to empiricism, takes a moderate view toward the rôle of past experience in learning.

It will not be necessary to point out that an anti-empiristic attitude does not mean the denial of the enormous value of experience. Not *that* it makes use of experience causes our objection to empiricism, but *how* it makes use of it.[10]

A favorite experiment repeatedly cited by gestalt psychologists in order to disprove the rôle of experience is that of Gottschaldt (1926, 1929). For example, if a picture of a letter *E* is presented 1000 times, and then a church window is exposed, are you any more likely to notice that some of the leaded lines in the windows could form a letter *E* than if *E* had been presented only once? I doubt if a jury of association psychologists or anyone else would expect experience to tear down a percept into the thousand and one possible parts unless there were some kind of search involved. If you looked for the hidden part, and found it, the finding would be easier the next time. Gottschaldt accepts this conclusion, and had evidence that the results of previous discovery were evident in later tests. It is familiar enough in the newspaper puzzles with faces hidden in the trees that once the face has been found it is more easily found again. Gottschaldt's

10 Koffka (1935), page 639n.

experiment reduces to the demonstration that camouflage hides familiar objects as effectively as it hides unfamiliar ones—provided we have no reason to be looking for the familiar objects. Gottschaldt's experiments are cited by gestalt psychologists as very damaging to associationist or empiricist positions. Because of the difference in conception as to what is important, the experiment has not impressed association psychologists as being a crucial refutation of their position.[11]

By the very nature of the case, it is not as easy for the gestalt psychologist to dismiss the rôle of experience in memory as it is to dismiss its rôle in perception. Memory so obviously depends upon prior experience that it would be foolhardy to deny it. Koffka is as puzzled as a non-gestalt psychologist over Wheeler's attempt to get rid of memory traces.[12] Koffka believes some trace theory essential, and proceeds to consider how the traces of past experiences can be reactivated by present processes.

The trace hypothesis is an involved one, and its full exposition requires over 100 pages of text.[13] The essential features of the theory are (1) a trace is assumed which persists from a prior experience, so that it represents the past in the present, (2) a present process is also posited, one which can select, reactivate, or in some manner communicate with the trace, and (3) there is a resulting new process of recall or recognition. The process and the trace are to be distinguished; they are localized in different parts of the brain. The trace system is organized according to the same laws applying in other fields, and the communication between process and trace follows these laws.

The trace concept has been further elaborated by Köhler (1938) and by Katona (1940). Katona makes a distinction between *individual* traces, referring to specific items, and *structural* traces, derived from the wholeness character of a process. The structural traces are said to be more adaptable and flexible, to be formed more quickly, and to persist longer than individual traces.[14]

By way of the doctrine of traces the gestalt psychologist is

[11] Moore (1930), Braly (1933) and Henle (1942) dispute Gottschaldt's interpretations.
[12] Wheeler's theory will be discussed later on (Chapter 9).
[13] Koffka (1935), pages 423-528.
[14] Katona (1940), pages 194-195.

able to represent a past event in the present. That is, of course, all that the association psychologist proposes to do. But the trace-system, if it is a system organized under gestalt laws, must undergo changes according to the law of *Prägnanz*. If these changes are of systematic sort it will be evidence against a theory of mere connections weakening in time or inhibited by new learning.

The experiments of Wulf (1922) and later experiments following up his suggestions will be reviewed among the illustrative experiments. The main point is that perceived figures are reproduced differently from the original model, and that the differences are systematic and progressive rather than random. The changes with successive reproduction correspond to the laws of organization, and move toward the "good" gestalt. A circle with a small opening tends to close, and an asymmetrical figure tends to become more symmetrical. There are two chief tendencies noted by Wulf: *levelling* and *sharpening*. The levelling tendency is that already described, a tendency to move according to the intrinsic character of the figure into symmetry and uniform relations of parts. Sharpening consists in the accentuating of details which serve as the discriminatory features of the pattern. For example, a saw-toothed figure may be reproduced with deeper and more striking teeth. Against the theory that memory leads to decay and fuzziness, the gestalt theory is that it leads to change but in the direction of greater clarity. A third tendency pointed out by Wulf is called *normalizing*. A figure which looks something like a familiar object tends on reproduction to be drawn more like such an object. All these changes (levelling, sharpening, and normalizing) are in the direction of a "good" gestalt.

To the extent that these systematic changes occur in the trace, there is a real addition which gestalt theory makes to other theories of memorial change.

New learning: the formation of traces. What happens as new traces get formed? It is to be recalled that Koffka distinguishes between the process and the trace. The process is that which goes on because of the present stimulating situation; the trace is the result of earlier processes.

1. Some processes are directly dependent upon stimuli. When such stimuli are presented a second time, the processes differ from those present the first time because the stimuli have been

reacted to before. For example, the second exposure may be recognized as "familiar." This difference suffices to show that learning took place with the first exposure. His illustrations are limited to perceptual ones, and it is apparently perceptual responses to which Koffka refers when he speaks of processes directly dependent upon stimuli.[15]

2. Processes may undergo transformation within a single sustained presentation. For example, when a series of sentences about mathematics is finally "understood" as a demonstration or proof, such a transformation has occurred. The insight experiments illustrate such transformations.[16]

3. Some processes are transformed by their consequences. This amounts to an acceptance by Koffka of the empirical "law of effect," but the explanation differs from Thorndike's. The transformation of process is at base the same as in the insight experiments, but it often occurs piece-meal as a consequence of the experimental arrangements. In the insight experiments all the data necessary for the transformation of process are present simultaneously, so that restructuring can take place at once. In the typical trial-and-error experiment, by contrast, the situation cannot be understood until the animal's activity has itself led to consequences—to food, to freedom, etc. Once success is achieved the process leading to success is transformed. It has a new meaning, a new rôle in the goal-directed activity.[17]

The effects of repetition: the consolidation of trace systems. The aggregate trace system resulting from repetition is always being transformed. With each repetition the trace organization left from preceding processes interacts with the present process to create something new. According to the principle of retroactive inhibition (which Koffka accepts) preceding individual traces are disrupted by the new learning. Repetition can still be beneficial, however, because the trace system becomes consolidated even while individual traces are destroyed. As the trace system becomes more fixed it becomes preëminent over process, and exerts more influence on future processes than such processes affect it. Such a trace system is said to become increasingly avail-

[15] Koffka (1935), pages 549-550.
[16] Koffka (1935), pages 555-556.
[17] Koffka (1935), page 552.

able; that is, it corresponds to what associationists think of as a habit system ready to function. A precaution is needed in the interpretation of availability, for conditions which make a trace more and more available for mere repetitions of one process may make it less available for other processes.[18] This is one of the dangers of too much drill in the school-subjects, because drill may have a narrowing or "blinding" influence.[19]

The treatment of the acquisition of skill by Koffka is sketchy and conjectural, for the problem has not been one of experimental interest to members of the gestalt group. But skill is made coherent with the process-trace theory through a line of thought somewhat as follows. The trace as part of the field of a process exerts an influence on the process in the direction of making it similar to the process which originally produced the trace.[20] This is close to Guthrie's statement that we tend to do what we last did in the same situation. Highly perfected skills can be repeated after periods of disuse because the process communicates with a stable trace system to which it then conforms. While the skill is being learned the trace is less stable. Through the interaction of trace and process, greater stability is achieved. This achievement of greater stability is what is meant by improvement in the skill. Because the trace system, obeying dynamic laws, also undergoes stabilizing changes over a period of no practice, the greater improvement with distributed practice than with massed practice is explained.

Restructuring the present field: insight. The contrast between trial-and-error and insight is a subject of some misunderstanding because there are empirical facts on the one hand and theories about these facts on the other. So far as empirical situations are concerned, there are experiments which demonstrate a maximum of fumbling, with gradual improvements and little understanding of how improvement takes place. These may be classified as experiments in which learning is by trial-and-error, without prejudging the processes to be invoked in explaining the learning. There are also experiments in which the learner obviously perceives a relationship which leads to problem solution, and the

---

[18] Koffka (1935), page 547.
[19] Luchins (1942).
[20] Koffka (1935), page 553.

experiment may be classified as an insight experiment. And there are situations which fall between, where there is partial insight combined with rather blind trial and error. The empirical grading of situations does not mean that the interpretations have to be so graded, i.e., that the trial-and-error behavior must be explained by a trial-and-error theory, insight by an insight theory, and mixed behavior by appropriate mixtures of the theories. This impression is occasionally given by writers taking a sensible middle-of-the-road position.

The problems which insightful learning set for learning theorists may be summarized around six characteristics of insightful learning. These are not the characteristics proposed by any of the gestalt writers, but result from a fairly matter-of-fact analysis of what happens in experiments in which insight is demonstrated.[21]

1. *Insight depends upon capacity.* The capacity for insight is limited by age, membership in a species, and by individual differences within a species. Younger children are less successful in solving "insight" problems than older ones. While the exact order has not been worked out, presumably animals higher in the phyletic scale (e.g., apes) achieve insightful solution more readily than those lower in the scale (e.g., guinea pigs).

2. *Insight depends upon relevant previous experience.* While insight depends upon sufficient previous experience, it is not guaranteed by the possession of that experience. Thus a child cannot get insight into a mathematics problem stated symbolically unless the conventional signs are understood, even if the problem were otherwise at his capacity level. But just because he knows the signs and can perform all the necessary mathematical operations it cannot be forthwith inferred that he can use this knowledge appropriately for the solution of the problem at hand. Association theories have implied that the mere possession of the needed past experience would somehow produce the solution, because nothing can be found in the solution but an assemblage of familiar operations previously learned. But that is like saying that in order to write a poem all you need is a vocabulary because the poem is nothing but words. The gestalt psychologists do not deny that previous experience is useful in insightful solution.

[21] The list draws heavily upon Yerkes' eight criteria of insight (Yerkes, 1927) but is somewhat differently organized.

They object to explanations in terms of previous experience which neglect the problem of organization. That more is needed than the necessary information was nicely demonstrated in Maier's (1930) early reasoning experiments. In one instance he provided his subjects with all the experience necessary for solving a problem, but only one of thirty-seven solved it. More is needed than the experience.

3. *Insight depends upon the experimental arrangements.* Insight is possible only if the learning situation is so arranged that all necessary aspects are open to observation. If a needed tool is hidden, its use in solution is made unlikely, or at least more difficult. In one form of the puzzle-box it is necessary for the rat to dig through a sawdust floor to discover a concealed tunnel which permits exit. Because the entrance to the tunnel is concealed beneath a uniform bed of sawdust, insight is impossible, and the first solution necessary occurs practically by chance—being aided only by the fact that sawdust-digging is within the rat's habitual action pattern. The parts which need to be brought into relationship for solution are assembled more easily if they are simultaneously present in perception, e.g., it is harder for an ape to learn to use a stick which lies on the side of the cage opposite the food than one which lies on the same side as the food.[22]

Skilled teachers are well aware of differences between situations in which understanding is arrived at easily and those in which it is achieved with difficulty—even though the same ultimate steps are involved and the same end-stage reached. In the favored arrangement the problem is so structured that significant features are perceived in proper relationship, and distracting or confusing features are subordinated. Some mathematics teachers make problem-solution difficult to grasp because they go through derivations step by step without an overview of where the steps are leading or what the articulating principles are. They teach the necessary operations, but the final insight eludes the students because of the manner in which the proof is arranged.

4. *Insight follows a period of fumbling and search.* In the presolution period the learner may make many false starts and be engaged in activity which can be characterized as trial-and-error. When insight shall come (if it does come) is not predictable.

[22] Jackson (1942).

These two features (initial fumbling and lack of predictability) have been used by opponents of insight either to assimilate it to associative learning because trial-and-error occurs, or to characterize it as mystical, non-scientific, or accidental because the moment of solution cannot be predicted.

The reply to those who find trial-and-error in insight experiments, and therefore wish to make insightful solution continuous with ordinary associative learning, is that fumbling in problem-solving is not *mere* trial and error. Even those who tend to favor trial-and-error interpretations have come to speak in terms of approximation and correction [23] or in other ways to indicate that the "try" is a real try and not just any old action in the behavior repertoire. In the case of adult insight experiments the "try" is often a plausible hypothesis which has to be rejected. A succession of such hypotheses may be tried before the appropriate one is hit upon. The more intelligent reasoner may actually take longer to solve a given problem because he commands a greater variety of hypotheses to bring to its solution. There is a theoretical distinction which ought to be made between blind fumbling and intelligent searching. Merely varied behavior is one thing; behavior testing hypotheses is varied also, but according to a different type of organization.

That random behavior and luck may further solution is illustrated by some behavior which I observed one summer while assisting Yerkes in an insight experiment with a young chimpanzee. The problem set the animal was to obtain a banana from a long hollow box, open at both ends.[24] The box, essentially a rectangular tube, was firmly fastened to the floor of a large cage. The banana was inserted through a trap door in the middle of the box under the watchful eye of the animal, then the trap door was securely padlocked. The chimpanzee, after a number of unsuccessful efforts to obtain the banana by direct attack—reaching in either end of the tube with hands and with feet, attempting to lift the tube from the floor—seemed to give up temporarily, or, as gestalt psychologists say, to "go out of the field." This extraneous behavior took the form of playful cavorting. In this mood the animal incorporated into her play the hoe handle

[23] Dodge (1931), Melton (1941*a*).
[24] The box is illustrated in Yerkes (1943).

which was standing in the corner of the room, climbing it, and throwing it. Once the handle fell with its end near the open tunnel. The chimpanzee stopped its play, became calm, looked reflective, and, for the first time in its history used the pole as a tool to push the banana out of the far end of the tube.

This first solution depended in part on "luck," on chance behavior which was not goal-directed, which was not a real "try." But was the ultimate solution insightful? The observers judged it to be, but the judgment was "anthropomorphic": the chimpanzee looked and acted about the way in which we might have acted if we had suddenly caught on. It could be called insightful only if it fulfilled the fifth condition, soon to be considered.

The lucky position of the hoe handle structured the situation perceptually to make solution easier. It brought the hoe handle in as a possibility, and gave direction to the problem-solving behavior. It did not add to the chimpanzee's past experience, but it made it easier to assemble the experiences appropriate to solution. Out of what was superfluous activity there thus developed a "hint" as to the direction of solution. An illustration of the way in which direct hints may aid solution is provided by Maier's (1930) experiment previously referred to. By giving a few "hints," in addition to the necessary past experience, solutions were obtained to the same problem by a much larger fraction of his subjects.

The objection to insight that it is unpredictable and therefore outside of science is lacking in force. The moment of insight is not the important feature in any case. Other features, such as reproducibility of the behavior and applicability to new situations are more important. But even though the moment of insight for a given animal confronted with a given problem is not predictable, it is possible to arrange problems in an order of difficulty so that the *degree of probability* that insight will occur is predictable. To assume that all predictions based on past occurrences (empirical probabilities) imply associative learning [25] is to make of association a term so broad as to be meaningless.

5. *Insightful solutions can be readily repeated.* The ape in the illustration just given was returned to the experimental room on

[25] The assumption is made by Guthrie (1935), page 193, and by Guthrie and Horton (1946), page 42.

the following day. Everything was arranged as before. When the banana was locked into position and the chimpanzee released, there was a single flip of the lock (it *might* have been unfastened!) and then the animal went directly for the hoe handle, carried it over a shoulder in a manner very different from the day before, and proceeded to use it appropriately as a tool, without any by-play or any dropping of it on the floor. This was satisfactory evidence that the previous day's solution was accompanied by insight.

6. *Insight, once achieved, can be used in new situations.* A solution once arrived at may be repeated promptly even though no insight had been present. Some of Guthrie and Horton's cats repeated their solution very promptly when next in the cage, but when the release pole was moved a few inches they were unable to use their prior pole-pushing habits.[26] They had evidently learned without insight. On the other hand, a chimpanzee which has learned with insight to obtain a banana with a stick will *search* for a stick when a banana is placed out of reach in a new situation. Having reacted to the more abstract relationship of stick-as-a-tool-to-obtain-banana, it is not disturbed by a slight change in the situation.

In the case of human learning, insight is often accompanied by a verbal formula which permits the principle to be applied readily to new problems. In a multiple choice problem, for example, in which one of a bank of telegraph keys is "correct" according to a pattern which has to be discovered, the subject may learn the formula: "It's the middle one." When a new bank of keys is exposed, the appropriate key can be selected promptly according to this verbal generalization.

Such applications of a perceived relationship to another situation in which it is applicable is the equivalent of transfer of training. The gestalt writers prefer to speak of it as *transposition*, on the pattern of a transposed melody. What is transferred is a relationship or a generalization, although the contents in the two situations may be entirely changed.

The fact of insight, descriptively represented by these six statements, is well established. Whether it is the *only* form of learning, or whether it is a complex form to be explained in other

[26] Guthrie and Horton (1946), page 17.

ways, is a further question. Insight is not itself the explanation of learning. It exemplifies rather more clearly than other forms of learning the applicability of the laws of organization. It is these laws which explain insight, and it is the gestalt contention that the same laws explain other forms of learning. Only in that sense is insight the typical or characteristic kind of learning.

Productive thinking. Wertheimer had lectured on thought processes for many years, but had published only a few fragmentary papers during his lifetime. He had, however, completed the manuscript of a small book just before his death. This has been edited by his friends and has appeared under the title *Productive thinking* (1945). In it a number of his experimental studies are summarized in his characteristic way, with penetrating qualitative analysis of simple situations serving to illustrate the differences between his approach and other approaches to which he is objecting.

The two chief competing alternatives to adopting the gestalt approach to thinking and problem solving are said to be formal logic on the one hand and association theory on the other. Both of these alternatives are believed to be too limited to encompass what actually happens when an individual confronted with a problem finds a sensible solution.

The distinction is made throughout between a blind solution, in which the learner applies a formula, and a sensible solution in which the learner understands what he is doing in relation to the essential structure of the situation. The blind solution is often an unsuccessful application of the formula to a situation not seen to be inappropriate. Experiments are cited, for example, in which school children are taught to demonstrate how to find the area of a parallelogram by dropping lines from two corners perpendicular to the base, thus converting the figure to a rectangle, whose area can be found. Children who could do the examples perfectly were baffled, however, when a parallelogram was presented in a new orientation, so that the "correct" steps of the procedure led to confusing results. They had learned the solution according to a blind procedure. By contrast, the solution of a five-and-one-half-year-old child is reported.

Given the parallelogram problem, after she had been shown briefly how to get at the area of the rectangle, she said, "I certainly don't know how to do *that*." Then after a moment of silence: "This is *no good here*," pointing to the region at the left end; "and *no good here*," pointing to the region at the right.

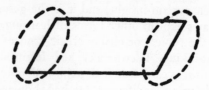

FIGURE 22. TROUBLESOME PARTS IN CHILD'S ATTEMPT TO APPLY RECTANGLE THEORY TO PARALLELOGRAM.
After Wertheimer (1945), page 48.

"It's troublesome, here and there." Hesitatingly she said: "I could make it right here . . . but . . . ." Suddenly she cried out, "May I have a scissors? What is bad there is just what is needed here. It fits." She took the scissor, cut vertically, and placed the left end at the right.[27]

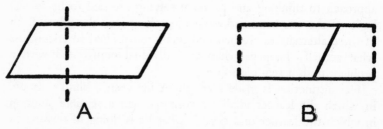

FIGURE 23. CHILD'S SOLUTION OF PARALLELOGRAM PROBLEM WITH A SCISSORS.
After Wertheimer (1945), page 48.

Another child, given a long parallelogram cut out of a piece of paper, remarked early that the whole middle was all right, but the ends—. She suddenly took the paper, and made it into a ring. She saw that it was all right now, since it could be cut vertically anywhere and made into a rectangle.

In cases such as these the solutions appear in an orderly way, in line with the true "structure" of the situation. It is this structural approach which Wertheimer emphasizes.

Children readily grasp such "structural" solutions unless they are badly taught in an atmosphere of blind repetitive drill. Given

[27] Wertheimer (1945), page 48.

figures such as those on the left in Figure 24 and those on the right, they can easily sort out the unsolvable ones from the solvable ones. It is futile to argue, says Wertheimer, that these dis-

A-Figures   **B-Figures**

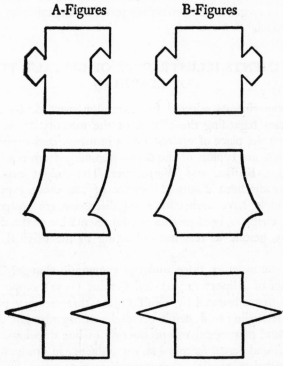

FIGURE 24. APPLICABILITY OF SOLUTION OF PARALLELOGRAM PROBLEM TO NEW FIGURES.

It is possible to change the A-figures sensibly so that they form rectangles. It is not possible to change the B-figures in this way. The ability of school children to solve the A-figures and to reject the B-figures is said to depend on something other than the familiarity of the figures. From Wertheimer (1945), page 20.

tinctions are made on the basis of familiarity, as the associationist seems to believe. Children make the distinctions because they know the essential nature of the solution. The structural features and requirements of the situation itself set up strains and stresses which lead in the direction of improving the situation, that is, to solving the problem.

The implications of Wertheimer's point of view for teaching are fairly clear. It is always preferable to proceed in a manner which favors discovery of the essential nature of the problematic situation, of the gaps which require filling in, so that, even at the cost of elegance or brevity, the proof is "organic" rather than "mechanical." [28]

EXPERIMENTS ILLUSTRATIVE OF GESTALT THEORY OF LEARNING

The experiments selected for discussion were devised to test hypotheses regarding the change of the memory trace, and to bear upon the place of understanding in memorization and retention. These are typical of the topics stemming from the interests of Köhler, Koffka, and Wertheimer. The insight experiments have already been discussed.[29] Some of the other experiments which might have been chosen for discussion are postponed to the next chapters, because they are representative of the direction given by gestalt writers not belonging to the original nuclear group.

Does the memory trace undergo systematic change? The experiments of Allport (1930) and Perkins (1932) supported the position first advanced by Wulf (1922) that memory processes change according to dynamic principles of organization. All used the method of successive reproduction of line drawings. Gibson (1929) found verbal factors a strong influence in producing what Wulf called normalizing, that is, becoming more like a real object on successive attempts to reconstruct what was seen. He therefore was somewhat critical of the theory of intrinsic factors within the memory trace producing the change. A number of other experiments are reviewed by Woodworth [30] and additional citations are given by McGeoch.[31]

All of the experimenters who have found the changes demanded by the theory have used the method of successive reproduction, which introduces the disturbing factor of being

[28] Duncker (1945), page 45.
[29] Reviews of additional experiments on insight may be found in Hartmann (1935) and Woodworth (1938).
[30] Woodworth (1938), pages 69-91.
[31] McGeoch (1942), pages 335-337.

affected by the second reproduction when the third reproduction is made, and so on. An extreme illustration of changes which can be made from one reproduction to another is that shown in Figure 25, from Bartlett (1932). If instead of the series of repro-

ORIGINAL   REPRODUCTION 1   REPRODUCTION 2

REPRODUCTION 3   REPRODUCTION 8   REPRODUCTION 9

REPRODUCTION 10   REPRODUCTION 15   REPRODUCTION 18

FIGURE 25. CHANGES IN FIGURES WITHIN THE METHOD OF SERIAL REPRODUCTION.
Each person views the reproduction by the person preceding him, and then passes his reproduction to the next person. There are progressive changes and elaborations, as in the series illustrated. From Bartlett (1932), pages 180, 181, by permission Cambridge University Press, England, and The Macmillan Company, publishers, N. Y.

ductions, there had been, say, only one reproduction spaced after the initial exposure by the time elapsed between it and the tenth picture in the series, it is most unlikely that anything like the tenth picture would have been made. It is well attested that in immediate reproduction changes such as those required by Wulf's theory occur. But this immediate change is related to the structure of the perceptual field. To use Koffka's term, the trace left by the process is already distorted according to the laws of dynamics, and the question remains whether or not anything happens to the trace with the passing of time.

In order to remedy the defect that experiments testing the theory used successive reproduction predominantly, Hebb and Foord (1945) arranged an experiment corresponding more nearly to ordinary retention experiments, in which there was only one retest for each learning, but the retest was made after a lapse of time different from one subject to another. The objects presented visually were a circle with a small portion of its circumference incomplete and an arrowhead figure. Presumably there would be a change either toward closure (levelling) or toward emphasizing the broken part (sharpening). The circle may be used for illustration. Testing was done by selecting from a series of broken circles the one which was said to have been seen before. While there was some variability, the trends were not in support of Wulf's theory, and there were no progressive changes evident with the passing of time.

The Hebb and Foord experiment is not entirely satisfactory, but it emphasizes the need for greater specification of the conditions under which the Wulf effect occurs. The reasons the experiment is not satisfactory are, first, that the broken circle was already a symmetrical figure, with the broken portion constituting a figure on a ground, and the tendencies to open and close the figure may have been nearly in balance; second, that recognition is objectively much more accurate in these situations than reproduction. Consider, for example, the primitive pictures of a man which a child will *draw* and label as a satisfactory picture of "Daddy," even though this same child is fully capable of selecting his own father's picture out of a gallery of photographs. The dynamics of this illustration are far from understood, but the differences between reproduction and recognition have to be reckoned with.

Bartlett's experiments on the repeating of stories over long intervals are perhaps more instructive in some ways than the experiments repeating line drawings. They reveal rather striking tendencies toward structuring the story so that it would "make sense," and as it grew older it got shorter and irrelevant details dropped out.

There is nothing to prevent association psychologists doing experiments like those of Wulf and his successors, but the suggestion that they be done came from a consideration of factors in figural organization in perception, at the heart of gestalt theory. They therefore serve as an illustration of the way in which theory influences the kind of experiments which get performed.

Drill versus understanding in memorization and retention. In his book on *Organizing and memorizing* (1940), Katona reports a number of experiments inspired by Wertheimer, who contributed the foreword to the book.

Katona attempts experimentally to define and characterize two types of processes leading to recall: rote memorizing and understanding. When a list of nonsense syllables is memorized, the learner is forced to use the former process, because there are no organizing principles which will permit understanding to help. On the other hand, there are many kinds of problems which illustrate principles; in such cases learning by understanding will have advantages. Simple and ingenious experiments were designed in which it was possible to commit the same material to memory with or without understanding, and then to test the results on new learning.

One experiment consisted in the teaching of simple match tricks of the kind illustrated in Figure 26. The problem is to move 3 lines and in so doing to have only 4 squares left. The possible solutions are shown in the figure. There is a simple principle involved in all solutions, which is that no side must be used for more than one square. (There are 16 matches making the original 5 squares; because these 16 matches are now to make 4 squares, it is evident that each side can be used but once.) A number of different tasks were used, all ringing changes on the same general pattern.

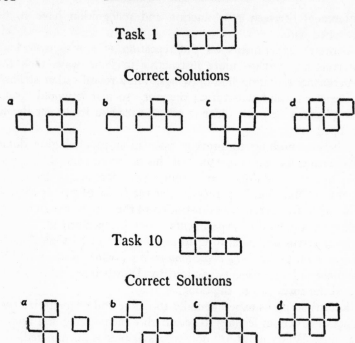

FIGURE 26. MATCH-STICK PROBLEMS.

The assigned problem is to make 4 squares instead of 5 by moving 3 matches (all matches to be used in the solution). Four solutions are shown for each of two tasks. From Katona (1940), page 120.

In his Experiment A, three groups were used, a control group, a memorization group, and a group practiced on examples. No preliminary practice was given the control group. The memorization group was shown the first problem (that of Figure 26), with one of its solutions. Then this same problem was presented in rotated form, and the same solution shown. The memorization group was thus shown essentially the same solution four times, with the problem very slightly rearranged geometrically. The group which had practiced on examples experienced six different transitions from one situation to another in their preliminary practice period, although no general principle was enunciated. Following this preliminary practice each of the three groups was given four tasks to solve; these were all new to the control group, but one of the four tasks was familiar to the memorization and examples group. There was a retest four weeks later, with a new control group. In this retest three new tasks were presented along with one of the originally practiced tasks. Successes on the practiced task were about alike for the two groups, in spite of the fact that the practiced task for the examples group was only one of three tasks practiced, while the memorization group had spent all of its practice period on this one task. The advantage of the examples group was more pronounced on new tasks, as shown below.

COMPARISON OF SCORES * ON NEW TASKS OF GROUPS PRACTICED IN
DIFFERENT WAYS
(Katona, 1940, page 86)

	Immediate Test	Retest After 4 Weeks
Control Group	1.06	2.20
Memorization Group	1.79	2.84
Group Practiced on Examples	3.92	6.24

* Weighted scores, with possible score of 10. The differences between the examples group and the others are statistically significant.

Why was the group practiced on examples superior? Presumably because the more varied experience had produced some measure of understanding. Verbal reports showed that this understanding was fragmentary, taking such forms as "filling up holes increases the number of squares;" "spreading it out decreases the number of squares." In any case, the method produced a more varied attack, and alternative solutions to the familiar problems were used in a way not true of the memorization group. Memorization sometimes tends to narrow rather than to increase the range of problem-solving.

Katona concludes that learning with understanding not only improves retention of that which is learned, but better qualifies the learner to move forward to new learning. Thus understanding is important for transfer. Some of Katona's conclusions have been criticized by Melton [32] on statistical grounds, but Melton accepts as demonstrated the following points on transfer following learning by understanding:

[32] Melton (1941b). For a reply see Katona (1942).

1. A group which has learned by rote memorization is little better than an unpracticed control group in the learning of new tasks, while a group which has learned with understanding learns new tasks much more readily.

2. When once tasks have been learned with understanding, repeated tests with new tasks result in progressive improvement in performance. By contrast, if the repeated tests are done with practiced tasks, the efficiency of performance on new tasks is reduced.

Katona concludes from all this that there is a real difference in what happens when meaningless memorization goes on and when learning takes place with understanding. He believes that the two kinds of learning are genuine and should be distinguished. This does not mean that he believes that there are two fundamental prototypes of learning, corresponding to the two types of arrangement under which learning takes place. According to him the underlying factor is organization. Only when better organization fails do you get the extreme picture of rote learning, which is itself a special form of organization resorted to with comparatively incoherent materials. The distinction in kind is not one of ease or of difficulty, for it is sometimes easier to learn by rote than to learn by understanding. The advantages of learning by understanding are that meaningful learning is applicable to new situations and is more enduring.

ESTIMATE OF GESTALT THEORY OF LEARNING

Gestalt theory and the typical problems of learning. The gestalt psychologists find a somewhat distorted emphasis in conventional treatments of learning, so that the typical problems as reviewed are not the most natural selection of problems from their standpoint. In order to maintain the symmetry of comparative study of the different positions, however, the same list will be followed which was used to summarize the associationist positions.

1. *Capacity*. Because learning requires differentiation and restructuring of fields, the higher forms of learning depend very much upon natural capacities for reacting in these ways. Poor methods of instruction, however, may be responsible for some inability to face new situations, for a "blindness" which might be confused with stupidity.

2. *Practice.* Changes go on within repetition, not as a result of repetition. Practically all psychologists now agree that this is so, but they differ with regard to the pertinent processes which go on within the repetitions. From the gestalt point of view, repetitions are successive exposures, bringing to light relationships to enter into restructurization. To Koffka, they also make possible the consolidation of trace systems, which is as near as any gestalt psychologist comes to saying that responses become fixed by repetition.

3. *Motivation.* Goals represent end-situations, and as such modify learning through the principle of closure. The processes leading to the successes or failures get transformed by their consequences. The empirical law of effect is accepted, but Thorndike's interpretation of the blind action of effect is denied.

4. *Understanding.* The perceiving of relationships, awareness of the relationships between parts and whole, of means to consequences, are emphasized by the gestalt writers. Problems are to be solved sensibly, structurally, organically, rather than mechanically, stupidly, or by the running off of prior habits.

5. *Transfer.* The gestalt concept most like that of transfer is *transposition*. A pattern of dynamic relationships discovered or understood in one situation may be applicable to another. This is in some respects like Judd's generalization theory of transfer.[33] There is something in common between the earlier learning and the situation in which transfer is found, but what exists in common is not identical piecemeal elements, but common patterns, configurations, or relationships. One of the advantages of learning by understanding rather than by rote process is that understanding is transposable to wider ranges of situations, and less often leads to erroneous applications of old learning.

6. *Forgetting.* Koffka relates forgetting to course of changes in the trace. Traces may disappear either through gradual decay (a possibility hard to prove or disprove), through destruction because of being part of a chaotic, ill-structured field, or through assimilation to new traces or processes. The last possibility is familiar as a form of theory of retroactive inhibition. Traces which continue to exist may at a given moment be unavailable. While little is known about this, Koffka believes it must have

[33] Judd (1908).

something to do with ego organization.[34] Finally, there are instances of forgetting in which a process fails to communicate with an otherwise available trace. The forgetting of an intention [35] would presumably classify here. This is also an ego problem.

In addition to such forgetting, there are the dynamic changes which take place in recall, so that what is reproduced is not earlier learning with some parts missing, but a modified trace which is productive as well as reproductive.

The interrelationship between perception and learning. Any estimate of the classical gestalt position would be incomplete which did not appraise the success with which the basic thesis has been defended that the dynamic laws of perception and of learning are alike. For the most part, these conjectures have been programmatic rather than worked out in convincing experiments. The point of view has been helpful to the extent that it has brought emphasis upon organization, meaningfulness, and understanding, and has called attention to the importance of the structure of the problematic situation. The laws of similarity (or equality), of proximity, of closure, and of good continuation, are not very convincing as laws of learning, and the attempts made by Koffka to summarize his point of view on learning in terms of them is not very successful. As we shall see in later chapters, the reintroduction of cognitive features into learning has been important, whatever one's judgment of the importance of the laws of organization may be.

Insight as an alternative to trial and error. It is implied in gestalt theory that a learner acts as intelligently as he can under the circumstances which confront him, so that insightful solution of problems is the typical solution, if the problem is not too difficult and the essentials are open to inspection. Fumbling and trial-and-error are resorted to only when the problem is too difficult, either intrinsically, or because of the way in which it is presented to the learner. This reverses the associationist position that trial-and-error is the typical method of attack and that reasoning is essentially "mental" trial-and-error. The empirical facts of insight are as satisfactory as the empirical facts of trial-and-error.

[34] Koffka (1935), pages 525-527.
[35] Birenbaum (1930).

Learning theorists are not yet in agreement on one of the three possibilities: (1) that all learning is of one kind, basically like trial-and-error, from which insightful learning can be derived; (2) that all learning is basically of one kind, like insightful learning, with trial-and-error a derivative form; or (3) that more than one kind of learning occurs, of which trial-and-error and insight are two illustrative examples. A strong case can be made for the gestalt point of view that blind learning is not the prototype of all learning. But this is one of the unresolved issues, to face us in succeeding chapters of this book.

In any case, the gestalt psychologists have sharpened the lines of cleavage in thinking about problems of learning, and by questioning most of what was conventionally accepted they have been of real service, regardless of whatever verdicts or compromises the future may produce.

SUPPLEMENTARY READINGS

BOOKS

Ellis, W. D. (1938) *A source book of gestalt psychology.*
Hartmann, G. W. (1935) *Gestalt psychology.*
Koffka, K. (1924) *Growth of the mind.*
Koffka, K. (1935) *Principles of gestalt psychology.*
Köhler, W. (1925) *The mentality of apes.*
Köhler, W. (1929) (1947) *Gestalt psychology.*
Köhler, W. (1940) *Dynamics in psychology.*
Wertheimer, M. (1945) *Productive thinking.*

SHORTER INTRODUCTIONS

Hartmann, G. W. (1942) The field theory of learning and its educational consequences. *Natl. Soc. Stud. Educ.*, 41st Yearbook, Part II, 165-214.
Heidbreder, E. (1933) *Seven psychologies*, 328-375.
Koffka, K. (1925) Mental development. In C. Murchison, edit., *Psychologies of 1925*, 130-143.
Köhler, W. (1930) Some tasks of gestalt psychology. In C. Murchison, edit., *Psychologies of 1930*, 143-160.

CRITICAL REVIEWS

Boring, E. G. (1930) The gestalt psychology and the gestalt movement. *Amer. J. Psychol.*, 42, 308-315.
Pratt, C. C. (1936) Review of Koffka's *Principles of gestalt psychology. Amer. J. Psychol.*, 48, 527-531.

Robinson, E. S. (1930) Review of Köhler's *Gestalt psychology*. *J. genet. Psychol.*, 37, 431-450.

Spence, K. W. (1941) Review of Köhler's *Dynamics in psychology*. *Psychol. Bull.*, 38, 886-889.

Vernon, P. E. (1935-1936) Review of Koffka's *Principles of gestalt psychology*. *Character & Pers.*, 4, 92-94.

REPRESENTATIVE EXPERIMENTS

Duncker, K. (1945) On problem-solving. *Psychol. Monogr.*, 58, No. 270, ix, 113 pp.

Gottschaldt, K. (1926) Über den Einfluss der Erfahrung auf die Wahrnehmung von Figuren, I. *Psychol. Forsch.*, 8, 261-317. [Translated and condensed as "Gestalt factors and repetition" in Ellis (1938), pages 109-122.]

Gottschaldt, K. (1929) Über den Einfluss der Erfahrung auf die Wahrnehmung von Figuren, II. *Psychol. Forsch.*, 12, 1-87. [Translated and condensed as "Gestalt factors and repetition" in Ellis (1938), pages 123-135.]

Gottschaldt, K. (1933) Der Aufbau des kindlichen Handelns. *Beih. Z. angew. Psychol.*, 68, 228 pp.

Harlow, H. F., and Settlage, P. H. (1934) Comparative behavior of primates. VII. Capacity of monkeys to solve patterned string tests. *J. comp. Psychol.*, 18, 423-435.

Harrower, M. R. (1932) Organization in higher mental processes. *Psychol. Forsch.*, 17, 56-120.

Köhler, W. (1918) Nachweis einfacher Strukturfunktionen beim Schimpansen und beim Haushuhn. *Abh. d. königl. Preuss. Ak. d. Wissen*, Phys. Math. Klasse, Nr.2, 1-101. [Translated and condensed as "Simple structural functions in the chimpanzee and in the chicken" in Ellis (1938), pages 217-227.]

Newman, E. B. (1939) Forgetting of meaningful material during sleep and waking. *Amer. J. Psychol.*, 52, 65-71.

Perkins, F. T. (1932) Symmetry in visual recall. *Amer. J. Psychol.*, 44, 473-490.

Restorff, H. von (1933) Analyse von Vorgängen im Spurenfeld. I. Über die wirkung von Bereichsbildungen im Spurenfeld. *Psychol. Forsch.*, 18, 299-342.

Wertheimer, M. (1925) Über Schlussprozesse im produktiven Denken. *Drei Abhandlungen zur Gestalttheorie*. Berlin: Erlangen, 164-184. [Translated and condensed as "The syllogism and productive thinking" in Ellis (1938), 274-282.]

Wulf, F. (1922) Über die Veränderung von Vorstellungen (Gedächtnis und Gestalt), *Psychol. Forsch.*, 1, 333-373. [Translated and condensed as "Tendencies in figural variation" in Ellis (1938), pages 136-148.]

Chapter 8

LEWIN'S TOPOLOGICAL AND VECTOR PSYCHOLOGY

Although a member of the Berlin gestalt group, Kurt Lewin early began to break new ground, especially in studies of motivation. Lewin's is not, strictly speaking, a psychology of learning. Only a small fraction of his own work and that of his students is devoted to problems of learning, but his conceptions of behavioral dynamics are critical of many current beliefs about learning. While the formulations are not presented as a theory of learning, they are relevant to such a theory.

THE BEGINNINGS OF LEWIN'S DYNAMIC CONCEPTIONS

The Lewin-Ach controversy. Ach belonged to the Würzburg school which had supplemented conventional association with sets, determining tendencies, and the like, thus adding something more dynamic to the standard theory of strengthening associations through repetition. He designed a series of experiments in which a habit of reproducing nonsense syllables was set up through repeated exposure, and then a determining tendency was introduced which might either facilitate or hinder the tendency created by practice. Thus "will" was set against "habit," and a possible quantitative measure of will proposed.[1]

There were three arrangements of nonsense syllables in the original learning experiments of Ach. One was the usual or normal arrangement of heterogeneous pairs, such as *bol-pid;* another arrangement called for a rhyming syllable, as *rik-tik;*

[1] Ach (1910).

the third called for inversion, as *kep-pek*. The subject learned one series of eight pairs of each of these kinds. The stimulus syllable of each pair was later used in test situations in which that syllable appeared with others. In the test series instructions were to reproduce what had been practiced, or to rhyme, or to invert. Thus the determining tendency could either sum with or contradict the associative reproductive tendency, or the reproductive factor could be present alone. Strength of reaction was inferred from latency of response. Ach found some results coherent with his theory, that the shortest reaction times were in the cases in which the associative (reproductive) tendency coincided with the determining tendency superimposed by instructions. His other results were somewhat irregular, but were interpreted by him as giving general support to his position.

Lewin's objection to Ach's work is not that he introduced the determining tendency, which Lewin essentially accepts, but that he added it to the conventional association theory without seeing that it was a foreign intrusion and led logically to the abandonment of the simple association theory. Lewin argued that the conflict which appeared in the experiment—and, indeed, conflict was convincingly demonstrated—was not between association and determining tendency, but between two determining tendencies. It was his belief that there is no "force" within mere association to lead to reproduction, that reproduction itself must be motivated and implies a set to reproduce.

Lewin's experiments [2] were much like Ach's, but a few modifications greatly changed the resulting interpretations. First a series of eight pairs of nonsense syllables was learned in which the second syllable rhymed with the first, *dak-tak*, *ged-ked*. Then a list of eight pairs was learned in which the response syllable was the stimulus-syllable spelled backward. Note that the only change in response syllables was in the consonants, the vowels being alike in both the rhyming and the reversed pairs.

The first test series consisted in instructing the subjects to respond to a set of syllables by changing the vowel. Syllables from the previously practiced series were inserted among unfamiliar syllables. If Ach's theory were sound, there should have been some conflict between "habit" and "determining tendency,"

[2] Lewin (1917) (1922).

but none was found. There were no wrong reactions, and the latent times for control and critical syllables were alike.

A second test, however, produced conflict and retardation, such as Ach found. When the subjects were told to rhyme a series including both syllables previously rhymed and syllables previously reversed, mistakes were made on the syllables previously reversed. Similarly, with instructions to reverse, errors were made in response to syllables previously rhymed when they were presented in the midst of syllables previously reversed. The interpretation is that the instruction to rhyme to syllables previously learned as rhymes was acted upon as though it had been an instruction to reproduce. When, then, a previously reversed syllable appeared, the faulty self-instruction to reproduce conflicted with the correct instruction to rhyme, and interference was shown.

The occurrence of conflict in one case and not in the other, although the prior habits fixed by association were equally strong before both tests, confirmed Lewin in his belief that the existence of an association (or, in his later terms, a cognitive structure) does not provide the "motor" for mental activity. There is always a tension system necessary for activity, including the activity of reproducing previously learned nonsense syllables.

Lewin's contention, while it remains cogent, has lost some of its force as interest has shifted from the artificially motivated habit of rote learning to habits more intimately tied up to need and tension systems. For example, a conditioned avoidance response, strengthened through repeated reinforcement, has a certain urgency about it, so that it breaks through contradictory instructions. It is possible to treat the conflict between "habit" and "determining tendency" in this case much as Ach did, and to find results which seem to support Ach's position.[3] The findings do not contradict Lewin's position, however, because in the case of conditioned avoidance responses there is a "motor" in the threat of punishment which is set against the verbal instructions not to respond. This "habit" is more than mere contiguous association leading to reproduction of associated items.

This early recognition of the dynamic organization of reproductive tendencies is reflected in later experiments on the rela-

[3] Hilgard (1938).

tionship between tension and retention, as shown in memory for finished and unfinished tasks,[4] and the tendency to resume unfinished tasks when the opportunity arises.[5]

Psychological tension-systems. Much that foreshadows his later systematic writings appears in an important paper by Lewin in 1926, shortly after Köhler's and Koffka's views were becoming known in America. Lewin was first introduced to American audiences by J. F. Brown (1929), three years after this paper appeared.

For one thing, Lewin set himself squarely in favor of a psychological analysis of the actual situation, and against what he called *accomplishment* concepts. The practice curve for typewriting, scoring typing according to words typed per minute or some other convenient unit, rises, shows a plateau, reaches a limit, and so on—as though all that happened could be described as "typewriting." A more psychological analysis would show that what the beginner is doing and what the skilled typist is doing are entirely different: the beginner's process is one of searching, but the searching process drops out as skill is mastered. This objection to accomplishment is to be compared with Guthrie's objections expressed in much the same way, several years later.[6] The difference is that Guthrie wishes to restrict his measurements to movements, which Lewin would class with accomplishments as lacking in sufficient psychological meaning.

The typical non-gestalt conception of psychological causation, says Lewin at this time, is *adhesion*. One thing is attached to another so that revival of the first brings forth the second. Gestalt psychology is sometimes misunderstood as correcting association by accepting the adhesion principle but permitting it to apply only to parts of wholes. This notion is flatly rejected. No mere coupling principle can provide the energy for psychical activity. Psychological behavior depends upon energy related to psychological tension systems.

Perception of the world of meaningful things and events does not provide the energy for activity, although activity aroused under need-tension systems may be *steered* by perception. This is

---

[4] Zeigarnik (1927).
[5] Ovsiankina (1928).
[6] Guthrie (1935), page 163.

not unlike Skinner's later notion of the role of the discriminated stimulus in operant behavior: the stimulus does not elicit the behavior, but it does set the occasion for it. The sequence of events from perception to satiation is as follows. The perception of an object or event may give rise to a psychological tension (e.g., a desire), or it may communicate with a state of tension already existing in such a way that this tension system thereupon assumes control over motor behavior. The aroused "valences" (attractions and repulsions of goal objects) act as environmental forces steering subsequent behavior. This behavior then leads to satiation or to the resolution of tension so that a state of equilibrium is approached.

At this early date (1926) Lewin goes to some pains to point out the ridiculousness for scientific purposes of saying that "everything depends upon everything else." While as a gestalt psychologist he is concerned with wholes, he recognizes as the most important problem the isolation of the "specific psychical units, personality spheres, and behavior wholes" in which one's activities, emotions, intentions, wishes, and hopes are embedded. Whatever psychical unity there may be in the "ego" system, it is a "weak" gestalt, and we are dealing in the personality with a great number of "strong" gestalts which in part are in communication with each other, in part disclose no genuine unity at all. In adults the possibility of organized behavior depends upon a relatively complete segregation of a number of different tension systems.

A number of pages are devoted to an analysis of "intentions," how they are fulfilled, why they are forgotten. He arrives at the conclusion that they are quasi-needs, because their satisfaction is like the satisfaction of other needs, not dependent upon particular occasions or particular actions. Substitute satisfactions may be found for intentions as for needs.

This paper introduces many of the concepts to be developed in the later attempts to formalize and metricize the system. There are the needs and quasi-needs; the tension-systems; perception (cognitive structure) as steering, but not as providing energy; valences; boundaries; a differentiated and complexly structured ego-system. It is a natural development to the later more formal system.

TOPOLOGICAL AND VECTOR PSYCHOLOGY

The more abstract and formal characteristics of Lewin's system were detailed in two books, *Principles of topological psychology* (1936), and *The conceptual representation and measurement of psychological forces* (1938). He later stated the relationship of his viewpoint to problems of learning.[7]

The words "topological" and "vector" refer to types of geometry borrowed because they appear to provide the mathematics appropriate to the structure of psychological situations. Any mathematics, like any language or any system of logic, may be used in science if it happens to fit. Plane geometry and trigonometry do for surveying, and spherical geometry is useful for navigation, but Einstein had to turn to a geometry of four dimensions to handle relativity problems. The problem of selecting appropriate mathematical tools is familiar in choosing the proper statistical formulas for a given set of data. In looking for a "fit" to his conception, Lewin hit upon topology and upon vectors.

Topology is a non-metrical geometry of spaces, in which concepts such as "inside" and "outside" and "boundary" are used. Lewin believes that many psychological situations are structured in that way. Sociologists have long talked of "in-groups and "outgroups." It is such a usage which Lewin is trying to formalize in topological concepts.

Vectors are borrowed from the mathematical system used in mechanics to describe the resolution of forces. Unlike topology, vectors are metrical. A vector is usually represented by an arrow, the length representing its force, the direction representing the line of application. The point of application may also be shown as a matter of convenience, but it does not belong as a property of the vector. Because much dynamic psychology can be described in terms of conflict and the resolution of conflict, the geometry of vectors finds appropriate application.

What Lewin intends by borrowing from topological and vector geometries is clear. He is searching for a mathematics which will be appropriate to psychological structure as he understands it. He has been attacked for using these mathematics in-

[7] Lewin (1942).

correctly, and for drawing improper analogies from them.[8] His system is no doubt vulnerable in some of these respects, but the relevance of his theories for the purposes of the present discussion does not rest upon the validity of his quantitative representations.

The psychological field: life space. The selection of geometry as an appropriate mathematics is natural because the psychological field is thought of as a space in which the person moves. This life space is psychological, not physical; it is represented mathematically by a spatial diagram, but that does not mean that it exists in such spatial relationships.

The conception of life space is a plausible one. It signifies that two people walking down the same street are going different places, and the worlds in which they are walking are to some extent different worlds. Or as I sit in revery and make plans for the morrow, I move in a world very different from that in which I sit. My life space is the space in which I live psychologically, as seen from my own viewpoint. It corresponds in many ways to the world about me, to the world of things, and people, and ideas, but it becomes my world always in edited and distorted forms. Even though psychological space is a space that somehow exists within me, it is a space in which I move, and it is possible to distinguish between the person and the environment in life space. The environment in life space is quasi-physical, quasi-social, quasi-conceptual. That is, it reflects many features of the physical and social environment, and of the environment of language and values and philosophies, but is never to be identified strictly with the outside factors which condition it and influence it.

Life space may be inferred; it does not depend upon subjective report. That is, life-space, while within the person, is not a strictly private affair open only to introspection. In fact, a person is not always able to introspect about the forces acting in his life space at a given moment. Life space is a construct, like other scientific constructs, to account for the psychological situation at a given moment.

Locomotion in life space is delineated by a geometrical representation of the selection of alternatives, the examining of possi-

[8] London (1944).

bilities, the setting out toward goals, the experiencing of frustration, and the like. It may or may not involve locomotion in the real world. If I move toward an object of choice in the real world, I am also moving in my life space, but the two motions are not to be identified; in life space we represent the psychological significance for the person of the motion in physical space. A typical life space diagram is shown in Figure 27.

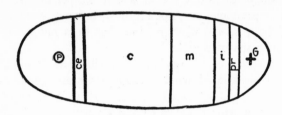

FIGURE 27. LIFE-SPACE.

The situation represented is that of a boy who wants to become a physician. The person (P) is shown separated from the goal region (+ G) by a number of regions with boundaries between them. The regions are college entrance (ce), college (c), medical school (m), internship (i), establishing a practice (pr). While the locomotion through these regions may take place in the future, they are in the present life-space as obstacles to the attainment of a goal which is now in view. By permission from *Principles of topological psychology*, by K. Lewin, Copyrighted 1936 by McGraw-Hill Book Co., Inc.

The person, while often represented as a point moving about in his life space, also has a structure which can be represented geometrically. There are more superficial and deeper (less accessible) layers of the personality; there are different degrees of complexity of organization and differentiation; some parts are in communication, others have strong barriers between them. The structure of the person is sometimes diagrammed as in Figure 28.

Occasionally life space corresponds very closely to the real world with which the person is in commerce. In that case he is said to be in touch with reality. At the other extreme we find individuals living in a world of fiction and phantasy—out of touch with reality. In order to describe these differences, Lewin proposes reality-irreality as a dimension of life space. The very young child may not distinguish between its hopes and wishes and the actual circumstances of life. Presumably there is a greater differentiation between reality and irreality as we grow older, although normal adults are fully capable of wishful thinking.

Another dimension of life space is that of "time-perspective."[9] The small child lives in the present, and as he grows he conforms his behavior to events in the more remote future. Part of the over-emotional reactions of adolescents may be due to the attempt to face adult problems before sufficient time-perspective

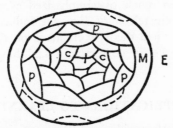

FIGURE 28. REPRESENTATION OF THE PERSON.

The motor and perceptual regions, because they have commerce with the environment (E), are represented at the boundary zone (M). The portion lying within represents the inner-personal region (I), which has more central parts (c) and more peripheral parts (p). Under different circumstances of stress, the inner-personal region undergoes differentiation or dedifferentiation ('primitivation'). By permission from *Principles of topological psychology*, by K. Lewin, Copyrighted 1936 by McGraw-Hill Book Co., Inc.

has developed. A momentary frustration is interpreted as an enduring defeat.

Behavior a function of the present life space. Perhaps even more forcefully than his gestalt colleagues, Lewin insisted that behavior depends upon the present, not upon the past or the future. Past events, like future events, do not exist now, and therefore in his sense, cannot have effects now. While past psychological fields are part of the origin of the present field, their relationship to the present is so indirect that their explanatory value is slight.

As pointed out earlier, the notion of contemporary causation is a sound one, and need not lessen the importance of a knowledge of the past in contributing to an understanding of the present. It is true, however, that in adopting a logical position there often go along with it certain overtones of interest and preoccupations not essential to the position. Lewin's whole-hearted

[9] L. K. Frank (1939).

insistence on the importance of the present accentuated his interest in conflict and other contemporaneous motivational situations, and lessened his interest in progressive changes, such as those studied in conventional learning situations or in the psychological clinic.[10]

Lewin justifies his neglect of learning on different grounds. He says that learning (i.e., the influence of the past on the present) has been much overemphasized as a reaction against earlier pre-scientific teleology (i.e., the influence of the future on the present). Field theory's emphasis on the present he believes to be a necessary corrective, establishing a preferred balance of interest.[11]

APPLICATIONS TO LEARNING

Learning as a change in cognitive structure. As one learns, one increases in knowledge. What does it mean to know more? It means to have a more highly differentiated life space, in which there are more subregions connected by defined paths. That is another way of saying that we know facts in their relationships; we know what leads to what.

A problematical situation represents an unstructured region of life space. We do not know how to get from the givens to the goal. We feel insecure until the region becomes structured. When it does become structured so as to permit problem-solution, we have learned.

A change in the structure of knowledge (cognitive structure) may occur with repetition. The situation may require repeated exposures before the structure gets changed. The important thing is that the cognitive structure gets changed, not that the repetitions occur. With better arrangements of the problem the structure may get changed with fewer repetitions. This is the lesson of the insight experiments. Too much repetition does not aid learning; on the contrary, repetition may lead to psychological satiation [12] with accompanying disorganization and dedifferentiation of the cognitive structure.

[10] A somewhat halting attempt to deal with progressive changes is made in Lewin (1943), although the importance of the present field is reaffirmed in the work.

[11] Lewin (1942), page 222.

[12] Karsten (1928).

Changes in cognitive structure come about, in part, according to the principles of patterning in perception, as previously discussed. These changes are due to "forces" intrinsic to the cognitive structure. But cognitive structure is also changed according to the needs of the individual. A psychological force corresponding to a need can have either of two consequences. It can lead to "locomotion" in the direction of the force. This means, in common language, that the need is satisfied in familiar ways; new learning is not required, and the cognitive structure may remain intact. Or the force can lead to a change in cognitive structure so that such a "locomotion" may be facilitated. That is, the relationships within the situation are seen in new ways, so that the need may be satisfied. In the latter case, motivated learning may be said to have taken place.

Reward and punishment. Those who accept law of effect or reinforcement theories have seldom analyzed in detail what the circumstances are which force the learner to confront the reward or the threat of punishment. Lewin is able to show that the situations are quite specific.

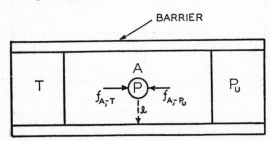

FIGURE 29. LIFE-SPACE IN THREATENED PUNISHMENT.
The person is caught between the tendency to avoid an unpleasant task (T) and the threat of punishment (Pu). Because of the conflict there will be a tendency to leave the situation (l) unless there are strong barriers to prevent this. Hence the punishment situation, to be effective, is necessarily prison-like. After Lewin (1942), page 233, by permission of the National Society for the Study of Education.

The usual situation in punishment is illustrated in Figure 29. The threat of punishment (Pu) is used to keep the learner at an intrinsically disliked task (T). A conflict situation is set up so that the individual is forced to choose between one or the other of the disagreeable possibilities. Under these circumstances, the tendency is to "leave the field," to avoid both of the tasks. In order to keep the learner in the conflict situation it is necessary to erect barriers (B). These in actual life are usually authoritarian; it is necessary to "police" a learning situation controlled by punishment. Because association psychologists have tended to perform their experiments in confining runways or with subjects strapped to the apparatus, they have usually overlooked important dynamic arrangements of their experiments. The importance of the barrier is not incorporated in their theories.

In a reward situation it is not necessary for the learner to be "walled in" because the attractiveness of the reward keeps him in the field. It is necessary, however, to keep a barrier around the reward, to prevent access by any route (such as W) other than by going through (performing) the disliked but requested activity (Figure 30). Because the reward is externally related to

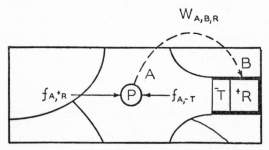

FIGURE 30. LIFE-SPACE IN OFFERED REWARD.

The person is in conflict because the approach to reward (R) is by way of the unpleasant task (T). While the tendency to leave the field is not present as it is in punishment, there is a tendency to approach the reward by way of a shortcut so as to avoid T, as by path $W_{A,B,R}$. Hence it is necessary to guard access to the reward to prevent approach by any path other than that through T. Some policing is necessary, but the situation is less prison-like than in the case of control by punishment. After Lewin (1946), page 811, reproduced by permission from *Manual of child psychology* edited by L. Carmichael, published by John Wiley & Sons, Inc.

activity T, there will always be a tendency to take shortcuts, if possible. Cheating by school-children is such an effort to obtain the reward without performing the demanded work.

The differences in structure between a reward and punishment situation are real, and to gloss over them, as writers like Guthrie and Hull do, is a real omission in their theories. One consequence of the different amounts of constraint in the two situations is that rewarded activities often become interesting and liked, so that motivation is no longer extrinsic, while activities controlled by the threat of punishment tend to become increasingly hated.[13]

Success and failure. When goals are intrinsic, it is more appropriate to think of the goal-activity as successful or unsuccessful rather than as rewarding or punishing.

The contrast between a "psychological" approach to psychological problems and a "non-psychological" approach is nowhere clearer than in the difference in treatment of *reward* and *success*. A reward is something tangible and external, which merely terminates a situation (Guthrie) or is associated with need reduction (Hull). A success experience has to be understood according to what the learner is trying to do, and the relationship between success and goal-achievement is a somewhat complex affair. Psychological analysis of success from the point of view of the learner shows at least the following possibilities: [14]

1. To reach a goal constitutes success. This is the usual interpretation of success. It is obviously satisfying to try for something and to achieve it.

2. To get within the region of the goal may be a success experience. Some goals are less well defined than others. A student may hope for an A grade, but be satisfied with a B; a person may wish an office, but take satisfaction in the fact that his fellow-members nominated him. The curious practice in India of signing a letter with the statement following the signature "B.A., failed," testifies to the fact that getting near enough to the goal to take the examination is a mark of esteem.

3. To make noticeable progress toward a goal may provide a success experience, even though the goal is remote. To pass freshman physics is not to be admitted to medical school, but it is a step along the way.

4. To select a socially approved goal may in itself be a success experience. To be the kind of student who carries books home over the Christmas holidays is a mark of serious intent and is bolstering to the ego, even though the books remain unopened.

[13] Lewin (1942), page 233.
[14] Hilgard (1942).

To own an encyclopedia is to be the kind of person you would like to be, whether or not the encyclopedia is consulted.

If such matters are talked about in the language of primary and secondary reinforcements, some of the vividness of the learner-goal relationship is bound to be lost. It is to Lewin's credit that he made a serious effort to deal with psychologically real problems, and then, as a second step, tried to find a mathematics appropriate to them. Too often the alternative is chosen of looking first for something which can be measured and counted, hoping that psychologically more interesting situations can be deduced from them later on. This leads to preoccupation with nonsense syllables, mazes, and conditioned responses, to the neglect of the problems of behavior in freer life situations in which the learner selects his own goals and redefines them as he goes along.

The experiments which pointed up the concepts used by Lewin and his students in discussing success and failure were those of Hoppe (1931) which introduced the companion notions of *ego-involvement* and *level of aspiration.*

Psychological success and failure depend upon ego-involvement in the task at hand. That is, the goals must be real to the learner, so that, if achieved, there is the elation of significant accomplishment, if not achieved, there is the chagrin or humiliation of defeat. As William James put it, our self-esteem may be expressed as the ratio between our success and our pretensions.[15]

Hoppe pointed out that there is a restricted region of difficulty within which success and failure are possible (Figure 31). Some tasks are much too easy. To succeed in them is not to experience success. A school-child is insulted if asked to spell words which are too easy or to make computations interpreted as "baby stuff." Some tasks are much too hard. If we are asked to give a construction in Russian grammar—and we make no pretense of knowing Russian—this is not a psychological failure. It is only within the range of uncertainty—where both success and failure are possible—that we can really succeed or really fail. Experienced teachers know how hard it is to keep tasks at an appropriate level of difficulty so that the learners remain ego-involved.

Individuals tend to set momentary goals within the range of

15 James (1890), page I, 310.

activities in which there is ego-involvement. The momentary goal is referred to as the *level of aspiration*. It is set according to the learner's interpretation of his own achievement, but there are wide individual differences in the manner of such goal-setting. Some learners are realistic, and set their goals near to what they have shown themselves capable of doing. Those who are un-

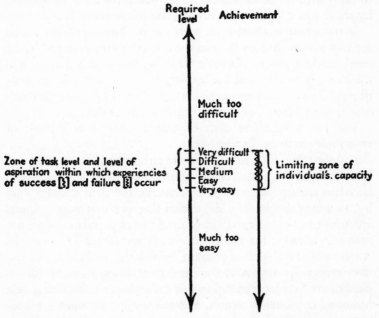

FIGURE 31. DIFFICULTY-LEVEL AND THE EXPERIENCE OF SUCCESS AND FAILURE. The psychological experience of success and failure can occur only in the region in which there is some possibility of objective achievement or lack of achievement. By permission from *A dynamic theory of personality*, by K. Lewin, Copyrighted 1935 by McGraw-Hill Book Co., Inc.

realistic may depart in either direction from their past achievements. Some are self-protective, and to avoid the possibility of failure set goals too low; others are hopeful, and set goals unrealistically too high.[16]

The interrelationships among past achievements, momentary goals, social atmosphere, and individuality, set a number of invit-

[16] P. S. Sears (1940) (1941).

ing experimental problems.[17] The flavor of these studies is legitimately compared with that of studies on reward, punishment and reinforcement, which represent the approach to the same subject-matter taken by the association psychologists. Regardless of how one may view the conceptual system within which the level of aspiration studies are framed, it is evident that they call attention to aspects of goal-directed activities which have been neglected by those preoccupied with reward and punishment.

Learning as a change in motivation. The repetition of an activity brings changes both in the cognitive structure and in the needs-tensions system. Often a desirable outcome is a change in the interests or values of the learner, that is, a change in the relative attractiveness of one goal over another. This goal-attractiveness is what Lewin calls *valence*, and valences change.

The following three cases of valence-change as a result of repetition are to be distinguished:

1. Attractive goals may lose their attraction if the activity related to them is repeated to the point of satiation. Monotony and boredom are familiar enough experiences, but their dynamics are by no means simple. The suggestion that every activity presents a barrier to its own repetition (one of Hull's postulates) does not suffice to account for the details which are found. For example, when tasks are graded as pleasant, unpleasant, or indifferent, and then repeated excessively, the unpleasant tasks, as might be expected, are first satiated.[18] But it is the pleasant tasks which next become impossible to repeat, and the indifferent tasks are consistently last. Because of less ego-involvement in the indifferent tasks, their endless repetition does not develop the resistances found for either pleasant or unpleasant activities. Psychological satiation is not to be confused with fatigue, even though fatigue symptoms are prominently present. Karsten showed that the symptoms often disappeared with a change of set, even though the same muscular activities might be involved in the new task. For example, a subject who had to quit a line-drawing task because of inability to hold the pencil any longer was asked to write out a description of the psychological processes which had

[17] For reviews of experiments concerned with level of aspiration, see J. D. Frank (1941) and Lewin, Dembo, Festinger, and P. S. Sears (1944).
[18] Karsten (1928).

been involved in the performance, and was able to pick up the pencil and write about the performance with ease, including demonstrations of the task which no longer could be performed!

2. Goals originally unattractive may become acceptable through a change in the meaning of the goal-related activity. There are many teaching techniques which depend upon this principle. Lewin gives a number of examples.[19] One is the changing of food-preferences by telling a story in which the disliked food is the favorite for the hero.[20] This is a common radio device for selling breakfast-foods. Another illustration is the changing of ideologies, as in the experiment of Bavelas (1942) in which relatively autocratic recreation leaders were changed into democratic ones. It was necessary for the cognitive structure of the field, "leadership behavior," to undergo changes so that what they were trying to do as leaders became changed.

3. The choice of goals is influenced by previous experiences of success and failure. This is most clearly shown in the experiments of Sears [21] in which she found that realistic goal-setting was characteristic of those who had experienced success. It is possible to attenuate the bad consequences of failure by teaching more appropriate adjustments to it, thus raising children who can tolerate frustration.[22] But this does not alter the fact that in addition to the problem of how goals affect behavior there exists the very important problem of how goals are chosen.

MEMORY FOR FINISHED AND UNFINISHED TASKS AS ILLUSTRATIVE OF EXPERIMENTS SUGGESTED BY LEWIN'S THEORY

The facts of amnesia show that forgetting and retention are incompletely understood according to our ordinary theories of forgetting through disuse or retroactive inhibition. That there are motivational and emotional factors at work has been emphasized in the Freudian theory of repression.[23] It is in this context

[19] Lewin (1942), pages 235-236.
[20] Duncker (1938).
[21] P. S. Sears (1940) (1941).
[22] Keister (1937).
[23] E.g., R. R. Sears (1936a), Rapaport (1942).

that Zeigarnik's (1927) experiment on the recall of finished and unfinished tasks is to be considered, for the experiment dramatically relates forgetting to tension-systems within the individual as a demonstration of Lewin's (1926) theory.

The subjects (variously students, teachers, children, 256 in all) were given simple tasks to perform. In the individual experiments there were usually 18 to 22 such tasks: modelling a figure from clay, laying out playing blocks in certain forms, solving simple puzzles, and so on. The experimenter interrupted the subject on half the tasks, waiting until the subject was deeply engrossed in it so that it would be a psychologically real interruption. Which tasks were interrupted differed from subject to subject according to conventional experimental practice.

After "tidying up" in order to remove all tools and other reminders of specific tasks, the experimenter asked the subject: "Please tell me what the tasks were upon which you worked during this experiment." Often a number of tasks were mentioned, then a pause would occur. After considerable effort a few more tasks might be recalled. For purposes of scoring, only those tasks were counted which were readily recalled, that is, before the pause. The difficulty of such recall is greater than might be supposed. In one series, 32 subjects recalled between 7 and 19 tasks out of 22 worked on, averaging 11, or just half the total; in another series, 14 subjects recalled between 7 and 16 of 20 tasks, averaging 10, again half the total.

When the relative success of recall for completed or interrupted tasks was examined, it was found that of the first 32 subjects, 26 remembered interrupted tasks better than completed ones, 3 remembered both equally well, and 3 remembered the completed tasks better.

A scoring ratio was devised to indicate the relative superiority of interrupted tasks recalled (I) over completed tasks recalled (C). If both were equally recalled, the ratio would be I/C=1.00. In the first experiment the ratio turned out to be 1.9, indicating that the interrupted tasks were recalled 90% better than the completed ones.[24] Most of the other ratios obtained from groups were

[24] Marrow (1938) has pointed out that the ratio of 1.9 is too high because it is an average of ratios. Corrected as a ratio of tasks recalled it is reduced to 1.6.

in the same direction, that is, above 1.0, although there were wide individual differences.

Zeigarnik went on to test several hypotheses to account for the greater retention of the unfinished tasks, and also to determine the circumstances under which finished tasks would be better recalled.

The first hypothesis tested was that the attention-value of the task might be enhanced by the shock of interruption. When, however, the task was interrupted early in the hour and completed later, it was forgotten like any other completed task, thus contradicting the hypothesis.

A second hypothesis was that the subjects expected the interrupted tasks to be resumed, and therefore made special note of them. However, a test situation in which one group was told that the tasks would be resumed and another that they would not, failed to result in a difference between the groups.

The remaining hypothesis, the one accepted, is that a task not completed leaves a state of tension, a quasi-need. Completing the task means resolving the tension, or discharging the quasi-need. The advantage in memory of the unfinished task is due to the continuation of the tension.

The advantage of unfinished tasks is not to be universally expected. Zeigarnik pointed out at least eight conditions under which the relative advantage is lost:

1. If a task, finished to the experimenter's satisfaction, is considered inadequately completed by the subject, it may be recalled as well as an interrupted task.

2. Tasks which are without a clear-cut completion stage, such as marking X's on a sheet of paper, have no advantage in memory following interruption. Interruption is in such cases not a psychological incompleteness; it is the mere calling of a halt to an endless activity.

3. Subjects who do not become at all involved in the individual tasks, but act according to command, remember finished and unfinished tasks equally well. A group of visiting school children who were set to work when they had come merely to see the laboratory were obedient in this way, and their recall ratio was $I/C=1.03$.

4. If the tasks are seen as leading to the satisfaction of a single

need, so that the boundaries between them are weakened, the individual effects of interruption are lost. One small group of subjects became engrossed in discovering the meaning of the experiment, so that the individual tasks were imbedded in this search for the secret of the experiment. The ratio was I/C=1.12. Another group of subjects was shown in advance all the tasks that were to be solved in the hour. By reducing the separateness of tasks the difference between interruption and completion was lost, with I/C=0.97.

5. If subjects were very tired when performing the experiment and rested when tested, or rested while performing and tired when tested, the memory advantage of unfinished tasks was lost; in fact, for the tired-fresh group, the finished tasks were better recalled (I/C=0.61). An ingenious explanation is offered. It is said that the tension-system cannot be maintained in a loosened, relatively fluid medium, hence memory for the uncompleted tasks is poor in a tired condition. On the other hand, under such circumstances relatively stable systems (finished tasks) persist in spite of the state of fatigue.[25]

6. After delays of 24 hours, the I/C ratio drops to about 1.00, so that there is no longer an advantage for the interrupted task. This is interpreted as due to intervening activity, not to time alone, because of the next observation.

7. If a highly emotional episode is introduced between the tasks and the retest, the same distortion occurs as with the passage of time. Six subjects tested in this way all showed better recall of finished tasks.

8. A task which the subject found too difficult was often forgotten, even thought it had been interrupted. The situation is considered to favor repression.

The practical implications of Mrs. Zeigarnik's findings are somewhat obscure. In the first place, the memory for the tasks performed is a very different matter from memory for what was learned or how to perform the task next time. It would be a mistake to assume that children should not be permitted to com-

[25] The tests were made after 13-15 hours, when the relative advantage of the interrupted task might have been lost in any case. If the conjecture holds, immediate retention after performing while tired should favor the completed tasks.

plete assignments, lest they forget them. They might forget what they *did* in the library on Tuesday afternoon and still remember what they *found out* there. In the second place, the phenomenon is so temporary, and so easily disturbed by other experiences, that its practical meaning is uncertain. It may be that the temporary nature of the effects is due to the triviality of the tasks; if that is so, it is important to have a comparable demonstration made with more significant tasks.

One of the more revealing of the later studies concerned with the problem of recall of the task, is that of Marrow (1938). He explained that he was trying out different sorts of materials, and that if he saw the subject was getting along all right he would stop him and give a new task. Only if the subject was taking unusually long, or having trouble, would he be permitted to finish the task. Under these circumstances, interruption was psychologically interpreted as success, non-interruption as failure. Recall was found to be higher for the *completed* tasks, that is, those which caused feelings of failure. While wholly in agreement with the position that ego-related aspects of the performance are important in the recall, the tension set up is not quite that of task-completion, although it may be related to it in the form: "If only I had another chance at it!"

The type of investigation started by Zeigarnik has proven a stimulus to a great deal of further work.[26] Some of the subsequent studies have been concerned with a slightly different problem—the resumption of the interrupted tasks. It is evident from these studies that correlated with the memory for the task is a tendency to resume it when the opportunity next arises.[27] These studies are consonant with the Lewin interpretation that a quasi-need has been set up as a result of the interruption.

ESTIMATE OF LEWIN'S POSITION

Lewin on the typical problems of learning. Because his is not essentially a psychology of learning, it is difficult to assign Lewin

[26] Illustrative are Abel (1938), Adler and Kounin (1939), Alper (1946), Marrow (1938), Martin (1940), Pachauri (1935), Rosenzweig (1933), Rosenzweig and Mason (1934), Sanford (1946). For summaries of experiments of this kind, see McGeoch (1942), pages 383-386.

[27] E.g., Harrower (1932), Nowlis (1941), Ovsiankina (1928), Rethlingshafer (1941).

a position on each of the standard problems. A large measure of conjecture necessarily enters.

1. *Capacity*. The life space of an adult is more highly differentiated than that of a child. Similarly the life space of an intelligent person is structured more highly than that of a less intelligent person. There are also differences in fluidity or rigidity.[28]

2. *Practice*. Learning may take place with repetition because the change in cognitive structure or in motivation may require repetition. There is, however, no one-to-one relationship between number of trials and the changes which constitute learning.

3. *Motivation*. The differences between reward and punishment are well represented in "topological" diagrams, which point out the difference in the amount of policing required in the two situations. This aspect of reward and punishment had been neglected by all the other writers considered. It is preferable to speak about success and failure rather than about reward and punishment. Then the concepts of ego-involvement and level of aspiration become important. Cognitive structure is both activated by and changed by aroused needs or tensions. Motivation is therefore of central importance within the theory.

4. *Understanding*. Because one of the chief characterizations of learning is as a change in cognitive structure, knowledge and understanding lie at the heart of learning.

5. *Transfer*. Probably the gestalt concept of transposition is acceptable to Lewin.

6. *Forgetting*. Motivated forgetting is important. The dynamics are rather complicated, with interruption in an ego-involved task leading usually to better retention and to attempts at resumption when the opportunity is offered. However, something like repression is accepted, in the forgetting of too difficult tasks.

A psychological theory of motivation essential to learning theory. The relationship of motivation to learning has been increasingly recognized by association theorists, but their usual solutions of the problem have been overly simple, and not well adapted to deal with the complexities of goal-setting, conflict, and problem-solving. The two solutions have been that of the law of effect (and related reinforcement theories), and the addition of set and determining tendencies to ordinary associative

[28] Kounin (1941).

processes. Lewin has made a real contribution by his more dynamic, in some real sense more "psychological," approach to the problem.

Historically there were others making similar proposals. Lewin was undoubtedly influenced by Freud, whose work he thought brilliant but methodologically unsound.[29] In America, McDougall[30] was the arch opponent of behaviorism until gestalt psychology came upon the scene. McDougall often inveighed against the errors of hedonism (in which he classed the law of effect) in placing too much emphasis on what happened in the presence of the goal, and too little on the satisfaction which derived from the striving. Woodworth, whose *Dynamic Psychology* as we have seen gave currency to the notion of drives, included the conception of activity itself becoming a drive. This is an anticipation of Lewin's tension-theory, although Lewin probably was not influenced by it. While Freud, McDougall, and Woodworth were not gestalt psychologists, they saw some of the limitations in contemporary learning theory which Lewin also saw and attempted to meet through his experiments and theories.

A satisfactory psychological theory of motivation is almost certain to include some kind of ego reference, that is, some incorporation of the present activity within the larger goals, values, or ambitions of the learner.[31] Lewin's motivational theories definitely take account of such problems.

The mathematical representation not entirely satisfactory. Lewin's use of vectors and valences leading to locomotion in life space represents a courageous attempt to find a mathematics with a natural "fit" to the kind of data with which he deals. The rather unsatisfactory state of this mathematical structure has been pointed out not only by those impatient with his approach,[32] but by those friendly to his point of view.[33] But the difficulties are

29 Lewin (1937).

30 E.g., McDougall (1923).

31 The problem is discussed by the contributors to a symposium on the ego and the law of effect, Allport (1946), Mowrer (1946), and Rice (1946).

32 E.g., London (1944).

33 E.g., Leeper (1943).

inherent in the early stages of theory construction, and need not prevent appreciation of Lewin's positive suggestions.

His general conception of the relationship between mathematics and the data of a science is sound. There is no question that some forms of mathematics are more appropriate than others. The geometry of spaces does usefully represent alternative routes, conflict, ambivalence, barriers, and many other psychologically real situations. It is the incorporation of metrical concepts of distance, direction, and the like, which causes the most trouble. The usual diagram also best represents the momentary life space. The conversion of this diagram into a third dimensional figure showing the changes in time—with which learning theories are commonly concerned—introduces some awkwardness. As in the case of Hull's mathematical model, a great deal of tinkering is possible in smoothing out the difficulties without destroying the essence of what it is trying to convey.

SUPPLEMENTARY READINGS

BOOKS

Lewin, K. (1935) *A dynamic theory of personality.*
Lewin, K. (1936) *Principles of topological psychology.*
Lewin, K. (1938) *The conceptual representation and the measurement of psychological forces.*

SHORTER INTRODUCTIONS

Leeper, R. (1943) *Lewin's topological and vector psychology, a digest and a critique.*
Lewin, K. (1942) Field theory and learning. *Natl. Soc. Stud. Educ.,* 41st Yearbook, Part II, 215-242.
Lewin, K. (1946) Behavior and development as a function of the total situation. In L. Carmichael, edit., *Manual of child psychology.* New York, Wiley, 791-844.

CRITICAL REVIEWS

Heidbreder, E. (1937) Review of Lewin's *Principles of topological psychology. Psychol. Bull.,* 34, 584-604.
Leeper, R. (1943) *Lewin's topological and vector psychology, a digest and a critique.*
Sears, R. R. (1936) Review of Lewin's *A dynamic theory of personality. Psychol. Bull.,* 33, 548-552.
Woodrow, H. (1939) Review of Lewin's *Conceptual representa-*

tion and the measurement of psychological forces. Psycho-metrika, 4, 175-176.

REPRESENTATIVE EXPERIMENTS

Barker, R. G. (1942) An experimental study of the resolution of conflict by children. In Q. McNemar and M. A. Merrill, edit. *Studies in personality, Contributed in honor of Lewis M. Terman.* New York: McGraw-Hill, 13-34.

Barker, R. G., Dembo, T., and Lewin, K. (1941) Frustration and regression: a study of young children. *Univ. Ia. Stud. Child Welf.*, 18, No. 1.

Bavelas, A. (1942) Morale and the training of leaders. In G. Watson, edit., *Civilian morale.* New York: Houghton Mifflin, 143-165.

Birenbaum, G. (1930) Das Vergessen einer Vornahme. *Psychol. Forsch.*, 13, 218-284.

Dembo. T. (1931) Der Ärger als dynamischen Problem. *Psychol. Forsch.*, 15, 1-144.

Festinger, L. (1942) Wish, expectation, and group standards as factors influencing level of aspiration. *J. abn. (soc.) Psychol.*, 37, 184-200.

Hoppe, F. (1931) Erfolg und Misserfolg. *Psychol. Forsch.*, 14, 1-62,

Karsten, A. (1928) Psychische Sättigung. *Psychol. Forsch.*, 10, 142-254.

Lewin, K., Lippitt, R., and White, R. K. (1939) Patterns of aggressive behavior in experimentally created "social climates." *J. soc. Psychol.*, 10, 271-299.

Ovsiankina, M. (1928) Die Wiederaufnahme unterbrochener Handlungen. *Psychol. Forsch.*, 11, 302-379.

Schwarz, G. (1927) Über Rückfälligkeit bei Umgewöhnung. *Psychol. Forsch.*, 9, 86-158.

Zeigarnik, B. (1927) Das Behalten erledigter und unerledigter Handlungen. *Psychol. Forsch.*, 9, 1-85.

Chapter 9

WHEELER'S ORGANISMIC PSYCHOLOGY

The strong biological flavor which Raymond H. Wheeler places upon his gestalt theory justifies its being called an organismic psychology. While neurologists and pathologists like Gelb and Goldstein [1] had been early affiliated with gestalt psychology, and other biologists have been friendly,[2] Wheeler became the spokesman for the embryological underpinnings for gestalt somewhat as Köhler was the spokesman for its support in the physical sciences.[3] His views are set forth most fully in a general textbook, *The science of psychology*,[4] and in a book intended as an educational psychology, *Principles of mental development*.[5] Because of the biological flavor in his central theories, it is important to examine the kinds of biological evidence which give support to gestalt-like principles.

BIOLOGICAL CONCEPTIONS OF DEVELOPMENT

Organization in amphibian embryos. Nowhere do holistic conceptions receive better support than in the studies of experimental embryology in which masses of cells are transplanted from one part of the developing organism to another, with consequent changes in the organ structures developing from these cells.

The classical work of Driesch (1891) on the sea urchin led him

[1] E.g., Gelb and Goldstein (1918); Goldstein (1939).
[2] E.g., Bertalanffy (1933).
[3] Köhler (1920).
[4] Wheeler (1929) (1940).
[5] Wheeler and Perkins (1932).

to his doctrine that cells are at first "equipotential," that is, can be made to form any portion of the organism. His experiments (without his vitalistic interpretations) have been extended by Spemann (1938) and others, especially with amphibian embryos.

To Spemann we owe the conception of the "organizer," a group of cells from the dorsal lip of the blastopore of the medium-aged gastrula. If a graft of these cells is made into the flank or belly of another developing embryo of about the same age, even one of a different species, the transplant develops into what is essentially a secondary embryo, utilizing the mesoderm of the host embryo along with its own cells. If the host is of a different species, the organs which develop are harmonious, but mottled in appearance, showing the two sources of origin of the cells. Within limits the cells of both transplant and host conform to the pattern induced by the field of the organizer. While the organizer produces a conspicuous and dramatic induction effect, other zones of the developing amphibian work in a somewhat similar manner with respect to more specific structures. The development is progressive, later fields being more specific than earlier ones. The following summary follows Weiss.[6]

The organizer establishes the medullary field. Gradually local subfields emerge, such as those of the eyes, lenses, ears, nose, gills, balancers, mouth, etc. The final outcome is a number of organ rudiments with a high degree of autonomy and self-differentiating power. Weiss concludes that the local subfields established within the "field district" of the organizer[7] are transitory stages as the germ moves from a state of indeterminacy of parts into a final stage where a maximum of definiteness has been acquired by each part.

The in-between stages are represented, for example, by limb buds, which, if transplanted to some inappropriate part of the organism, nevertheless develop as limbs. However, the fate of individual cells is not yet fully determined, for if the limb bud is split in two, two complete limbs develop. Or, if the extra bud

---

[6] P. Weiss (1939), page 356.

[7] Weiss prefers the descriptive designation "chorda-mesodermal field district" to the term "organizer" to avoid the implication that one region has a monopoly on organization.

is superimposed on a normal limb rudiment, only one uniform limb develops.[8]

The problems involved are of great complexity. It is necessary to distinguish between the activating or excitation factors (which account for the influence of transplants of dead tissue or of inert substances), and the organizing field factor which requires a living transplant.[9] But in any case, the use made of the cellular potentials for development is relative to situational factors, and meaningless except in organizational terms.

Among the simpler models to account in part for these complexities is that of the *physiological gradient,* proposed and studied by Child.[10] The gradient corresponds to levels of metabolic activity. Many of the lower invertebrates, such as hydroids and worms, can regenerate after considerable loss of tissue. Intermediate sections of the body, bounded at both head and tail ends by cut surfaces, regenerate a head and a tail according to the original polarity of the organism. It is not necessary that there be some sort of "seed" for a head or a tail; according to the gradient principle, head and tail develop according to the fields created by the gradient, just as a bar magnet if cut develops positive and negative poles like the original magnet.

While this is not the place to consider the problems which these illustrations set for the biologist, the phenomena themselves, however explained, give support to the principle that the whole is more than the sum of its parts, that the part functions in relation to its surrounds, that a part has a number of roles which it can play, if it comes under the influence of differing fields. There is also a developmental arrow in the direction of increasing specificity of the action of the parts as the wholes become more highly evolved and differentiated.

Maturation of behavior patterns in amphibia. Coghill,[11] in his studies of the correlation between growth and behavior in salamanders (amblystoma) came to the conclusion that the organism reacts as a whole, maintaining its integrity at each stage of its development. More specialized bits of behavior, such as re-

[8] The related experiments, by Harrison and others, are cited by P. Weiss (1939), pages 328-329.
[9] P. Weiss (1939), pages 372-373.
[10] E.g., Child (1924).
[11] Coghill (1929) (1933).

flexes, are *differentiated* out of more massive behavior. The conventional position was that habits were developed out of combinations of reflexes, that walking was a combination of reflexes of the legs, trunk, breathing, etc. Coghill's view is that swimming, or walking, come first; out of them are developed the finer coordinations. The primacy of the whole is, of course, one of the foundation stones of gestalt thinking.

The order of new coordinations in the developing embryo is a matter of growth, foreshadowed in anatomy before the behavior appears. Thus a muscle begins to grow and a nerve begins to grow toward it. Not until they are in contact does the muscle function. But this function was already laid down in the pattern of growth. The growth pattern thus anticipates behavior. Many things which might appear to be learned are actually the products of growth. Coghill is impressed by the overgrowth of nervous tissue as providing the structural counterparts of future behavioral forms:

> . . . it is conceivable that in this continuously growing embryonic matrix, neural mechanisms of specific behavior value may arise which have no possibility of immediate expression. Such mechanisms must be organized out of elements of experience, but they are essentially new creations as regards their real identity. They represent such factors of behavior as attitudes which can come to an issue only in the more or less distant future, but which, at the appropriate time, issue in decisive, essentially predetermined action. This predetermination may be regarded, in mechanistic terms, as an act of will. It may arise within the constantly expanding conditioning mechanism by a process of individuation in the same manner as the limb reflex emerges within an expanding total behavior pattern. In the latter case the mechanism is in process of creating a definite end-result for a long period before the end-result is attained. So, also, in the conditioning mechanism it is conceivable that similar creative acts of growth may be in process of eventuation in behavior far in the future. Growth, accordingly, may be conceived as the creative function of the nervous system, not only with regard to the form of the behavior pattern, but also with regard to its control. The creative component of thought, upon this hypothesis, is growth.[12]

With this support from an eminent biologist for a maturational conception of adult processes, Wheeler moved to a full-fledged identification of learning with growth.

[12] Coghill (1929), pages 108-109.

MATURATION AND LEARNING

Learning identified with maturation. All behavior is said by Wheeler to be the result of growth. This includes learned behavior. If salamander embryos "learn" to swim, young birds "learn" to fly, and chicks "learn" to peck by growing older, so also man learns to talk and to play tennis by growing into such modes of behaving. But the later illustrations involve influences not prominent in the earlier ones, for a person learns to talk the specific language which he hears, and learns to play tennis only if given the opportunity and the arbitrary rules of the game.

There is inferred a principle which may be called *stimulation-induced maturation*.[13] That is, in addition to the maturation which takes place through intrinsic growth factors as a result of getting older, as in the case of developing embryos, there is a supplementary growth process induced by the conditions of stimulation. It is this latter growth which is said to underlie learning. "The difference between one performance and the next during a learning process transcends repetition; it is the result of an emergent, creative process of growth, or maturation." [14]

The one kind of maturation, that which is correlated with age, may be referred to as *age-maturation*. That the older child has capacities not found in the younger child is almost a truism, and while theories of maturation are a source of controversy, the general facts of age-maturation are accepted by all. The second kind of maturation, induced by stimulation, is more controversial, especially as applied to short practice periods over which age-maturation remains essentially constant. The presence of growth underlying learning in this second sense must be accepted as a bold hypothesis. The possibility has occurred to other writers before Wheeler. William James, for example, tacitly accepted both kinds of maturation. His doctrine of the transitoriness of instinct ("striking while the iron is hot") implied age-maturation; his suggestion that we learn to swim in winter and to skate in summer implied stimulation-induced maturation.[15]

[13] Doré and Hilgard (1937).

[14] Wheeler (1940), page 244. By permission Thomas Y. Crowell Co.

[15] James (1890). Transitoriness of instinct is discussed on pages II, 398-402; the statement about swimming and skating, credited to an unnamed German author, appears on page I, 110.

The results of some experiments testing the hypothesis of stimulation-induced maturation will be reported later in this chapter as illustrative of the kind of studies to which Wheeler's theory leads.

Pacing. The relationship between an imposed task (like learning to speak or to read English or to play chess) and growth is emphasized in the concept of *pacing*. Pacing refers to adjusting the task to the learner's present level of capacity (his level of insight), increasing the difficulty of the task as the learner grows. Under proper arrangements, he would learn without error, for errors and fumbling are indications that the presented task is beyond the learner's insight level.

Pacing is a plausible enough principle, regardless of one's theory. The advantages of distributed over massed practice are so nearly universal for motor skills that the generalization is one of the best established in the experimental study of learning. But there is no completely satisfactory theory as to the precise advantage to be expected from rests between trials. Wheeler's principle suggests that within a fairly wide range of conditions there ought to be growth at a rate characteristic of the individual. The growth potential may be raised by stimulation, so that growth takes place which would not take place without practice. Overstimulation, however, easily leads to poor conditions of learning.

The advantages of rest, after a condition of stimulation, are: (1) to allow the energy supply to be replenished, (2) to overcome the effects of any overstimulation, and (3) to permit maturation.[16] Overstimulation results in faulty energy distributions. These are evidenced in irradiation patterns, as described by Snoddy (1920). In motor learning these patterns are shown in tenseness and incoördination. To some extent the energy distribution has become more diffuse, reversing the maturational trend. Maturation results in more highly differentiated energy patterns.

There are really two aspects to the problem of pacing, related to the two sorts of maturation. At any given age, there are problem situations appropriate for the learner and others inappropriate. Such a conception is widely accepted by educators in the construction of school curricula, under such names as reading readiness, grade placement, scope and sequence, and so on.

[16] Wheeler and Perkins (1932), page 341.

Except for matters of details, there is no controversy here. The older child is capable of a wider range of activities than the younger child, and it is foolhardy to introduce activities too early. The second aspect refers to learning over much shorter time spans. Then the problem becomes that of interpreting the gains within a few practice trials as evidence of maturation. It is this conception of maturation which is foreign to usual thinking about learning.

LEARNING AND THE LAWS OF DYNAMICS

The laws and their use in prediction. In keeping with the scientific outlook of the classical gestalt writers, Wheeler sees his task as that of promoting a new conception of nature. The laws of learning are to be thought of as merely specifications within the laws of dynamics which apply not only within perception, emotion, and the other fields of psychology, but within all of natural science. The laws, briefly characterized, were as follows in 1932: [17]

1. The law of field properties. "A whole is more than the sum of its parts."
2. The law of derived properties. "Parts derive their properties from wholes."
3. The law of determined action. "The whole determines the activities of its parts."
4. The law of individuation. "Parts of wholes come into existence through an emergence process called individuation, or structurization, or differentiation."
5. The law of field genesis. "Wholes evolve as wholes."
6. The law of least action. "Units of energy multiplied by units of time are, for a given set of conditions, a minimum."
7. The law of maximum work. "First, . . . any influence affecting a system of energy affects it throughout . . . Second, in an energy system a maximum amount of energy, for any given set of conditions, will be expended in the course of maintaining balance."
8. The law of configuration. "A system of energy always functions as a unit, and always adjusts itself to a multitude of disturbing influences."

The set of laws underwent a slight modification in 1940, the law of field genesis being omitted, and the law of reciprocal

[17] Wheeler and Perkins (1932), pages 18-33.

change appearing as a newcomer. The new law is not given a succinct statement, but the following quotation expresses its gist:

The expression "reciprocal change" comes from the fact that parts structured very much alike in the same whole (homogeneity of the whole) behave in a manner very much unlike one another (their paths or functions are dissimilar—heterogeneity of action); whereas, when the parts become specialized in their structure and function (heterogeneity) they "cooperate" in the execution of a single (homogeneous) act. Heterogeneity and homogeneity exchange places.[18]

These organismic laws or laws of dynamics have a very different flavor from, say, Hull's postulates, or the Carr-Robinson laws of association. They reflect the results of experimental embryology in respect to the relationships between wholes and parts, and of modern physics in respect to energy interchanges. This is an audacious proposal for the organization of psychological knowledge, with some a priori considerations in its favor. The difficulties which it confronts are those of specification, in order that the application of the laws to psychological problems may be logically firm and not on the basis of gross analogy. Wheeler anticipates these criticisms by arguing for stages in scientific prediction, the first of which does not require the precision of the later stages.

Scientific predictions, according to Wheeler, may occur at any of three stages. A *Stage One* prediction is based on a gross and rather undifferentiated comprehension of the situation, but permits the assertion that an event will or will not occur. That a body when dropped will fall, that a rat long deprived of food will eat, are illustrative of Stage One predictions. *Stage Two* predictions introduce a crude mensuration by introducing judgments of "more than" or "less than." Thus to predict that a rat deprived of food for twenty-four hours will run faster than one deprived of food for twelve hours is such a prediction. Most of our quantitative experiments in psychology are Stage Two predictions, because they depend on critical ratios which tell us only that one condition is "probably" more favorable than another. Finally, there are *Stage Three* predictions which specify events with precision. Of the writers considered, only Hull really attempts Stage Three prediction.

[18] Wheeler (1940), page 274. By permission Thomas Y. Crowell Co.

The laws of dynamics as applied to psychology do not all permit Stage Three predictions. To ask this of them is not only asking too much, but is also misunderstanding the way in which scientific predictions are actually made.

The primacy of wholes over parts. In the original set of laws, the first five of the eight ring changes on the principle that wholes take precedence over parts. Wholes exist in their own right (law of field properties); they regulate the properties and activities of their parts (laws of derived properties and determined action); parts are differentiated out of wholes (law of individuation); wholes emerge as wholes (law of field genesis). The eighth law might also be added to these. The whole responds as a whole to disturbances (law of configuration).

All of these laws make predictions at Stage One. They state only the more general circumstances by which it can be predicted whether or not an event will occur. Thus learning will occur only if the wholes present are such as will be grasped as wholes by the learner; parts will be learned only if their meanings as derived from the whole are understood, and so on. The laws are all essentially corollaries of the main principle that wholes have primacy over parts.

The whole-part problem is the source of much confusion as between association and field theories. The difficulties are in part linguistic, but they go deeper than that. To say that wholes result from the integration of parts or that they result from closure *could* mean the same thing, but as used by the two groups of writers there is a difference. The difference lies in the identifiability of the part after it is integrated into the whole. The conventional association-type theories suppose that the part retains its identity, so that if several habits cooperate, their strengths are additive, according to some sort of formula (not necessarily direct algebraic addition). A separate weakening of one habit of the complex will weaken the complex by the amount attributed (by formula) to that component. The theory is somewhat that of multiple correlation, in which each of the test components is given its weight in a regression equation. This logic of summation, with the part identifiable and separable as a part, is the logic of the association position. The equations of interaction may, to be sure, provide for considerable complexity beyond algebraic summation, as they do, in fact, in a multiple regression equation. In a multiple regression equation, a higher or lower score on a given test enters directly into the equation, as the summative logic suggests. But if the same test is repeated twice, the score is not entered at double its original value but allowance is made for reliability and test intercorrelations. The technique of empirical validation thus makes the necessary corrections. Therefore the whole is somewhat different from the sum of its parts, even in this situation.

The closure theory of the formation of wholes rejects the logic of summation, for the part is *lost* in the whole, as a drop of mercury is lost when it coalesces with another drop. By *weight*, the new drop is the sum of the old drops, but by *number* of drops the parts are lost. The new drop may be made into any number of new droplets. The quality of being a "drop" is the result of closure. If one sticks to measuring "weights" instead of "drops," the summation principle is satisfactory.

It is not the facts in this situation which cause the controversy, but the implications for psychology. Reduced to simplest terms we might ask, Are habits more like "weights" or like "drops"? The answer, as in the story of the blind man and the elephants, is that habits are like both, and the question as stated is unanswerable. So another question has to be asked: Is it scientifically more fruitful to treat behavior according to concepts like "weight" or according to concepts like "drops"? It is here that we come to the parting of the ways.

The associationists in general were clearly on the side of "weights." Perhaps the clearest denouncement of the opposing point of view was that of A. P. Weiss, who accused some modern physicists of misunderstanding their own science by accepting emergent ("droplike") concepts.[19] Unless science deals with things that can be scaled, and enter into equations in which the variables remain identified, how can there be a science? The argument that the properties of water (H_2O) cannot be inferred from a knowledge of hydrogen and oxygen is beside the point. Have not physics and chemistry advanced further by treating water as H_2O than as something wet which can be frozen into ice?

[19] A. P. Weiss (1929), page 55.

The argument by gestalt and organismic psychologists must take the form that it is *scientifically more fruitful* to treat the data of psychology in accordance with its emergent wholeness characters. Nobody denies these characters, and it is futile to argue the point that a triangle is more than three lines or that an organism is more than the stuff into which it could be analyzed in the chemist's laboratory. There is a choice as to the level of analysis to be attempted; which choice is made must be defended according to its consequences, not because it is the only choice permitted by the facts of nature. Nature does not determine that mercury is to be measured in drops or in grams, but there is a stubborn and somewhat coercive character about the kinds of events in nature which can be ordered under one or the other kind of measurement. Just as Skinner finds a reflex unit the one most natural for his analysis, gestalt psychologists find organized and isolatable wholes the most natural units for their analysis. The ultimate success in system-making whereby all the facts are dealt with coherently and parsimoniously is the final criterion of choice. Before that ultimate showdown, personal preferences enter into the choice.

By accepting a higher level analysis, one nearer to the level of organization at which our own more interesting behavior goes on, organismic psychology is ready to surge ahead with the analysis of problem-solving and linguistic behavior—problems late in the program of the one who builds from the bottom up, from more "weight"-like concepts instead of "drop"-like ones. Whether one approach can ever be translated into the other, *i.e.*, satisfactorily account for the same order of phenomena, remains to be seen.

In any case, the relationship between wholes and parts is to be taken seriously *as a relationship*. It solves the problem no more to say that wholes have primacy over parts than to say that wholes are composed of parts. There is an interaction between wholes and parts which constitutes the real problem, and whether one starts with wholes or starts with parts, there will undoubtedly be some kind of meeting-place as the essential interaction is recognized. Thus every medical specialist has to be increasingly aware that he is treating a whole organism, and he can be greatly misled if he treats isolated symptoms. The person who comes to the eye doctor may need psychiatric advice instead of spectacles; but he sometimes needs spectacles. If the specialist, concerned with the part, understands the relationship of the part to the whole, his specialty is useful. The ophthalmologist need not throw away his box of lenses because someone says that we must always treat the whole organism.

The transplantation and regeneration experiments upon which Wheeler so greatly leans for evidence on the primacy of wholes are themselves good illustrations of the cautions needed, and the importance of not riding one alternative to the exclusion of another. In the contrast between preformation and epigenesis, the evidence leans increasingly toward epigenesis,[20] which is the position which Wheeler favors. Yet it would be a mistake to suppose that the cellular material is entirely indifferent, or, in other words, that the part does not matter. In many experiments, a transplant conforms to the formative tendencies of the area in which it is placed, but in other cases the tissue develops in such a manner as to conform to the donor region from which the graft was taken rather than to the host region into which it was put.[21]

The following summary of an experiment is instructive:

The head of the young larva of the *newt* carries ventrolaterally two rod-like excrescences, the so-called *balancers*. The larva of the *axolotl*, on the other hand, lacks them. The problem was to find out whether the balancer field of the newt, if confronted with undetermined axolotl ectoderm would be able to make these latter cells of a balancerless species form a balancer. Thus, belly ectoderm from a young axolotl germ was grafted over the lateral head region of a newt larva prior to the time when the balancer was due to appear. *No balancer developed in the strange skin graft.* The axolotl cells apparently did not know how to respond to the strange newt demand. In the reciprocal experiment, however, *belly ectoderm of a newt* (the balancered species) *when grafted over the head region of the axolotl* (the normally balancerless form) *did develop a balancer.*[22]

This concession must be made to the influence of the part: "*A field cannot make any cell produce any specific response unless that cell is intrinsically prepared to do so.*"[23]

[20] E.g., P. Weiss (1939), page 478.
[21] P. Weiss (1939), pages 356-373.
[22] P. Weiss (1939), pages 362-363. From *Principles of Development* by Paul Weiss. Copyright, 1939, by Henry Holt and Company, Inc.
[23] P. Weiss (1939), page 359.

Somewhat the same precautions are needed in the interpretation of the developmental sequences of behavior as studied by Coghill. In higher forms there are many more segmental activities than Coghill found in amblystoma. The first activities in the chick or the guinea pig are found to be specific movements, not massive responses.[24]

In other words, the service which gestalt psychologists do in calling attention to organizational principles is useful if it brings into focus the many problems in the relationships between wholes and parts. If, however, all that happens is to shift a preference from the primacy of parts to the primacy of wholes, many important experimental findings will be glossed over.

Energy interchanges. The remaining laws in Wheeler's original list are those of least action and maximum work, both concerned with energy interchanges, deriving from physics rather than from biology. The law of least action is considered central to scientific prediction. "This is nature's universal law of economy or parsimony. It is with this law (and its corollaries) that the scientist makes his predictions at Stages Two and Three." [25]

The law of least action is stated: *When action is defined as units of energy multiplied by units of time, movement occurs from one position to the other, over the shortest possible path.*[26] This is a law in physics, holding for isolated systems, but Wheeler believes its significance to be much more general: ". . . it makes no difference whether we express the Law of Least Action as the physicist does nowadays by an equation or whether we express it as its founders did centuries ago in ordinary words, *it is the same law.*" [27] This ordinary law is that under a given set of conditions only one course of action will occur. In that form it is, indeed, part of the scientist's credo.

While the physicist is able to make Stage Three predictions under these energy laws, the psychologist must content himself with Stage Two predictions. He will thus predict a preference for one path in a maze over another, without dealing with the actual energy interchanges. This is Wheeler's reply to such crit-

[24] Orr and Windle (1934), Carmichael (1934), Carmichael (1946).
[25] Wheeler (1940), page 40.⎫
[26] Wheeler (1940), page 40.⎬By permission Thomas Y. Crowell Co.
[27] Wheeler (1940), page 55.⎭

icisms as those of Guthrie that the psychologist does not deal with isolated energy-systems.[28]

Rats in mazes, other things equal, do tend to take the shorter of two paths to a goal, and to choose the confinement compart-

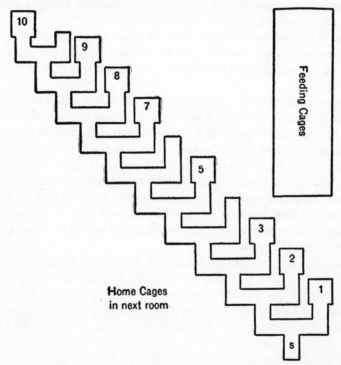

FIGURE 32. MAZE IN WHICH RATS TAKE THE LONGER PATH TO FOOD.
In the choice between food in box 10 and in any of the boxes 3, 5, 7, or 9, open on the right, rats preferred the longer path. From Snygg (1936) as reproduced in Wheeler (1940), page 263. By permission Thomas Y. Crowell Co.

ment which means less delay toward the goal. Wheeler is not alone in seeing this principle of parsimony as an important one.[29]

The principle is a useful one to illustrate the difference between a field law and an association law. This is distinctly a field-type of law, making predictions on the basis of very general

[28] Guthrie (1935), pages 15-18.
[29] Helson (1927), Gengerelli (1928), Adams (1931), Tolman (1932b), Waters (1937), have all accepted a principle like least effort.

relationships within the total organism-environment interaction. The contrary approach is illustrated in Hull's derivation of the preference for the shorter of two paths on the basis of principles making use of no such general tendency to take the easier way. Running along the shorter paths simply gets more strongly reinforced, and so wins out in the competition.[30]

An experiment of Snygg (1936) in which rats took the longer path to food is, paradoxically enough, better support for Wheeler's principle than for Hull's. The maze design was that pictured in Figure 32.

Suppose, for example, that food may be found either in Box 5 or in Box 10. The path to Box 5 is of course shorter. But will the rat choose that path? It is easier for the rat to follow the left wall, and not to have to "count" than it is for it to find Box 5, which is nearer. Therefore the rat takes the longer path. The controls that are needed are the number of trials to learn when either one box is open. If it is easier to learn to go to Box 10, the prediction then follows: Snygg showed both that it was easier to learn to go to Box 10 and that that was what the rat would do if given a chance.

A strict test of the reinforcement hypothesis would require that the length of the path actually run by the rat when going to Box 5 during training was shorter than that taken to Box 10. But of course there are features which Hull can also invoke, such as the more regular anticipatory tendencies which may get strengthened when all turns are to the left.

The law of maximum work is stated: *For any given set of conditions all of the available potential energy of the whole will be expended in the course of maintaining a condition of equilibrium or balance, i.e., in preserving its status quo.*[31]

This law of self-preservation does not contradict the law of least action. It signifies the amount of energy available for expenditure under the principle of least action.

The law of maximum work is plausible on clinical grounds, but it is difficult to state it precisely for experimental work. It is like Cannon's principle of homeostasis,[32] which states that the

[30] Hull (1932).
[31] Wheeler (1940), page 104. By permission Thomas Y. Crowell Co.
[32] Cannon (1929).

regulatory mechanisms of the body get mobilized to preserve the internal state of equilibrium, such as the normal temperature. A drowning man will not save his energy for the hike he was planning for the next weekend. When there is a serious enough threat, all resources of energy are called upon to maintain or restore equilibrium. Like the law of least action, it is a good representative of field-type laws, which might be tailored in such a manner as to make a real contribution to problems of motivation.

The newcomer to the list of laws—the law of reciprocal change—is hard to classify, although it is also a law of wholes and of parts. It presumably refers to such a contrast as that between anarchy, in which every man is king (homogeneity of structure, heterogeneity of action) and a totalitarian state, in which there is division of labor, but in the service of a highly integrated common end (heterogeneity of structure, homogeneity of action). The attempt to deal by means of this law with the randomness in early trials of trial-and-error learning and the predictability of part-actions later is not very successful, although there is some analogy between the learning illustration and the political illustration above. Before control is achieved, one movement is as good as another; after control is achieved, a variety of specific movements fall into line with the total activity pattern.

Wheeler's laws, on the surface, are more inviting than the laws of organization proposed by the gestalt psychologists following Wertheimer, as described in Chapter 7. They are not bound as closely to visual perception, and have a somewhat richer dynamic setting. They are used so loosely, however, that despite the excuses that predictions are at Stages One or Two, it is not possible to infer at present what could be done with such a set of laws if they were worked over carefully, somewhat after the manner of Hull's use of his postulates. A good set of organismic laws would aid greatly in the systematization of psychological knowledge. But such a set of laws requires statement in mutually exclusive form, and in sufficient precision to permit refutation or emendation as empirical data require. Wheeler's laws are not stated in this way, nor are they used in this self-correcting manner.

EXPERIMENTS RELEVANT TO WHEELER'S HYPOTHE-
SIS OF STIMULATION-INDUCED MATURATION

One of the most practical proposals which Wheeler has made is that of the appropriate arrangement of practice which he calls *pacing*. It is plausible that material to be learned should be adjusted to the learning rate of the individual, and this practical suggestion does not actually depend for its value on a further implication of the concept of pacing. This further implication is that learning rate has some of the properties of growth, that is, that it is a process characteristic of the individual which goes along at its own rate *within wide limits of stimulation*. All maturation doctrines assume that the organism is affected by its environment to some extent, at least to the point of maintaining its nutrition. But the maturation concept, as usually understood, is that within wide ranges of environment, the intrinsic growth potential is still exhibited. If practice is delayed for one of two equivalent learners, the later learner "catches up" in spite of the excessive stimulation received by the first (e.g., J. R. Hilgard, 1933).

The hypothesis of stimulation-induced maturation differs from the usual maturation hypothesis only in that it proposes that a specific kind of maturation can be imposed upon the general maturational attainment. In other words, learning how to typewrite or to send telegraph code does not arise as a consequence simply of growing older; it requires a specific kind of stimulation. But this stimulation induces growth which is not unlike general maturation. Just as the child learns to walk when it is old enough and not before (assuming sufficient food and exercise prior to this attainment), so the learner can type sixty words per minute when he has been exposed to typewriters long enough and not before (assuming sufficient practice, but within a wide range of tolerance).

Wheeler sometimes solves the problem carelessly by definition. All change is growth. Learning is change. Therefore, learning is growth. But the hypothesis can be stated in a form to make prediction. The form of statement is as follows: *For any given learner, the rate of improvement in a specialized perceptual-*

motor function within wide limits of practice and rest corresponds more nearly to the total time elapsed from the beginning of practice than to the fraction of this total time spent in practice.

Some looseness enters into what shall be considered "wide limits of practice and rest," but this is permissible at Stage Two. For different tasks these limits might be very different. Nobody would argue for wide differences if the amounts of practice were barely discriminable. But if it turns out that of two learners of equal capacity and previous training one practices twice or three times as much as another and ends after a period of elapsed time with about the same score, this will be acceptable evidence. Beyond these limits it is supposed that there are two extremes, one of understimulation, another of overstimulation. The extreme of understimulation is no practice at all; under these circumstances no growth is expected. There must then be both threshold and marginal conditions below the range of "normal" growth. This would correspond in the case of bodily growth to diets which permitted life to be maintained, but dwarfed the organism. At the other extreme is overstimulation which interferes with normal growth through producing what Wheeler describes as irradiation patterns. Whether there is a nutritional analogy is not clear, though it is a not unreasonable conjecture that greatly overfeeding a young organism might also interfere with its normal growth and development. Related phenomena are those of getting stale through overpractice or getting muscle-bound through overexercising in certain ways.

Prediction according to the hypothesis of stimulation-induced maturation is more precise than according to the principle that distribution is to be favored over massing, for it suggests *how much* advantage favorable distribution should bring. Within a wide range, improvement should follow the same general curve of improvement when measured in units of *elapsed time*, even though one arrangement is more favorable than another in units of *trials*. The uniform time curve thus serves to predict the amount of advantage to be found in the trials curve.

Experiments with the pursuit rotor. While some preliminary experimentation was done on the problem of stimulation-induced maturation in the Kansas laboratory under Wheeler's supervision, it did not come to publication. The first experiment to be de-

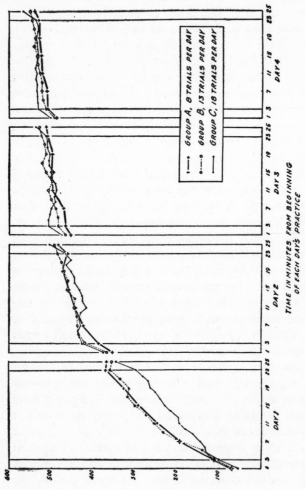

FIGURE 33. SCORES ON THE PURSUIT ROTOR WHICH CORRESPOND MORE NEARLY TO ELAPSED TIME THAN TO NUMBER OF TRIALS SPENT IN PRACTICE.

During the first day the overcrowding effect depresses the scores of the group with the greatest amount of time in practice, but with the shortest rest periods. Scoring level becomes essentially alike on the later days, although by the end of practice the groups have had 3^2, 5^2, and 72 trials, respectively. From Hilgard and Smith (1942).

signed for the express purpose of testing the hypothesis was that of Doré and Hilgard (1937). Although the practice period was a single hour, the relationships predicted by the hypothesis held fairly well, as shown below. The second column shows the usual

TOTAL MINUTES OF PRACTICE AND TOTAL ELAPSED TIME REQUIRED TO ACHIEVE A STANDARD GAIN IN SCORE WITH DIFFERENT DISTRIBUTIONS OF PRACTICE AND REST *

Arrangement of Practice and Rest	Minutes of Practice Required to Gain 200 Score Points	Minutes of Elapsed Time Required to Gain 200 Points
A: 1-minute practice, 11 minutes rest	3	36
B: 1-minute practice, 3 minutes rest	4	16
C: 1-minute practice, 1 minute rest	8	16
D: 3-minute practice, 1 minute rest	12	16

* Doré and Hilgard (1937). Modified from Table 2, p. 252.

results of experiments with distributed practice. That is, the more closely trials are crowded together, the more trials are required for a comparable gain. But the last column bears directly on the hypothesis. Except for Group A, which would represent a case of understimulation, the other three groups all gain at the same rate in time (i.e., the same gain in 16 minutes) in spite of amounts of practice differing from 4 to 8 to 12 trials of the same length. This greater correspondence with elapsed time than with number of trials, over a range of stimulation, is exactly what the hypothesis of stimulation-induced maturation would predict.

Because the experiment all takes place within a single hour, it seems somewhat bizarre as a test of growth. But there is no a priori reason why growth should not take place fairly promptly, as indeed it must if it is to underlie learning.

In order to answer any objections arising out of the short practice period in the experiment of Doré and Hilgard, another experiment of similar sort was done over a four-day period, each subject maintaining his same distribution of practice and rest within the day.[33] The performance curves for three groups of subjects over the four-day period are shown in Figure 33.

[33] Hilgard and Smith (1942).

The groups end essentially alike, although Group A has had a total of 32 trials, Group B a total of 52 trials, and Group C a total of 72 trials by the end of the fourth day. Group C, the deviant group on the first day, showed the deleterious effects of *over*stimulation. But these bad effects were recovered from before the end of the experiment. It will be recalled that in the Doré and Hilgard experiment the unfavored group was due to *under*stimulation. Within these two experiments, then, we have something of the definition of the favorable amounts of stimulation. One-minute trials with rest intervals of 1 to 3 minutes result in essentially comparable progress; if the rest interval is reduced to 20 seconds, scores are reduced (at least during the first hour); if the rest intervals are increased to 11 minutes, scores are also reduced (at least during the first hour). Intervals between 3 and 11 minutes have not been studied, so that 3 minutes is not an outside limit for favorable score changes.

These two experiments, although illustrative of the principle and not contradictory to it, have one important flaw. That is that the total time in the experimental room is constant for all learners, and overnight rests are equal in length for all. The hypothesis is not confirmed when a single rest of 1 minute to 36 hours is introduced between two trials of a 20-trial series. Then the final scores after 20 trials correspond more nearly to the number of trials than to the total elapsed time.[34] Human learning is too complicated to be explained by a single hypothesis. This does not mean necessarily that the hypothesis is to be rejected, but that it can stand only if supplementary hypotheses can be found to square those facts which it does not comprehend. Bell's experiment definitely contradicts the hypothesis as stated, and the contradiction is serious because it is within the same sort of learning as that studied by Doré and Hilgard and by Hilgard and Smith.

Mirror-vision coordination. Another experiment offers data which can be analyzed for agreement or disagreement with the hypothesis. That is the experiment on mirror-star-tracing reported by Snoddy (1945). The subject moves a stylus through a notched path around a star-shaped figure viewed in a mirror, attempting to avoid contact with the sides of the path. The scoring system used results in a rising curve, roughly of logarithmic

[34] Bell (1942).

form, such as the curves obtained on the pursuit rotor. One group made one circuit of the star per day for each of the 40 days. Another group made 10 continuous circuits per day, but worked only on alternate days. Under the circumstances the usual advantages of distributed practice were found, the group with one trial per day being ahead on all circuit-by-circuit comparisons after the first circuit.[35] Because the experiment covered so many days it is a convenient one to use for a test of the hypothesis of stimulation-induced maturation. Are the scores at the beginning of a day later in practice more nearly a function of the amount of preceding practice or of the amount of elapsed time?

The answer is given in Figure 34, reconstructed from Snoddy's data. The correspondence between the two curves is nearly perfect, thus conforming to the hypothesis. Because one group made a single circuit each day, and the other 10 circuits each day, comparison can be made strictly for only the first trials on days when both groups were practicing. Groups A and B gain similar amounts over 5 days although one has had 5 circuits, the other 21 at the time of the comparison; they gain similar amounts in 7 days of experimentation, although by then Group A has had 7 trials, Group B, 31 trials. This is an arrangement superior to that of the pursuit rotor experiments because longer time intervals are allowed between practice periods. It is complicated by the variation at once of the length of the practice session and the inter-session interval. A more satisfactory agreement with the stimulation-maturation hypothesis could not be asked for. Under two different conditions, scores are much more alike when expressed according to elapsed time than when expressed according to trials.

As in the case of the pursuit experiment, many of the arrangements of the mirror-drawing experiments yield data which do not support the hypothesis.[36] Recent experiments with nonsense syllable learning also have failed to verify the hypothesis.[37] The reality of the phenomena implied by the hypothesis of stimu-

[35] Snoddy (1945), page 406.
[36] Unpublished recomputations of the data in Snoddy (1935) by the author show the same sorts of contradiction between data and hypothesis as those in Bell's data.
[37] Taylor and Wright (1947).

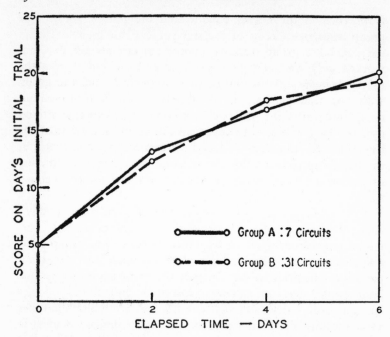

FIGURE 34. SCORES IN A MIRROR-VISION COORDINATION EXPERIMENT WHICH CORRESPOND MORE NEARLY TO ELAPSED TIME THAN TO NUMBER OF TRIALS SPENT IN PRACTICE.

The trials plotted are the first which occurred at the stated number of days from the start of practice, although one group had 10 trials every other day, while the second group had a single trial every day. Scores are essentially alike despite the difference in amount of time spent in practice. Curves constructed from data presented in different form by Snoddy (1945).

lation-induced maturation are therefore seriously in doubt, unless plausible accounts can be given of the many exceptions to its predictions.

The reasons for selecting this particular hypothesis and the experiments testing it are two. First, several of the experiments were definitely suggested by Wheeler's theory. It is one of the advantages of a theory to be fertile enough to propose experiments testing its suggestions. Second, the fact that the experiments tend in some measure to refute the hypothesis shows that it is possible to state a theory like Wheeler's in specific enough form to be subject to experimental correction. It is characteristic of useful hypotheses that experiments may either support or challenge them.

There is a further lesson to be learned from these experiments. A few cases of agreement are not enough to establish an hypothesis. Agreement with the hypothesis of some of the data from pursuit learning and mirror drawing makes it more interesting, but does not make it true. Hypotheses are never confirmed. They are only made increasingly plausible if, after many tests, they are still in the running. The search for the crucial experiment, while not doomed to failure, is an arduous one, and comes best after science is far along systematically.

ESTIMATE OF WHEELER'S POSITION

The typical problems of learning. Wheeler has given more direct discussion of the problems of learning than any other gestalt psychologist, so that his position can be summarized with somewhat greater assurance than that of the others.

1. *Capacity*. Capacities are the result of maturation, but maturation is itself induced by stimulation. Therefore Wheeler is more of an environmentalist than most gestalt psychologists.

2. *Practice*. Within repetitions there is stimulation to maturation. Once a process is started, it keeps going unless something stops it; habits persist because of inertia. Growth may take place between repetitions.

3. *Motivation*. All learning is goal-seeking. If rewards are to be effective they must really be identified with the goal. "Mastering a task in an adequate and efficient fashion, for the sake of the knowledge and use that the mastery of the task is to give the individual, should be the true reward of the learning process." [38] Feelings are not to be interpreted as motives; they are symptoms. Pleasure and annoyance should be used as signs as to how the learning process is going, not as a method of promoting learning.

4. *Understanding*. All learning is meaningful, insightful. Therefor, it is essentially cognitive. Insight has an "expanding, emerging" character, so that insightful learning leads to further insightful learning.

5. *Transfer*. Transfer requires making the same response in a

[38] Wheeler (1940), page 37.

new situation which was made in an older one. " 'Transfer' can take place, then, only when the two tasks are so similar that the learner can apprehend them in the same whole, that is, perceive that the responses learned in the first task fit the second." [39]

When transfer occurs, it is the whole system conditioning the activities of its parts. Wheeler sets this principle in oppostition to the principle of identical elements.

6. *Forgetting.* Wheeler objects to the memory-trace theory as proposed by Köhler and Koffka. His "non-process" theory is said to be one having to do exclusively with the present. This makes little difference in practice, for some representation of the past remains to influence the present perceptual fields. Forgetting is said to be an active learning process, an effort to continue learning under adverse conditions, i.e., in the absence of sufficient cues.

The phenomena of retroactive inhibition are accepted, interpreted as negative transfer.

The laws of dynamics used uncritically. Because he plays up every contrast, familiarity with Wheeler's system is a useful antidote for those who find no essential difference between associationist and organismic thinking. It is unfortunate for his own case that the hortatory and polemic style leads to extravagance of statement and provokes resistance in the reader. The system is a provocative one, and might in other hands have become an elegant one as well. The laws are so extended by analogy that their edges are blurred, and illustrations cannot be used to discover the separate principles intended by each of the laws. The energy laws, which are given the most precise statement, are used without evidence of reflection upon the difficulties to be encountered in their application to psychological data. They are presented as true and as of exceptionless validity. In the present state of psychological science, what is needed is provisional laws, held subject to tests of their validity in relation to the data and events which we seek to understand.

Intimacy between growth and learning. The vigorous manner in which Wheeler has called for acceptance of the findings of experimental embryology, and the implications of such findings, is wholesome. There are indeed "fields" in the growing organism

[39] Wheeler and Perkins (1932), page 321.

which have to be treated in terms of organization and not in terms of composition. That similar processes go on in the adult organism is not a bizarre suggestion. Maturation has usually been studied as one of the competitors to learning in the development of behavior. Wheeler has attempted in his own way to assimilate such concepts to each other, especially through the principle of pacing. While experiments on stimulation-induced maturation give ambiguous or negative results, there are practical schoolroom experiments which add some validation to the close correspondence between learning rate and growth rate.[40]

More down-to-earth experimentation needed. There is a balance between audacious theorizing and cautious empirical investigation which will in the end help us in our quest for a science of learning. Experimentation upon learning within gestalt psychology of the classical school (Wertheimer, Köhler, Koffka) and within Wheeler's Americanized version, has been all too much concerned with illustrating a point of view already adopted rather than with filling in the gaps of knowledge about the relationship of learning outcomes to the numerous variables known to affect such outcomes. In order for the teachings of gestalt psychology to be assimilated to the ongoing body of scientific knowledge about learning, someone needs to do for gestalt psychology what Hull has been doing for behaviorism, that is, to state the laws or postulates more clearly and precisely, and then to design experiments which will true up these laws for the purposes of scientific prediction in terms of the detailed circumstances under which learning occurs.[41] The suggestions by the gestalt psychologists have been sufficiently fertile that the carrying out of such a program of extension and validation holds rich promise.

[40] Olson and Davis (1941).

[41] Wheeler states that we have been struggling to get our guiding principles clear, and that the years ahead call for "a much more accurate set of predictions made available by painstaking experimental work" (Wheeler, 1940, page 417).

SUPPLEMENTARY READINGS

BOOKS

Wheeler, R. H. (1929) (1940) *The science of psychology.*
Wheeler, R. H. (1932) *The laws of human nature.*
Wheeler, R. H. and Perkins, F. T. (1932) *Principles of mental development.*

SHORTER INTRODUCTIONS

Wheeler, R. H. (1935) Organismic vs. mechanistic logic. *Psychol. Rev.,* 42, 335-353.
Wheeler, R. H. (1935) A set of postulates for educational theory. I. The background. *J. educ. Res.,* 28, 321-333.

CRITICAL REVIEWS

English, H. B. (1934) Review of Wheeler and Perkins' *Principles of mental development. Amer. J. Psychol.,* 46, 348-350.
Lanier, L. H. (1931) Review of Wheeler's *The science of psychology. Amer. J. Psychol.,* 43, 146-150.
McGeoch, J. A. (1933) The configurational psychology of learning. *J. appl. Psychol.,* 17, 83-96.

REPRESENTATIVE EXPERIMENTS

Baldwin, O. B. (1933) The maturation of the college student as evidenced by retests with the National Council tests. *Psychol. Monogr.,* 44, 233-262.
Brigden, R. L. (1933) Goal activity in the white rat. *Psychol. Monogr.,* 44, 88-97.
Brigden, R. L. (1935) The dynamics of spiral movement in man. *J. comp. Psychol.,* 20, 59-74.
Lewis, M. H. (1930) Elemental vs. configural response in the chick. *J. exp. Psychol.,* 13, 61-75.
Patton, E. K. (1933) The problem of insightful behavior. *Psychol. Monogr.,* 44, 98-124.
Perkins, F. T. (1933) A study of cerebral action currents in the dog under sound stimulation. *Psychol. Monogr.,* 44, 1-29.
Perkins, F. T., and Wheeler, R. H. (1930). Configurational learning in the goldfish. *Comp. Psychol. Monogr.,* 7, No. 31, 50 pp.
Snoddy, G. S. (1935) *Evidence for two opposed processes in mental growth.* Lancaster, Pa., Science Press, 103 pp.
Snygg, D. (1936) Mazes in which rats take the longer path to food. *J. Psychol.,* 1, 153-166.
Wheeler, R. H. (1946) Climate and human behavior. In P. L. Harriman, edit., *Encyclopedia of psychology.* New York, Philosophical Library, 78-86.

Chapter 10

TOLMAN'S SIGN-GESTALT THEORY

In his sign-gestalt theory Edward C. Tolman has achieved a synthesis of many trends within systematic psychology. The complex affiliations of Tolman's system—with Watson's behaviorism, McDougall's hormic psychology, Woodworth's dynamic psychology, gestalt psychology, in both classical and Lewin's forms, and, finally, with Brunswik's act-psychology—make almost any feature or suggestion one which derives from a distinguished relative. The major presentation of his systematic position, *Purposive behavior in animals and men* (1932) acknowledges all these affiliations except the last, which became clear later.[1] The variety of influences incorporated in his system does not mean that Tolman is an eclectic. He is as earnest about system-making as anyone, and what he has learned from others is fitted in with his own contributions in a way which is always highly original and results in a whole which is new and significant.

There are three points on which Tolman always stands firm, regardless of what amusingly admitted misgivings he has from time to time about aspects of his system.

1. His system is a genuine *behaviorism*, and as such rigidly rejects introspection as a method and "raw feels" as data for psychological science. When he makes reference to consciousness, to inventive ideation, and the like, he is talking about interpretations of observed behavior. He does not accept "verbal report" as a dodge by which to smuggle consciousness in through the back door.

2. The system is a *molar*, rather than a *molecular* behaviorism.

[1] Tolman and Brunswik (1935).

261

An act of behavior has distinctive properties all its own, to be identified and described irrespective of whatever muscular, glandular, or neural processes underlie it. The molecular facts of physics and physiology upon which behavior rests have identifying properties of their own, which are not the properties of behavior as molar. This means for Tolman an independence from physiology, a characteristic which he shares with several of the writers whom we have considered.

3. The system is a *purposivism*, but of a sort to avoid the implications of a teleological metaphysics. It is a purposivism because it recognizes that behavior is regulated in accordance with objectively determinable ends. It is not mentalistic; purposes are not those of a self-conscious mind. It is not in agreement with teleological points of view which make effects take precedence over and determine their causes.

The strongest rejection is of American structuralism, because structuralism was dependent upon introspection of the most offensive sort, that known as *Beschreibung*. Watsonian behaviorism is almost as vigorously rejected, because it was not only molecular but tended to neglect the problems of goal-seeking behavior.

THE SYSTEMATIC POSITION

Behavior as molar. The descriptive properties of molar behavior are the most general characteristics of behavior which would impress themselves upon a naive but intelligent onlooker, prior to any attempt to explain how the behavior comes about.

First, behavior is goal-directed. It is always a getting-toward something, or a getting-away from something. The most significant description of any behavior is what the organism is doing, where it is going. The cat is trying to get out of the box, the carpenter is building a house (or earning a living), the musician is seeking acclaim. The particular movements involved are less descriptive of the molar behavior than the goal toward which or away from which the movements lead. This feature characterizes molar behavior as *purposive*.

Second, the behavior makes use of environmental supports as means-objects toward the goal. The world in which behavior goes on is a world of paths and tools and obstacles with which the organism has commerce. The manner in which the organism makes use of paths and tools in relation to its goals characterizes molar behavior as *cognitive* as well as purposive.

Third, there is a selective preference for short or easy means activities as against long or difficult ones, called the *principle of least effort*. This preference has been met before in Wheeler's law of least action.

Fourth, behavior, if it is molar, is *docile*. That is, molar behavior is characterized by teachableness. If it is mechanical and stereotyped, like a spinal reflex, it belongs at the molecular level. Docility is said to be a mark of purpose.[2]

Intervening variables. The complete act of behavior is initiated by environmental stimuli and physiological states. Certain processes intervene, and behavior emerges. Programmatically, this is the formula which Hull has taken over from Tolman. The problem of psychological analysis at the molar level is to infer the processes which intervene between the initiation of action in the world of physics and physiology and the resulting observable consequences, again in the world of physics and physiology. Because all of the data are rooted in this world, the system remains a behaviorism.

In spite of his methodological behaviorism, Tolman is clearly seeking to make a "psychological" as against a "physiological" analysis. The intervening variables include such processes as cognitions and purposes, so that, in its spirit, Tolman's position belongs with the gestalt psychologists who have been characterized as "centralists," rather than with the stimulus-response psychologists characterized as "peripheralists." [3]

The precise variables entering into behavior determination have not remained fixed in Tolman's later discussions, but the logic of system-making has remained the same. The set of terms used in his presidential address before the American Psychological Association in 1937 [4] may serve as illustrative.

The background of physiology and physics with which

---

[2] In this Tolman follows Perry (1918).

[3] Murray (1938); Leeper (1944).

[4] Tolman (1938a).

choice-point behavior begins is defined by environmental and individual difference variables:

I. ENVIRONMENTAL VARIABLES

M—Maintenance schedule
G—Appropriateness of goal object
S—Types and modes of stimuli provided
R—Types of motor response required
Σ(OBO)—Cumulative nature and number of trials [5]
P—Pattern of preceding and succeeding maze units

II. INDIVIDUAL DIFFERENCE VARIABLES

H—Heredity
A—Age
T—Previous training
E—Special endocrine, drug or vitamin conditions

It is possible to study the effect of such variables on resulting behavior. The usual learning curve is a plot of the functional relationship under stated conditions. These are the behavioral "facts" about learning. It is the effort to explain the facts which leads to theories.

Tolman's explanation rests on intervening variables. These are inferred processes between the independent variables (stimuli, etc.) and the dependent variables (responses, etc.). The preliminary list as presented coordinates one intervening variable with each of the environmental variables.

Intervening Variable			Environmental Variable
Demand	correlated with		Maintenance schedule
Appetite	"	"	Appropriateness of goal object
Differentiation	"	"	Types and modes of stimuli provided
Motor skill	"	"	Types of motor response required
Hypotheses	"	"	Cumulative nature and number of trials
Biases	"	"	Pattern of preceding and succeeding maze units

[5] Σ(OBO) is a shorthand formula which means some consequence or summation of previous experiences in which one occasion (O) has led through behavior (B) to another occasion (O). The occasions are such features as a choice point, a goal at the left, and so on.

Although the intervening variables sound subjective, each can be given objective definition and measurement, through a defining experiment in which everything else is held constant except the correlative environmental variable while that one is systematically varied. Demand, for example, may be expected to increase with the number of hours since feeding, but the relationship between food deprivation and demand is not a simple one. It must be studied empirically. The same holds for each of the intervening variables.[6]

Having thus established a basis for inferring the value of the intervening variable from the antecedent conditions, the next stage in theory construction is to find the equations relating intervening variables to behavioral outcomes, as these intervening variables are simultaneously varied. Tolman asserts that association psychologists imply that these equations are those of simple algebraic summation. Tolman objects to this, and asserts that he believes dynamic concepts like those of Lewin will prove most useful in working out these final equations.[7]

In spite of the clear outline of what a systematic theory ought to be, Tolman has nowhere attempted quantitative predictions paralleling those of Hull, so that his conjectures have not in that sense been put to the test.[8] This does not mean that his experiments are unrelated to his theory. There are, in fact, many predictions, but they assert that one path will be preferred to another, that under one set of circumstances the problem will be easier than under another set, and so on. The dimensional analysis which completes the function is not provided.

[6] A useful distinction has been made by MacCorquodale and Meehl (1947) between "intervening variables" and "hypothetical constructs." Functionally defined "intervening variables" like those of Tolman do not imply a "state" or "neural process" remaining to be discovered and described by physiologists. Some of Hull's intervening variables are, on the other hand, "hypothetical constructs" because they suggest existences such as neural traces, anticipatory responses, inhibitory increments, and so on, which might eventually be described ostensively, that is, through direct experimentation. "Hypothetical constructs" usually have some properties attributed to them beyond those of the functional equations through which such constructs are defined.

[7] Tolman (1938a), page 23.

[8] Some starts have been made, e.g., Tolman (1939) (1941).

SIGN LEARNING

Sign learning as an alternative to response learning. Stimulus-response theories, while stated with different degrees of sophistication, imply that the organism is goaded along a path by internal and external stimuli, learning the correct movement sequences so that they are released under appropriate conditions of drive and environmental stimulation. The alternative possibility is that the learner is following signs to a goal, is learning his way about, is following a sort of map—in other words, is learning not movements but meanings. This is the contention of Tolman's theory of sign learning. The organism learns sign-significate relations; it learns a behavior-route, not a movement-pattern. Many learning situations do not permit a clear distinction between these two possibilities. If there is a single path with food at the end and the organism runs faster at each opportunity, there is no way of telling whether its responses are being stamped in by reinforcement or whether it is guided by its immanent purposes and cognitions.

Because both stimulus-response and sign learning so often predict the same behavioral outcome, it is necessary to design special situations in which it is possible to favor one theory over the other. Three situations give strong support to the sign learning alternative. These are experiments on reward expectancy, on place learning, and on latent learning.

1. *Reward-expectancy.* One of the earliest and most striking observations on reward-expectancy was that of Tinklepaugh (1928). In his experiment, food was placed under one of two containers while the monkey was looking. Later the monkey was permitted to choose between the containers, and showed skill in choosing correctly. The behavior which is pertinent here occurred when, after a banana had been hidden under one of the cups, the experimenter substituted for it a lettuce leaf (a less preferred food). The monkey rejected the lettuce leaf and engaged in definite searching behavior. Somewhat the same sort of behavior was found by Elliott (1928) when the food in the goal box of a rat maze experiment was changed from bran mash to sunflower seed. More systematic experiments have been carried

out since with chimpanzees.[9] There is little doubt that animals have some sort of precognition or expectancy of specific goal objects. Under those circumstances, other goal objects produce signs of behavior disruption. Such behavior means that the sign-learning theory is appropriate; it does not, of course, mean that other theories may not attempt to deduce the behavior from other principles.

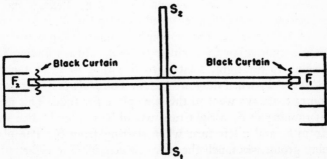

FIGURE 35. MAZE USED TO TEST THE RELATIVE EASE OF LEARNING A RESPONSE WHICH BRINGS REWARD OR THE PLACE AT WHICH REWARD IS FOUND.

By starting irregularly at S_1 and S_2, but finding reward at the same food box each time, one group of rats turns now to the right, now to the left, to find food always at the same location. These are the place learners. By starting at either S_1 or S_2, but always finding food as a result of turning the same way (right or left), another group is taught always to make the same response, but to find food at different places, depending upon the starting point. Place learning, under the conditions of the experiment, is found to be easier than response learning. From Tolman, Ritchie, and Kalish (1946b), page 223.

2. *Place learning.* Experiments on place learning are designed to show that the learner is not moving from start to goal according to a fixed sequence of movements such as would be predicted from reinforcement theories, but is capable of behavior which is varied appropriately to changed conditions, as though he "knows" where the goal is. There are three subtypes of these experiments.

The first subtype of the place-learning alternative to response-learning leaves the form of the path intact but interferes with the movement sequences in getting from start to goal. In one experiment, rats following cerebellar damage were unable to run

[9] Cowles and Nissen (1937).

the maze except in circles, but even so were able to run without error.[10] They could not have been running off the earlier learned sequences of kinesthetic habits. In another, rats were able to demonstrate what they had learned by swimming the correct path after having been trained in wading it.[11]

The second subtype of place-learning experiment sets a movement habit against a spatial habit, and determines which is the more readily learned. In a recent experiment, Tolman and his collaborators [12] arranged an elevated maze in the form of a cross, as shown in Figure 35. The response-learning group was started in random alternation from either S_1 or S_2, always finding food by turning to the right. That is, food was at F_1 when the start was S_1 and at F_2 when the start was S_2. The place-learning group, by contrast, always went to the same place for food. This meant that if running to F_1, a right turn would be required when starting from S_1 and a left turn when starting from S_2. The place-learning group was much the more successful. The eight rats of the place-learning group all learned within 8 trials, so that the next 10 trials were without error. None of the eight rats of the response-learning group learned this quickly, and five of them did not reach the criterion in 72 trials. Under the circumstances of an elevated maze with many extra-maze cues, it is clearly demonstrated that place-learning is simpler than response-learning.

The third subtype of place-learning experiment involves the use of unfamiliar paths when a practiced path is blocked. Another experiment from Tolman's laboratory [13] shows how well the rat can adjust to this situation. First the rat was taught to go to the goal by a fixed path. After some preliminary training, each rat ran five times to the food box along this path, this training requiring 4 days. On the fifth day a single trial was given with the old path blocked. On this day there were available for the first time a series of radiating paths from the circular table top from which the original path departed. One of these radiating paths, at a considerable angle from the original, led in the goal direction. Of 56 rats tested, three failed to make a choice on the

[10] Lashley and Ball (1929).
[11] Macfarlane (1930).
[12] Tolman, Ritchie, and Kalish (1946*b*), (1947*b*).
[13] Tolman, Ritchie, and Kalish (1946*a*).

test day, and were discarded. Of the other 53, the preferred choice was the path leading in the goal direction. This was chosen by 19 rats, while only 4 rats chose the path just to the left of the original and only 1 the path just to the right. These are the paths starting off most like the blocked path. Instead of choosing them, the animals tend to choose the directly goal-pointing path. The experiment shows rather clearly that the animal is oriented in space, that it "knows its way around." It has learned not just how to run along a path, but where the goal is in the experimental room. It is important to remark again that such a demonstration, while it accords fully with Tolman's theory, does not necessarily exclude alternative explanations. Hull, for example, has attempted to deduce just such behavior upon the basis of habit-family hierarchies built up through experience in free space. When one member of a habit-family is blocked (as in this experiment), the other preferred members come into play. The conception of habit-family is so much like that of cognitive structure that it might be argued that Hull has in fact capitulated to Tolman's theory, although Hull believes himself to have deduced it from more elementary principles.[14]

Another arrangement of the blocked-path experiment is that of Tolman and Honzik (1930*a*) which is said to demonstrate inferential expectation, or insight. The main features of the arrangement are as follows. There are three paths (1, 2, and 3), in that order of length from shortest to longest, and hence in that order of preference (Figure 36). In preliminary training, when path 1 was blocked, a preference was established between paths 2 and 3 for the shorter of these paths. Only when path 2 was blocked also, did they run by path 3. We may somewhat oversimplify by saying that a familiarity with all paths and a preference for them in the order 1, 2, 3 was established in preliminary training. An important feature of the maze design, crucial for the test, was that paths 1 and 2 had a common segment leading to the goal. Previously the block in path 1 had been placed before this common path; then the rat, after backing up from the block, ran by path 2. Now in the test the block was placed farther along path 1, so that it fell in the common path. Would the rat in backing out again run by the second prefer-

[14] Hull (1934*a*) (1938).

ence, path 2, and be frustrated, or would it "see" that path 2 was also blocked? What the rats did, predominantly, was to avoid path 2, and to take the path ordinarily least preferred, the long path 3, but the only one open. Again the hypothesis is supported

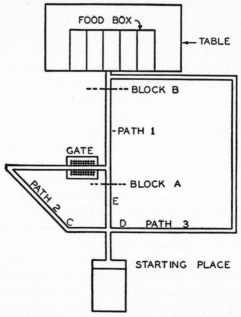

FIGURE 36. MAZE USED TO TEST INSIGHT IN RATS.

The paths become established as a hierarchy according to length, Path 1 preferred to Path 2, Path 2 to Path 3. If Path 1 is closed by Block A, the rats run by Path 2. If Path 1 is closed by Block B, the rats run by Path 3 if they have "insight" that the barrier closes Path 2 as well as Path 1. From Honzik and Tolman (1930a), page 223.

that the rat acted in accordance with some sort of "map" of the situation, and not according to blind habit, or according to the automatic running off of habits in hierarchical order.[15]

3. *Latent learning.* In addition to the experiments on reward-expectancy and on space learning, a third set of experiments bear

[15] The Tolman and Honzik experiment has been criticized by other experimenters who have shown that the results, while reproducible, are easily disturbed by the manipulation of experimental variables such as alley width which would not be expected to make insight impossible. See Evans (1936), Harsh (1937), Keller and Hill (1936), Kuo (1937).

importantly on sign learning. These are the experiments on latent learning to be described more fully later in this chapter. In essence they show that an animal can learn by exploring the maze, without food reward, so that, when reward is later introduced, performance is as good as that of rats with many previously rewarded trials. The "latent learning" consisted of knowledge of the maze, not revealed in choice of the shortest path from entrance to exit until the rat was motivated to make that choice. The experiments, beginning with those of Blodgett (1929),[16] throw considerable doubt upon explanations of learning of the "law of effect" type, since reward appears to be more nearly a matter of performance than of learning. In other words, the learner shows what he "knows" only when motivated to do so; the relationship between the motivation and the learning is not at all direct.

All of these experiments—reward-expectancy, space learning, and latent learning—yield results which conform well to Tolman's theory, and put other theories under strain to derive them.

Can a more precise formulation be made of the sign learning theory? It has sometimes been characterized as a theory of "what leads to what," a theory of signs, significates, and behavior routes. Morris has recently incorporated it into his philosophical analysis of signs.[17] There are the two problems, which Lewin also faced: first, the nature of the "expectancy" or "cognitive structure," second, the "activation" or manner in which behavior is made to occur in accordance with the cognitive structure.

Expectancies and hypotheses. The nearest thing to a simple habit which the sign learning theory accepts is a *sign-gestalt expectation*, or, more simply, an *expectancy* that given behavior will result in a goal object. What repetition does is to increase the probability that an expectancy will be fulfilled. The result in behavior is faster running, exactly as if a habit were being strengthened by reward. In order to provide an operational distinction between the learning of a running habit and the acquiring of an expectancy, Tolman, Ritchie and Kalish make a formal statement which puts their experiment into words:

[16] Historical priority is sometimes assigned to Szymanski (1918).
[17] Morris (1946).

When we assert that a rat expects food at location L, what we assert is that *if* (1) he is deprived of food, (2) he has been trained on path P, (3) he is now put on path P, (4) path P is now blocked, and (5) there are other paths which lead away from path P, one of which points directly to location L, then he will run down the path which points directly to location L.

When we assert that he does not expect food at location L, what we assert is that, under the same conditions, he will *not* run down the path which points directly to location L.[18]

This is characteristic of particularist definitions which are so clear as actually to lose some of the meaning intended. This definition says that an expectation to be an expectation must operate perfectly; if the rat makes good errors (e.g., by taking a path near the direct-pointing one) he does not have an expectation of food at the location L. However, the intent is clearly to define an expectation as the learner's having a serviceable map of the surroundings, so that the goal can be approached via any goal-pointing path. The purpose of the definition is to distinguish between having a map and a running-habit, which is the alternative. Behavior which shows that the rat knows what leads to what along a fixed path might also be used to show that it has a running habit; therefore, the need to distinguish between an expectation and a habit in terms of goal-pointing paths not previously traversed.

There is another quality of expectancy not covered in this definition. That is its provisional nature. In a very stimulating paper Tolman and Brunswik (1935) propose that the causal texture of the environment is not such as to permit the firm expectations of the definition, but that predictions must often be made on the basis of probabilities. In an experimental test of the proposal, Brunswik (1939) presented his rats with such a contingent environment, in which food might sometimes be found on the right, sometimes on the left. He found that there was some measure of agreement between the choices of the rat and the probability that food would be where he went for it.[19]

[18] Tolman, Ritchie, and Kalish (1946a), page 15.

[19] The constancy of the "extinction ratio" in Skinner's periodic reconditioning could be interpreted as an adjustment of rate of response to the probability of being reinforced, thus supporting Brunswik's findings. This suggestion was made to me by Dr. Paul E. Meehl.

In order to compare an expectancy theory with a reinforcement theory, Humphreys performed several experiments of the conditioned response type. In human eyelid conditioning, it had already been shown that conditioned discrimination was more rapid when subjects knew which stimulus of a pair was to be positive, which negative, than when the probabilities had to be established through experience with the stimuli.[20] The conjecture that the subjects were responding according to their expectations was a plausible one. Humphreys went on to show that random alternation of reinforcement and non-reinforcement led not only to as much conditioning as reinforcement every trial, but was followed also by greater resistance to extinction.[21] During extinction, responses increased in frequency at first, and then fell off. This would be anticipated on an expectancy theory because the likelihood of reinforcement was great after a non-reinforcement during the body of the experiment, and greater still after two non-reinforcements because there were never more than two successive non-reinforcements during the training sessions. But even after this high point, extinction was gradual. Humphreys conjectured that a shift from intermittent reinforcement to uniform non-reinforcement must have led with difficulty to the hypothesis of uniform non-reinforcement. Because the experiment was done with human subjects, a direct test was possible on the verbal level, and Humphreys designed and carried out a simple experiment which confirmed his conjecture.[22]

For the study of verbal expectations, two lights were arranged on a board. When one of these lights was turned on, the subject was asked to guess whether or not it would be followed by the other light. Half the subjects were "trained" with the second light invariably following the first. They came gradually to guess in a high percentage of the cases that the first light would be followed by the second, in agreement with their experience. The other half had the second light turned on only in random alternation, so that half the time it did not appear. They guessed at chance level. The training trials are as in the case of the conditioning experiment. The results differ in that within the conditioning

[20] Hilgard, R. K. Campbell, and W. N. Sears (1938).
[21] Humphreys (1939a).
[22] Humphreys (1939b).

experiment the intermittent reinforcement group performed like the group uniformly reinforced. This difference does not invalidate the comparison. On the contrary, it is an essential part of it, because it is necessary to distinguish between performance and expectation. In the conditioning experiment, uncertainty leads to conditioned responses as well as certainty because it is a punishment situation; blinking is as easy as refraining from blinking, and there is no penalty for an "erroneous" response, that is, for blinking to the conditioned stimulus alone. In the verbal situation, response is more nearly representative of "pure" expectation, because a false guess is subjectively interpreted as a mistake in a way in which a false conditioned response is not.

The crucial portion of the experiment is that in which extinction is simulated, that is, in which the first light is never again followed by the second. Humphreys' results are plotted in Figure 37. It is seen that the group which had been trained on the every-trial "reinforcement" quickly developed the hypothesis of uniform non-reinforcement, and ceased to expect the second light. The group trained with intermittent "reinforcement" showed the rise in expectation which the theory demands, and the slow acceptance of the hypothesis that there would be no more second lights.

These results of Humphreys with human subjects are unequivocally in favor of a principle like expectancy. Experiments similar to the conditioning ones with human subjects have been done with rats by Humphreys[23] and extended by Mowrer and Jones.[24] The results turn out about the same, that is, satisfactory conditioning under intermittent reinforcement and greater resistance to extinction. Mowrer and Jones make an ingenious application of reinforcement theory, but they do not in fact circumvent the difficulties faced also by Skinner in the explanation of the results of reinforcement at a fixed ratio.

A provisional expectancy is an hypothesis. When a situation is not yet structured so that path-goal relationships become clear, behavior in relationship to the situation may either be "random" or "systematic." If it is systematic, it may be said to accord with an hypothesis. Score averages from groups of animals tend to

[23] Humphreys (1943b).
[24] Mowrer and Jones (1945).

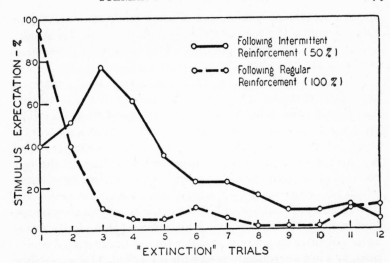

FIGURE 37. A PHENOMENON LIKE EXTINCTION IN AN EXPERIMENT ON VERBAL
EXPECTATIONS.

Prior to yielding the data in this figure, one group had regularly experienced a second light following a signal light, and had developed the expectation that a second light would regularly follow. This condition simu-
lates 100 per cent reinforcement in a conditioning situation. For the second
group, the signal light had been followed by the 'expected' light only half
the time. This condition is like 50 per cent reinforcement in conditioning,
and leads to uncertainty as to whether or not the signal will be followed
by a second light. Beginning with the trials shown in the figure, the signal
light was never followed by the second light, thus simulating extinction.
What is recorded is the per cent of subjects guessing on each trial that the
second light would occur. Following regular reinforcement the change to
the expectation of regular non-reinforcement occurs more readily than
following intermittent reinforcement. After Humphreys (1939b).

conceal the differences between chance approaches and more
orderly approaches, because one animal's responses cancel another's unless they happen to correspond to the experimenter's
plan as to what will be counted correct. By studying the presolution behavior of individual animals, systematic attempts at
solution can often be discovered, solutions of the order: "turn
right," "alternate," "go to the dark." These are not mere fixed
preferences, because after one pattern has been used for a while,
the animal learner may shift to another one. Krech named such
systematic attempts at solution "hypotheses," and studied them

under a number of conditions.[25] Their possible rôle in discrimination learning led to a controversy with those taking a more strictly stimulus-response position. This controversy is discussed briefly in the next chapter.

The full-fledged conception of expectancy thus includes a good deal more than the recent definition by Tolman, Ritchie and Kalish. The following aspects are all relevant: (1) The organism brings to a problematic situation various systematic modes of attack, based largely on prior experiences. (2) The cognitive field is provisionally organized according to the hypotheses of the learner, the hypotheses which survive being those which best correspond with reality, that is, with the causal texture of the environment. These hypotheses or expectancies are confirmed by successes in goal achievement. (3) A clearly established cognitive structure is available for use under altered conditions, as when a frequently used path is blocked. This availability of cognitive structure distinguishes it from habit strength, for which transfer possibilities are limited.

Motivation and sign learning. Because Tolman has been at such pains to protest against the law of effect and the principle of reinforcement as essential to learning, it is in order to inquire what rôle he assigns motivation in learning.

One rôle assigned to motivation is in relation to performance. Learning is *used* when drives are active. Lewin's distinction between the perceptual field and the "motor" or "activator" of the performance is paralleled by Tolman's cognitive structure leading to behavior under appropriate conditions of drive. When drives are aroused, a state of tension ensues, leading to demands for goal objects. These tensions lead to activity, guided by the expectancies or cognitive structures available. In this rôle, then, motivation is not really a factor in learning at all. It is related to performance, not to acquisition. Because this rôle of motivation is made much of in the criticisms of reinforcement theories, the impression is given that learning, the acquiring of cognitive structures, is independent of motivation. This is not true in fact, nor is it true in Tolman's theory.

The second rôle of motivation is in the acquisition of cognitive structures. In one of the experiments critical of the law of effect,

[25] Krechevsky (1932a, 1932b, 1933a, 1933b).

the suggestion was made that what appeared to be the principle of effect might better be considered the influence of *emphasis*.[26] That is, motivation affects those features of the environment which interest the learner, and to which he pays attention. Such factors are influential in perceptual acquisitions, which are the genuine substance of place learning. Causal sequences of the environment are not all spatial. Some are temporal; some are logical or systematic or arbitrary. The goal-object, by its presence or absence, verifies or refutes hypotheses. Hence the goal-object is essential for the establishment of some features of cognitive structure. Latent learning, which dramatizes a relatively unmotivated, incidental type of learning, is an extreme case of the relationship of goal-behavior to learning, and is probably not a typical case.

The importance of something like emphasis is well brought out in the series of experiments by Muenzinger and his associates,[27] in which punishment or obstacles to be overcome, even on the side of the correct choice, aid learning. Whether or not punishment will be an aid to learning thus depends upon what influence it has on the cognitions of the learner. It may be helpful as an emphasizer or harmful as a distractor.

The importance of goal-behavior in the acquiring of social techniques is described in Tolman's book concerned with problems of social motivation.

Consider a chimpanzee or a nursery-school child. The little animal (partly by accident and partly as a result of innate propensity) chances, let us say, to embark upon dominance behavior. He engages in a few fights and establishes a high dominance-status in his group. He therewith discovers *(that is, learns)* the instrumental fact that this establishing of high dominance status is a *means* to obtaining practically all of a limited food supply, or to obtaining an especially prized toy, if he be the nursery-school child. He discovers that his basic biological drives of hunger or of play become thereby better satisfied. On the other hand, in some other quite different situation he may learn the instrumental value of using collective techniques instead . . . Learning is thus a "reasonable" activity which tends to keep the individual well-adjusted to the actual environmental realities.[28]

[26] Tolman, Hall, and Bretnall (1932).
[27] Muenzinger and others, 1934-1938.
[28] Tolman (1942), pages 59-60.

This quotation, with slight changes in wording, might be used to describe socialization according to a reinforcement theory like Miller and Dollard's or Hull's. The regulatory rôle of the "reward" is somewhat similar in both cases, although the interpretation differs. According to Tolman the learner acquires knowledge of a means-end relationship; according to reinforcement theory he learns behavior which is followed by reward. In any case, it would be most misleading to interpret Tolman's position as if reward influenced performance only, and not learning. All that he insists upon is that learning and performance cannot be equated, and the rôle of motivation in learning differs in some respects from its rôle in performance. This conclusion, originally proposed by Lashley (1929b), can scarcely be doubted.

LAWS OF LEARNING

Tolman's laws of learning are not much emphasized within his systematic writings. They have nothing of the centrality of Hull's postulates, or of Wheeler's laws of dynamics. They are merely topics within which lawful relationships may be found, the laws thus being left in much the form in which Skinner and Robinson leave their laws. Beneath all their differences there are many similarities among these three representatives of pragmatism.

Learning theorists commonly select one kind of learning problem or situation as typical, and then proceed to develop a theory appropriate to this reference situation. Having constructed a set of principles in this way, they attempt to show by a logical process that other kinds of learning are really at base like the typical one, and hence explicable in the same terms. Recognizing this tendency, Tolman selects for review three kinds of learning experiments, with their three corresponding doctrines. These are conditioned reflex learning (Pavlov), trial-and-error learning (Thorndike), and inventive learning (Köhler). He then gives a sign-gestalt interpretation of each of the three kinds of learning as alternative to the usual theory associated with each. He finds it useful to preserve the typical experiments, which represent a kind of hierarchy from stupidity to intelligence. The laws applicable to the more stupid situations have to be supplemented by additional laws for the higher forms of learning.

In the 1932 version there are three groups of laws: capacity laws, laws relative to the nature of the material, and laws relative to the manner of presentation.

1. *Capacity laws.* Only organisms can learn. It is evident, therefore, that what the organism can learn must depend on what kind of an organism it is. That is the reason for capacity laws.

The list of capacity laws is as follows: [29]

a. Formal means-end-capacities
b. Discriminating and manipulating capacities
c. Retentivity
d. Means-end-capacities needed for alternative routes, detours, etc.
e. Ideational capacities
f. Creative instability

In order to learn conditioned reflexes the learner must have the necessary capacities to form and act in accordance with "sign-gestalt-expectations." That is, the conditioned stimulus serves as a sign that the unconditioned stimulus is about to appear and the conditioned behavior is appropriate to the sign. This capacity is named a "means-end-capacity." In his later writings Tolman has dropped a number of the hyphenated terms which made his book clear, entertaining, but also somewhat forbidding. In the list of laws which we have given above, his terms have been freely paraphrased to make for easier reading, although there may be some loss involved. In addition to the general capacity for sign learning, conditioning requires special capacities for discriminating and manipulating features of the environment. Finally retentivity is implied, if the results of earlier conditioning trials are to influence later ones. Only capacity laws *a*, *b*, and *c* apply to conditioning.

The capacities needed for trial-and-error learning are the same as those required for conditioning, except that additional means-end-capacities are needed because more alternatives are open to the learner. The field relationships of alternate routes, detours, final common paths, are involved. Additional capacities of ideational sort, permitting comparison of alternatives (a mental "run-

[29] Tolman (1932*b*), pages 376-377.

ning-back-and-forth") are probably helpful in trial-and-error learning.

Inventive learning requires all the capacities of the other varieties of learning plus *creative instability*. This is a capacity to break out into new lines of activity which have never occurred to the learner before in the situation.

The need for capacity laws seems evident enough, once they are proposed, though they have been neglected in most learning theories. Even Thorndike, strongly identified with the study of individual differences, neglects capacity laws in his learning theory. Such a statement as "Any response of which the organism is capable can become attached to any stimulus to which it is sensitive" [30] implies only sensitivity capacity and response capacity, and neglects any capacity to establish relations between them. It would be grossly unfair to say that Thorndike did not recognize differences in learning ability, but it is true that he slighted the different kinds of capacities needed for different kinds of learning, because all learning was merely the forming of bonds. Hull, who also in one of his earlier research interests contributed to the psychology of individual differences,[31] has only recently begun to consider individuality as something to enter into his learning theory.[32]

2. *Laws relating to the nature of the material.* In Tolman's discussion of these topics, he calls attention to certain "gestalt-inducing-conditions" and suggests that they are of the sorts emphasized in gestalt studies of perception.

The list follows: [33]

a. Togetherness
b. Fusibility
c. Other gestalt-like laws
d. Interrelations among the spatial, temporal and other characters of the alternatives
e. Characters in the material favoring new closures and expansions of the field

In relation to conditioned reflex learning these laws suggest that there must be a "togetherness" of essential signs and their means-end relationship to the thing signified. Tolman states that

30 Thorndike (1913*b*), page 15.
31 Hull (1928).
32 Hull (1945*b*).
33 Tolman (1932*b*), pages 378-385.

this is about what Thorndike has called "belongingness." Tolman adds a somewhat similar law of fusibility of sign, significate and signified means-end-relationship by which he means a certain naturalness about the situation which makes it easier to form a gestalt of the whole. He provides in a third law for the possibility of new discoveries. He adds one law *d* for trial-and-error learning and one for inventive learning *e*, to suggest that some arrangements must be easier than others. He points to Köhler's observation that the ape could learn to use the stick more easily to rake in the food if the stick and food were perceived together.

These laws show the same sort of catholicity as Robinson's list, except that there is no ordering principle among them. "Spatial, temporal, and other" can scarcely be said to arrange things dimensionally. They do make a definite bow to the important fact that perceptual principles must be understood if the relative ease or difficulty of problematic situations is to be made comprehensible.

3. *Laws relative to the manner of presentation.* These are the laws inherited largely from association psychology, the ones for which abundant evidence can be found recorded in McGeoch's book (1942). The list is as follows: [34]

a. Frequency, recency
b. Revival after extinction, primacy, distributed repetition, etc.
c. Motivation
d. Not "effect" but "emphasis"
e. Temporal orders and sequences in the presentation of alternatives
f. Temporal relations between the presentation of certain of the already given alternatives and the true solution

Of these, the first four belong to conditioned reflex learning, the first five to trial-and-error learning, and all six to inventive learning.

The principles of frequency and recency are accepted in the following form: "The more frequently and more recently the actual sequence of sign, means-end-relation and significate have been presented, the stronger, other things being equal, this resulting sign-gestalt will tend to be." [35] That is, only in a situation favorable to sign-gestalt formation will frequency be effective. The other laws provide opportunity again to raise the question

[34] Tolman (1932*b*), pages 385-389.
[35] Tolman (1932*b*), page 386.

of the law of effect, and to make some observations descriptive of favorable conditions in trial-and-error and multiple-choice experiments.

As a set, the laws are rather disappointing. They serve as a useful reminder of the main tenets of the point of view, and of its criticisms of prevailing doctrines. They leave much to be asked for on the positive side in their lack of sufficient precision of statement so that they can be called true or false.

Leaving the laws in this form makes everything a matter of correlations between situation and behavior and does not get at the formal problem of rigorous definition and measurement of intervening variables. This lack has not yet been made up, in spite of later reworkings of the list of laws.[36]

EXPERIMENTS ON LATENT LEARNING

The issue is fairly sharp as between reinforcement theory and sign-learning theory. Reinforcement theory proposes that habits are strengthened by reinforcement; sign-learning theory says that expectancies become established, and that habit (that is, performance) is secondarily correlated with expectancy. While several varieties of experiment bear on the choice between these theories, none is more important than latent learning. In a symposium on the law of effect, Tolman chose latent learning as his main argument against the Thorndikian principle.[37] Because of its centrality, therefore, the evidence is worth examining in some detail.

Tolman and Honzik's experiment. Following up the work started by Blodgett (1929), Tolman and Honzik (1930b) studied the effect of introduction of reward in a rat maze experiment after the animals had run several days without food. The control group, fed each day in the maze, gained much more rapidly than the non-fed group, but when food was introduced for the latter group, error scores and time scores became alike for both groups. Thus the non-fed group had apparently profited as much by its earlier trials as the fed group. Since this profiting did not show in performance, the learning taking place is said to be "latent." The results for error elimination are shown in Figure 38.

[36] New lists of laws may be found in Tolman (1934) (1937).
[37] Tolman (1938b).

There were three groups: two control groups, one rewarded throughout, the other non-rewarded throughout, and the experimental group, non-rewarded until the eleventh trial. On the twelfth day, the experimental group, having been fed but once in the maze, made as few errors as the group which had received food in the maze each of the preceding days.

There are several comments to be made on this situation, in its bearing on other theories as well as on Tolman's. The maze used

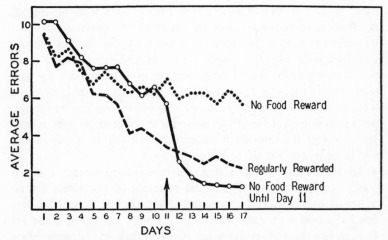

FIGURE 38. EVIDENCE FOR LATENT LEARNING IN THE MAZE.

With no food reward there is some reduction in errors, but not as great a reduction as with regular food reward. Despite the higher error scores prior to the introduction of food, the group rewarded only from the 11th trial immediately begins to do as well as the group had been regularly rewarded. The interpretation is that some learning went on within the first 10 trials which did not show in performance until the food incentive activated it. After Tolman and Honzik (1930b).

was a 14-unit one of multiple-T type,[38] arranged with doors between each unit to prevent retracing. The rat without food at the end still progressed through the maze, so that, according to such a theory as Guthrie's, learning conditions were ideal. The rat had no opportunity to unlearn what it last did in each segment, which was of course to go through the door to the next one. The results are critical of Guthrie's theory not because the

[38] Stone and Nyswander (1927).

rat shows latent learning but because it does not show enough learning when there is no food at the end of the maze. (It is to be recalled that the Guthrie and Horton cats often did not eat when they left the problem-box; their behavior was said be fixed because they left the box.) The Guthrie explanation is not sufficient, because the fed rats learned much better than the unfed ones.

Theories which relate reinforcement to actual behavior-sequences have occasionally tried to argue that there really was some reward in the non-rewarded runs. There was, of course, satisfaction of curiosity, and escape from the maze. And there was some reduction in errors, as shown by the control curves. But these theories cannot have their cake and eat it too. If there was a reward, it should have served as rewards do, by the strengthening of the rewarded behavior. Such rewards as there were sufficed to produce as much learning as was shown by the performances in the control trials. To say that there was a concealed effect of reward in addition would be to concede the whole argument for latent learning.

Tolman's explanation is that the non-reward situation was a good one for learning the spatial relations of the maze. Every unit had one dead end and another end with a door. The last thing done in each case was to go through the door. Recency (which is accepted as favoring sign-gestalts) would strengthen the cognition that the door was the way from one segment to the next, though under non-reward conditions there was no reason for the rat to show what it "knew." The substitution of the food at the end of the maze, a highly demanded goal-object, led the rat to use its cognitive map, to take the turns which led from one unit to the next. Hence the sudden reduction in errors. That the group with late introduction of reward had a tendency to do even better than the regularly rewarded group may conceivably have been due to a more thorough exploration of the maze in the early trials by the non-rewarded group, with consequent better orientation when finally running toward the goal.

Some controversial experiments. The conditions under which latent learning is found are not fully known, and experiments throwing doubt upon latent learning have appeared along with others supporting it.

One of the supporting experiments is that of Buxton (1940) in which the effort was made to meet some of the criticisms of earlier experimental procedures. Rats were permitted to live at night for several nights in a conventional 12-unit T-maze. They were placed into the maze from different positions, and removed in the morning from different exits, so that no learning of entrance or exit factors was involved in their explorations prior to the experiment proper. After 48-hours of food deprivation each rat was fed for 20-30 seconds in the food-box in the maze—the first experience of eating in the maze. The rat was then started at the entrance to the maze in the usual fashion, though gates were now in place to prevent retracing. About 50 per cent of the rats reached the food box with 3 errors or less on the first run, although it was estimated from the records of a control group that not more than 5 per cent would be expected to achieve that good a score. Hence latent learning appears to have been demonstrated. For those animals making such good scores (3 errors or less) it was found that there was a gradient of running speed on this very first trial very much like that which Hull (1932) would expect to appear on later trials from the backward influence of the reward upon the approach behavior. In this situation, no opportunity for such rewarding effect could have operated, so that Buxton attributes his findings to a general pattern or field set up in the rat through previous explorations, and now influencing running speed by the experience of eating in a known part of the maze. Although Buxton's experiment is well designed, and convincing so far as latent learning is concerned, the handling of the data leaves much to be desired when it comes to interpreting his gradients of running speed. Not enough information is given about the performances of the animals within the experimental group which did not meet the criterion of 3 errors or less, nor is information given about the animals within the control group which happened to run the maze in the first trial with few errors. Lacking such information, the skeptical reader is not able to try out his hunches.

Reynolds (1945b) did a critical repetition of Blodgett's experiment, and failed to demonstrate latent learning. The suggestion was made that the form of the curve of learning is different for reward and non-reward learning, and if Blodgett had waited before introducing reward the non-reward rats would have caught up with the rewarded ones in any case. In view of the control group in the Tolman and Honzik experiment, however, this explanation is insufficient. Blodgett (1946) has presented a satisfactory reply to Reynolds' experiment.

Spence and Lippitt (1946) have reported a failure to obtain latent learning under conditions which seem favorable to it. In a Y-maze, with a single choice point, food was always present at the end of one wing, water at the end of the other. Rats deprived of water were forced to run to the food side as often as to the water side. Under the circumstances, there was as much exposure to the food-place as to the water-place, so that place-learning of both was possible. Reinforcement conditions favored the water side, however, since the animals were thirst motivated. The crucial test was made by having the animals hungry instead of thirsty. Which way would they run? All ran to the water side, in spite of the opportunity to go to the place where food had been frequently observed. They thus performed the reinforced act rather than the appropriate act according to a cognition of what-leads-to-what which would be expected according to the principle of latent learning. It is necessary for the believer in latent learning to assert that the thirsty animals were not interested in paying attention to food, and hence did not form the appropriate cognitive structure to be used in the demonstration of latent learning.

That something of the sort is indeed applicable is indicated in the abstract of a further study by Spence and Lippitt (1940) in which they permitted rats neither hungry nor thirsty to explore the maze containing the food and water. Under such circumstances, when motivated by food deprivation or water deprivation, they did show latent learning, that is, they went to the appropriate side for the goal object appropriate to the drive state.

Another Iowa experiment, by Kendler (1946), is consonant with the interpretation that latent learning will be formed so long as the drive conditions during latent learning are either low, permitting "curiosity" to be in the ascendancy, or balanced, so that interest is distributed among the available possibilities. Kendler's rats learned under conditions of both hunger and thirst. A single-choice T-maze had food on one side, water on the other. Animals motivated by both hunger and thirst were trained for four trials a day, the first and third trial being a free choice, but the second and fourth being forced runs to the side opposite the choice. Hence they had equal experience of eating on the food side when hungry and thirsty, and drinking on the water side when hungry and thirsty. The test series consisted of one daily trial on each of four days, when only one of the motives operated. On the first and fourth day the rat was motivated for one goal-object (food or water) and on the second and third day for the other goal-object. The choices on the critical trials were correct in 98 per cent of the opportunities when thirst motivated and in 73 per cent of the opportunities when food motivated.

While the experiments of Kendler are not latent learning experiments, strictly speaking, the results favor a similar consideration of the rôle of motivation in the utilization of habits. That is, spatial arrangements learned under one condition of drive are available for selective use under other conditions of drive. The experiments were designed to test suggestions by Hull and Leeper on the basis of their experiments. Leeper's interpretation, which is like Tolman's, is more satisfactory than Hull's.

In an experiment designed to isolate what is going on during latent learning, Karn and Porter (1946) compared a number of pretraining procedures: (1) habituation to handling, (2) familiarity with the maze, (3) familiarity with the maze and goal orientation, and (4) habituation to being detained in an enclosure similar to the starting compartment in the maze. In general, the more pretraining the animals received the more rapidly they learned when reward was introduced. The authors interpret their data as critical of latent learning because they believe that objective signs of learning can be found during the pretraining period. Thus learning would be manifest rather than latent. The fact of some objective signs of learning during the prereward period does not suffice to disprove latent learning. It does not explain the sudden gains when reward is introduced, nor the results in the reverse experiment—the losses when a new goal-object is substituted.

While more must be found out about latent learning, as an experimental fact it appears to be securely established. It is one of the strongest supports for Tolman's theory, and a matter of considerable embarrassment for reinforcement theories.[39]

ESTIMATE OF TOLMAN'S SIGN LEARNING

Tolman's position on the typical problems of learning. Because it is a system with some aspirations toward completeness, there are statements within Tolman's writings relevant to most of the problems raised by other writers.

1. *Capacity.* In his clear statement of the necessity for capacity laws, Tolman is one of the few systematic writers on learning to focus upon this aspect of learning. The matter interests him chiefly because of the possible graduation of learning tasks from those requiring least to those requiring most intelligence. It is natural that one who makes predictions about what animals will do in problem-solving situations is confronted with the limitations of one organism as compared with another. Tolman believes that the high degree of specificity of capacities in the rat is due to the lack of influence of a culture which prizes certain behaviors over others. Hence one of the contributions of animal studies may be to show processes at a sub-cultural level.[40]

2. *Practice.* The law of exercise is accepted in the sense of the frequency with which the sign, the significate, and the behavioral relation between the two, have been presented. Exercise is not the cause of the initial selection of the right response. Mere frequency without "belonging" does not establish a connection. After a response has been learned, overexercise tends to fix it, making it unduly resistant to change.[41]

3. *Motivation.* Rewards and punishment tend to regulate performance, rather than acquisition, although they are related to acquisition also because they serve as "emphasizers" and because goal-objects confirm or refute hypotheses. Because of the demonstration of latent learning, the law of effect in its usual sense (reward as a strengthener of response tendencies) is not accepted.

4. *Understanding.* Cognitive processes are of the very essence

[39] Among additional experiments on latent learning is that of Herb (1939), which gives an experimental reply to those who argue that the animal does what it last did. See also Seward (1947).

[40] Tolman (1945).

[41] Krechevsky and Honzik (1932).

of molar behavior and learning. Hence Tolman is friendly to learning by creative inference, inventive ideation, and so on. He repeatedly states, however, that he does not wish to imply "introspectively get-at-able conscious contents." The prototype of learning is sensible, reasonable adjustment according to the requirements of the situation; stupid learning occurs as a limiting case when the problem is unsuited to the learner's capacities or is set up in inaccessible form. Insightful learning is not limited to the primates; it is characteristic of rat behavior as well.

5. *Transfer.* The problem of transfer of training as such has been of relatively slight interest to those experimenting with animals. To some extent all the experiments on change of reward, change of drive, place learning, latent learning are experiments on problems related to transfer, that is, the ability to use something learned in one situation in relation to another. All cognitive theories expect a large measure of transfer, provided the essential relationships of the situation are open to the observation of the learner.

6. *Forgetting.* Tolman has not treated the problem of retention, except as a capacity. Having earlier experimented in the field of retroactive inhibition,[42] it is probable that he is friendly toward some theory of retroactive inhibition, and he has indicated that he accepts the Freudian mechanism of repression.[43]

Molar behavior as a field concept. The contention of the student of molar behavior is that there can be a psychological science or behavioral science in its own right, not waiting for its progress upon advances in other sciences. While there is some controversy about this, it is a position which can be defended by both associationists and field psychologists. Hull is able to adopt a concept of molar behavior by this definition.

Beyond the matter of level of discourse there lies the question as to whether molar behavior is essentially a field concept. The question might be put another way. To what extent is Tolman's sign-gestalt theory a true gestalt psychology? Koffka, in his review of Tolman's book, welcomed the friendliness to gestalt, but deplored some limitations which he detected in Tolman's

---

[42] Tolman (1917).
[43] Tolman (1942), pages 63-64.

variety of gestalt.[44] He believed that the distinction between molar and molecular did not go far enough, because the reality of the molecular was acknowledged. Koffka would wish field principles applied to physiology as well as to psychology, so that all explanatory concepts should be molar. Furthermore, Tolman's preoccupation with behavior sequences and historical interpretations makes sign-gestalts only a limited illustration of the variety of possible gestalts.

This disadvantage, from Koffka's point of view, may actually be interpreted as a gain because of the ease of comparison between Tolman's experiments and those done under the influence of other theories. Since the experiments are done with rats in mazes and discrimination situations they are directly comparable to the experiments in the typical American animal laboratory. Therefore Tolman challenges prevailing conceptions such as those of Thorndike and Guthrie and Hull more vividly than the more orthodox gestalt writers, whose situations are often so different as to be incommensurate.

Tolman makes so many generous acknowledgments to Lewin and Adams that there is no doubt of the affiliations between their systems, as third parties have made clear.[45] Their differences became adjusted in a brief and friendly controversy.[46]

The conception of molar behavior is consonant with prevailing conceptions of science, in which some degree of arbitrariness is recognized in the abstractions to be made from the totality of natural events for the purposes of any given science. Natural laws can be formulated in many different ways to cover aspects of occurrences. Tolman has undoubtedly done a service to psychology in joining with those who see the importance of a "psychological" psychology, that is, one whose concepts are appropriate to the level of its descriptions and predictions.

Intervening variables. The distinction between performance and learning, which must be accepted in one form or another, requires that learning be inferred from performance. These inferences are always being made, even in the most "objective" sorts of observations, because only "relevant" physical or physiological

[44] Koffka (1933).
[45] E.g., White (1943).
[46] Tolman (1932a), Lewin (1933b).

occurrences are recorded. There is nothing especially new about Tolman's intervening variable, except that he points out clearly and insistently that the intervening variable is there, and is not out of place in a behavioral science. The logical mistake is easily made of supposing that the physical and physiological terms to which the intervening variables are anchored are themselves independent of theories, which they are not. The kinds of experiments which are performed, the kinds of measurements which are taken, always involve selection by the experimenter. The data, even though reproducible, are not "pure" facts of nature. The question may therefore be raised whether the intervening variables are going to be anything not found in the experimental relationships directly. It is doubtful if a satisfactory answer can be given until the intervening variables are identified with quantities. If there are derived constants, interchangeable from one situation to another, then the intervening variable becomes a scientific construct of some importance.

Explanations according to intervening variables are fruitful at an early stage of theory construction, if only to emphasize again what Lewin has distinguished as *genotypical* versus *phenotypical* explanations.[47] A genotypical explanation goes beneath the surface phenomena to detect an underlying dynamic explanation; a phenotypical explanation tends to stay with surface phenomena, treated statistically or actuarially. The intervening variable is a genotypical sort of explanation.

As previously pointed out, Hull has adopted the intervening variable also, so that the logic is common to the differing points of view. The difference lies in the sorts of intervening variables chosen.

Is rat psychology sufficient? In spite of a vigorous defense of rat psychology as the proper place to find principles of learning laid bare, there are limitations to a theory built exclusively upon rat behavior. In his *Drives toward war*, Tolman points out the great importance of the so-called "dynamisms," deriving from Freudian psychology. Elsewhere, he is impressed by the immensely important bearing that cultural influences have upon human behavior and learning.[48] It is in part to avoid these com-

47 Lewin (1931).
48 Tolman (1945).

plications that a rat psychology is useful, but the recognition of the significance of cultural influences means that a psychology limited to animals below man will always fall short. There is, however, a useful division of labor, and at this stage of our science none can deny that rat psychology has made important contributions to our knowledge about learning.

A comparison with Lewin's work, the system's nearest affiliate, shows many problems which it is possible to attack with human subjects that would be difficult to duplicate with animals. These include the studies of retention of completed and incompleted tasks, the forgetting of intentions, goal-setting. Again, human learning is complicated by verbal factors. If it be true that these are complicating, they are ever-present, and if we are really to understand human learning, we are going to have to study it.

A psychological behaviorism. The important philosophical contribution which Tolman is making is to show that a sophisticated behaviorism can be cognizant of all the richness and variety of psychological situations, and need not be restrained by an effort to build an engineer's conception of the learning machine.

There is a question whether there is any point in being insistent upon a behaviorism. A non-behavioristic pragmatism like that of Carr and Robinson can be fully as verifiable and objective as one which continues the older strictures against the intrusion of verbal reports on relevant private experiences. But among behaviorisms, one like Tolman's opens the way for preserving a psychological outlook toward the subject-matter of psychology.

SUPPLEMENTARY READINGS

BOOKS

Tolman, E. C. (1932) *Purposive behavior in animals and men.*
Tolman, E. C. (1942) *Drives toward war.*

SHORTER INTRODUCTIONS

Spence, K. W. (1942) Theoretical interpretations of learning. In F. A. Moss, edit., *Comparative psychology* (Revised edition), 280-329. (Tolman's theory is treated on pages 284-297.)

Tolman, E. C. (1934) Theories of learning. In F. A. Moss, edit., *Comparative psychology*, 367-408.

Tolman, E. C. (1938) The determiners of behavior at a choice point. *Psychol. Rev.*, 45, 1-41.

CRITICAL REVIEWS

Adams, D. K. (1933) Three theories of learning. *J. gen. Psychol.*, 8, 485-497.

Koffka, K. (1933) Review of Tolman's *Purposive behavior in animals and men. Psychol. Bull.*, 30, 440-451.

Young, P. T. (1933) Review of Tolman's *Purposive behavior in animals and men. Amer. J. Psychol.*, 45, 177-178.

REPRESENTATIVE EXPERIMENTS

Blodgett, H. C. (1929) The effect of the introduction of reward upon the maze performance of rats. *Univ. Calif. Publ. Psychol.*, 4, 113-134.

Brunswik, E. (1929) Probability as a determiner of rat behavior. *J. exp. Psychol.*, 25, 175-197.

Buel, J., and Ballachey, E. L. (1934) Choice-point expectancy in the maze running of the rat. *J. genet. Psychol.*, 45, 145-168.

Crutchfield, R. S. (1939) The determiners of energy expenditure in string-pulling by the rat. *J. Psychol.*, 7, 163-178.

Geier, F. M., and Tolman, E. C. (1943) Goal distance and restless activity. I. The goal gradient of restless activity. *J. comp. Psychol.*, 35, 197-204.

Hall, C. S. (1936) Emotional behavior in the rat. III. The relationship between emotionality and ambulatory activity. *J. comp. Psychol.*, 22, 345-352.

Honzik, C. H., and Tolman, E. C. (1936) The perception of spatial relations by the rat: A type of response not easily explained by conditioning. *J. comp. Psychol.*, 22, 287-318.

Krechevsky, I. (1932) "Hypotheses" versus "chance" in the presolution period in sensory discrimination learning. *Univ. Calif. Publ. Psychol.*, 6, 27-44.

Ritchie, B. F. (1947) Studies in spatial learning. III. Two paths to the same location and two paths to different locations. *J. exp. Psychol.*, 37, 25-38.

Tolman, E. C., Hall, C. S. and Bretnall, E. P. (1932) A disproof of the law of effect and a substitution of the laws of emphasis, motivation and disruption. *J. exp. Psychol.*, 15, 601-614.

Tolman, E. C., and Minium, E. (1942) VTE in rats: Overlearning and difficulty of discrimination. *J. comp. Psychol.*, 34, 301-306.

Tolman, E. C., Ritchie, B. F., and Kalish, D. (1947) Studies in spatial learning. IV. The transfer of place learning to other starting paths. *J. exp. Psychol.*, 37, 39-47.

Chapter 11

THEORIES INFLUENCED BY FIELD CONCEPTIONS

The full impact of a new point of view is felt slowly. There are at first a few converts who promote the new position, a few conservatives who find it important enough to refute. But there are many others fitting neither of these extremes, who learn what is to be learned, and gradually assimilate much of the new, often retaining the old in slightly modified form. Gestalt psychology has had somewhat that history in America. There were a few who swung enthusiastically into line, some who set themselves in active opposition, others whose views have gradually incorporated much of the new theory. When the signs of influence are particularly marked, as in the theories of Lewin and Tolman, it is perhaps permissible to designate the theories as gestalt psychologies, even though they depart from the classical formulations of Wertheimer, Köhler, and Koffka. A number of writers represent related points of view which might be described as *neogestalt* positions. There is no one spokesman for the group because of differences in emphasis among them.

SOME THEORISTS WITH FIELD-LIKE CONCEPTIONS

Many of those influenced by gestalt psychology have worked primarily upon topics other than learning, topics such as perception or social psychology. Among those whose interests have been largely in learning a few have been selected for discussion. Because the boundaries of the position are ill-defined, the choice for listing is very arbitrary. Our purpose is an expository one. If it were historical or biographical, others would have just as much reason for inclusion.

Donald K. Adams. After completing his doctorate under Yerkes at Yale, Adams studied in Berlin, where he became much impressed by Lewin. His doctoral dissertation on the adaptive behavior of cats, was critical of Thorndike, and favorable to gestalt concepts. In 1931, after his European study, he wrote a paper on learning theory which set the problems of learning in relation to psychobiological fields, following many of Lewin's suggestions. The "psychobiological field" is the antecedent of "cognitive structure" or "life space." It is a representation within the organism of the environmental field as related to the organism's needs, sensitivity, and retentivity. The field is remade as the organism encounters barriers in the way of satisfying its needs. The process of need satiation is regulated by a principle called "parsimony." That is a preference for short-cuts, described by others as the principle of least action. Briefly, learning depends upon the capacity of the organism to discriminate, and to be influenced by its prior discriminations through its retentivity; the behavior of the organism is directed by its needs under the controlling principle that it will satisfy its needs as economically as possible.

Adams, with his colleague Zener, later translated one of Lewin's books,[1] and has continued close to his original position. Zener has also contributed an interpretation of learning, which he proposes as a "sign-urge" theory.[2] This is in many respects like Tolman's theory of sign-gestalt.

George Humphrey. If modern field physics is to be taken seriously, psychology cannot get along in a world of Euclidean three-dimensional space with a Newtonian time dimension. This is the contention of Humphrey's system-theory [3] which proposes that the organism represents a four-dimensional space-time integration. Learning is one of the integrations in which the time-dimension is more important than the other dimensions, which happen to be more important, for example, in perception.

Learning may be graded from the simple to the complex. Habituation (negative adaptation) is the simplest. Next in order of complexity is the conditioned response. Finally, there are the

[1] Lewin (1935).
[2] Zener (1937).
[3] Humphrey (1930, 1933, 1937).

types of learning represented by the maze and by problem-solving.

An important principle of which much use is made is that of Le Chatelier, which states the conditions of equilibrium for reversible chemical reactions. For example, under high temperature a reaction will move to the side of the equation on which heat is absorbed, under low temperature to the side under which heat is evolved. There is thus a kind of buffer reaction whereby the temperature is kept as constant as possible against the changes in the environment. The organism is said to react according to similar principles of equilibrium. The principle as applied to organisms is somewhat like that proposed by Cannon, who named it "homeostasis."

Karl S. Lashley. Although he had earlier been an avowed behaviorist, Lashley's experiments on cerebral mechanisms in learning led him away from a reflex doctrine toward more field-like concepts. By the time of his presidential address before the American Psychological Association, delivered at the 1929 International Congress of Psychology,[4] he was ready to propose a mechanism of neural action more nearly in accord with gestalt principles. While the generality attributed to mass action, equipotentiality, and vicarious functioning has become limited by later experiments, he and the students working with him have frequently favored interpretations of learning which might classify as neo-gestalt theories. Among the post-doctoral psychologists who worked in his laboratories, gestalt-like interpretations are evident in the interpretations of Klüver, Krech, Leeper, and Maier,[5] to mention but a few who have taken strong positions.

In a review of neurological theories of learning, Lashley (1929b) was one of the first to emphasize the importance of the distinction between learning and performance, a distinction upon which associationists and field psychologists have tended (until recently) to divide. Once the distinction is emphasized, the way is open for learning as a change in knowledge, or cognitive structure, or some equivalent "central" rather than response-evoking ("peripheral") process.

Apart from his work on cerebral processes, with which this

[4] Lashley (1930a).
[5] E.g., Klüver (1933), Krechevsky (1938a), Leeper (1943), Maier (1932).

book is not concerned, Lashley's later work on learning has revolved largely around the problems of discrimination. He invented the discrimination apparatus in which the rat has to jump to one of a pair of cards.[6] If the correct one is selected, the card falls over, and the animal finds itself on a feeding platform. If the incorrect one is chosen, the animal finds the card fastened, bumps its nose, and falls into a net. This apparatus has proven very convenient for the study not only of what the rat can discriminate, but of the behavioral consequences of reward and punishment in general, including the circumstances giving rise to abnormal seizures, sometimes called experimental neuroses.

In the controversy between Spence and Krech over the interpretation of discrimination learning, to be discussed shortly, Lashley has entered on the side of Krech.[7] Lashley's own theory is somewhat loosely formulated, but it is a theory strongly emphasizing cognitive or perceptual factors:

1. The mechanism of nervous integration is such that when any complex of stimuli arouses nervous activity, that activity is immediately organized and certain elements or components become dominant for reaction while others become ineffective. Such an organization is in part described by gestalt principles of perception, in part by principles of attention.

2. In any trial of a training series, only those components of the stimulating situation which are dominant in the organization are associated. Other stimuli which excite the receptors are not associated because the animal is not set to react to them.[8]

In the later paper referred to, the point is made that the "dimensions" of a stimulus, upon which generalization may be based, are determined by comparison of two or more stimuli. The dimensions are said not to exist until established by differential training.

Norman R. F. Maier. When Maier returned from his study in Berlin he brought back with him the reasoning experiment, which had been undertaken in relation to gestalt theory by Duncker (1926). Working also with Lashley, he began doing reasoning experiments with rats, relating his findings to cerebral

[6] Lashley (1930b).
[7] Lashley (1942); Lashley and Wade (1946).
[8] Lashley (1942), page 242.

damage. These studies, and a series of studies on abnormal behavior in the rat, give a significant place to Maier and his students in the literature of neo-gestalt psychology.

In his collaborative writings with Schneirla,[9] a two-fold classification of learning situations is accepted. Learning is either associative (as in conditioning) or selective (as in trial-and-error). The twofold classification is the one made familiar by Thorndike's distinction between associative shifting and trial-and-error, and by Skinner's types S and R. Maier and Schneirla object to attempts to assimilate simple conditioning to the reinforcement type of situation as advocated by Hull (1943a) and Stephens (1942). The further step in analysis which they take consists in showing that within the course of the typical Pavlov situation there is a shift from simple conditioning to rewarded learning. That is, conditioned salivation is first produced by simple association. Once the form of response has been determined by association, it can be reinforced by the food-eating sequence, and so fall under the principles of selective learning. The unconditioned stimulus thus has a dual rôle: early in the experiment it serves to determine both the occurrence and the form of the conditioned response, while late in the experiment it serves as a reward, just as in trial-and-error learning. While Culler (1938) had earlier pointed out these two possible rôles of a reinforcing agent, he had failed to note that there is a shift from one rôle to the other within the experiment.

The simple conditioning to which Maier and Schneirla refer is near to simple sensory association, in a form which Tolman might accept.[10] The new process is not a sensory-motor connection, but a modified sensory integration. Trial-and-error learning, regulated by rewards and punishments, goes on, but this does not mean that for this process Maier and Schneirla accept a simple reinforcement or law of effect theory. Maier, as we shall see later, has much to criticize in trial-and-error theories which make predictions upon the basis of the cumulative effects of reward, punishment and generalization.

While some forms of problem-solving occur through the processes of trial-and-error, supplemented by equivalence reactions,

---

[9] Maier and Schneirla (1935, 1942).
[10] Tolman (1938b).

the kind of problem-solving which involves spontaneous integrations is classified by Maier as reasoning, and is not included as a form of learning. The distinctiveness of reasoning is one of Maier's most vigorously defended beliefs.

Karl F. Muenzinger. In appraising the influences upon his system, Muenzinger cites particularly the influence of George Herbert Mead. He recognizes the similarity of his position to that of Tolman, but this may be the result either of some direct influence through Tolman's writings, or a parallel development "as the inevitable outcome of the method used." [11]

The necessity for a unit of description is felt, much as it is recognized by Skinner. Instead of an *S-R* relationship, however, Muenzinger settles upon an *S-E* unit. What this means is an abstracted unit of behavior in which there is a constant direction from a *starting-phase S* to an *end-phase E.* The problem of psychology as Muenzinger sees it, is "to discover and describe the facts that bring about and determine the psychological movement from start to end-phase." [12] He finds it convenient to describe each such unit in terms of motivation, discrimination, performance, and affectivity. [13]

Learning is defined either as the discovery of new patterns of meanings or as the change in efficiency of performance. The words "reorganization of the situation" are also used to describe the discovery of new patterns of meanings. These phrases suggest the cognitive features of Muenzinger's system, which brings it into relationship with gestalt views, although it is scarcely a gestalt psychology.

Support for a position like Tolman's has come through a series of studies on motivation,[14] mostly critical of a simple law of effect situation, and through studies of "vicarious trial-and-error" [15] which Tolman has taken over and extended. The moti-

[11] Muenzinger (1942), page ix.
[12] Muenzinger (1942), page 21.
[13] The four categories of description used by Muenzinger bear an interesting equivalence to the fractionation of the learning process by Miller and Dollard (1941). The equivalent terms expressed as pairs are: motivation-drive, discrimination-cue, performance-response, and affectivity-reward. The two sets of categories, despite the family resemblance, are quite independent.
[14] See the list of studies by Muenzinger and his associates, 1934 to 1938.
[15] Muenzinger (1938b).

vational studies show, among other things, that punishment after correct choice can improve performance, suggesting that something like "paying attention" is important. The vicarious trial-and-error studies show the importance of "looking back-and-forth" before choice, as though performance is somehow catalyzed through these successive comparisons.

These brief descriptions of several positions suffice to suggest something of the range and variety of the family of viewpoints being described. They have in common chiefly a rejection of simple associations between stimuli and responses in favor of some kind of organizational processes usually described as perceptual or cognitive. They may or may not be out-and-out field theories.

ASPECTS OF PROBLEM-SOLVING

Problem-solving is a major interest among this group of learning theorists, and it is a useful place to look for their distinctive contributions. Because he has treated the problem most extensively, what follows leans primarily upon the work of Norman R. F. Maier.

According to Maier (1940) there are three major ways in which problem-solving goes on. It may go on, first of all, because the organism varies its behavior. Having varied its behavior, the correct response is hit upon, and learning appears to be by trial-and-error. Or, on the basis of previous experience, the organism may react to a new situation as equivalent to an old one. This may lead to immediate solution, in which case the problem-solving is appropriately described as transfer. The third method of problem-solving requires spontaneous integrations of two or more separate experiences. Such experiments are usually described as detour or insight experiments. Maier prefers to call the process reasoning. Some of the experimental complications within studies of variability and stereotypy, equivalence, and reasoning will now be examined.

Variability: A need and an ability. A general plasticity of habits is what is usually meant by variability in behavior, so that, for example, in a checkerboard maze rats may use a number of routes in random alternation. Another possible meaning is preference for variation over routine, for novelty over stereotypy. Maier (1939 *b*) believes evidence in experiments with rats justifies the distinction between the need or preference for variety, on the one hand, and the ability to vary behavior in a given situation. He draws heavily in his discussion upon three experiments by Krech.

The first experiment,[16] using a Dashiell checkerboard maze, showed normal animals to use 5.5 different routes in 15 runs, while rats with brain lesions took an average of 3.0 different routes. The difference in variability is clear, but from these data it cannot be determined whether the difference depends upon ability or preference.

In the second experiment there were two routes to the goal. One was a fixed and shorter route, the other was a variable and longer route.[17] Normal rats, in spite of the well-known tendency to prefer shorter paths, under these conditions chose the variable path, even though it was longer. Rats with brain lesions, however, chose the shorter fixed route. The operated animals were thus able to make the discrimination between longer and shorter routes, but lacked the preference for variation shown by the normal animals. Krech repeated his experiment [18] using a similar maze but making the variable path the shorter one. Now all rats chose the shorter path. The rats with brain lesions were able to run with the variations demanded, and still choose the shorter path. This supports the contention of Maier that in the previous experiment there was a difference in preference between the normal and operated animals. With reduced intelligence (as with brain lesions) there is also some loss in the ability to vary as shown by the variety of "hypotheses" or alternative systematic position habits used by normal and operated rats.

As learning occurs, variability is usually reduced. When the problem has been solved, a specific pattern of behavior may replace the initial variability. This may account for Guthrie's finding stereotypy the most general characterization of associative learning. But according to Maier stereotyped adaptive behavior

[16] Krechevsky (1937*a*).
[17] Krechevsky (1937*b*).
[18] Krechevsky (1937*c*).

of this kind can be changed readily when new alternatives are presented.

Stereotypy as a result of frustration. Another kind of reduction of variability is to be distinguished from that which results from a preference for one pattern of behavior over another. This is the kind which Maier calls an *abnormal fixation*. When under appropriate conditions such a fixation has been established, it is no longer modified by presenting an alternative. The fixed mode of behavior has to be destroyed by appropriate means before a new pattern can be established. These fixed modes of behavior found in rat experiments are especially interesting for the light which they may throw ultimately upon compulsive symptoms in man. It is well known clinically that compulsive symptoms are very resistant to psychotherapy. They may be dynamically similar to the abnormal fixations in the laboratory which cannot be changed by the usual methods of reward and punishment, but which can nevertheless be broken by proper procedures.

Two chief experimental situations give rise to fixations in the rat. The first of these is the insoluble problem in a discrimination apparatus of the Lashley jumping type. Two windows are presented, but the card which is free and hence falls on the food platform when the rat jumps appears now on the right and now on the left, so that no matter what the rat does it strikes a latched card half the time and is punished by a fall into the net. In this frustrating situation the animal has to be forced to jump by an air-blast or other such device. When forced to respond it develops a fixation, most commonly a position preference. That is, it will jump invariably to the left window or to the right window. In some cases a discrimination preference is developed, so that it jumps to one of the exposed cards no matter which window it appears in, and in spite of punishment half the time.[19] The second method of producing fixations was earlier noted by Hamilton and Krechevsky (1933). When a shock is presented at the choice point in the alley type of discrimination box, a learned discrimination may be converted into a fixation, i.e., a position habit. Such a fixation is comparable to that in the insoluble situation.[20]

[19] Maier, Glaser, and Klee (1940).
[20] Kleemeier (1942).

These fixations are different from strong habits in that they are unusually resistant to modification by ordinary reward and punishment procedures. Once a fixation has been set up it persists in spite of punishment every trial for hundreds of trials, in spite of long vacations, and in spite of metrazol shocks.[21]

It is quite possible to obtain regularized responses which are the result of learning and represent strong habits, and to contrast them experimentally with fixations, which they superficially resemble. Whether they are habits or fixations can be determined by their subsequent history when the attempt is made to alter them.

In the first experiment of the series, Maier, Glaser and Klee (1940) showed not only that fixations differ from habits in their resistance to change, but showed that the fixation persisted *even when the animal gave evidence that it had learned the discrimination.* The first stage consisted in establishing a position habit, either through rewarding jumping to one of the two windows, or through presenting the animal with the insoluble problem (i.e., punishment half the time, regardless of which card is chosen). There were 31 animals which established the position habit, so that 98 per cent of the last 160 trials were responses to position. The cards themselves were alternated in random order, so that with the position habit a discrimination habit could not be developed.

After the position habit was well established, all rats were presented with a discrimination problem. The card with a black circle on a white background was made the positive (rewarded) stimulus, and the card with the white circle on black background was negative (punished). The animal, in order to knock over the card and reach the food platform, had to jump to the positive card whether it was on the right or the left, so that persistence in the position habit would lead to punishment half the time. Under these circumstances the rats which had formed position habits in the insoluble problem learned the discrimination problem less easily than those which had been rewarded for position responses. It may be noted, however, that the objective change between the two problems was not as striking for them. The rewarded rats shifted from 100 per cent reward to 50 per cent punishment

[21] Maier and Klee (1941).

between the position problem and the discrimination problem, while the rats trained on the insoluble problem received 50 per cent punishment during the establishment of the position preference and continued to receive 50 per cent punishment during the discrimination problem though now the punishment always followed a given card. It is surprising that any of them learned to discriminate under these circumstances; it is to be expected that those which learned were slower than the other groups.

The findings of the experiment with which we are now concerned have to do with the nature of the continued preference for the position habit, even with 50 per cent punishment, on the part of 13 of the 31 rats which failed to learn the discrimination problem. In the effort to break the position habit after it had continued unaltered through the discrimination cycle, each of the 13 rats now received 100 trials (10 per day) in which the position response was punished every time. Not one of the rats broke the position habit. This is taken as evidence that the fixation is abnormal, and does not conform to the usual principles of learning and unlearning.

That these 13 rats which continued their position preference throughout the discrimination trials (and against 100 per cent punishment) were paying attention to the cards and had actually formed the necessary associations was evidenced in two ways. One was the greater resistance to jumping to the negative card than to the positive card when it appeared in the aperture of the preferred side. A rating was devised on the basis of delay against increasing intensity of the air-blast used to force the jump. By this rating, resistance to the positive card decreased somewhat during the course of the discrimination trials, but it increased markedly in the presence of the negative card. A second measure of discrimination was the number of abortive jumps. When the animal has in a sense "given up" and is prepared to fall into the net, the jump is often not directly at the card. Not infrequently the animal strikes the card with its side. These abortive jumps, about equal in frequency to the positive and negative card at the beginning of the discrimination training, disappeared almost entirely in the presence of the positive card, but increased markedly in the presence of the negative card. The course of discrimination according to these criteria is shown in Figures 39 and 40. Of the 13 rats, 9 expressed their differentiation both in their resistance and in their abortive behavior, 3 in their resistance behavior only, and 1 in its abortive behavior only. Every animal which did not show in its choices that it had learned the discrimination,

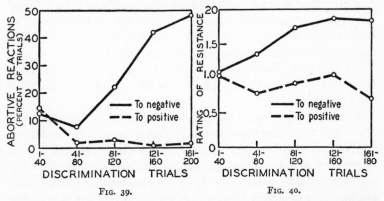

FIG. 39. FIG. 40.

FIGURE 39. EVIDENCE FOR DISCRIMINATION AS SHOWN BY ABORTIVE REACTIONS.

The curves represent the mean results for 13 rats which did not learn to discriminate according to the ordinary criteria of appropriate response to positive and negative cards. Although slaves to a position habit, they gave evidence of discrimination by turning sideways while jumping (preparing to fall into the net?) when the negative card was exposed to them, although they jumped straight ahead when the positive (safe) card was exposed. That the discrimination was progressive is shown by the separation of the curves as learning proceeded. Based on a recomputation of the data presented by Maier, Glaser and Klee (1940).

FIGURE 40. EVIDENCE FOR DISCRIMINATION AS SHOWN BY RESISTANCE TO JUMPING.

The same rats whose abortive jumps are recorded in Figure 39 also showed evidence of discrimination through greater resistance to jumping when the negative (dangerous) card was exposed than when the positive (safe) card was exposed, even though they continued to jump according to a persistent position habit. Based on a recomputation of the data presented by Maier, Glaser and Klee (1940).

showed in these secondary ways that it differentiated rewarded from punished card. Yet it was so mastered by its compulsion that it could not act in accordance with its knowledge.

Further tests were made with some of the rats. For two of them, the position habit persisted unaltered through 460 discrimination trials. They were then given guidance to break the fixation. The window opposite the position preference was left without a card, and the rat was guided to jump through the open window. This guidance was manual. That is, the experimenter pointed the rat toward the window, gently corrected any orientation back to the old window, rather in the manner of an animal trainer. After 20 such trials, the positive card was placed in the window. The rats now chose the positive card and continued to choose it for the next 120 trials regardless of the side on which it appeared. Once the fixation was broken, they showed that they had learned the differentiation called for in the 460 discrimination trials which had preceded. Now they were able to use what they had learned.

The breaking of fixations was later followed up by Maier and Klee (1945), who compared guidance with trial-and-error methods. As in the experiments just described, position preferences were established either through rewarding regular jumping to the originally preferred side or by confronting the rat with the insoluble problem. Then a discrimination problem was taught either by the usual trial-and-error method (rewarding correct responses and punishment of incorrect ones) or by a combination of guidance and trial-and-error, in which manual guidance was used to break fixated position responses.

The trial-and-error method showed that habits established on the basis of reward are more easily modified than those adopted as fixations in the frustrating insoluble situation. Of 29 rats which had established the position habit through motivated learning, 20 solved the discrimination problem without special guidance. By contrast, of the 28 rats which developed position habits in the frustrating situation, only 7 learned the subsequent discrimination unaided. The rest of the animals in both groups persisted in the position habit throughout 200 trials.

Guidance procedures succeeded admirably in breaking fixations and in permitting the new discriminatory choices to appear for other groups of rats whose preliminary training was similar to those above. Of 30 rats which learned position preferences under the influence of reward, all learned the subsequent discrimination problem when guidance was included as part of their training. Of the 29 rats which acquired fixed preferences in the insoluble problem, all but 3 learned the discrimination problem, and all of these non-learners were in the first cycle of the experiment in which arrangements were not ideal. In the second cycle, when guidance and trial-and-error were alternated in the training, there were no animals which failed to learn the discrimination.

Additional evidence of the course of discrimination favors the view that guidance is an effective technique for breaking an old response, for making the animal face an alternative to a fixated response, but it is not highly effective for teaching a new response. The trial-and-error method, on the other hand, is favorable for learning new responses, but not effective for breaking old ones. Thus the two methods, used together, are most practical in retraining.

The advice which emerges has been expressed as follows:

. . . the results show that guidance is primarily effective for breaking a fixation and relatively ineffective for establishing a new response. This suggests that guidance could be discontinued as soon as the old response is broken . . . By using guidance in its most effective role (breaking the old response) and trial-and-error in its most effective role (learning a new response), one should be able to facilitate the learning of new adjustments. Alternating trial-and-error and guidance trials permits one to determine when guidance is no longer necessary and this would seem to make it the preferable method. The amount of guidance can be adapted to the needs of the individual case, thus permitting it to be adapted to the strengths of the fixations or of the habits which are being broken.[22]

These results are taken to be critical of quantitative theories such as those of Spence (1936) which reduce changes in behavior to modifications in the relative strengths of competing tendencies. Two aspects of habit change have to be distinguished: freeing the animal from the old response and utilizing the new. Unless qualitative distinctions are made carefully enough, a quantitative approach is bound to be very limited in its predictive value.

The upshot of these experiments is that frustrating agents must be avoided in learning if abnormally rigid habits are to be avoided and teachability not interfered with. Punishment may be a negative incentive, and so aid in ordinary learning, but it is also likely to be a frustrating agent and hence interfere with adaptive adjustments.[23] When an undesirable or persistent response is to be

[22] Maier and Klee (1945), page 155.
[23] Maier and Klee (1943).

broken, it is important to diagnose its origin. If it originated in frustration it cannot be changed as easily as if it is merely the consequence of strong habit.

Maier has hypothetically extended these findings to the interpretation of social movements.[24] He distinguishes between frustration-instigated movements, which have some of the characteristics of abnormal fixations, and goal-motivated movements, which correspond more nearly to adaptive learning. He makes it appear plausible that frustration-instigated movements are likely to be the more powerful, although goal-motivated movements are no doubt the more desirable. There is a more primitive organization under frustration, so that the leader in a dictatorship has excessive power. He determines the pattern according to which the energies are expressed, and gives unity to a movement which attracts fanaticism of varying origins. Such unity is much harder to achieve around rational goals. When striving for goals people are more far-sighted and do not concern themselves over immediate difficulties. The movement toward socialism, motivated around a goal, has little vigor; communism contains the feature of frustration, which gives it more vitality. It is the same sort of difference which Maier believes makes nations more effective in waging wars than in constructing a peace program.

Equivalence reactions and transfer. The equivalence of perceived patterns is one of the primary emphases of gestalt psychology. It is from such transposable qualities that the theory derived its name. Part of the attack on association theory was based on the criticism that association implied a response to *absolute* characteristics of a stimulus, whereas gestalt psychology emphasized *relational* characters. One of the oft-quoted experiments is that of Köhler (1918) with the hen, in which the hen learned to react to the darker of two grays, rather than to the absolute brightness.

In theories such as those of Spence (1937) and Hull (1939a), equivalences are based on dimensional similarities, such as may be scaled on a psychophysical continuum, and on habit strength engendered as a result of prior learning. How the organism will react to a novel stimulus will depend upon the place along these intersecting dimensions where the stimulus is found, each dimen-

[24] Maier (1942).

sion contributing its own portion of excitation or inhibition to the resulting compound excitatory tendency. While both Hull and Spence have been able to make ingenious predictions upon the basis of their theory, they have been vigorously opposed by those leaning toward field theory.[25]

The opposing theory is that the organization of habit tendencies is not nearly as simple as the Hull-Spence theory suggests. The Hull-Spence theory makes no allowance for the importance of comparisons between stimuli in setting up the psychophysical dimensions, although the operational definition of the dimensional continuum (in j.n.d.'s) assumes that the subject can discriminate along the dimension, and depends upon the psychophysical experiment in which such comparisons are important. The Hull-Spence theory also minimizes what the organism brings to the situation in the way of "hypotheses" or "expectations," although Hull and Spence may recognize "preparatory" responses.[26]

Lashley has designed several experiments to refute the Hull-Spence interpretation.

In one experiment [27] he trained rats to respond to the larger of two circles, then substituted a large triangle for the circle. The rats reacted to the triangle, presumably on the basis of size of pattern. Having reacted on the basis of size, the question is whether or not triangularity will be learned if the triangle is repeatedly rewarded as the positive stimulus. Further practice was given with the large triangle as positive and the small circle as negative. Then a test situation was presented in which the choice had to be made between a circle and a triangle of equal area. Presumably the rat has two trained "dimensions" along which it might choose: size or triangularity. Size is eliminated because the two stimuli are equal by this dimension; if size is the basis of choice, results will conform to chance. Triangularity remains as a possible choice, because the triangle has always been positive. Circularity was previously positive also, although the small circle was consistently negative and the small triangle never so. What the rats did was to respond on a chance basis. Lashley interprets

<hr />

[25] Krechevsky (1937d, 1938c), Lashley (1942), Lashley and Wade (1946), Leeper (1944), McCulloch (1939) and Maier (1939a). For a summary of the controversy to the time of his writing, see Spence (1945).

[26] Spence (1937).

[27] Lashley (1942).

this to mean that they had been reacting to size all along, and rewarding the triangle produced no preferences along the dimension of triangles-of-different-size. When trained to size, the rats "paid no attention" to triangularity.[28]

In later experiments,[29] rats were first trained to respond positively to a white circle opposed to a black card. Then another discrimination was learned, involving two white circles, one larger than the other, one of the circles having been reinforced in the first experiment. Lashley and Wade found that it did not matter in the second discrimination whether the circle reinforced was the one reinforced in the preceding experiment or not. According to the Hull-Spence theory it would be supposed that the preceding reinforcements would have favored that circle. Not only was the previously reinforced figure not preferred in the next discrimination, but there was some slight evidence "statistically unreliable but . . . consistent in all ten experiments" that the new discrimination was formed more rapidly when the initial reaction to the familiar member of the pair had to be extinguished. Tests with chimpanzees, monkeys, and man, are interpreted as supporting the point of view that the neo-Pavlovian interpretation of generalization as a result of training is false. What generalization is found in conditioning is said to be a failure of association, rather than an indication of it.

The argument over discrimination and stimulus equivalence has two aspects. On the one hand, there is the problem of the cumulative effect of previous experience. This is the issue over continuity-discontinuity, the Hull-Spence position being that present learning is continuous with (that is, predictable from) past learning, while the neo-gestalt position is that there may be sudden turning points, in which the past experience is restructured in new ways relatively independent of the frequency of prior reinforcements and extinctions, and significantly related to the present patterning of the stimuli. On the other hand, there is the

[28] The question of relative difficulty of response to "size" and to "triangularity" may be raised. The complementary experiment should be performed in which response to triangularity is first learned (with size constant), then the subsequent training is to a triangle as the larger of two figures, the other a circle. A test with a large circle and a small circle, on Lashley's theory, should result in chance responses.

[29] Lashley and Wade (1946). For a reply see Hull (1947).

problem of response to the absolute versus the relative properties of the stimuli. This is not independent of the preceding point, because a simple accumulation of response tendencies and their dimensional generalization requires response to the absolute properties of the stimulus. Hence the attack upon the Hull-Spence position takes two forms: (1) the criticisms of the reinforcement principle, with its assumptions of the cumulative effects of reward and punishment, and (2) the insistence upon responses to the relational character of stimuli. Because the argument still goes on, with new data on both sides, it is difficult to render a decision. It is possible that some sort of compromise will eventually clarify the situation.

Reasoning. Reasoning has as its distinguishing characteristic the reorganization of two or more isolated experiences in such a manner that a goal is achieved. How this reorganization is achieved is somewhat obscure, but one of the aspects is a dynamic process which Maier calls *direction*. A direction may be present when integrations do not occur (and may, in fact, block solution). Direction is not therefore identical with the successful reorganization process.

The origin of the stresses within the problematic situation which lead to reorganization is important theoretically. The somewhat orthodox gestalt viewpoint is that forces within the problematic situation set up a field of stress leading to the restructuring of the experiences involved without any outside force entering.[30] Maier disagrees, in that he believes direction to be something which the organism brings to the situation, and is therefore something in addition to the experiences themselves.

A distinction is needed between *reproductive* thinking and *productive* thinking.[31] Reproductive thinking is that in which subjective identity in past learning and the demands of the problem are present at the outset, so that the problems are solved by the process of equivalent stimuli. Habitual directions suffice to produce old solutions. Such habitual directions correspond to Krech's *hypothesis*, Ach's *determining tendency*, and Woodworth and Sells' *atmosphere effect*.

Productive thinking involves changes or restructuring of past

[30] Duncker (1945).
[31] Duncker (1926), Maier (1945).

experience. Habitual directions do not lead to creative thinking; new directions are needed. The new direction must give rise to a new combination and a new product. Often the sudden change of meaning introduces a surprise element, what Bühler (1916) calls the *Aha!-Erlebnis*. This constitutes the experience of insight. "Insight thus becomes a consequence rather than a cause of problem-solving."[32]

The common meaning of learning is to profit by experience, to improve through repeated trials or exposures to the problem. In order to emphasize that reasoning is essentially a contemporary process, a spontaneous combination of isolated experiences, Maier insists that reasoning be considered a process separate from learning.[33] The experiences which are reorganized are, of course, learned, but enough experience does not always mean a reasoned solution to the problem upon which that experience bears. The essence of reasoning is what goes on at the time the learner is confronted with the problem.

Rats were taught problems which could be solved by reasoning alone, and others in which prior experience of solution (learning) either aided or hindered the solution by reasoning.[34] It was found that those rats whose brains had been damaged showed greater loss in reasoning ability than in learning ability, thus confirming Maier's belief in the separability of the processes.

In Figure 41 there is a schematic representation of the problem used to test reasoning, and in Figure 42 the variation used in the testing of reasoning and learning. As reasoning problems both are essentially alike. The rat is given two experiences, the first of which is general familiarity with the tables and the paths from one to the other. The second experience is that of being fed on one of the tables. Then placed at one of the other tables as a starting point, the problem is to combine the knowledge of the total situation with the knowledge of the food location, and to act accordingly, that is, to make the correct choice of the single alternative before it. If these separate experiences are integrated in this manner, without repeated reward for running a fixed path,

[32] Maier (1945), page 51.
[33] Maier (1931*a*, 1937).
[34] Maier (1932). These experiments have provoked criticism and reply, Wolfe and Spragg (1934), Maier (1935).

the solution is said to be by reasoning. If, however, the rat has once learned to go from one table to another for food, and this opportunity is then again presented, the experience is one of learning. Running along the path has been rewarded, and the association therefore established through experience.

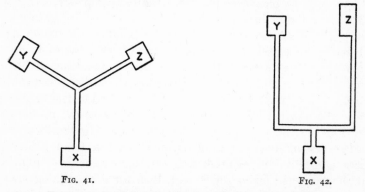

FIG. 41.   FIG. 42.

FIGURE 41. APPARATUS FOR STUDYING REASONING IN RATS.

The three platforms are discriminable in shape and in texture. The rat is said to exhibit reasoning if through experiencing food on one platform it can return to this platform without error by starting from either of the others. From Maier (1929).

FIGURE 42. APPARATUS FOR STUDYING REASONING VERSUS LEARNING IN RATS.

The apparatus is logically similar to that in Figure 41, but one platform regularly served as the starting-point, and the choice of end-point was always between the other two. By regularly finding food on one side in 10 consecutive trials a "habit" could be set up, opposite to the "information" in a single trial at the beginning of the test day. Returned to the starting point, the rat could either "reason" that food would be where it had just been found, or he could follow the dictates of habit, which would lead to error. From Maier (1932).

The first situation was used as a reasoning problem. At the beginning of each run the rat was given a period of exploration, then fed on one of the tables, then permitted to start from one of the others. Each day this was repeated, but the food table and the starting table were different from the day before, and the rat had therefore to combine the experiences just presented to it. This is called the reasoning test (R).

The second situation was used for the combination of reasoning and learning. The experiences to be combined by reasoning were the same as before, except that table A was always used as the starting-place, and feeding was either at B or at C. Following the preliminary experiences, which gave the essentials for solution by reasoning, the rat was given seven additional rewarded runs along the same pathway, thus adding learning to reasoning. If the same problem was presented the following day, the first solution would be benefitted both by the previous day's learning, and by the experiences sufficient for solution by reasoning. Hence the first trial of such a day is considered a test of R + L (reasoning plus learning). Every third day the reasoning problem was made to conflict with prior learning by feeding the animal on the side opposite that to which it had learned to run to food. Now the solution by reasoning had to overcome the effects of previous practice in running to the other table. Hence this is said to be a test of R − L (reasoning minus the interference due to learning). Successes, as predicted, were higher for R + L than for R alone, and lower for R − L than for R alone. Algebraic determination of the relative contribution of reasoning and learning (admittedly a somewhat crude computation) showed the reasoning ability to fall off strikingly with increasing cortical damage, while the learning ability remained more nearly constant. That is, the relative contribution of learning and of reasoning changed with brain lesions, learning playing a relatively greater role in rats with more severe brain damage. The results are summarized in the table. The computed values for R agree fairly well with the experimentally obtained values, but they suggest that the pure reasoning experiment was somewhat harder than the reasoning aspect of the experiment involving both reasoning and learning. This is plausible in view of the fact that in the pure reasoning experiment the starting point was shifted as well as the food platform, while in the other experiment the starting point remained the same throughout. Thus the rat was confronted with only two cognitive alternatives altogether instead of six alternatives presented two at a time. In view of the later finding [35] that the reasoning problem, if mastered prior to operation, could be retained beyond it, Maier seems to have demonstrated that reasoning ability is differentiated from learning ability as he defines them.

[35] Maier (1938).

RELATIVE IMPORTANCE OF REASONING AND OF LEARNING IN THE SOLUTION OF
PROBLEMS INVOLVING BOTH AS AFFECTED BY CEREBRAL LESIONS
(Maier, 1932)

	Number of Rats	Correct Runs in Per Cent (Chance = 0)			Computed Values ‡	
		R	R + L	R − L	R	L
Normal	19	80.7	89.1	70.1	79.6	9.5
Smaller lesions *	13	49.6	73.0	45.2	59.1	13.9
Larger lesions †	18	4.1	34.9	10.5	22.7	12.2

* Lesions less than 17 per cent of cortex.
† Lesions from 18 to 41 per cent of cortex.
‡ Computed algebraically from R + L and R − L.

At the time of writing, Maier has published four experimental papers on adult human reasoning.[36] The last of these may serve to illustrate his approach to the problem.

The question attacked is the role of past experiences (memories) relative to the role of contemporaneous experiences (perceptions) in productive thinking and reasoning.

One possibility in problem-solving is that the solution is all a matter of transfer. In that case whether or not a person solves a problem depends solely on what he has learned previously. Thorndike's theory of identical elements or the gestalt theory of equivalence or transposition would then account for problem solution. Under the circumstances the task of the teacher would be to predict what situations the learner is likely to face and to provide situations equivalent to them. There is an alternative possibility, however, favored by Maier, and to be subjected to test. This is the possibility that a thinker may reconstruct his earlier experience so as to *create* an equivalence not there before. The reconstruction or reorganization of experience is the essence of reasoning. In this reconstruction process the contemporary situation must play a decisive role.

There were three main groups of adults in the experiment, solving the same problem in different contextual backgrounds. Group 1 was given an experience with the string problem previously used,[37] but in connection with this experience there were

[36] Maier (1930, 1931*b*, 1933, 1945).
[37] Maier (1930).

some properties to be made use of in the next problem, the hat-rack, presently to be described. The hint toward solution is contained in a structure of sticks and clamps, called the prop structure. With the essential prop structure still standing, and thus in the perceptual field, the new hatrack problem was presented. Group 2 was given the same sort of experience with the string problem, but before the hatrack problem was presented the prop structure was removed. Therefore, in order to draw upon its principles, it had to be recalled. Group 2 brought memories to

FIGURE 43. STRING-PROBLEM USED IN THE STUDY OF REASONING.
The prop-structure is incidental to hanging the strings from the ceiling. The ends of the string are to be tied together. The principle of the pendulum is involved in the solution. After Maier (1930) as reproduced in Maier (1945).

the new task, whereas Group 1 had the advantage of perceiving what Group 2 remembered. Group 3 was given the hatrack problem without the prior experience of the string problem or of the prop structure which was part of it. Before turning to the results, we must first describe the string problem and the hatrack problem.

The arrangement of the experimental room for the string problem is shown in Figure 43. The subject assisted the experimenter in arranging the structure to support the strings against the ceiling without marring the ceiling. It was erected from boards and clamps as shown. These boards and clamps were to enter the next problem, but they were introduced quite incidentally at this point as a way of arranging the strings. The problem presented the subject was that of tying together the ends of the strings. They are too far apart for the subject to reach them both at once and tie them as usual. Solution consists in fastening a pliers to the longer string and transforming it into a pendulum. When it is started swinging the subject can hold the other string, catch the pendulum at the end of its swing, and solve the problem. Experiences have to be transformed in this solution. The string which is at first judged simply as short or long must be transformed into a pendulum, even though this requires shorten-

FIGURE 44. HATRACK PROBLEM USED IN THE STUDY OF REASONING.

It is necessary to see the clamp and sticks in a new functional relationship, although the physical structure is that experienced four times in the string-problem of Figure 43. From Maier (1945).

ing a string already too short. The pliers which is intended for other purposes must be transformed into a weight, suitable as the bob of a pendulum. In the earlier experiments [38] this problem was studied in detail. Here suggestions were given so that the solution was obtained within ten minutes. The subject was told that he would have to solve the next problem by himself.

The hatrack problem uses the same physical construction principles as in the string problem. The subject is given two sticks and a clamp and told to make a structure suitable for a hatrack. The solution is shown in Figure 44. Actually four such "hatracks" had been made, with the experimenter's assistance, in supporting the strings against the ceiling.

[38] Maier (1931b, 1933).

The chief difference between the supports in the string experiment and the hatrack is the way in which they are perceived. In the string problem, the sticks support the top rod, which in turn supports the string. In the hatrack problem, the ceiling supports the sticks. This is a shift in perception much like the reversal of figure and ground. The question is whether or not this shift can be made more easily if the possibilities are present in perception or only in memory. The results were clearly in the predicted direction, as shown below.

SOLUTIONS TO THE HATRACK PROBLEM
(Maier, 1945)

	Number of Subjects	Number Who Solved	Per Cent Who Solved
Group 1. Prop-structure visibly present	25	18	72
Group 2. Prop-structure experienced but removed	25	12	48
Group 3. Prop-structure not experienced	25	6	24

In order to check on the equivalence between the hatrack structure and the prop structure prior to the stress of the problem-situation, a further group of 180 subjects watched the experimenter clamp two poles together and wedge them to the ceiling. Then they were asked to write down what useful functions the structure could possibly serve. Three-quarters of the group saw the structure as a prop or brace. By the most generous estimate, not over one-quarter saw the structure as something upon which things might be hung or tied to or leaned against. Thus direct equivalence out of past experience could account perhaps for some of the solutions by those who had experienced the props in other connections, but for the most part the equivalence must have been created under the stress of the problem.

The table shows that it was easier for this reorganization of experience to occur when the elements of the solution were perceptually present than when they were recalled, but in either case there was an advantage arising out of the immediately prior experience.

An additional reason for supposing that the solution required the reorganization of experience rather than mere equivalence was the fact that solutions were often delayed. If there were equivalence, it would be expected to lead to immediate solutions. Out of 36 solutions, only 17 occurred within the first five minutes. Among these 5 subjects had offered an alternative solution before arriving at the correct one. None of the other 19 solutions occurred within the first 10 minutes after the problem was presented.

As further support to the notion that reorganization takes place more easily when aspects are present perceptually, nine of the subjects of Group 2 who failed to solve the problem were asked to write out what they remembered of the string problem and to draw the structure as they remembered it. With the drawing before them, 7 of the 9 solved the problem.

Past experience can be an inhibiting factor as well as an aid to reasoning. In one of Maier's experiments [39] solutions were increased when subjects were told to refrain from using habitual approaches to solution. No direction at all may be better than a false one. Maier believes that we may discover methods of teaching which will free people from enslavement to past experience, and in so doing encourage a more effective use of reasoning. One method is that of training people to react to different aspects of a situation, for example, to see the ceiling as holding up the pillar while the pillar holds up the ceiling. Under such circumstances solutions by equivalence can be increased because the problem-solver is accustomed to discover and create new equivalences.

Because human reasoning is "mental" if any processes are, the question arises as to the relative value of controlled experimentation and retrospective verbal reports in studying the process in man. In part because of his desire to treat lower animals and human beings comparatively, Maier prefers not to depend upon introspective techniques. But this preference is influenced also by what he discovered in a study of the representation in conscious awareness of the steps in solution.[40] The crucial act of

[39] Maier (1933).
[40] Maier (1931b).

integration is, in fact, lost to the reasoner, and his report on what happened is often misleading. False directions, which have hindered solution, may be reported as helpful, whereas the hints which led to solution may have been picked up without awareness of their significance.

COMMON CHARACTERISTICS OF THE VIEWPOINTS INFLUENCED BY FIELD THEORY

The position of the writers under consideration is a resultant of a friendliness and openmindedness toward the kinds of experimental relationships discovered by or emphasized by gestalt psychologists, combined with a positivistic eclecticism foreign to classical gestalt writers. It is not surprising that among the neo-gestalt writers one does not find the clarity or forcefulness of position to be found among those more loyal to one or the other of the contemporary cults in psychology. A positivist background means that one is tolerant of some looseness, some multiplicity, some pluralism, within the system. Tolman [41] can recognize seven varieties of learning, Muenzinger can experiment on "the Thorndike effect" or on VTE, Maier accepts associative learning, selective learning, and reasoning, Lashley speaks in both the language of attention and of organization. Hence there is a *rapprochement* between contemporary functionalists and the neo-gestalt group, with the stricter stimulus-response psychologists forming a more evident opposition. The orthodox behaviorists tend to favor a blindly mechanical model, rather than a merely pragmatic one. This forces them to refuse to accept certain categories of description easily acceptable to the functionalist group.[42]

But within the breadth and looseness of position represented by these writers, there are some common characteristics.

Learning distinguished from performance. The distinction between learning and performance, if it is emphasized, leads inevit-

[41] Tolman's position can be considered as within this family of unorthodox gestalt-like views.

[42] Many experimenters within conditioning find it possible to use concepts like those of Tolman and Lashley rather than those of Guthrie, Hull, or Skinner (e.g., Wickens, 1940). In other words, a given type of experimentation does not require systematic rigidity. Woodworth illustrates as clearly as anyone that gestalt-like concepts may be incorporated into a functionalist system.

ably to the rejection of a theory which makes learning the strengthening of response tendencies, whether through simple conditioning or through reinforcement. Learning becomes instead a matter of sensory reorganization or association or redintegration, secondarily related to performance by way of motivation. It is a common belief of those under consideration that perceptual features in learning are important, that something like cognitive structure is required.

In a brief statement of his alternative to Hull's theory, Leeper (1944) analyzes learning as a four-fold process involving (1) perceptual organization, (2) redintegration, (3) fusion of redintegrative material with current perceptual material, and (4) final effector activity. It is evident that a large role is assigned perception and perception-like processes, while the response (effector) processes come in late. The organism uses "whatever effector activities are at his command and seem appropriate to him as a means of dealing with the particular objective situations."

Motivational relationships believed to be too complicated for the law of effect. While the empirical law of effect holds as a crude approximation, closer experimental study shows an enormous complication in the actions of rewards and punishments upon learning. These writers, more than any others, have given experimental evidence that it is not possible to count the number of reinforcements and non-reinforcements, apply some kind of formula to them (along with an interpretation of generalization), and explain what happens. The positive stimulus may have more weight than the negative stimulus, punishment may have any number of effects whether given before or after choice, for the correct or for the incorrect response, or in an insoluble situation. The "dimensions" of the stimuli to which the organism reacts may not be natively given, but may result from comparison stimuli available. Pattern of reinforcements may be as important as cumulative frequencies.

Field reorganization makes for discontinuities in learning. A concept of sudden restructuring of a field, leading to problem solution, as in insight or reasoning experiments, does not mean a denial of the role of experience in learning, but it does mean that the utilization of that experience is regulated by contemporary factors not completely expressed in the prior habits of response. Prior habits of response there are, and there are biases and preferences, and temporary sets and directions—all of these are brought to the situation. But the structuring of the situation itself adds something to all of this, which makes prior learning more or less accessible, which makes the problem easier or harder. A neo-gestalt theorist would prefer to supplement a statement of prior history with this contemporaneous analysis in predicting what will happen. Because this contemporary structuring intro- duces new patterns of stresses and strains, there will be features in the behavior which are by ordinary standards discontinuous with what has gone before, that is, there will be a large measure of novelty in the adjustments. This does not preclude prediction of what will occur in a given situation, for the novelty is not completely fortuitous and whimsical. It will preclude prediction based solely on inferences from habit strengths associated with isolated features of the situation.

Some of the restructuring occurs within learning trials, so that there is some uncertainty in prediction. But this is equally true in other theories which require multiple responses. The order in which alternatives are tried out cannot in fact be fully predicted. Hence the recognition of discontinuity in the learning process does not give up whatever success in prediction there may be by any other method.

Conventional neurology criticized. Many of this group have worked with Lashley, who is best known for his criticisms of conventional reflex-arc conceptions of the action of the nervous system. Lashley came to his field-like position by way of his cerebral studies. The contemporary position appears to be one of skepticism rather than one of assurance:

At the present time nothing whatever is known concerning the nature of the alterations in the nervous system which constitute memory traces. Knowledge of cerebral physiology is in fact so limited that it does not even lend greater plausibility to one than to another of the many speculations concerning the organic basis of memory with which the literature is burdened. Association with direction of flow of nervous excitation or with a ratio of excitation is neither more nor less fantastic than is association between hypo- thetical conditioned-reflex arcs. The only relevant facts are those of psychology. . . .[43]

[43] Lashley and Wade (1946), page 86. See also Marquis (1942).

This paragraph is perhaps sufficient basis for the neglect of the neurophysiological theories in this book. The problems are important, but at the present time do not mediate among the psychological theories of learning. It is true that Lashley and Wade go on to say:

... the phenomena of stimulus equivalence and generalization are much more consistent with the former than the latter alternative.

That is, the facts of psychology suggest an interpretation of the way in which the nervous system acts more readily than knowledge of the nervous system suggests what psychological activities should occur. And these facts, according to Lashley, favor a field type of theory, association with the direction of flow of nervous impulses or with ratios of excitation.

SUPPLEMENTARY READINGS

BOOKS

Humphrey, G. (1933) *The nature of learning in its relation to the living system.*

Lashley, K. S. (1929) *Brain mechanisms and intelligence.*

Maier, N. R. F. and Schneirla, T. C. (1935) *Principles of animal psychology.*

Muenzinger, K. F. (1942) *Psychology: The science of behavior.*

SHORTER INTRODUCTIONS

Adams, D. K. (1931) A restatement of the problem of learning. *Brit. J. Psychol.,* 22, 150-178.

Humphrey, G. (1930) Learning and the living system. *Psychol. Rev.,* 37, 497-510.

Lashley, K. S. (1930) Basic neural mechanisms in behavior. *Psychol. Rev.,* 37, 1-24.

Maier, N. R. F. (1939) The specific processes constituting the learning function. *Psychol. Rev.,* 46, 241-252.

Muenzinger, K. F. (1938) The law of effect. *Psychol. Rev.,* 45, 215-218.

CRITICAL REVIEWS

Except for that by Humphrey, the books listed above cover many topics other than learning theory, and reviews of them are not central to the topic of this chapter. For a critical review of Humphrey, see:

McGeoch, J. A. (1934) Review of Humphrey's *The nature of learning in its relation to the living system. Psychol. Bull.*, 31, 220-222.

REPRESENTATIVE EXPERIMENTS

Adams, D. K. (1929) Experimental studies of adaptive behavior in cats. *Comp. Psychol. Monogr.*, 6, No. 27, 168 pp.

Humphrey, G. (1928) The effect of sequences of indifferent stimuli on a reaction of the conditioned response type. *J. abn. (soc.) Psychol.*, 22, 194-212.

Klüver, H. (1933) *Behavior mechanisms in monkeys.*

Krechevsky, I. (1938) An experimental investigation of the principle of proximity in the visual perception of the rat. *J. exp. Psychol.*, 22, 497-523.

Lashley, K. S. (1938) The mechanism of vision. XV. Preliminary studies of the rat's capacity for detail vision. *J. gen. Psychol.*, 18, 123-193.

Lashley, K. S. (1942) An examination of the "continuity theory" as applied to discriminative learning. *J. gen. Psychol.*, 26, 241-265.

Leeper, R. (1935) The role of motivation in learning; a study of the phenomenon of differential motivational control of the utilization of habits. *J. genet. Psychol.*, 46, 3-40.

Leeper, R. (1935) A study of a neglected portion of the field of learning—the development of sensory organization. *J. genet. Psychol.*, 1935, 46, 41-75.

Maier, N. R. F. (1939) Qualitative differences in the learning of rats in a discrimination situation. *J. comp. Psychol.*, 27, 289-331.

Maier, N. R. F. (1941) The effect of cortical injuries on equivalence reactions in rats. *J. comp. Psychol.*, 32, 165-189.

Muenzinger, K. F. (1938) Vicarious trial and error at a point of choice. I. A general survey of its relation to learning efficiency. *J. genet. Psychol.*, 53, 75-86.

Zener, K. (1937) The significance of behavior accompanying conditioned salivary secretion for theories of the conditioned response. *Amer. J. Psychol.*, 50, 384-403.

Chapter 12

A POINT OF VIEW

The array of theories presents an unfavorable picture of the state of systematic knowledge about learning. How can psychologists be helpful to other social scientists or to practical people if they disagree among themselves on these fundamental matters? There are several considerations which temper this adverse judgment. For one thing, there is a great deal of empirical knowledge about learning which is independent of the major points of view. For another, there are, in addition to the general theories, a number of special theories, more closely related to particular experimental situations. These special theories are tested and corrected in a matter-of-fact manner cutting across the preferences of the major viewpoints. Finally, discipleship in one or another of the major schools is not characteristic of most psychologists working in the field of learning. There are strong tendencies toward mediating positions. Many writers find the major contributions of the different schools largely reconcilable.[1]

The disadvantages of conflicting points of view are balanced to some extent by the motivation which a strong position provides for its proponent and by the challenge it issues to its adversary. Out of the heat of controversy there is eventually scientific advance.[2] Even in the midst of controversy, it is not necessary for the theorist to set aside reasonableness or critical powers.[3] Theoretical differences show up most markedly where the data remain ambiguous, so that preferences hold sway over evidence. As the

[1] E.g., Dashiell (1935), Kellogg (1938), McConnell (1942).
[2] Boring (1929).
[3] The point is well made by Dennes (1946).

data become more securely established it becomes increasingly possible to translate one system into another.

While the situation is not therefore as bad as the parade of points of view makes it out to be, it is still rather unsatisfactory. There are no laws of learning which can be taught with confidence. Even the most obvious facts of improvement with practice and the regulation of learning under reward and punishment are matters of theoretical dispute. Are there reasons for this unsatisfactory state of learning theory?

WHY LEARNING THEORIES ARE UNSATISFACTORY

Psychology has too long used the excuse that it is a young science, and therefore cannot be expected to have its house in order. The study of learning has been, next to perception, the most active field of investigation in experimental psychology ever since the send-off by Ebbinghaus in 1885. This is sufficient time for knowledge to accumulate in an active field. Prestige has been granted the investigators and theorists. It cannot be said that the field has been unattractive to able members of the psychological profession.[4]

Concepts not yet in order for a satisfactory comprehensive theory. A generally satisfactory theory awaits a set of concepts which will be appropriate to all that is known about learning. While each major theorist believes his concepts to be the appropriate ones, their propriety often depends upon that theorist's interest primarily in some segment or aspect of the total learning situation. Some are interested in the initial adjustment, as in insight or problem-solving, others are interested in improvement with practice, as in rote memorizing, others are interested in the predictability of performance under varied conditions of motivation, and so on. We need a more careful delineation of the *kinds* of learning which take place (each of which may have "laws" of its own), and an acceptable fractionation of the *aspects* of learn-

---

[4] Among the presidents of the American Psychological Association since 1925 a central interest in learning has been shown in the work of at least Carr, Dashiell, Guthrie, Hollingworth, Hull, Hunter, Lashley, Marquis, Peterson, Stone, Tolman, and Woodrow. Earlier presidents included Dunlap, Thorndike, Woodworth, Watson, and Yerkes, all contributors to the literature of learning.

ing which make demands upon theory. Some theories are different largely because they are concerned with different problems
to begin with. This search for the appropriate concepts is not
merely an exercise in definition or classification. It requires a
high order of theory construction, based on openminded acceptance of demonstrated relationships, and in addition contributing
to the ordering of such relationships into a system.

It may be that the stage of advance has been reached when a
return to naturalistic observations would help in rounding out
the concepts needed for a complete theory of learning.[5] A few
observations of a whipped dog returning to lick the hands of its
master would suffice to show that the ordinary treatment of the
effects of punishment in our textbooks is not rich enough.
Watching a child learning to brush its teeth or to assemble a
radio receiver or to play hop-scotch makes most of our learning
principles seem inadequate.

The inadequacy of contemporary theories is most apparent in
matters of motivational control of learning. So many of the
motives are personal—emulative, defiant, aggressive, appealing—
that a social psychology of learning would almost certainly be
called for if a fresh start were made in the study of learning, beginning with behavior diaries or logs of the situations in which
learning occurs.

Inappropriate quantification. As psychology became divorced
from philosophy, it had to prove its scientific status by stating its
problems in experimentable and quantifiable form. This was indeed an advance. It is a mark of the scientist to be able to select
a problem which is small enough that he can work on it and get
verifiable results, even though the results may not at first appear
world-shaking.

But there are dangers in the desire for quantities, and the history of learning experimentation well illustrates them. Ebbinghaus, fitting a logarithmic curve to his plot of the course of
retention, started a fashion which led to many futile efforts to
discover the "true" form of the learning curve. The aim was
admirable enough, but the qualitative processes composing the
learning curve were insufficiently analyzed, so that scores at one
part of the curve did not mean the same as scores at another part,

[5] This suggestion is extended later in this chapter.

and the empirical curve of best fit had no theoretical significance.

The more sophisticated approach of Hull shows how quantification collapses when the underlying processes are not understood. His efforts to predict the form of the serial position curve seemed rather promising when a crude approximation was accepted,[6] but when the details were taken seriously an enormously complicated *ad hoc* system was needed.[7] This did not meet the test of interchangeable constants, and the whole enterprise has ended in a stalemate.

It is easy to be misunderstood at this point. I believe that the logic of Hull's approach is the correct one, and that learning science must ultimately be written quantitatively very much as he writes it—though with a different content. The reason that I speak of quantification as inappropriate is that it leads to preoccupation with the wrong kind of experiment. It is the insistence upon easily obtained quantities which has led to too much experimentation on rote memorizing, maze learning, conditioning, and rat lever-pressing. If quantification diverts attention from important problems of learning to trivial ones, it does as much harm as it does good. It produces what might be called a "scientifics" of learning instead of a science of learning.

Preoccupation with the comparative method. Relatively few workers with animals in the laboratory are interested in animal learning as such. In fact, professional psychologists have contributed rather little to the training of seeing-eye dogs, or racehorses, or circus performers—fields in which animal learning is of interest in its own right. Psychologists are interested instead in the more general problems of comparative psychology, with the outlook of evolutionary theory in the background. Ultimately the knowledge of animal learning is to be placed on a continuum with human learning.

The use of animal subjects is very important, dramatically so in relation to some kinds of problems. Notable among these are problems involving brain surgery, as made familiar by the work of Lashley. Important also are the studies of inheritance, which permit an experimenter to work with many generations—something quite impossible with human subjects. Also, special controls

[6] Hull (1935a).
[7] Hull and others (1940).

of the environment are possible which for social reasons would not be acceptable with human children.

There are some methodological advantages in having a learner which is not too bright, so that the learning process is more open to inspection, and in having one which cannot talk, so that there will not be the temptation to ask questions. These advantages are possessed by young children, however, so that animal subjects are not unique in these respects.

A price is always paid for the convenience of a given approach to a problem. The price to be paid for overmuch experimentation with animals is to neglect the fact that human subjects are brighter, are able to use language—*and probably learn differently because of these advances over lower animals.*

It is time that we reinterpret what we mean by comparative psychology. It might mean about what it means in pharmacology. That is, the pharmacologist uses animal subjects in the try-out stages, to the extent that he finds that animals react somewhat comparable to man. He rests finally, however, only when he has established his findings on man. A peculiar twist is sometimes given to psychological thinking which takes the form that a process, in order to be scientifically reputable, must be demonstrated to occur in lower animals. If it occurs only in man, it is excused away because man possesses verbal or related abilities. It would be better to reverse this viewpoint: *Only if a process demonstrable in human learning can also be demonstrated in lower animals is the comparative method useful in studying it.* This would not limit the role of the comparative psychologist very much, for there are many continuities. Where there are discontinuities, it is human learning which should be studied. The chief aim of the comparative method, in psychology as in pharmacology, is ultimately to understand the human being.

SUGGESTIONS TOWARD AN ACCEPTABLE THEORY

Learning capacities. The extreme form of generalization from comparative studies is that there are no differences, except quantitative ones, between the learning of lower animals and primates, including man.[8] While this position is more often implied than

[8] E.g., Hull (1945*b*).

asserted, it is strange that the opposite point of view is not more often made explicit—that at the human level there have emerged capacities for retaining, reorganizing, and foreseeing experiences which are not approached by the lower animals, including the other primates. No one has seriously proposed that animals can develop a set of ideals which regulate conduct around long-range plans, or that they can invent a mathematics to help them keep track of their enterprises. Because a trained dog shows some manifestations of shame, or a chimpanzee some signs of cooperation, or a rat a dawning concept of triangularity, it does not follow that these lower organisms, clever as they are, have all the richness of human mental activity.

The problem of emerging types of learning ability must be pushed farther back. Language in man is perhaps the clearest of the emergents which carries with it a forward surge in what may be learned. It seems plausible enough that other advances in the ability to learn must have come about as the nervous system evolved through successive stages below man. The prevailing learning theories have had remarkably little to say about the different processes which together make up the functional changes which are classified together as learning.[9] There are probably a number of different kinds of learning which have emerged at different evolutionary periods, with the more highly evolved organisms using at once several of them. It is quite probable that the different kinds of learning follow different laws.

Learning capacity can be assigned a quantitative meaning only when the several learning capacities are identified. Factor analysis is a useful tool in this direction, although it cannot be used blindly. It may be that some of the primary factors are the results of emphases within our social heritage.[10]

The doubt about the influence of the culture upon the primary abilities as isolated from test scores raises another fundamental problem about learning capacity, the problem as to the extent to which the ceiling of ability is itself modified by training. It is evident that without appropriate prior experiences there are learnings within his capacity that the learner will never acquire.

[9] Maier (1939a, 1939b) and Tryon (1940) have stressed similar points.
[10] Tolman (1945).

Without appropriate linguistic or mathematical tools, for example, there are kinds of problems which cannot be solved, regardless of the requisite native intelligence. After these tools are acquired, the learning ability rises, without any necessary inference that the ceiling of ability was raised.

The obstacle to a precise scientific statement of the problem lies in the difficulty of assigning a limit until one is approached. The notion of a physiological or psychological limit as taught in our elementary textbooks is a convenient fiction. The records of athletic contests suffice to show how impractical it is to assign definite limits, because records are made by improving methods as well as by the speed of conduction of neural impulses. When the bamboo pole was introduced into pole-vaulting, for example, records increased by a full foot, but improvements in technique have led to their regular improvement beyond this. Kantor [11] has made much of the interbehavioral meaning of abilities. He would argue that both typewriters and poles must enter into the equations defining typing speed and vaulting records. The difficulty exists, and must be taken account of. There is, however, an asymmetry between the learner and his instrument. It is not the typewriter or the pole which does the learning, and there ought to be some way of getting at what the limit would be for a given typist with a given typewriter or a given vaulter with a given pole. Until the ceiling of ability gets a satisfactory theoretical-empirical definition, such problems as the effect of practice on individual differences can receive only superficial answers.

Perceptual learning. If it were not sensitive to its environment, an organism could not learn. Therefore the problem of perceptual discrimination is a central one for learning theory. There is some uncertainty as to the manner in which perception is natively organized, but at a primitive level there are undoubtedly some discriminations of continuity and discontinuity, of change and succession, of boundary phenomena, of proximity and remoteness. There is an old controversy between those who believe that the organization of perception is essentially unlearned, and those who believe that practically everything within perception

[11] E.g., Kantor (1941).

is learned.[12] It is not necessary to enter this controversy in order to point out that the learning theorist must be aware of the learning within perception as well as of the rôle of perception in learning.

The perception of objects suffices to show that there is at least some learning in perception. A cake of ice *looks* cold; the red tip of the poker *looks* hot. The properties of cold and hot, not present to the senses, are present in the perception as a result of prior experiences. They are not judgments or deliberate inferences from perceptual data, but are given as immediately as any other of the properties of the perceived objects.

The process whereby identifying signs are used to represent a total situation previously experienced is called *redintegration*.[13] The ice looks cold because the previous experiences of felt cold are redintegrated by its appearance. The paramnesic experience (sometimes referred to as *déja vu*) is probably of this sort. That the process occurs is evident, but its explanation is not easy.

The relationship between motivation and perceptual achievements has never been well worked out, although there have been many suggestions that momentary sets or preoccupations determine the manner in which things are perceived. If some such motive as curiosity is allowed (Pavlov called it the "what-is-it?" reflex), then the goal of perception is to achieve clarity. This ordinarily involves structuring the perceptual field either geometrically (as in figure-ground relationships) or in accordance with familiar objects.

That the achievement of objects appears as an important goal of perception is illustrated by the experiments on size-constancy. Objects seen at a distance do not look as much smaller as the geometry of perspective would require; in the conflict between perspective-size and object-size, they remain closer to object-size.[14] In other words, perception is not a high-fidelity reproduction of stimuli impinging upon the receptors, but is reproductive of the objects which those stimuli suggest. Every act of perception incorporates redintegrative experiences along with the

---

[12] The contrasting positions are represented by Koffka (1930) and Carr (1935).

[13] Hollingworth (1928).

[14] Brunswik (1940).

contributions of present discriminated stimuli. Heidbreder's finding that object-like concepts are the most easily attained supports the position that "thing-ness" is a goal of mental organization.[15]

Because of the importance of motivational and other organizational features within the act of perception, redintegration should not be understood as a function of mere contiguity. Not just any contiguous item can serve to redintegrate the experiences with which it was present. Only features which were discriminated in the original perception can serve in this way. Even though a passing automobile was in sight when a train whistled, the whistle later redintegrates the train, not the automobile—unless perhaps the train and the car were seen in a relationship, such as a threatened collision. How integrated the original perceptual pattern must have been is not clear, for occasionally very casual experiences serve as cues to redintegration. A Stanford alumnus, returning to the campus after several years in other parts of the country, said that he could tell with his eyes closed that he was back in California. Only after careful consideration of cues he realized that the sense of familiarity was being caused by the odor of eucalyptus trees, of which, up to the time of mentioning the feeling of familiarity, he had been unaware.

Selective factors operate at the time of redintegrative reinstatement, and what is revived does not flow automatically from what is retained of an earlier perception. Many cues are ambiguous, and redintegrate at once a number of possibilities. The different interpretations of the Rorschach ink-blot are illustrative. It is supposed that persistent personality preferences favor one sort of redintegration over another in this situation. The temporary set at the moment may also call forth a consonant experience. It has been shown, for example, that food references are seen more frequently in ambiguous figures when the subject is hungry.[16] Motivation, involved in original perception, also acts differentially at the time of redintegrative recall.

While perceptual learning is here treated as distinguishable from motor learning, it is not inferred to be a merely passive process based upon exposure to stimuli. Discussions of latent learning have occasionally been so insistent upon the relationship

[15] Heidbreder (1945, 1946).
[16] Sanford (1936, 1937), Levine, Chein, and Murphy (1942).

of motivation to performance that they have neglected the extent to which motivation affects cognitive processes.[17]

The release of action. Were it unable to do anything about its discriminations, an organism's perceptual achievements would be futile. Once the distinction between perception and performance is reintroduced, some of the nineteenth century problems again emerge, for the convenient identification of perception with motor response breaks down. William James considered the evidence for *dynamogenesis* and *ideo-motor action*, and finally came to the conclusion that a thought led immediately to action so long as there were no inhibiting thoughts in the way. This solution is not a very satisfactory one, but the problem it intended to solve still exists.

The theory of simple conditioning is an inviting one. It says in effect that partial cues reinstate stimulus-response situations just as fully as they reinstate perceptual ones—that what was *done* in the presence of the stimuli as well as what was *perceived* tends to recur in their presence. Despite all the attention commonly given to simple conditioning in learning theory, the evidence for it is very fragmentary. There is no doubt that learning takes place under the arrangements of the conditioned response experiment, but the results may usually be given alternative explanations. The fact is that *there is little evidence that the simultaneous or nearly simultaneous occurrence of an incidental stimulus and an unconditioned response is the sufficient condition for establishing a sensori-motor association between them.* The conditioning of muscle twitches in spinal preparations comes nearest to the pure case, but it is scarcely typical.[18]

If simple conditioning is not accepted as the rule, the alternative is to find the contingencies which give rise to results looking like simple conditioning. The usual solution is to find the stimulus-response sequences related to an on-going goal-directed activity, whether this be described as proximity to a reinforcing state of affairs, or as part of a field tension-system. It is undeniable that in many instances the learner will do what he last did

[17] Proshansky and Murphy (1942) have experimented upon the relationship between reward and punishment and perception.
[18] P. S. Shurrager and H. C. Shurrager (1946).

in the presence of given stimuli because similar motives are operating, and what he did last time achieved the goal.

Some types of direct action release—weeping at a letter bearing sad news, fainting at the sight of blood—appear to conform to a simple conditioning formula, but the full consideration of what is happening involves motives like anxiety, making these cases not unlike other illustrations of learning with tension-release. Action systems which seem to be directly released by perceived stimuli are usually either of low threshold or supported by strong motives. Some people weep easily, so that tears to a letter would be a matter of low thresholds; others would weep only if the letter reported the loss of someone deeply loved. Some reaction systems, such as salivation and neurocirculatory changes, are in unstable equilibrium most of the time, so that they are easily disturbed by a wide range of perceptual experiences. Because these actions can occur without environmental support they may be activated independently of dominant on-going activity at the time.

While allowance must be made for some relatively automatic associated movements released by perceived stimuli, in the more usual case these movements are integrated with goal-directed activity. This follows because the motives which support the goal-seeking activity serve also to lower the thresholds for the perceptually aroused concomitants. Hence the hungry dog is likely to salivate while nosing up the lid to the food-box. Because the dog is hungry the threshold for salivation is low, and the sight of food or food-related objects is likely to lead to salivation.

The differences between the point of view here adopted and that of simple conditioning, which it resembles, are three. (1) The aroused perception (not the conditioned stimulus) is said to be related to the movement. (2) The direct release of movement systems in the presence of stimuli, taken to be general and universal in simple conditioning, is here accepted as a principle of limited applicability. (3) The goal-directed activity need not depend upon these redintegratively released responses for its integration, as it does in the theories of Guthrie and Hull.

The provisional try. Many learning situations require the selection of one or another possible mode of action in order to reach a goal. Because alternatives are selected one after another until the correct one is stumbled upon, this learning is commonly described as trial-and-error. This designation is descriptively appropriate to several standard laboratory experiments. In motor skill experiments acceptable responses have to be discovered within a range of movement possibilities; in the problem-box there is usually one correct response among many unspecified possibilities; in discrimination experiments selection is to be made from among fixed alternatives; in the maze and multiple discrimination experiments successive choices must be integrated in proper order.

Two main theoretical problems arise: the problem of the nature of the original adjustment ending in the correct act, and the problem as to how this adjustment is facilitated when the situation is repeated.

Thorndike's explanation has tended to separate the two problems. The initial adjustment is a result of the tendency of the organism to vary its responses ("law of multiple response"). The acts within its repertory run off more or less by chance until the correct one is hit upon. Then the second principle comes into play. The correct response is stamped in ("law of effect"). When the situation recurs, the rewarded response has a favored position in relation to the rest of the possible multiple responses, and tends to occur earlier than before. Because prior experiences will have established preferential orders of response even in a situation relatively novel, the multiple responses will never, in fact, be purely random. Hull has worked out a theory like Thorndike's, giving an orderly account of these possibilities.

The alternative is that the original behavior is not the running off of earlier habits in the new situation, but is a genuine attempt at discovering the route to the goal. Past experience is used, but in a manner appropriate to the present. Such an interpretation makes the original adjustment a *provisional try*, to be confirmed or denied by its success or failure. What is here being called a provisional try corresponds to what Tolman and Krech have called "hypothesis" behavior. The theory supposes that a provisional behavior route is kept in suspension until its consequences change its provisional status; if it is confirmed it is an appropriate path of action to be followed under like circumstances, if it is not confirmed it is inappropriate. All that is required is some sort of memorial representation of what was done, so that on the next occasion it can be repeated or not repeated. Such an interpretation takes all the mystery out of the backward action of effect.

Within many situations there is little or no basis of choice between the alternatives of running off of habits according to their strengths and of making genuine tries. If one stimulus has been more often followed by reward than another it will be preferred either because it has been more strongly reinforced or because it has been more frequently confirmed as a good sign. Generalization of prior learning to new stimuli may depend upon the same features of equivalence in both theories.[19]

Within other situations there is a difference. Three kinds of evidence support the interpretation of the initial adjustment as a provisional try rather than as the selection according to conditioning principles of previously acquired sensori-motor habits.

1. *Approximation and correction in motor skills.* The conception of the provisional try is especially appropriate when the movement called for is not clearly specified by the apparatus. In mirror-drawing or pursuit-learning or ball-tossing the performance called for is a pattern of movements correct in direction and (in some cases) in rhythm. The general character of the correct movement is understood at the outset, but it cannot be produced without considerable fumbling. This fumbling is a real try. The learner does not act in chance fashion, no matter how clumsy his movements may be. In this kind of situation either Dodge's designation *approximation and correction* or Woodworth's *trial-and-check* is appropriate.[20] Theories of spontaneous movement and of conditioning of previous responses have never been successful in dealing with the detailed movements which occur in manual skill. The suggestion that any new movements must be compromises between movements elicited as old responses to familiar stimuli does not take the problem seriously. The movements are new integrations at first crudely adapted to the situation at hand, presently becoming better adapted.

It may be that a learner at some early stage in its development

[19] Despite different approaches there are striking similarities between the accounts of Spence (1937) and Tolman (1939), (1941).

[20] Dodge (1931), page 113, Woodworth (1947).

has to learn how to try,[21] but by the time it is ready for the usual laboratory experiments it has learned, and its behavior is probably not greatly unlike the human learner acquiring a skill. The cat's behavior in the problem-box is best described by saying that the cat is trying to get out of the box. When the cat quits trying, and, as Lewin says, "goes out of the field," its not-trying is evident also. It may lie down, lick itself, appear to be relaxed, then suddenly return to a state of tension and again begin to try.

2. *Perceptual organization dominant over frequency of reinforcement.* Prior experiences establish the probability that a given behavior-route will lead to a goal, and hence a cognitive theory leads to the same prediction as reinforcement theory, when only the simple case is considered. When patterning of reinforcement is introduced, however, reinforcement theory, without many supplementary assumptions, has difficulty in accounting for what occurs. There are some old experiments of Gengerelli,[22] in which rats fed successively for 25 trials on one wing of a single choice-point maze would reverse their runs and go to the other wing when food was omitted but two or three times in the familiar feeding box. One or two extinction trials ought not to counteract 25 reinforcements, if it is merely sensori-motor responses which are controlled by reinforcement and non-reinforcement. Theories emphasizing perceptual control can accept this dramatic re-organization of the cognitive situation when after uniform reinforcement there is a sudden change to non-reinforcement.

Other experiments critical of simple reinforcement theory (latent learning experiments, reward expectancy experiments, experiments on intermittent reinforcement) similarly suggest that perceptual organization may take precedence over the cumulative frequencies of reinforcement and non-reinforcement.

3. *Generalization may be along discriminated dimensions.* If in discrimination experiments the learner is making provisional tries, these may be tested by the introduction of new stimuli, equivalent in some respects to the original ones. According to reinforcement theory, generalization ought to be predictable according to whatever dimensions of the stimuli there may be to which the

[21] Hull (1937) shows the possibility of deriving "striving" from more elementary principles.
[22] Gengerelli (1928).

organism can react; according to the theory of genuine trying, the dimensions along which generalization will occur will depend upon what the organism has been trying to do. The experiments and conclusions of Lashley and Wade (1946), if acceptable, support the latter interpretation. More evidence is needed. The most frequently quoted experiments on generalization of conditioned responses have been done with human subjects for whom conventional dimensions of discrimination have been much practiced.

There are a number of objections to the principle of the provisional try. One is that it is a high-level principle which ought to be derived from simpler kinds of learning. Those who offer this objection do not deny its occurrence. The reply is that once its occurrence is admitted, it must be looked for in a great many places where it is not usually looked for—as in conditioning and discrimination experiments—and care must be taken lest it be "explained" by situations in which it is already found. A second objection is that behavior is often more stupid and stereotyped than a theory of genuine trying suggests. The problem of fixity of habit requires further discussion.

Overlearning and stereotypy. A theory which assumes that behavior is regulated reasonably on the basis of available information is put to it to account for the persistence of habits in situations in which they are no longer adaptive.

One kind of stereotypy, normally adaptive, is a consequence of overlearning. By overlearning is meant the facilitation of response with repetition *after* the essential learning has been mastered. Memorization furnishes convenient illustrations. A series of digits can be learned in a single presentation so that it can be correctly repeated if recall is immediate. But if the series is long enough to be near the limit of immediate memory, more repetitions are needed to fix the list so that it can be recalled after greater lapse of time. The most evident effect of overlearning is this one upon recall. It provides the explanation for the long retention of overlearned skills like swimming or bicycle riding.

But overlearning has other consequences than guaranteeing retention. These have been little studied, and only a few suggestions are available. One possible result is a mechanization of habit, leading to a loss of "docility." Oft-repeated activities take on some measure of goal-character, perhaps through a process like secondary reinforcement. The learner is then "blinded" to new possibilities.[23] Rats which have learned a path including a jump appear to prefer that path to other more economical ones after they have been overtrained on it.[24] Maier and his associates interpret some of their data to show that habits learned in accordance with original preferences are more easily altered than habits built up against original preferences.[25] If this be generally true, it may account in part for the persistent preferences by adults for highly artificial ways of doing things learned as children.[26]

The familiar way of doing things is commonly economical, and there is no special mystery to its persistence. It has had motivational support according to any theory. There are other instances of stereotyped fixations, however, which have had no such history of support as adaptive habits. Their occurrence raises additional problems.

One source of fixated behavior is the insoluble problem. There is no way in which to make a reasonable adjustment, because the order of events in the environment is chaotic. There is no basis for choice, and a ritualistic fixed choice is adopted. Such a ritualistic performance represents a giving up of the attempt to predict the occurrence of reward on the basis of "correct" behavior. The environment is unresponsive to the trying by the learner. It is not surprising that such a pattern of behavior persists against punishment. Maier's finding that there was evidence that positive and negative cards were in fact discriminated, even though the position habit remained fixed, means in cognitive terms only that the organism finds the situation too difficult. The problems which experimenters set animals are often fairly complex when translated into our own experiences. In this situation the animal learner, in adopting the fixated habit, has rejected the second window as no better than the first, since its provisional tries were frustrated as frequently one place as the other. Because there now develops a pattern of predictable success and failure at the first window does not mean that things would be any better at the other one. A human parallel might be as follows. Suppose

[23] Luchins (1942), Wertheimer (1945).
[24] Gilhousen (1941).
[25] Maier, Glaser, and Klee (1940).
[26] Holt (1931) attributes this fixity of familiar ways of doing things to "canalization" in childhood.

that in long experience the front door and the rear door of the laboratory had always been unlocked together. Even though one knows about both doors, he might sit a long time before the front door, waiting for it to be opened, before trying the back door, even though on that day a careless attendant had unlocked one door and neglected the other. To the visitor from Mars this waiting might appear to be very stupid and fixated behavior. It may be, as Maier believes, that these fixations are compulsions to which the animal is a slave. An alternative interpretation is that the situation is misinterpreted in the light of the learner's experience, and the sense of alternative has been lost. The ease with which the alternative can be brought back into the animal's behavior field through guidance suggests that some such interpretation is sound.

The other source of fixated behavior is excessive punishment at the moment of choice. The general frustration probably interferes in this case with orderly cognitive processes, so that the learner falls back on stereotyped responses. The reduction in cognitive clearness under intense emotion is what is proposed in the expression "blind with rage."

Still another form of stereotypy is that in the Guthrie and Horton experiment. This conforms neither to overlearning nor to Maier's fixation. The interpretation of their experiment according to the principle of the provisional try would be somewhat as follows. A successful try often occurs in the midst of a response which is not being made to the crucial aspect of the situation at all. The trying by a cat in the Guthrie and Horton experiment may be backing up (not backing into the post). It strikes the post, however, and the door opens. Its behavioral try next time may be quite inappropriate, because it was simply backing up when the door opened. Some of the cats apparently never got it cognitively clear that responding to the post had anything to do with opening the door. Under those conditions they were led to repeat in stereotyped fashion the sort of trying that was going on when the door last opened. Those which responded directly to the pole were less stereotyped because their tries included moving the pole. They were better able to adjust to the pole in a new position. The direct tries of practically all the cats were oriented toward the escape door. The pole was struck in some posture toward the door. It is doubtful if the relation of pole to door was ever clearly cognized. In such a situation the organism behaves in stereotyped fashion.[27]

Overlearned, fixated, and stereotyped behavior can be made coherent with the theory of the provisional try if two assumptions are accepted. One assumption is that after sufficient overlearning the learner no longer tries, unless something dramatic again arouses his searching behavior. Otherwise the old ways of doing things are preferred. The other assumption is that stereotypy results when situations are cognitively too difficult. Here again the organism stops trying, and adopts a patterned mode of response without regard to the environmental consequences.

Ideation. Because learning is under cognitive control does not mean that it always proceeds with full understanding. A correct response may be made time and again in a situation without the learner's awareness of what is being done. The probabilities of a situation may be estimated without the learner's making any computations. The experiments of Thorndike and his collaborators on learning without awareness are of this sort.[28] The subjects made discriminations on the basis of the probabilities of the situation, but could not tell what they had done. Yet their responses were predictable in terms of the arrangements of the learning situation. The experiments are used to substantiate a blind law of effect interpretation, but they may be explained equally well on the basis of cumulative discriminations among real tries.

While there is a tendency to achieve clarity and to learn with understanding when that is possible, there is a limit to the learner's curiosity, and it is not true as implied in some gestalt writings that learning takes place with all the understanding which the situation and the capacities of the learner permit. The understanding which the learner wishes in a problematic sitution is knowledge of the essentials to economical goal-achievement, and nothing more can be counted on. The mistake is sometimes made in teaching school children (or college students) of assuming that they wish to understand what lies behind a process which

[27] An interpretation of the Guthrie and Horton experiment somewhat along these lines was suggested to me in a private communication from N. R. F. Maier.

[28] E.g., Thorndike and Rock (1934). For a different sort of criticism, see Irwin, Kauffman, Prior, and Weaver (1934).

is for them just a tool. They wish to know how to use the tool to reach immediate goals; the further curiosity is related to different goals, which may be goals for the teacher but not for them.

Because all learning is to some extent cognitively controlled, the distinction between blind learning and learning with understanding becomes one of degree. There is a point, however, at which understanding takes on new prominence. That is in the kind of creative attack on a problem in which experience does not provide solutions ready-made, but the solutions have to be discovered or invented through a reconstruction of experience appropriate to the problem at hand. This is not completely specified by experiments on insight, but it is suggested by them.

There are several alternatives. One is to treat all problem solving and reasoning as a form of trial-and-error learning, with some transfer to account for shortcut solutions. This is the position of Carr (1925) endorsed by McGeoch (1942). This position fails to grant any reality to the reconstruction of experience present in the act of reasoning which makes the "try" something other than the running off of varying habits. A second alternative, that of Hull (1935c), is to recognize that the mechanism for assembling prior experiences appropriate to problem solution has in it characteristics different from ordinary trial and error learning. Hull attempts to derive such behavior from other processes. This derivation depends upon discrimination among fractional anticipatory responses which are common to several experiences and have to be integrated in order to solve the problem.

Stimulus-response psychologists, under the restraint of Lloyd Morgan's principle of parsimony,[29] have assigned as little as possible to ideation, but they have usually recognized that some behavior is controlled by ideas. Thorndike called ideas by that name, and granted their occurrence; Hunter recognized a "symbolic process" necessary to account for behavior in delayed reaction and double alternation experiments;[30] Hull infers "pure-stimulus acts," that is, responses whose sole function is to furnish stimuli to guide or integrate behavior sequences; Guthrie's position is about like Hull's, with great emphasis upon movements

[29] Morgan (1894).
[30] Hunter (1924).

(especially implicit speech) as the substance of thought. Tolman, in behaviorist spirit, makes of ideation a "mere 'behavior-feint' at running-back-and-forth," without specifying the precise nature of the feint.

Is there any gain, having accepted ideation, in seeking a palpable basis for ideas? A scientific construct does not have to be something you can hold in your hand or cut with a scissors. To assert that the organism can discriminate between the sensory consequences of two kinds of anticipatory salivation more readily than between two perceptual redintegrations is no great gain, except for the logical possibility of discovering by separate techniques the presence of two kinds of salivation. Because both perceptual redintegrations and stimuli from anticipatory responses are, in fact, inferred, it is as possible to be logically strict about one as the other—*and the evidence used in the inference for one has to be as good as the evidence for the other*. The benefit of the doubt need not go to the one with preference for inferring tangibles. There is some concealing of ignorance in attributing specific substantive bases to psychological functions such as drives, sets, images, and thoughts. If we are critical about accepting the results of experiments, then stomach contractions are *not* the basis of appetite, eye movements are *not* the cause of the Müller-Lyer illusion, kinesthetic cues are *not* the preferred ones in maze learning, tongue movements are *not* the basis for thinking. The burden of proof is on those who believe otherwise. That there are some movement concomitants of thought is insufficient evidence that these movements (and their consequences) are the sufficient condition for the occurrence of the thought. The argument that inferring movements will make easier the task of the neurophysiologist does not hold. It is no harder to make a brain model for perceptual redintegration than for the pattern of discrimination among the proprioceptive consequences of anticipatory responses.

The integration of behavior-choices remote from a tension-reducing goal object is usually accounted for on the basis of some sort of internalized stimulus-response sequences, supported by secondary reinforcements. Hull, who has been most meticulous in stating precisely what the theory involves, finds it necessary to assert that secondary reinforcing agents need not bring about tension reduction in order to be reinforcing. This is almost a complete concession to cognitive control, and weakens greatly the centrality of the reinforcement principle. In describing the essential similarities between secondary reinforcement theory and cognitive theory, it is clearer to state that Hull reformulates the cognitive theory than to assert that the cognitive theory is just another way of talking about secondary reinforcement.[31]

The alternative to trial-and-error and reinforcement theories is to make allowance for a genuine reconstruction of experience appropriate to problem solution, as proposed by Tolman (1932*b*) in his principle of creative instability and by Maier (1931*a*) in his separation of reasoning from other kinds of learning. An organism capable of functioning at different levels does not keep his abilities in abeyance to be brought out to suit the convenience of an experimenter. Therefore if a given ability is shown in clear outline in one experimental situation, it may be supposed that if looked for it might also be found in other situations in which it is not as clearly exhibited.[32] Thus the reconstruction of experience goes on to some extent in every act of redintegration. When ice is seen as cold, or a distant object as a motorcycle, the perceptions are not photographic, nor are they simply revivals of past experiences. They are perceptual achievements molded out of past experience and present sensory discriminations. It is only the more striking recombinations of previous experiences and present perceptions which we call reasoning. These more striking instances reveal aspects of the process which might otherwise be overlooked.

One aspect of the detour or roundabout experiment emphasized by Köhler is the turning away from the ends of action to the means. The direct path to the goal may be blocked. A stupid animal will continue to make a direct attack, but a more intelligent one is able to turn its back and to take the long way around. Discovering a long route which already exists is one way of solv-

---

[31] The increasing prominence attributed to secondary reinforcement in the explanation of events difficult to explain by primary reinforcement is illustrated in the papers of Denny (1946) and of Spence (1947).

[32] Note this inversion of Lloyd Morgan's canon. As now inverted it might be paraphrased: "An organism capable of ideational problem-solving may also use ideas in learning situations in which they would be theoretically unnecessary."

ing such a problem. It is trial-and-error behavior, but in a direction against the attraction of the goal. Another solution is that of discovering or creating some sort of tool which then becomes a means to the goal. This often requires a reconstruction of experience, perhaps by putting some familiar object to unfamiliar use: making a pliers into a pendulum-bob, a clamp into a hat-hanger, a Bunsen-burner tube into a blow-pipe, and so on. It is this reconstruction aspect rather than the detour aspect which is most significant in reasoning experiments.

The reconstruction of experience follows certain lines of solution which Maier calls "direction." If there is a flame to be blown out, one "direction" is to find some way to direct a jet of air upon it, another direction is to use water, still another is to smother it with something solid. Each of these suggestions directs the search for appropriate objects to convert into means. In one of the psychological laboratories during the war a glass plate was being used in a piece of apparatus in such a way that it was to be looked through and also used as a mirror, somewhat as in the Dodge tachistoscope. There were troublesome double images of a small fixation object due to reflections from both the front and the back surfaces of the glass. The first hypothesis was that the glass could be made so thin that the images would fuse. Successively thinner sheets of glass were used in following out this "direction," but without solving the problem. The idea emerged of making the glass much thicker, so that the images could be drawn apart and one of them screened off. This worked. The direction "if we can make it thin enough" was one hypothesis used until the other hypothesis "if we can make it thick enough" supervened.[33] It is this sudden restructuring which gives the subjective experience of insight.

Understanding and inference may be used in unsuccessful solutions as well as in successful ones. The flash of insight is not evidence of unusual heights to which intelligence has soared, but of an aptness of the solution suggested. A solution may be achieved with understanding without any such experience of insight. For example, in fitting mathematical functions to a given set of points it is often necessary to try out curves from several families to see which will achieve the best fit. Such a solution to

[33] I am indebted to S. Smith Stevens for this illustration.

a problem goes on at a high level of skill and of understanding, but when the best fit is found there is no necessary experience of insight. Insight is experienced only when there is an integration of experiences, a restructuring, a seeing of things in a new light, appropriate to the problem at hand.

Because the integration and reconstruction of experience go on in many acts of learning, reasoning need not be made a separate category as done by Maier. This does not mean that there may not be one or more special capacities involved in reasoning ability and in other sorts of creativity. But there may be different learning processes below the reasoning level as well. In order to avoid artificial boundaries, it is preferable to include together in one family of processes all forms of problem-solving and reasoning, subject to later determination of the kinds and number of processes involved.

Motivation. Thorndike deserves credit for bringing into the foreground the relationship between learning and motivation in his law of effect, a factor which had been neglected in studying the associative processes in memorizing and in acquiring skills. The problem is now a central one for learning theories.

The drive-incentive paradigm became accepted as activity-cage studies began to parallel maze studies. The internal state of the animal controlled its restlessness in the activity cage; this restlessness determined the first run through the maze; the reward at the end of the maze was appropriate to the drive condition which evoked the activity, and hence had its effect through the satiation which it brought about. Studies of stomach contractions in hunger gave support to the interpretation that the drive produced *stimuli*, so that the restlessness in a state of aroused drive was stimulus-response activity like any other. This epitome of the deprivation-drive-satiation-learning relationship seemed so plausible that it became firmly entrenched. Mowrer (1940) designed a punishment situation to provide the parallel between relief from shock-tension and relief from hunger-tension, and the reinforcement pattern appeared to be complete.

Doubts about this basic pattern for reinforcement theory have been expressed frequently throughout the preceding chapters. Some of them may be recapitulated briefly:

1. The great importance attributed by supporters of reinforce-

ment theory to secondary reinforcements weakens the paradigm that reinforcement depends upon tension reduction. If reinforcement depends upon discriminated *stimuli* (and not upon their motor consequences) as it does in Skinner's system, or in Hull's secondary reinforcement, reinforcement theory is close to cognitive theory. Miller and Dollard find it preferable to attribute reinforcing power to any consequence which facilitates learning. This departs completely from the basic pattern of aroused drive and consummatory reaction.

2. Skinner (who would be critical of Hull's position) prefers to think of drive as a *state*, rather than as a source of stimuli. He points out that it has been necessary to do great violence to the term stimulus in order to make other drives parallel the case of hunger. Even of hunger he says: "Hunger cannot enter into the present formulation with the dimensions of a stimulus and could be regarded as such only with the greatest confusion." (Skinner, 1938, p. 375.)

3. Latent learning and similar experiments are critical of simple reinforcement theories.

4. Experiments on the pattern of reward and punishment—at the time of, before, and after choice, intermittent and periodic reinforcement—all cast doubt on the fundamental picture of reinforcement.

That there are goal-tensions, and that the goal-situation is an end state which makes a change (either toward relaxation or elation) cannot be denied, but the reinforcement principle in orthodox form does not provide a satisfactory statement of what takes place. The ancillary principle of spread of effect or gradient of reinforcement is also subject to question.

The conception of the provisional try, which defines the goal cognitively, substitutes for the reinforcement principle. It allows for the kinds of behavior which reinforcement theory predicts, and is at the same time more coherent with the facts which are contradictory to reinforcement theory.

Especially in human learning, and perhaps also in animal learning, it is important to know what the learner is trying to do. If there is any teaching which has come from Freudian psychology it is that motives are organized in some sort of hierarchy within the individual, resulting in a value-system expressed in behavior.

This system may go by such names as "character-structure" or "ego," but whatever it is called, it becomes very important for the learning of that individual. A sophisticated learning theory, however it conceives its primary data or principles, must take into account the organization of motives in the individual. Hence concepts like ego-involvement and level of aspiration, as introduced by Lewin and his followers, become important supplements to theories of reward and punishment. A case has been made for this point of view by Allport, in a recent symposium.[34]

The necessary distinction between performance and learning does not require that motivation be assigned to one of the terms and not to the other. The problem is an empirical one, but the goals and purposes of the individual surely affect both learning *and* performance. The effect is not symmetrical. A starved person may be motivated to eat, but not to learn table manners. Table manners are probably learned better when the hunger drive is less strongly aroused.

Stimulus-response concepts not essential. It is a carry-over from the prestige of Sherrington and Pavlov that stimulus-response concepts are bandied about as they are. Yet the whole history of stimulus and response has been one of compromise and amendment. Dewey early criticized the reflex arc concept, and Thurstone later repeated his criticism.[35] Woodworth gradually shifted from his S-R motto to an S-O-R one. Thorndike began to talk about situation and response instead of stimulus and response. Skinner dared to introduce the notion of emitted behavior, refusing to follow the lead of others in inferring stimuli when none could be discovered. Robinson talked of instigators and instigatable processes, departing from the stimulus-response pattern.

It may be that the stimulus-response language has outlived its usefulness, now that molar psychologies have freed themselves from the necessity of explanation according to physiological mechanisms. Patched up as it is with drives, sets, tensions, secondary reinforcing agents, it is a way of talking carried over from reflex physiology when reflex physiology is no longer the model for psychological study. It would perhaps be a wholesome rec-

---

[34] Allport (1946).
[35] Dewey (1896), Thurstone (1923).

ognition of the change which has come in psychological thinking to talk about behavior in the presence of certain objects rather than about reaction to stimuli. Nothing need be lost. The organism is still confronted by environmental objects and acts in the presence of them. Correlations may be stated between psychologically real processes or their indicators without carrying the illusion that we are dealing with physical energy on the one hand and muscular contraction on the other. It is surprising how little the concepts of stimulus and response are needed in the description of what is actually done in learning experiments. We usually plot products of behavior (scores, errors, words per minute) against frequency of repetition or elapsed time—not responses against stimuli. The rest is inferred from our measurements.

A new theory can be written just as quantitatively and just as objectively as one in stimulus-response terms. The beginnings in this direction by Tolman and Lewin are indicative of possible directions.

A broad functionalism provides the common ground. If one asks what kind of theory this is, it is best described as a functionalism like that of Carr or Robinson or Woodworth, supplemented by additional borrowing from the cognitive theories of writers like Lashley, Muenzinger, Tolman and the rest.

The merit of the broad functionalist position is the willingness to accept new dimensions as they are discovered, to tolerate some theoretical inconsistencies rather than fly in the face of well-demonstrated experimental relationships. Such a positivistic attitude has worked well in other sciences. Even an elegant science like physics has stumbled along for a good while with inconsistent theories like the wave theory and the quantum theory of light. Biologists do not worry too much that their gene theories and their theories of embryological development are not yet satisfactorily integrated.

The difficulty with functionalism is that it does not satisfy the esthetic desire for a neat system. The motivation to seek for a few postulates, to find interchangeable constants, to be able to move logically from one part of the system to another has worked well in the physical sciences, and there is every reason to expect it to work well in psychology also. Functionalism has no quarrel with this possibility, and it is entirely possible to seek systematic elegance within the tolerance of a functionalist position. In the end, we shall know more and find more convenient ways both of expressing what we know and of finding out still more. That is ultimately what we are after, however that end is achieved.

AN EXPERIMENTAL PROGRAM

In the foregoing suggestions toward a theory of learning the erroneous impression may easily be given that the concepts represent a return to the pre-experimental period of psychologizing about learning. Acceptance of such a point of view might be interpreted to mean turning our backs upon the advances which have come through rejecting mentalistic and mystical concepts in favor of objective behavioral ones. In order to allay such fears and correct misapprehensions, I wish to propose what appear to me to be the needed directions of research upon learning.

Naturalistic observations. Because the search must continue for the most appropriate concepts to be used in the study and description of learning, it is desirable to keep flexibility in the approaches and to welcome novelty as well as precision. In urging consideration for a concept like the provisional try, I have not intended to discard the results of experimentation which have been obtained under other concepts, but only to break through the rigidity which makes us think of nonsense syllable lists, mazes, conditioning experiments and target-practice as exhausting the phenomena of learning.

The common acknowledgment of the ingenuity and originality of the experiments by Lewin and his students (even by those most devastatingly critical of his conceptual system) leads to a search for the roots of this freshness of approach. The answer probably lies in Lewin's tendency to pick problems out of real life situations, instead of choosing examples which would fit a previously learned method of study. It is out of real life that one finds problems like the forgetting of an intention, the tendency to resume interrupted tasks, and so on. Such problems are not thought up by students whose only concern is to counterbalance practice effects in a standard experiment in such a manner as to add an additional decimal point to the determination.

Somewhat the same thing might be said about Freud's contributions. Because Freud was listening to real people in their efforts to recall and to come to grips with their recollections, he discovered facts about repression and memorial distortion which were unknown to the followers of Ebbinghaus.

It would probably be desirable for someone to do for learning what Brunswik has recently been doing for perception [36]—that is, to take a notebook and follow a child around for hours at a time. What are the circumstances under which he learns? What performances provide for recall? for recognition? for problem-solving? What tasks are left half-finished? What kinds of forgetting are there? What motives can be inferred? Such observations would be like a breath of fresh air in most learning laboratories. To be sure, many observers would see only what they were taught to see. Some would find nothing but trial-and-error, others would see the child doing only what he last did, others would be impressed by the child's insight. But of a group who started out in this manner one or two would probably come back with suggestions as fertile as those of Lewin and his students. Such suggestions would help break the sterility of contemporary learning theories, and would help in the search for appropriate new concepts.

Physiological changes concomitant with learning. Because this book has neglected physiology does not mean that it is anti-physiological. On the contrary, it is a blot upon our scientific ingenuity that after so many years of search we know as little as we do about the physiological accompaniments of learning.

Learning theories may be developed at a molar level, independent of neurophysiology. It is preferable that the division of labor between psychology and physiology be recognized, and that psychological theories be developed objectively and self-consistently at the molar level, without recourse to a hypothetical neurology or a physiology not grounded in demonstrated relationships. Once the possibility of such a learning theory is granted—and there appears to be increasing agreement on this point—then an appropriate position with respect to neurophysiology can be established. The learning theorist does not have to *wait* for physiology in order to go ahead on firm scientific ground, but this

[36] Brunswik (1940, 1944).

does not mean that he will not welcome any advance in knowledge in this field, nor that he will not wish to contribute to such
knowledge through appropriate experiments.

One of the most crying needs is for a crucial experiment identifying specifically a change in neural tissue (or in bio-electrical
fields related to such tissue) as learning takes place. Possibly the
first task is to find an organism as appropriate for this purpose as
the fruit-fly has been for genetics. The white rat is probably too
complicated. Perhaps a simpler organism like amblystoma should
be chosen, in which the nervous elements are few enough to be
under direct inspection with modern techniques. It is possible to
teach larval amblystoma simple habits,[37] and it ought to be possible to find out what sort of "trace" these habits leave. To refuse
to search for such a change would be like refusing to look for
the micro-organism causing malaria just because an objective
plot could be made of the temperature fluctuations in the patient
as a means of identifying the disease. It can be stated with reasonable confidence that there are changes in the nervous system
accompanying learning, and, if there are, then there are surely
no insurmountable obstacles to the detecting of such changes.
It is a surprising thing that with all the interest in learning this
direct identifying step has not been taken more successfully.

The other possibilities, besides the study of the simpler organism, include the study of special preparations, such as the spinal
animal. Electrical methods of exploring the cortex may succeed,
but they, like behavioral studies, are likely to be at a molar level
from which the identifying steps still have to be made inferen-
tially.

Much that is known and can be found out about learning
will not be altered by changes in neurophysiological knowledge.
This is the basis of the argument for learning theories which dis-
pense with physiology, and it is sound. But it would be foolhardy
to suppose that a knowledge of the physical substratum of learning would not be helpful in further advancing of our theories
and in achieving control over the learning process. Such knowledge is indeed so important that psychologists interested in learning will wish to continue in the future, as they have in the past,
to share with physiologists and neurologists in experimentation

[37] Moore and Welch (1940).

designed to get at the changes in the organism which go along with manifest behavior.

Miniature systems. In what he chose to call a "miniature system," Hull set an important model for system-making at this stage of knowledge about learning.[38] Such a miniature system isolates from the totality of psychological phenomena a few interrelated variables, and then gives a coherent systematic account of these. Such systems have been prominent in the development of the physical sciences. The gas laws, prior to the kinetic theory, were already a miniature system relating temperature, pressure and volume. By way of the kinetic theory they were related to Newton's laws of mechanics, and thus became integrated with a larger system. Galileo's laws of the pendulum and of falling bodies represent another miniature system, later also integrated into the Newtonian laws of motion. The hope is that the miniature system, if well studied, may by appropriate transformations become part of a larger system. In the meantime, it serves to aid in the discovery of the concepts appropriate to that more inclusive systematization.

An advantage of the miniature system is that it permits the use of *ad hoc* (or heuristic) concepts, and allows the concepts to go through preliminary testing and purification before they are universalized. The disadvantage that there result a great many concepts with different ranges of applicability is a temporary one only, for if the miniature system is a good one, its concepts can be easily transformed through appropriate equations when the time comes.

There are many useful starts which have been made in the direction of such miniature systems within learning, and they should be encouraged. Hull and his collaborators have provided the best worked out illustration in the rote-learning theory, where the events which are interrelated all take place within the anticipation method of serial memorization of nonsense syllables.[39] Skinner moves in this direction by describing the functional relationships within rat lever-pressing.[40] Spence has done a useful service in his deduction of events within discrimination

[38] Hull (1935a).
[39] Hull and others (1940).
[40] Skinner (1938).

experiments.[41] Tolman and his collaborators are making a system of spatial learning.[42] Melton and his coworkers have followed McGeoch in establishing the relationships within and around retroactive inhibition.[43] The problem of motivated forgetting, as studied by Zeigarnik and followed up by others now becomes almost a miniature system, or could become one.[44] Pursuit learning has a sufficient complexity of interrelationships to merit special systematic study, as illustrated in the work of Bell and the theoretical analysis by Ammons.[45] The level of aspiration experiments begin to crystallize out as a series of interrelationships.[46]

Having previously complained against inappropriate quantification, I wish now to defend my support of miniature systems. Their saving grace lies in their being "miniature." They should make no pretense of solving at once all the problems of learning. They seek rather to try to make sense of a body of quantified material by mathematical treatment *appropriate to that material*. The relationships are close at hand, and conjectures within the miniature system can be readily put to test. The charge that any one system is remote from ordinary learning or that it studies highly specialized aspects of learning can be true without being embarrassing, as long as there are many other miniature systems trying out a variety of conceptual approaches.

How does a good miniature system come about and what is it like? It can come about as soon as there are enough quantitative experiments to define with assurance some of the functional relationships. These relationships are then ordered in some appropriate manner, and gaps filled in. Usually there are some predictions made and tested, in order to be sure that there is a "tightness" to the system. The interrelationships are expressed in mathematical form, by equations of which the constants have rational meaning. This meaning may be conjectural, either as "intervening variable" or as "hypothetical construct," but the equation must

[41] Spence (1936, 1937).

[42] Tolman, Ritchie, and Kalish (1946*a*, 1946*b*, 1947*ab*), Ritchie (1947).

[43] Melton and Irwin (1940), Melton and Von Lackum (1941), Underwood (1945).

[44] See the references cited on page 229.

[45] Bell (1942), Ammons (1947).

[46] Lewin and others (1944).

be more than the result of empirical curve fitting. A merely empirical or "actuarial" curve may be useful at an exploratory stage, but the relationships take on a systematic character when the constants in the equations have meaning. Ultimately the same constants begin to crop up in different equations. When that happens within the equations of two or more miniature systems, these systems can be integrated into a more comprehensive system. One difficulty with "dimensional" analysis is that it tends to stress the variables within experiments instead of stressing the constants.[47] When learning theory has matured, constants representing an individual's plasticity or retentivity (or whatever may prove to be fundamental) should be possible of insertion in equations which will tell how much he will profit by spaced practice over massed practice, and so on.

What the quest boils down to is not immediately the statement of the quantitative laws of learning but the discovery of the most appropriate concepts by means of which to describe and understand learning. A multitude of miniature systems will give many concepts a chance to be tried. There is probably no shortcut, although a brilliant systematizer may come along to accelerate the process. This brilliant theorist will be immeasurably aided if the rest of us have provided raw materials in the form of systematic interrelationships carefully worked out around identifiable bodies of data.

Research on applications to practical situations. A study of the history of science will show that there is no uniform relationship between pure and applied science as they develop. The practice of extracting ores preceded the appropriate understanding of chemistry by centuries. Diets upon which people grew to maturity were chosen for ages before there was a science of nutrition. As theoretical and experimental science mature the relationship between science and invention becomes more intimate. Gunpowder could be invented before physical science advanced, but the atomic bomb could not have been made with-

---

[47] A constant as here described epitomizes a tie between empirical data and theoretical formulation because it has measured size (making it empirical) and fits interchangeably into equations (making it systematic). Illustrations from physical sciences would include gravitational acceleration, the speed of light, Planck's constant, and so on—each stated in units which have required measurements, each appearing in many different equations.

out calling upon the resources of pure science. The scientific study of learning is today in an intermediate position. While its results can be helpful to educators and parents, there are many problems in the practical guidance of learning which cannot yet be handled upon the basis of well-established principles.

At any one time, scientists in experimental and theoretical fields can work only on the problems upon which they are prepared to work with the conceptual and material tools at hand. These may or may not be appropriate to the practical problem calling for solution. Mothers must feed and rear their children as best they can while the children are growing up, and physicians have to treat their patients when they are sick. Practical pursuits cannot wait. Hence some sorts of adjustment are made in the practical world, while the scientists go about their business. Children may have rickets because nothing is known about vitamins, and patients may die because a new curative drug has not yet emerged from the laboratory. The scientists are not to be blamed if their science had not yet discovered vitamins or was not yet prepared to synthesize the new drug.

Because scientists have to develop appropriate methods and concepts before their results can become efficient regulators of practice, their concerns for a time may appear to be remote from practical affairs, and some of their disputes will seem to be quibbling over distinctions which do not matter. All this suggests the need for patience and tolerance toward experimentation which pushes back the boundaries of the known and toward theory construction which attempts to sharpen the conceptual tools with which scientists can work.

There is one faulty interpretation of the relationship between pure and applied science which is to be avoided. This is the interpretation that applications, if they are to have any verifiable basis, must wait until there is a pure science ready to be applied. A corollary of this interpretation is the confident hope that once the pure science is in order, applications will follow automatically. Neither the interpretation nor the corollary corresponds to reality, for it is quite possible to do applied research before the problems of pure science are settled, and it is seldom if ever possible to apply scientific principles directly to practical situations without some empirical tailoring to make them fit.

The ideal situation calls for a better relationship between the scientific knowledge of learning principles and the practical knowledge of their applications in real life situations. It is an improper use of the prestige of science to bolster a practice which, while coherent with the scientific theory, has developed independently and has had no rigorous scientific testing. For example, it is sometimes asserted that young children should construct large things rather than small because the order of motor development is from large gross movements to finer ones. The general principle, while probably useful, does not provide a rule for determining just what size construction is appropriate at any given age. Real learning situations are controlled and limited by the acquired motivational patterns of the learners, by the specific social context in which learning occurs, by the constraints of time, equipment, and leadership available. This is no different in other technologies. A new motor car model has to be given a road test in spite of all the advances in thermodynamics, metallurgy, and streamlining, and usually changes in design are made as a result of such preliminary tests.

An adequate research program in the applied psychology of learning would rest in part upon the findings in the experimental studies of learning, but it would consist in much more than the making of suggestions on the basis of general principles. There must finally be experimental testing in the school, or on the playground, or in the shop—wherever the application is to be made.

If in the end a principle has to be experimented upon at the point of application, it might be asked, why do laboratory research at all? If what we do with animals has to be repeated with children, why not work with children in the first place? There are several answers. For one thing, we do some things with animals which we cannot do with children. For another thing, we make many false starts in the laboratory, and it would be wasteful to subject school children to all the things we try in the laboratory. Again, in the laboratory we are able to control conditions as we are not able to control them in the school. *A principle once discovered in a better controlled situation can be validated in a less well-controlled one.*[48] Even though the sole aim of learning

[48] This is well illustrated by experiments on diet. It would be difficult to start out to detect dietary deficiencies by analyzing the whole bill of fare

experimentation were practical, it might prove economical to work in the laboratory in order to find the leads worth testing in practice.

Research on practical problems, if well done, not only adjusts theory to practice, but contributes to substantiating, refuting, or extending theoretical knowledge. It is a mistake to distinguish too sharply between pure and applied research, if both are good research. It is true, however, that much applied research is necessarily concerned with problems bound to specific times and places, and so lacks the universality of pure research. It is these local and temporary features which lead to the judgment that applied research is inferior, and tend to reduce the prestige of the applied scientist relative to the pure scientist. When the relationships between pure and applied research are properly worked out, the requisite skills are of a high order however the labor is divided, and there is no reason why prestige should not be more equitably distributed.

A FINAL WORD

The erroneous impression may be left that little is known about learning. The factual knowledge does in reality bulk large. McGeoch's selected bibliography of human learning, published in 1933, contained 1,200 titles. Razran's bibliography of conditioning, published in 1937, included 1,111 titles. Neither of these references covers the general field of learning experiments done with animals or done within the fields of application.

It is the consistent ordering of this voluminous material into a compact and agreed-upon systematic structure which is lacking. Because this book has been concerned with these more theoretical problems, the areas of disagreement have been emphasized above the areas of agreement. Many plain facts about learning, important in practice, have nothing of controversy in them, and are not interesting in the theoretical context. There

of subjects with a varied diet, but once dietary essentials have been discovered in the laboratory it is possible to supplement otherwise varied diets (lacking in some essentials) and so validate the laboratory findings that this factor is indeed essential.

is a common ground of understanding based upon an accepted logic of experimental inquiry and demonstrations, so that factual disagreements are readily arbitrated in the laboratory. Such disagreements over empirical fact as there are need not persist for long.

The time is ripe for a concerted attack upon the major points of disagreement within facts and theories. The next twenty years may well lead to a clearing of issues which will make obsolete the occasion for a book of this kind.

SUPPLEMENTARY READINGS

ECLECTICISM IN LEARNING THEORY

Dashiell, J. F. (1935) A survey and synthesis of learning theories. *Psychol. Bull.*, 32, 261-275.

Kellogg, W. N. (1938) An eclectic view of some theories of learning. *Psychol. Rev.*, 45, 165-184.

McConnell, T. R. (1942) Reconciliation of learning theories. *Natl. Soc. Stud. Educ.*, 41st Yearbook, Part II, 243-286.

Melton, A. W. (1941) Learning. In W. S. Monroe, edit., *Encyclopedia of educational research.* New York, Macmillan, 667-686.

Schlosberg, H. (1937) The relationship between success and the laws of conditioning. *Psychol. Rev.*, 44, 379-394.

Wickens, D. D. (1940) Conditioned response data and the holistic point of view. *Psychol. Rev.*, 47, 155-168.

THE NATURE OF THEORY CONSTRUCTION IN PSYCHOLOGY

Boring, E. G., Bridgman, P. W., Feigl, H., Israel, H. E., Pratt, C. C., Skinner, B. F. (1945) Symposium on operationism. *Psychol. Rev.*, 52, 241-294.

Brunswik, E. (1943) Organismic achievement and environmental probability. *Psychol. Rev.*, 50, 255-272.

Hull, C. L. (1943) The problem of intervening variables in molar behavior theory. *Psychol. Rev.*, 50, 273-291.

Kantor, J. R. (1941) Current trends in psychological theory. *Psychol. Bull.*, 38, 29-65.

Lewin, K. (1943) Defining the 'field at a given time.' *Psychol. Rev.*, 50, 288-290; 292-310.

Snygg, D. (1941) The need for a phenomenological system of psychology. *Psychol. Rev.*, 48, 404-424.

Spence, K. W. (1944) The nature of theory construction in contemporary psychology. *Psychol. Rev.*, 51, 47-68.

Stevens, S. S. (1939) Psychology and the science of science. *Psychol. Bull.*, 36, 221-263.

Tolman, E. C. (1938) The determiners of behavior at a choice point. *Psychol, Rev.,* 45, 1-41.

Woodrow, H. (1942) The problem of general quantitative laws in psychology. *Psychol. Bull.,* 39, 1-27.

ILLUSTRATIONS OF MINIATURE SYSTEMS USING A VARIETY OF CONCEPTS

Ammons, R. B. (1947) Acquisition of motor skill. I. Quantitative analysis and theoretical formulation. *Psychol. Rev.,* 54, 263-281.

Buxton, C. E. (1940) Latent learning and the goal gradient hypothesis. *Contrib. Psychol. Theor.,* 2. No. 6, 75 pp.

Cartwright, D., and Festinger, L. (1943) A quantitative theory of decision. *Psychol. Rev.,* 50, 595-621.

Gibson, E. J. (1940) A systematic application of the concepts of generalization and differentiation to verbal learning. *Psychol. Rev.,* 47, 196-229.

Gulliksen, H., and Wolfle, D. L. (1938) A theory of learning and transfer. *Psychometrika,* 3, 127-149; 225-251.

Hilgard, E. R. (1938) An algebraic analysis of conditioned discrimination in man. *Psychol. Rev.,* 45, 472-496.

Householder, A. S., and Landahl, H. D. (1945) *Mathematical biophysics of the central nervous system.*

Hull and others (1940) *Mathematico-deductive theory of rote learning.*

Melton, A. W. and Irwin, J. McQ. (1940) The influence of degree of interpolated learning on retroactive inhibition and the overt transfer of specific responses. *Amer. J. Psychol.,* 53, 173-203.

Miller, N. E. (1944) Experimental studies in conflict. In J. McV. Hunt, edit., *Personality and the behavior disorders.* New York, Ronald, 431-465.

Spence, K. W. (1937) The differential response in animals to stimuli varying within a single dimension. *Psychol. Rev.,* 44, 430-444.

Tolman, E. C. (1941) Discrimination vs. learning and the schematic sowbug. *Psychol. Rev.,* 48, 367-382.

REFERENCES AND AUTHOR INDEX

The numbers in italics following each reference give the text pages on which the paper is cited. Abbreviations of journal titles are given in accordance with the conventions of the *World list of scientific periodicals*, 2d ed., Oxford University Press, 1934, as adopted by the journals of the American Psychological Association. Citations in the text are made by date of publication.

ABEL, T. M. (1938) Neuro-circulatory reaction and the recall of unfinished and completed tasks. *J. Psychol.*, 6, 377-383.—*229*

ACH, N. (1910) *Über den Willensakt und das Temperament: Eine experimentelle Untersuchung.* Leipzig: Quelle and Meyer, xi, 324 pp.—*209*

ADAMS, D. K. (1929) Experimental studies of adaptive behavior in cats. *Comp. Psychol. Monogr.*, 6, No. 27, 168 pp.—*65, 324*

ADAMS, D. K. (1931) A restatement of the problem of learning. *Brit. J. Psychol.*, 22, 150-178.—*247, 295, 323*

ADAMS, D. K. (1933) Three theories of learning. *J. gen. Psychol.*, 8, 485-497.—*293*

ADLER, D. L., and KOUNIN, J. (1939) Some factors operating at the moment of resumption of interrupted tasks. *J. Psychol.*, 7, 255-267.—*229*

ALLPORT, G. W. (1930) Change and decay in the visual memory image. *Brit. J. Psychol.*, 21, 134-148.—*198*

ALLPORT, G. W. (1937) *Personality: a psychological interpretation.* New York, Holt, xiv, 588 pp.—*159*

ALLPORT, G. W. (1946) Effect: a secondary principle of learning. *Psychol. Rev.*, 53, 335-347.—*231, 349*

ALPER, T. G. (1946) Task-orientation vs. ego-orientation in learning and retention. *Amer. J. Psychol.*, 59, 236-248.—*229*

ALPER, T. G., *see also* Postman and Alper (1946).

AMMONS, R. B. (1947). Acquisition of motor skill: I. Quantitative analysis and theoretical formulation. *Psychol, Rev.*, 54, 263-281.—*355, 361*

ANGELL, J. R. (1906) Review of *Studies in philosophy and psychology* (Garman Commemorative Volume). *J. Phil. Psychol. sci. Meth.*, 3, 637-643.—*160*

BALDWIN, O. B. (1933) The maturation of the college student as evidenced by retests with the National Council Tests. *Psychol. Monogr.*, 44, 233-262.—*260*

BALL, J., *see* Lashley and Ball (1929).

BALLACHEY, E. L., *see* Buel and Ballachey (1934).

BARKER, R. G. (1942) An experimental study of the resolution of conflict by children: time elapsing and amount of vicarious trial-and-error behavior occurring. In Q. McNemar and M. A. Merrill, edit., *Studies in personality; Contributed in honor of Lewis M. Terman.* New York, McGraw-Hill, 13-34.—*233*

BARKER, R. G., DEMBO, T., and LEWIN, K. (1941) Frustration and regression: a study of young children. *Univ. Ia. Stud. Child Welf.*, 18, No. 1, xv, 314 pp.—*233*

BARTLETT, F. C. (1932) *Remembering.* Cambridge, Cambridge Univ. Press, x, 317 pp.—*199*

BAVELAS, A. (1942) Morale and the training of leaders. In G. Watson, edit., *Civilian morale.* Boston, Houghton Mifflin, 143-165.—*225, 233*

BAVELAS, A., *see also* Seashore and Bavelas (1941).

BELL, H. M. (1942) Rest pauses in motor learning as related to Snoddy's hypothesis of mental growth. *Psychol. Monogr.*, 54, No. 243, v, 38 pp.—*254, 355*

BERGMANN, G., and SPENCE, K. W. (1941) Operationism and theory in psychology. *Psychol. Rev.*, 48, 1-14.—*91*

BERNSTONE, A. H., *see* Muenzinger and others (1938).

BERTALANFFY, L. von. (1933) *Modern theories of development.* New York, Oxford Univ. Press, vii, 204 pp.—*234*

BILLS, A. G., and STAUFFACHER, J. C. (1937) The influence of voluntarily induced tension on rational problem solving. *J. Psychol.*, 4, 261-271.—*176*

BIRENBAUM, J. (1930) Das Vergessen einer Vornahme. Isolierte seelische Systeme und dynamische Gesamtbereiche. *Psychol. Forsch.*, 13, 218-284.—*206, 233*

BLODGETT, H. C. (1929) The effect of the introduction of reward upon the maze performance of rats. *Univ. Calif. Publ. Psychol.*, 4, 113-134.—*271, 282, 293*

BLODGETT, H. C. (1946) Reynolds' repetition of Blodgett's experiment on latent learning. *J. exp. Psychol.*, 36, 184-186.—*286*

BORING, E. G. (1929) The psychology of controversy. *Psychol. Rev.*, 36, 97-121.—*325*

BORING, E. G. (1930) The gestalt psychology and the gestalt movement. *Amer. J. Psychol.*, 42, 308-315.—*207*

BORING, E. G. (1933a) *The physical dimensions of consciousness.* New York, Appleton-Century, xii, 251 pp.—*154*

BORING, E. G. (1933b) Review of Robinson's *Association theory today. Psychol. Bull.*, 30, 451-455.—*176*

BORING, E. G., BRIDGMAN, P. W., FEIGL, H., ISRAEL, H. E., PRATT, C. C., and SKINNER, B. F. (1945) Symposium on operationism. *Psychol. Rev.*, 52, 241-294.—*360*

BRALY, K. W. (1933) The influence of past experience in visual perception. *J. exp. Psychol.*, 16, 613-643.—*186*

BRETNALL, E. P., see Tolman and others (1932).

BRIDGMAN, P. W., see Boring and others (1945).

BRIGDEN, R. L. (1933) Goal activity in the white rat. *Psychol. Monogr.*, 44, 88-97.—*260*

BRIGDEN, R. L. (1935) The dynamics of spiral movement in man. *J. comp. Psychol.*, 20, 59-74.—*260*

BRITT, S. H. (1935) Retroactive inhibition: a review of the literature. *Psychol. Bull.*, 32, 381-440.—*161, 166*

BROGDEN, W. J. (1939) The effect of frequency of reinforcement upon the level of conditioning. *J. exp. Psychol.*, 24, 419-431.—*112*

BROWN, J. F. (1929) The methods of Kurt Lewin in the psychology of action and affection. *Psychol. Rev.*, 36, 200-221.—*212*

BROWN, J. F., and FEDER, D. D. (1934) Thorndike's theory of learning as gestalt psychology. *Psychol. Bull.*, 31, 426-437.—*34, 50*

BROWN, M. A., see Robinson and Brown (1926).

BROWN, T. (1820) *Lectures on the philosophy of the human mind.* 16th edition, 4 vols., Edinburgh, William Tait, 1846.—*148*

BRUCE, R. W. (1933) Conditions of transfer of training. *J. exp. Psychol.*, 16, 343-361.—*176*

BRUNSWIK, E. (1939) Probability as a determiner of rat behavior. *J. exp. Psychol.*, 25, 175-197.—*112, 272, 293*

BRUNSWIK, E. (1940) Thing constancy as measured by correlation coefficients. *Psychol. Rev.*, 47, 69-78.—*332, 352*

BRUNSWIK, E. (1943) Organismic achievement and environmental probability. *Psychol. Rev.*, 50, 255-272.—*352, 360*

BRUNSWIK, E. (1944) Distal focussing of perception: Size-constancy in a representative sample of situations. *Psychol. Monogr.*, 56, No. 254, v, 49 pp.—*352*

BRUNSWIK, E., see also Tolman and Brunswik (1935).

BRYAN, W. L., and HARTER, N. (1897) Studies in the physiology and psychology of the telegraphic language. *Psychol. Rev.*, 4, 27-53.—*2*

BRYAN, W. L., and HARTER, N. (1899) Studies on the telegraphic language. The acquisition of a hierarchy of habits. *Psychol. Rev.*, 6, 345-375.—*2*

BUEL, J., and BALLACHEY, E. L. (1934) Choice-point expectancy in the maze running of the rat. *J. genet. Psychol.*, 45, 145-168.—*293*

BÜHLER, K. (1916) *Die geistige Entwicklung des Kindes.* Jena, Gustav Fischer (6th ed., 1930, xx, 494 pp.).—*312*

BUXTON, C. E. (1940) Latent learning and the goal gradient hypothesis. *Contrib. psychol. Theor.*, 2, No. 6, 75 pp.—*285, 361*

CAMPBELL, A. A., *see* Hilgard and Campbell (1936).

CAMPBELL, R. K., *see* Hilgard and others (1938).

CANNON, W. B. (1929) Organization for physiological homeostasis. *Physiol. Rev.*, 9, 399-431.—*248*

CARMICHAEL, L. (1934) An experimental study in the prenatal guinea-pig of the origin and development of reflexes and patterns of behavior in relation to the stimulation of specific receptor areas during the period of active fetal life. *Genet. Psychol. Monogr.*, 16, 337-491.—*246*

CARMICHAEL, L. (1936) Review of Guthrie's *The psychology of human learning. J. gen Psychol.*, 14, 490-492.—*75*

CARMICHAEL, L. (1946) The onset and early development of behavior. In L. Carmichael, edit., *Manual of child psychology*. New York, Wiley, 43-166.—*246*

CARNAP, R. (1936) Testability and meaning. *Philos. Sci.*, 3, 419-471. —*95*

CARNAP, R. (1937) Testability and meaning. *Philos. Sci.*, 4, 1-40.—*95*

CARR, H. A. (1925) *Psychology, a study of mental activity*. New York, Longmans Green, v, 432 pp.—*153, 156, 157, 343*

CARR, H. A. (1930) Teaching and learning. *J. genet. Psychol.*, 37, 189-219.—*155, 173*

CARR, H. A. (1931) The laws of association. *Psychol. Rev.*, 38, 212-228.—*147, 176*

CARR, H. A. (1933) The quest for constants. *Psychol. Rev.*, 40, 514-532.—*156*

CARR, H. A. (1935) *An introduction to space perception*. New York, Longmans Green, xi, 413 pp.—*332*

CARR, H. A. (1938) The law of effect. *Psychol. Rev.*, 45, 191-199.—*157*

CARTER, L. F. (1936) Maze learning with a differential proprioceptive cue. *J. exp. Psychol.*, 19, 758-762.—*75*

CARTER, L. F. (1941) Intensity of conditioned stimulus and rate of conditioning. *J. exp. Psychol.*, 28, 481-490.—*75*

CARTWRIGHT, D., and FESTINGER, L. (1943) A quantitative theory of decision. *Psychol. Rev.*, 50, 595-621.—*361*

CASON, H. (1932) Review of Thorndike's *Human learning. J. abnorm. (soc.) Psychol.*, 27, 214-222.—*51*

CASON, H., *see also* Trowbridge and Cason (1932).

CHEIN, I., *see* Levine and others (1942).

CHILD, C. M. (1924) *Physiological foundations of behavior*. New York, Holt, xii, 330 pp.—*236*

COGHILL, G. E. (1929) *Anatomy and the problem of behavior*. New York, Macmillan, xii, 113 pp.—*236, 237*

COGHILL, G. E. (1933) The neuro-embryologic study of behavior: principles, perspective and aim. *Science*, 78, 131-138.—*236*

COLE, L. E. (1939) A comparison of the factors of practice and knowledge of experimental procedure in conditioning the eyelid response of human subjects. *J. gen. Psychol.*, 20, 349-373.—*112*

COOK, S. W., and SKINNER, B. F. (1939) Some factors influencing the distribution of associated words. *Psychol. Rec.*, 3, 178-184.—*144*

COOK, T. W. (1941) Mirror position and negative transfer. *J. exp. Psychol.*, 29, 155-160.—*176*

COURTS, F. A. (1939) Relations between experimentally induced muscular tension and memorization. *J. exp. Psychol.*, 25, 235-256.—*176*

COWLES, J. T., and NISSEN, H. W. (1937) Reward expectancy in delayed responses of chimpanzees. *J. comp. Psychol.*, 24, 345-358.—*267*

CRUTCHFIELD, R. S. (1939) The determiners of energy expenditure in string-pulling by the rat. *J. Psychol.*, 7, 163-178.—*293*

CULLER, E. A. (1938) Recent advances in some concepts of conditioning. *Psychol. Rev.*, 45, 134-153.—*298*

DALLENBACH, K. M., *see* Jenkins and Dallenbach (1924), Minami and Dallenbach (1946).

DASHIELL, J. F. (1935) A survey and synthesis of learning theories. *Psychol. Bull.*, 32, 261-275.—*325, 360*

DAVIS, S. I., *see* Olson and Davis (1941).

DEMBO, T. (1931) Der Ärger als dynamischen Problem. *Psychol. Farsch*, 15, 1-144.—*233*

DEMBO, T., *see also* Lewin and others (1944).

DENNES, W. R. (1946) Conflict. *Phil. Rev.*, N. Y., 55, 343-376.—*325*

DENNY, M. R. (1946) The role of secondary reinforcement in a partial reinforcement situation. *J. exp. Psychol.*, 36, 373-389.—*112, 113, 345*

DEWEY, J. (1896) The reflex arc concept in psychology. *Psychol. Rev.*, 3, 357-370.—*349*

DODGE, R. (1931) *Conditions and consequences of human variability.* New Haven, Yale Univ. Press, x, 162 pp.—*192, 337*

DOLLARD, J., *see* Miller and Dollard (1941).

DORÉ, L. R., and HILGARD, E. R. (1937) Spaced practice and the maturation hypothesis. *J. Psychol.*, 4, 245-259.—*238, 253*

DOVE, C. C., *see* Muenzinger and Dove (1937).

DREIS, T. A. (1933) Two studies in retroaction: I. Influence of partial identity. II. Susceptibility to retroaction at various grade levels. *J. gen. Psychol.*, 8, 157-171.—*162*

DRIESCH, H. (1891) Entwicklungs-mechanische Studien I. Z. *wiss. Zool.*, 53, 160-184.—*234*

DUNCKER, K. (1926) A qualitative study (experimental and theoretical) of productive thinking (solving of comprehensible problems). *J. genet. Psychol.*, 33, 642-708.—*297, 311*

DUNCKER, K. (1938) Experimental modification of children's food preferences through social suggestion. *J. abnorm. (soc.) Psychol.,* 33, 489-507.—*225*

DUNCKER, K. (1945) On problem solving. (Trans. by L. S. Lees from the 1935 original.) *Psychol. Monogr.,* 58, No. 270, ix, 113 pp.— *198, 311*

EBBINGHAUS, H. (1885) *Memory.* (Trans. H. A. Ruger and C. E. Bussenius.) New York, Teachers College, 1913, viii, 123 pp.—*2, 326*

ELLIOTT, M. H. (1928) The effect of change of reward on the maze performance of rats. *Univ. Calif. Publ. Psychol.,* 4, 19-30.—*266*

ELLIS, W. D. (1938) *A source book of gestalt psychology.* New York, Harcourt Brace, xiv, 403 pp.—*207*

ELLSON, D. G. (1938) Quantitative studies of the interaction of simple habits. I. Recovery from specific and generalized effects of extinction. *J. exp. Psychol.,* 23, 339-358.—*114*

ENGLISH, H. B. (1934) Review of Wheeler and Perkins' *Principles of mental development. Amer. J. Psychol.,* 46, 348-350.—*260*

ESTES, W. K. (1944) An experimental study of punishment. *Psychol. Monogr.,* 57, No. 263, iii, 40 pp.—*129, 136-141*

ESTES, W. K., and SKINNER, B. F. (1941) Some quantitative properties of anxiety. *J. exp. Psychol.,* 29, 390-400.—*145*

EVANS, S. (1936) Flexibility of established habit. *J. gen. Psychol.,* 14, 177-200.—*270*

FEDER, D. D., *see* Brown and Feder (1934).

FEIGL, H., *see* Boring and others (1945).

FESTINGER, L. (1942) Wish, expectation, and group standards as factors influencing level of aspiration. *J. abnorm. (soc.) Psychol.,* 37, 184-200.—*233*

FESTINGER, L., *see also* Cartwright and Festinger (1943), Lewin and others (1944).

FINAN, J. L. (1940*a*) Quantitative studies in motivation. I. Strength of conditioning in rats under varying degrees of hunger. *J. comp. Psychol.,* 29, 119-134.—*107*

FINAN, J. L. (1940*b*) Review of Skinner's *Behavior of organisms. J. gen. Psychol.,* 22, 441-447.—*145*

FINGER, F. W. (1942*a*) The effect of varying conditions of reinforcement upon a simple running response. *J. exp. Psychol.,* 30, 53-68. —*112*

FINGER, F. W. (1942*b*) Retention and subsequent extinction of a simple running response following varying conditions of reinforcement. *J. exp. Psychol.,* 31, 120-133.—*112*

FITCH, E. E., *see* Smith and Fitch (1935).

FITCH, F. B., *see* Hull and others (1940).

FLETCHER, F. M., *see* Muenzinger and Fletcher (1936, 1937).

FOORD, E. N., *see* Hebb and Foord (1945).

FRANK, J. D. (1941) Recent studies of the level of aspiration. *Psychol. Bull.*, 38, 218-226.—*224*

FRANK, L. K. (1939) Time perspectives. *J. soc. Phil.*, 4, 293-312.—*217*

GATES, A. I. (1942) Connectionism: Present concepts and interpretations. *Natl. Soc. Stud. Educ.*, 41st Yearbook, Part II, 141-164.—*50, 158*

GEIER, F. M., and TOLMAN, E. C. (1943) Goal distance and restless activity. I. The goal gradient of restless activity. *J. comp. Psychol.*, 35, 197-204.—*293*

GELB, A., and GOLDSTEIN, K. (1918) Zur Psychologie des optischen Wahrnehmungs- und Erkennungsvorganges. *Z. ges. Neurol. Psychiat.*, 41, 1-143. [Condensed and translated as "Analysis of a case of figural blindness" in Ellis (1938), pages 315-325.]—*234*

GENGERELLI, J. A. (1928) Preliminary experiments on the causal factors in animal learning. *J. comp. Psychol.*, 8, 435-457.—*53, 247, 338*

GIBSON, E. J. (1940) A systematic application of the concepts of generalization and differentiation to verbal learning. *Psychol. Rev.*, 47, 196-229.—*361*

GIBSON, J. J. (1929) The reproduction of visually perceived forms. *J. exp. Psychol.*, 12, 1-39.—*198*

GILHOUSEN, H. C. (1931) An investigation of "insight" in rats. *Science*, 73, 711-712.—*340*

GLASER, N. M., *see* Maier and others (1940).

GOLDSTEIN, K. (1939) *The organism: A holistic approach to biology derived from pathological data in man.* New York, American Book Company, xviii, 533 pp.—*234*

GOLDSTEIN, K., *see also* Gelb and Goldstein (1918).

GOTTSCHALDT, K. (1926) Über den Einfluss der Erfahrung auf die Wahrnehmung von Figuren, I. *Psychol. Forsch.*, 8, 261-317. [Translated and condensed as "Gestalt factors and repetition" in Ellis (1938), pages 109-122.]—*185, 208*

GOTTSCHALDT, K. (1929) Über den Einfluss der Erfahrung auf die Wahrnehmung von Figuren, II. *Psychol. Forsch.*, 12, 1-87. [Translated and condensed as "Gestalt factors and repetition" in Ellis (1938), pages 123-135.]—*185, 208*

GOTTSCHALDT, K. (1933) Der Aufbau des kindlichen Handelns. *Beih. Z. angew. Psychol.*, No. 68, 228 pp.—*208*

GRICE, G. R. (1942) An experimental study of the gradient of reinforcement in maze learning. *J. exp. Psychol.*, 30, 475-489.—*114*

GULLIKSEN, H., and WOLFLE, D. L. (1938) A theory of learning and transfer. *Psychometrika*, 3, 127-149; 225-251.—*361*

GUTHRIE, E. R. (1930) Conditioning as a principle of learning. *Psychol. Rev.*, 37, 412-428.—*75*

GUTHRIE, E. R. (1933) Association as a function of time interval. *Psychol. Rev.*, 40, 355-367.—*75, 92*

GUTHRIE, E. R. (1935) *The psychology of learning.* New York, Harper, viii, 258 pp.—*3, 57, 60-64, 73, 75, 193, 212, 247*

GUTHRIE, E. R. (1936a) Psychological principles and scientific truth. *Proc. 25th Anniv. Celebr. Inaug. Grad. Stud.*, Univ. Southern Calif., 104-115.—*63*

GUTHRIE, E. R. (1936b) Thorndike's concept of "belonging." *Psychol. Bull.*, 33, 621.—*34*

GUTHRIE, E. R. (1938) *The psychology of human conflict.* New York, Harper, ix, 408 pp.—*61, 75*

GUTHRIE, E. R. (1942) Conditioning: A theory of learning in terms of stimulus, response, and association. *Natl. Soc. Stud. Educ.*, 41st Yearbook, Part II, 17-60.—*57, 64, 73, 75*

GUTHRIE, E. R., see also Smith and Guthrie (1921), Yacorzynski and Guthrie (1937).

GUTHRIE, E. R., and HORTON, G. P. (1946) *Cats in a puzzle box.* New York, Rinehart, 67 pp.—*65-70, 75, 193, 194, 341*

HALL, C. S. (1936) Emotional behavior in the rat. III. The relationship between emotionality and ambulatory activity. *J. comp. Psychol.*, 22, 345-352.—*293*

HALL, C. S., see also Tolman and others (1932).

HALL, M., see Hull and others (1940).

HAMILTON, G. V. (1916) A study of perseverance reactions in primates and rodents. *Behav. Monogr.*, 3, No. 13, 65 pp.—*69*

HAMILTON, J. A., and KRECHEVSKY, I. (1933) Studies in the effect of shock upon behavior plasticity in the rat. *J. comp. Psychol.*, 16, 237-253.—*302*

HARDEN, L. M. (1929) A quantitative study of the similarity factor in retroactive inhibition. *J. gen. Psychol.*, 2, 421-430.—*162*

HARLOW, H. F., and SETTLAGE, P. H. (1934) Comparative behavior of primates. VII. Capacity of monkeys to solve patterned string tests. *J. comp. Psychol.*, 18, 423-435.—*208*

HARROWER, M. R. (1932) Organization in higher mental processes. *Psychol. Forsch.*, 17, 56-120.—*208, 229*

HARSH, C. M. (1937) Disturbance and "insight" in rats. *Univ. Calif. Publ. Psychol.*, 6, 163-168.—*270*

HARTER, N., see Bryan and Harter (1897, 1899).

HARTMANN, G. W. (1935) *Gestalt psychology.* New York, Ronald Press, xiii, 325 pp.—*198, 207*

HARTMANN, G. W. (1942) The field theory of learning and its educational consequences. *Natl. Soc. Stud. Educ.*, 41st Yearbook, Part II, 165-214.—*207*

HEBB, D. O., and FOORD, E. N. (1945) Errors of visual recognition and the nature of the trace. *J. exp. Psychol.*, 35, 335-348.—*200*

HEIDBREDER, E. (1933) *Seven psychologies*. New York, D. Appleton-Century, viii, 450 pp.—*18, 176, 207*

HEIDBREDER, E. (1937) Review of Lewin's *Principles of topological psychology*. *Psychol. Bull.*, 34, 584-604.—*232*

HEIDBREDER, E. (1945) Toward a dynamic theory of cognition. *Psychol. Rev.*, 52, 1-22.—*333*

HEIDBREDER, E. (1946) The attainment of concepts. *J. gen. Psychol.*, 35, 173-189; 191-223.—*333*

HELSON, H. (1927) Insight in the white rat. *J. exp. Psychol.*, 10, 378-396.—*247*

HENLE, M. (1942) An experimental investigation of past experience as a determinant of visual form perception. *J. exp. Psychol.*, 30, 1-22.—*186*

HENLE, M., *see also* Wallach and Henle (1941) (1942).

HERB, F. H. (1939) Latent learning—non-reward followed by food in blinds. *J. comp. Psychol.*, 29, 247-256.—*288*

HERON, W. T., *see* Robinson and Heron (1922), Skinner and Heron (1937).

HERON, W. T., and SKINNER, B. F. (1937) Changes in hunger during starvation. *Psychol. Rec.*, 1, 51-60.—*145*

HERON, W. T., and SKINNER, B. F. (1940) The rate of extinction in maze-bright and maze-dull rats. *Psychol. Rec.*, 4, 11-18.—*145*

HILGARD, E. R. (1935) Review of Guthrie's *The psychology of learning*. *Psychol. Bull.*, 32, 306-309.—*75*

HILGARD, E. R. (1938) An algebraic analysis of conditioned discrimination in man. *Psychol. Rev.*, 45, 472-496.—*211, 361*

HILGARD, E. R. (1939) Review of Skinner's *The behavior of organisms*. *Psychol. Bull.*, 36, 121-125.—*145*

HILGARD, E. R. (1940) Review of *Mathematico-deductive theory of rote learning*: The psychological system. *Psychol. Bull.*, 37, 808-815.—*98, 104, 114*

HILGARD, E. R. (1942) Success in relation to level of aspiration. *Sch. & Soc.*, 55, 423-428.—*221*

HILGARD, E. R., *see also* Doré & Hilgard (1937).

HILGARD, E. R., and CAMPBELL, A. A. (1936) The course of acquisition and retention of conditioned eyelid responses in man. *J. exp. Psychol.*, 19, 227-247.—*59*

HILGARD, E. R., CAMPBELL, R. K., and SEARS, W. N. (1938) Conditioned discrimination: the effect of knowledge of stimulus-relationships. *Amer. J. Psychol.*, 51, 498-506.—*273*

HILGARD, E. R., and MARQUIS, D. G. (1940) *Conditioning and learning*. New York, D. Appleton-Century, xi, 429 pp.—*4, 18, 56, 58, 90, 93, 108, 110, 114, 119, 123, 125*

HILGARD, E. R., and SMITH, M. B. (1942) Distributed practice in motor learning: score changes within and between daily sessions. *J. exp. Psychol.*, 30, 136-146.—*252, 253*

HILGARD, J. R. (1933) The effect of early and delayed practice on memory and motor performances studied by the method of co-twin control. *Genet. Psychol. Monogr.*, 14, 493-565.—*250*

HILL, L. M., *see* Keller and Hill (1936)

HOLLINGWORTH, H. L. (1928) General laws of redintegration. *J. gen. Psychol.*, 1, 79-90.—*332*

HOLLINGWORTH, H. L. (1931) Effect and affect in learning. *Psychol. Rev.*, 38, 153-159.—*34*

HOLT, E. B. (1931) *Animal drive and the learning process.* New York, Holt, vii, 307 pp.—*340*

HONZIK, C. H. (1931) Delayed reaction in rats. *Univ. Calif. Publ. Psychol.*, 4, 307-318.—*109*

HONZIK, C. H. (1936) The sensory basis of maze learning in rats. *Comp. Psychol. Monogr.*, 13, No. 64, 113 pp.—*58*

HONZIK, C. H., *see also* Tolman and Honzik (1930a, 1930b).

HONZIK, C. H., and TOLMAN, E. C. (1936) The perception of spatial relations by the rat: a type of response not easily explained by conditioning. *J. comp. Psychol.*, 22, 287-318.—*293*

HOPPE, F. (1931) Erfolg und Misserfolg. *Psychol. Forsch.*, 14, 1-62.—*222, 223, 233*

HORTON, G. P., *see* Guthrie and Horton (1946).

HOUSEHOLDER, A. S., and LANDAHL, H. D. (1945) *Mathematical biophysics of the central nervous system.* Bloomington, Ind., Principia Press, 124 pp.—*361*

HOVLAND, C. I. (1937) The generalization of conditioned responses. IV. The effects of varying amounts of reinforcement upon the degree of generalization of conditioned responses. *J. exp. Psychol.*, 21, 261-276.—*111*

HOVLAND, C. I. (1938) Experimental studies in rote-learning theory. III. Distribution of practice with varying speeds of syllable presentation. *J. exp. Psychol.*, 23, 172-190.—*101, 102*

HOVLAND, C. I. (1939) Experimental studies in rote-learning theory. IV. Comparison of reminiscence in serial and paired associate learning. *J. exp. Psychol.*, 24, 466-484.—*114*

HOVLAND, C. I., *see also* Hull and others (1940).

HUDGINS, C. V. (1933) Conditioning and the voluntary control of the pupillary light reflex. *J. gen. Psychol.*, 8, 3-51.—*120*

HULL, C. L. (1917) The formation and retention of associations among the insane. *Amer. J. Psychol.*, 28, 419-435.—*104*

HULL, C. L. (1928) *Aptitude testing.* Yonkers-on-Hudson, World Book Company, xiv, 535 pp.—*280*

HULL, C. L. (1930) Knowledge and purpose as habit mechanisms. *Psychol. Rev.*, 37, 511-525.—*105*

HULL, C. L. (1931) Goal attraction and directing ideas conceived as habit phenomena. *Psychol. Rev.*, 38, 487-506.—*105*

HULL, C. L. (1932) The goal gradient hypothesis and maze learning. *Psychol. Rev.*, 39, 25-43.—*93, 248, 285*

HULL, C. L. (1933) Differential habituation to internal stimuli in the albino rat. *J. comp. Psychol.*, 16, 255-273.—*86*

HULL, C. L. (1934*a*) The concept of the habit-family hierarchy and maze learning. *Psychol. Rev.*, 41, 33-54; 134-152.—*95, 269*

HULL, C. L. (1934*b*) The rat's speed-of-locomotion gradient in the approach to food. *J. comp. Psychol.*, 17, 393-422.—*114*

HULL, C. L. (1935*a*) The conflicting psychologies of learning—a way out. *Psychol. Rev.*, 42, 491-516.—*98, 328, 354*

HULL, C. L. (1935*b*) The influence of caffeine and other factors on certain phenomena of rote learning. *J. gen. Psychol.*, 13, 249-274.—*114*

HULL, C. L. (1935*c*) The mechanism of the assembly of behavior segments in novel combinations suitable for problem solution. *Psychol. Rev.*, 42, 219-245.—*105, 343*

HULL, C. L. (1935*d*) Special review of Thorndike's *The fundamentals of learning*. *Psychol. Bull.*, 32, 807-823.—*37, 44, 51*

HULL, C. L. (1937) Mind, mechanism, and adaptive behavior. *Psychol. Rev.*, 44, 1-32.—*95, 338*

HULL, C. L. (1938) The goal-gradient hypothesis applied to some "field-force" problems in the behavior of young children. *Psychol. Rev.*, 45, 271-299.—*94, 95, 105, 269*

HULL, C. L. (1939*a*) The problem of stimulus equivalence in behavior theory. *Psychol. Rev.*, 46, 9-30.—*85, 308*

HULL, C. L. (1939*b*) Simple trial and error learning—an empirical investigation. *J. comp. Psychol.*, 27, 233-258.—*114*

HULL, C. L. (1942) Conditioning: outline of a systematic theory of learning. *Natl. Soc. Stud. Educ.*, 41st Yearbook, Part II, 61-95.—*82, 114*

HULL, C. L. (1943*a*) *Principles of behavior*. New York, D. Appleton-Century, x, 422 pp.—*3, 80-96, 106, 107, 111-113, 133, 135, 298*

HULL, C. L. (1943*b*) The problem of intervening variables in molar behavior theory. *Psychol. Rev.*, 50, 273-291.—*360*

HULL, C. L. (1945*a*) The discrimination of stimulus configurations and the hypothesis of afferent neural interaction. *Psychol. Rev.*, 52, 133-142.—*82*

HULL, C. L. (1945*b*) The place of innate individual and species differences in a natural-science theory of behavior. *Psychol. Rev.*, 52, 55-60.—*104, 280, 329*

HULL, C. L. (1947) The problem of primary stimulus generalization. *Psychol. Rev.*, 54, 120-134.—*85, 310*

HULL, C. L., HOVLAND, C. I., ROSS, R. T., HALL, M., PERKINS, D. T., and FITCH, F. B. (1940) *Mathematico-deductive theory of rote learning*. New Haven, Yale Univ. Press, xii, 329 pp.—*87, 96-104, 106, 113, 328, 354, 361*

HUMPHREY, G. (1928) The effect of sequences of indifferent stimuli on a reaction of the conditioned response type. *J. abnorm. (soc.) Psychol.*, 22, 194-212.—*82, 324*

HUMPHREY, G. (1930) Learning and the living system. *Psychol. Rev.*, 37, 497-510.—*295, 323*

HUMPHREY, G. (1933) *The nature of learning in its relation to the living system.* New York, Harcourt Brace, vii, 296 pp.—*295, 322*

HUMPHREY, G. (1937) A note on system-theory. *Psychol. Rev.*, 44, 346-348.—*295*

HUMPHREYS, L. G. (1939a) The effect of random alternation of reinforcement on the acquisition and extinction of conditioned eyelid reactions. *J. exp. Psychol.*, 25, 141-158.—*112, 273*

HUMPHREYS, L. G. (1939b) Acquisition and extinction of verbal expectations in a situation analogous to conditioning. *J. exp. Psychol.*, 25, 294-301.—*273, 275*

HUMPHREYS, L. G. (1940) Extinction of conditioned psychogalvanic responses following two conditions of reinforcement. *J. exp. Psychol.*, 27, 71-75.—*112*

HUMPHREYS, L. G. (1943a) Measures of strength of conditioned eyelid responses. *J. gen. Psychol.*, 29, 101-111.—*90*

HUMPHREYS, L. G. (1943b) The strength of a Thorndikian response as a function of the number of practice trials. *J. comp. Psychol.*, 35, 101-110.—*112, 274*

HUNTER, W. S. (1913) The delayed reaction in animals and children. *Behav. Monogr.*, 2, No. 6 86 pp.—*109*

HUNTER, W. S. (1924) The symbolic process. *Psychol. Rev.*, 31, 478-497.—*343*

IRION, A. L. (1946) Retroactive inhibition as a function of the relative serial positions of the original and interpolated items. *J. exp. Psychol.*, 36, 262-270—*161, 165*

IRWIN, F. W., KAUFFMAN, K., PRIOR, G., and WEAVER, H. B. (1934) On "Learning without awareness of what is being learned." *J. exp. Psychol.*, 17, 823-827.—*342*

IRWIN, J. McQ., *see* Melton and Irwin (1940).

ISRAEL, H. E., *see* Boring and others (1945).

JACKSON, T. A. (1942) Use of the stick as a tool by young chimpanzees. *J. comp. Psychol.*, 34, 223-235.—*191*

JAMES, W. (1890) *The principles of psychology.* New York, Holt, I, xii, 689 pp.; II, vi, 704 pp.—*222, 238*

JENKINS, J. G., and DALLENBACH, K. M. (1924) Oblivescence during sleep and waking. *Amer. J. Psychol.*, 35, 605-612.—*164*

JENKINS, W. O. (1943) Studies in the spread of effect. *J. comp. Psychol.*, 35, 41-72.—*45*

JENKINS, W. O., and SHEFFIELD, F. D. (1946) Rehearsal and guessing habits as sources of the "spread of effect." *J. exp. Psychol.*, 36, 316-330.—*41, 44*

JONES, H., *see* Mowrer and Jones (1945).

JUDD, C. H. (1908) The relation of special training to general intelligence. *Educ. Rev.*, 36, 28-42.—*205*

KALISH, D., *see* Tolman and others (1946*a*, 1946*b*, 1947).

KANTOR, J. R. (1941*a*) Review of Hull and others, *Mathematico-deductive theory of rote learning*. *Amer. J. Psychol.*, 54, 300-304. —*114*

KANTOR, J. R. (1941*b*) Current trends in psychological theory. *Psychol. Bull.*, 38, 29-65.—*331, 360*

KAPPAUF, W. E., and SCHLOSBERG, H. (1937) Conditioned responses in the white rat. III. Conditioning as a function of the length of the period of delay. *J. genet. Psychol.*, 50, 27-45.—*92*

KARN, H. W., and PORTER, J. M., Jr. (1946) The effects of certain pre-training procedures upon maze performance and their significance for the concept of latent learning. *J. exp. Psychol.*, 36, 461-469.—*287*

KARSTEN, A. (1928) Psychische Sättigung. *Psychol. Forsch.*, 10, 142-254.—*218, 224, 233*

KATONA, G. (1940) *Organizing and memorizing*. New York, Columbia Univ. Press, xii, 318 pp.—*186, 201-203*

KATONA, G. (1942) Organizing and memorizing: a reply to Dr. Melton. *Amer. J. Psychol.*, 55, 273-275.—*203*

KAUFFMAN, K., *see* Irwin and others (1934).

KEISTER, M. E. (1937) The behavior of young children in failure: an experimental attempt to discover and to modify undesirable responses of pre-school children to failure. *Univ. Ia. Stud. Child Welf.*, 14, 28-82.—*225*

KELLER, F. S. (1941) Light-aversion in the white rat. *Psychol. Rec.*, 4, 235-250.—*145*

KELLER, F. S., and HILL, L. M. (1936) Another "insight" experiment. *J. genet. Psychol.*, 48, 484-489.—*270*

KELLOGG, W. N. (1938) An eclectic view of some theories of learning. *Psychol. Rev.*, 45, 165-184.—*325, 360*

KENDLER, H. H. (1946) The influence of simultaneous hunger and thirst drives upon the learning of two opposed spatial responses of the white rat. *J. exp. Psychol.*, 36, 212-220.—*86, 286*

KENNELLY, T. W. (1941) The role of similarity in retroactive inhibition. *Arch. Psychol., N. Y.*, 37, No. 260, 56 pp.—*162*

KIMBLE, G. A. (1947) Conditioning as a function of the time between conditioned and unconditioned stimuli. *J. exp. Psychol.*, 37, 1-15. —*58*

KLEE, J. B., *see* Maier and others (1940), Maier and Klee (1941, 1943, 1945).

KLEEMEIER, R. W. (1942) Fixation and regression in the rat. *Psychol. Monogr.*, 54, No. 246, v, 34 pp.—*302*

KLÜVER, H. (1933) *Behavior mechanisms in monkeys.* Chicago, Univ. Chicago Press, xvii, 387 pp.—*296, 324*

KOCH, S. (1944) Review of Hull's *Principles of behavior. Psychol. Bull.*, 41, 269-286.—*114*

KOFFKA, K. (1924) *The growth of the mind.* (Trans. by R. M. Ogden) London, Kegan Paul, Trench, Trubner & Co., Ltd., xvi, 383 pp.—*177, 180, 184, 207*

KOFFKA, K. (1925) Mental development. In C. Murchison, edit., *Psychologies of 1925.* Worcester, Mass., Clark Univ. Press, 130-143.—*207*

KOFFKA, K. (1930) Some problems of space perception. In C. Murchison, edit., *Psychologies of 1930.* Worcester, Mass., Clark Univ. Press, 161-187.—*11, 332*

KOFFKA, K. (1933) Review of Tolman's *Purposive behavior in animals and men. Psychol. Bull.*, 30, 440-451.—*290, 293*

KOFFKA, K. (1935) *Principles of gestalt psychology.* New York, Harcourt Brace, xi, 720 pp.—*181-189, 206, 207*

KÖHLER, W. (1917) *Intelligenzprufungen an Menschenaffen.* (See Köhler, 1925.)—*178*

KÖHLER, W. (1918) Nachweis einfacher Strukturfunktionen beim Schimpansen und beim Haushuhn. *Abh. d. königl. Preuss. Ak. d. Wissen*, Phys. Math. Klasse, Nr. 2, 1-101. [Translated and condensed as "Simple structural functions in the chimpanzee and in the chicken" in Ellis (1938), pages 217-227.]—*208, 308*

KÖHLER, W. (1920) *Die physische Gestalten in Ruhe und in stationären Zustand, Eine naturphilosophische Untersuchung.* Braunschweig, Vieweg, xx, 263 pp. [Portions condensed and translated in Ellis (1938), pages 17-54.]—*234*

KÖHLER, W. (1925) *The mentality of apes.* (Trans. by E. Winter) New York, Harcourt Brace, viii, 342 pp.—*177, 207*

KÖHLER, W. (1929) *Gestalt psychology. New York,* Liveright, x, 403 pp.—*153, 207*

KÖHLER, W. (1930) Some tasks of gestalt psychology. In C. Murchison, edit., *Psychologies of 1930.* Worcester, Mass., Clark Univ. Press, 143-160.—*207*

KÖHLER, W. (1938) *The place of value in a world of facts.* New York, Liveright, ix, 418 pp.—*186*

KÖHLER, W. (1940) *Dynamics in psychology.* New York, *Liveright*, 158 pp.—*170, 207*

KÖHLER, W. (1943) Review of McGeoch's *The psychology of human learning. Amer. J. Psychol.*, 56, 455-460.—*176*

Köhler, W. (1947) *Gestalt psychology.* New York, Liveright, 369 pp. *—207*

Kounin, J. (1941) Experimental studies of rigidity. I. The measurement of rigidity in normal and feeble-minded persons. *Character & Pers.,* 9, 251-272.*—230*

Kounin, J., *see also* Adler and Kounin (1939).

Krechevsky, I. (1932*a*) 'Hypotheses' in rats. *Psychol. Rev.,* 39, 516-532.*—276*

Krechevsky, I. (1932*b*) 'Hypotheses' versus 'chance' in the presolution period in sensory discrimination-learning. *Univ. Calif. Publ. Psychol.,* 6, 27-44.*—276, 293*

Krechevsky, I. (1933*a*) Hereditary nature of 'hypotheses'. *J. comp. Psychol.,* 16, 99-116.*—276*

Krechevsky, I. (1933*b*) The docile nature of 'hypotheses'. *J. comp. Psychol.,* 15, 429-443.*—276*

Krechevsky, I. (1937*a*) Brain mechanisms and variability: I. Variability within a means-end-readiness. *J. comp. Psychol.,* 23, 121-138.*—301*

Krechevsky, I. (1937*b*) Brain mechanisms and variability: II. Variability when no learning is involved. *J. comp. Psychol.,* 23, 139-163.*—301*

Krechevsky, I. (1937*c*) Brain mechanisms and variability: III. Limitations of the effect of cortical injury upon variability. *J. comp. Psychol.,* 23, 351-364.*—301*

Krechevsky, I. (1937*d*) A note concerning "The nature of discrimination learning in animals." *Psychol. Rev.,* 44, 97-104.*—309*

Krechevsky, I. (1938*a*) Brain mechanisms and *Umweg* behavior. *J. comp. Psychol.,* 25, 147-173.*—296*

Krechevsky, I. (1938*b*) An experimental investigation of the principle of proximity in the visual perception of the rat. *J. exp. Psychol.,* 22, 497-523.*—324*

Krechevsky, I. (1938*c*) A study of the continuity of the problem-solving process. *Psychol. Rev.,* 45, 107-133.*—309*

Krechevsky, I. (1939) Review of Skinner's *Behavior of organisms. J. abnorm. (soc.) Psychol.,* 34, 404-407.*—145*

Krechevsky, I., *see also* Hamilton and Krechevsky (1933).

Krechevsky, I., and Honzik, C. H. (1932) Fixation in the rat. *Univ. Calif. Publ. Psychol.,* 6, 13-26.*—288*

Kuo, Z. Y. (1937) Forced movement or insight? *Univ. Calif. Publ. Psychol.,* 6, 169-188.*—270*

Lamoreaux, R. R., *see* Mowrer and Lamoreaux (1942).

Landahl, H. D., *see* Householder and Landahl (1945).

Lanier, L. H. (1931) Review of Wheeler's *The science of psychology. Amer. J. Psychol.,* 43, 146-150.*—260*

LASHLEY, K. S. (1929a) Brain mechanisms and intelligence. Chicago, Univ. Chicago Press, xiv, 186 pp.—323

LASHLEY, K. S. (1929b) Learning: I. Nervous mechanisms in learning. In C. Murchison, edit., The foundations of experimental psychology. Worcester, Mass., Clark Univ. Press, 524-563.—278, 296

LASHLEY, K. S. (1930a) Basic neural mechanisms in behavior. Psychol. Rev., 37, 1-24.—296, 323

LASHLEY, K. S. (1930b) The mechanism of vision: I. A method for rapid analysis of pattern-vision in the rat. J. genet. Psychol., 37, 453-460.—297

LASHLEY, K. S. (1938) The mechanism of vision. XV. Preliminary studies of the rat's capacity for detail vision. J. gen. Psychol., 18, 123-193.—324

LASHLEY, K. S. (1942) An examination of the "continuity theory" as applied to discriminative learning. J. gen. Psychol., 26, 241-265. —297, 309, 324

LASHLEY, K. S., and BALL, J. (1929) Spinal conduction and kinesthetic sensitivity in the maze habit. J. comp. Psychol., 9, 71-105.—268

LASHLEY, K. S., and WADE, M. (1946) The Pavlovian theory of generalization. Psychol. Rev., 53, 72-87.—111, 297, 309, 310, 322, 323, 339

LEEPER, R. (1935a) The role of motivation in learning; a study of the phenomenon of differential motivational control of the utilization of habits. J. genet. Psychol., 46, 3-40.—86, 324

LEEPER, R. (1935b) A study of a neglected portion of the field of learning—the development of sensory organization. J. genet. Psychol., 46, 41-75.—181, 324

LEEPER, R. (1943) Lewin's topological and vector psychology, a digest and a critique. Eugene, Ore., Univ. Oregon Press, ix, 218 pp.—231, 232, 296

LEEPER, R. (1944) Dr. Hull's Principles of behavior. J. genet. Psychol., 65, 3-52.—82, 114, 263, 309, 321

LEVINE, R., CHEIN, I., and MURPHY, G. (1942) The relation of the intensity of a need to the amount of perceptual distortion: a preliminary report. J. Psychol., 13, 283-293.—333

LEWIN, K. (1917) Die psychische Tätigkeit bei der Hemmung vons Willensvorgängen und das Grundgesetz der Assoziation. Z. Psychol., 77, 212-247.—210

LEWIN, K. (1922) Das Problem der Willensmessung und das Grundgesetz der Assoziation. Psychol. Forsch., 1, 65-140; 191-302.—210, 213

LEWIN, K. (1926) Vorsatz, Wille, und Bedürfnis (Mit Vorbemerkungen über die psychischen Kräfte und Energien und die Struktur der Seele). Psychol. Forsch., 7, 294-385. [Translated and condensed as "Will and needs" in Ellis (1938), pages 283-299.] —212, 226

LEWIN, K. (1931) The conflict between Aristotelian and Galileian modes of thought in contemporary psychology. *J. gen. Psychol.*, 5, 141-177.—*291*

LEWIN, K. (1933*a*) Environmental forces. In C. Murchison, edit., *A handbook of child psychology*. Worcester, Mass., Clark Univ. Press, 590-625.—*94*

LEWIN, K. (1933*b*) Vectors, cognitive processes, and Mr. Tolman's criticism. *J. gen. Psychol.*, 8, 318-345.—*290*

LEWIN, K. (1935) *A dynamic theory of personality*. (Trans. by D. K. Adams and K. E. Zener) New York, McGraw-Hill, ix, 286 pp. —*94, 223, 232, 295*

LEWIN, K. (1936) *Principles of topological psychology*. (Trans. by F. Heider and G. M. Heider) New York, McGraw-Hill, xv, 231 pp.—*214, 216, 217, 232*

LEWIN, K. (1937) Psychoanalysis and topological psychology. *Bull. Menninger Clin.*, 1, 202-211.—*231*

LEWIN, K. (1938) The conceptual representation and measurement of psychological forces. *Contr. psychol. Theor.*, I, No. 4, 247 pp. —*214, 232*

LEWIN, K. (1942) Field theory and learning. *Natl. Soc. Stud. Educ.*, 41st Yearbook, Part II, 215-242.—*214, 218, 219, 221, 225, 232*

LEWIN, K. (1943) Defining the 'field at a given time'. *Psychol. Rev.*, 50, 288-290; 292-310.—*218, 360*

LEWIN, K. (1946) Behavior and development as a function of the total situation. In L. Carmichael, edit., *Manual of child psychology*. New York, Wiley, 791-844.—*220, 232*

LEWIN, K., DEMBO, T., FESTINGER, L., and SEARS, P. S. (1944) Level of aspiration. In J. McV. Hunt, edit., *Personality and the behavior disorders*. New York, Ronald, 333-378.—*224, 355*

LEWIN, K., LIPPITT, R., and WHITE, R. K. (1939) Patterns of aggressive behavior in experimentally created 'social climates'. *J. soc. Psychol.*, 10, 271-299.—*233*

LEWIS, M. H. (1930) Elemental vs. configural response in the chick. *J. exp. Psychol.*, 13, 61-75.—*260*

LIPPITT, R., *see* Lewin and others (1939), Spence and Lippitt (1940, 1946).

LONDON, I. D. (1944) Psychologists' misuse of the auxiliary concepts of physics and mathematics. *Psychol. Rev.*, 51, 266-291.—*215, 231*

LORGE, I. (1936) Irrelevant rewards in animal learning. *J. comp. Psychol.*, 21, 105-128.—*51*

LORGE, I., *see also* Thorndike and Lorge (1935).

LUCHINS, A. S., (1942) Mechanization in problem solving. The effect of *Einstellung*. *Psychol. Monogr.*, 54, No. 248, vii, 95 pp.—*189, 340*

LUH, C. W. (1922) The conditions of retention. *Psychol. Monogr.*, 31, No. 142, 87 pp.—*176*

LUMSDAINE, A. A. (1941) Measures of individual differences in susceptability to conditioning. *J. exp. Psychol.*, 28, 428-435.—*90*

McCONNELL, T. R. (1942) Reconciliation of learning theories. *Natl. Soc. Stud. Educ.*, 41st Yearbook, Part II, 243-286.—*325, 360*

McCONNELL, T. R., and OTHERS (1942) *The psychology of learning.* Natl. Soc. Stud. Educ., 41st Yearbook, Part II, xiv, 502 pp.—*18*

McCORD, F. (1939) The delayed reaction and memory in rats. I. Length of delay. *J. comp. Psychol.*, 27, 1-37.—*109*

McCULLOCH, T. L. (1939) Comment on the formation of discrimination habits. *Psychol. Rev.*, 46, 75-85.—*309*

McDONALD, W. T., *see* McGeoch and McDonald (1931).

McDOUGALL, W. (1923) *Outline of psychology.* New York, Scribner, xvi, 456 pp.—*11, 231*

McGEOCH, J. A. (1932*a*) The comparative retention values of a maze habit, of nonsense syllables, and of rational learning. *J. exp. Psychol.*, 15, 662-680.—*176*

McGEOCH, J. A. (1932*b*) Review of Robinson's *Association theory today. J. gen. Psychol.*, 7, 231-237.—*176*

McGEOCH, J. A. (1933*a*) The configurational psychology of learning. *J. appl. Psychol.*, 17, 83-96.—*260*

McGEOCH, J. A. (1933*b*) The psychology of human learning: a bibliography. *Psychol. Bull.*, 30, 1-62.—*359*

McGEOCH, J. A. (1933*c*) Review of Thorndike's *The fundamentals of learning. J. gen. Psychol.*, 8, 285-296.—*51*

McGEOCH, J. A. (1934) Review of Humphrey's *The nature of learning in its relation to the living system. Psychol. Bull.*, 31, 220-222. —*324*

McGEOCH, J. A. (1936) The vertical dimensions of mind. *Psychol. Rev.*, 43, 107-129.—*155*

McGEOCH, J. A. (1942) *The psychology of human learning.* New York, Longmans Green, xvii, 633 pp.—*18, 152, 161, 164, 169, 171, 175, 198, 229, 343*

McGEOCH, J. A., and McDONALD, W. T. (1931) Meaningful relation and retroactive inhibition. *Amer. J. Psychol.*, 43, 579-588.—*165*

MacCORQUODALE, K., and MEEHL, P. E. (1947) On a distinction between hypothetical constructs and intervening variables. *Psychol. Rev.* (To appear)—*91, 265*

MACFARLANE, D. A. (1930) The role of kinesthesis in maze learning. *Univ. Calif. Publ. Psychol.*, 4, 277-305.—*268*

MAIER, N. R. F. (1929) Reasoning in white rats. *Comp. Psychol. Monogr.*, 6, No. 29, 93 pp.—*313*

MAIER, N. R. F. (1930) Reasoning in humans. I. On direction. *J. comp. Psychol.*, 10, 115-143.—*191, 193, 315, 316*

MAIER, N. R. F. (1931*a*) Reasoning and learning. *Psychol. Rev.*, 38, 332-346.—*6, 312*

MAIER, N. R. F. (1931*b*) Reasoning in humans. II. The solution of a problem and its appearance in consciousness. *J. comp. Psychol.*, 12, 181-194.—*315, 317, 319*

MAIER, N. R. F. (1932) The effect of cortical destruction on reasoning and learning in white rats. *J. comp. Neurol.*, 54, 45-75.—*296, 312, 313, 315*

MAIER, N. R. F. (1933) An aspect of human reasoning. *Brit. J. Psychol.*, 24, 144-155.—*315, 317, 319*

MAIER, N. R. F. (1935) In defense of reasoning in rats: a reply. *J. comp. Psychol.*, 19, 197-206.—*312*

MAIER, N. R. F. (1937) Reasoning in rats and human beings. *Psychol. Rev.*, 44, 365-378.—*312*

MAIER, N. R. F. (1938) A further analysis of reasoning in rats. III. The influence of cortical injuries on the process of "direction." *Comp. Psychol. Monogr.*, 15, No. 73, 44-80.—*314*

MAIER, N. R. F. (1939*a*) Qualitative differences in the learning of rats in a discrimination situation. *J. comp. Psychol.*, 27, 289-331. —*309, 324, 330*

MAIER, N. R. F. (1939*b*) The specific processes constituting the learning function. *Psychol. Rev.*, 46, 241-252.—*301, 323, 330*

MAIER, N. R. F. (1940) The behavior mechanisms concerned with problem solving. *Psychol. Rev.*, 47, 43-58.—*300*

MAIER, N. R. F. (1941) The effect of cortical injuries on equivalence reactions in rats. *J. comp. Psychol.*, 32, 165-189.—*324*

MAIER, N. R. F. (1942) The role of frustration in social movements. *Psychol. Rev.*, 49, 586-599.—*308*

MAIER, N. R. F. (1945) Reasoning in humans. III. The mechanisms of equivalent stimuli and of reasoning. *J. exp. Psychol.*, 35, 349-360.—*311, 312, 315-318*

MAIER, N. R. F., GLASER, N. M., and KLEE, J. B. (1940) Studies of abnormal behavior in the rat. III. The development of behavior fixations through frustration. *J. exp. Psychol.*, 26, 521-546.—*302, 303, 305, 340*

MAIER, N. R. F., and KLEE, J. B. (1941) Studies of abnormal behavior in the rat. VII. The permanent nature of abnormal fixations and their relation to convulsive tendencies. *J. exp. Psychol.*, 29, 380-389.—*303*

MAIER, N. R. F., and KLEE, J. B. (1943) Studies of abnormal behavior in the rat. XII. The pattern of punishment and its relation to abnormal fixations. *J. exp. Psychol.*, 32, 377-398.—*307*

MAIER, N. R. F., and KLEE, J. B. (1945) Studies of abnormal behavior in the rat. XVII. Guidance versus trial and error in the alteration of habits and fixations. *J. Psychol.*, 19, 133-163.—*306, 307*

MAIER, N. R. F., and SCHNEIRLA, T. C. (1935) *Principles of animal psychology.* New York, McGraw-Hill, xiii, 529 pp.—*298, 323*

MAIER, N. R. F., and SCHNEIRLA, T. C. (1942) Mechanisms in conditioning. *Psychol. Rev.*, 49, 117-134.—*298*

MANGOLD, A. (1931) Versuche zur Analyse der Entwicklung des Haftfadens bei Urodelen; ein Beispiel für die Induktion artfremder Organe. *Naturwissenschaften*, 19, 905-911.—*245*

MARHENKE, P. (1940) Review of *Mathematico-deductive theory of rote learning:* The logical system. *Psychol. Bull.*, 37, 815-817.—*114*

MARQUIS, D. G. (1942) The neurology of learning. In F. A. Moss, edit., *Comparative psychology.* (Revised edition) New York, Prentice-Hall, 153-177.—*322*

MARQUIS, D. G., *see also* Hilgard and Marquis (1940).

MARROW, A. J. (1938) Goal tensions and recall. *J. gen. Psychol.*, 19, 3-35, 37-64.—*226, 229*

MARTENS, D. (1946) Spread of effect in verbal serial learning. (Abstract.) *Amer. Psychologist*, 1, 448-449.—*38*

MARTIN, J. R. (1940) Reminiscence and gestalt theory. *Psychol. Monogr.*, 52, No. 235, v, 37 pp.—*229*

MASON, G., *see* Rosenzweig and Mason (1934).

MEEHL, P. E. (1945) An examination of the treatment of stimulus patterning in Professor Hull's *Principles of behavior. Psychol. Rev.*, 52, 324-332.—*82, 111*

MEEHL, P. E., *see also* MacCorquodale and Meehl (1947).

MELTON, A. W. (1941*a*) Learning. In W. S. Monroe, edit., *Encyclopedia of educational research.* New York, Macmillan, 667-686.—*155, 176, 192, 360*

MELTON, A. W. (1941*b*) Review of Katona's *Organizing and memorizing. Amer. J. Psychol.*, 54, 455-457.—*203*

MELTON, A. W., and IRWIN, J. McQ. (1940) The influence of degree of interpolated learning on retroactive inhibition and the overt transfer of specific responses. *Amer. J. Psychol.*, 53, 173-203.—*166-169, 355, 361*

MELTON, A. W., and STONE, G. R. (1942) The retention of serial lists of adjectives over short time-intervals with varying rates of presentation. *J. exp. Psychol.*, 30, 295-310.—*101*

MELTON, A. W., and VON LACKUM, W. J. (1941) Retroactive and proactive inhibition in retention: evidence for a two-factor theory of retroactive inhibition. *Amer. J. Psychol.*, 54, 157-173.—*355*

MILLER, J. (1939) The rate of conditioning of human subjects to single and multiple conditioned stimuli. *J. gen. Psychol.*, 20, 399-408.—*75*

MILLER, N. E. (1935) A reply to "Sign-gestalt or conditioned reflex?" *Psychol. Rev.*, 42, 280-292.—*114*

MILLER, N. E. (1944) Experimental studies in conflict. In J. McV. Hunt, edit., *Personality and the behavior disorders.* New York, Ronald, 431-465.—*361*

MILLER, N. E., and DOLLARD, J. (1941) *Social learning and imitation.* New Haven, Yale Univ. Press, xiv, 341 pp.—*77-79, 299*

MINAMI, H., and DALLENBACH, K. M. (1946) The effect of activity upon learning and retention in the cockroach. *Amer. J. Psychol.*, 59, 1-58.—*161, 164*

MINIUM, E., *see* Tolman and Minium (1942).

MOORE, A. R., and WELCH, J. C. (1940) Associative hysteresis in larval amblystoma. *J. comp. Psychol.*, 29, 283-292.—*353*

MOORE, M. G. (1930) Gestalt vs. experience. *Amer. J. Psychol.*, 42, 453-455.—*186*

MORGAN, C. L. (1894) *Introduction to comparative psychology.* London, Scott, xiv, 382 pp.—*343*

MORRIS, C. (1946) *Signs, language and behavior.* New York, Prentice-Hall, xii, 365 pp.—*271*

MOWRER, O. H. (1940) Anxiety-reduction and learning. *J. exp. Psychol.*, 27, 497-516.—*107, 115, 347*

MOWRER, O. H. (1946) The law of effect and ego psychology. *Psychol. Rev.*, 53, 321-334.—*231*

MOWRER, O. H., and JONES, H. (1945) Habit strength as a function of the pattern of reinforcement. *J. exp. Psychol.*, 35, 293-311.—*112, 113, 274*

MOWRER, O. H., and LAMOREAUX, R. R. (1942) Avoidance conditioning and signal duration—a study of secondary motivation and reward. *Psychol. Monogr.*, 54, No. 247, iii, 34 pp.—*107*

MUENZINGER, K. F. (1934a) Motivation in learning. I. Electric shock for correct response in the visual discrimination habit. *J. comp. Psychol.*, 17, 267-277.—*277, 299*

MUENZINGER, K. F. (1934b) Motivation in learning. II. The function of electric shock for right and wrong responses in human subjects. *J. exp. Psychol.*, 17, 439-448.—*277, 299*

MUENZINGER, K. F. (1938a) The law of effect. *Psychol. Rev.*, 45, 215-218.—*323*

MUENZINGER, K. F. (1938b) Vicarious trial and error at a point of choice. I. A general survey of its relation to learning efficiency. *J. genet. Psychol.*, 53, 75-86.—*299, 324*

MUENZINGER, K. F. (1942) *Psychology: The science of behavior.* New York, Harper, xi, 441 pp.—*299, 323*

MUENZINGER, K. F., BERNSTONE, A. H., and RICHARDS, L. (1938) Motivation in learning. VIII. Equivalent amounts of electric shock for right and wrong responses in a visual discrimination habit. *J. comp. Psychol.*, 26, 177-185.—*277, 299*

MUENZINGER, K. F., and DOVE, C. C. (1937) Serial learning: I. Gradients of uniformity and variability produced by success and failure of single responses. *J. gen. Psychol.*, 16, 403-413.—*44*

MUENZINGER, K. F., and FLETCHER, F. M. (1936) Motivation in learning. VI. Escape from electric shock compared with hunger-food tension in the visual discrimination habit. *J. comp. Psychol.*, 22, 79-91.—*277, 299*

MUENZINGER, K. F., and FLETCHER, F. M. (1937) Motivation in learning. VII. The effect of an enforced delay at the point of choice in the visual discrimination habit. *J. comp. Psychol.*, 23, 383-392. —*277, 299*

MUENZINGER, K. F., and NEWCOMB, H. (1935) Motivation in learning. III. A bell signal compared with electric shock for right and wrong responses in the visual discrimination habit. *J. comp. Psychol.*, 20, 85-93.—*277, 299*

MUENZINGER, K. F., and NEWCOMB, H. (1936) Motivation in learning. V. The relative effectiveness of jumping a gap and crossing an electric grid in a visual discrimination habit. *J. comp. Psychol.*, 21, 95-104.—*277, 299*

MUENZINGER, K. F., and WOOD, A. (1935) Motivation in learning. IV. The function of punishment as determined by its temporal relation to the act of choice in the visual discrimination habit. *J. comp. Psychol.*, 20, 95-106.—*277, 299*

MÜLLER, G. E., and PILZECKER, A. (1900) Experimentelle Beiträge zur Lehre vom Gedächtnis. *Z. Psychol.*, Erbgd. 1, 300 pp.—*161*

MURPHY, G., *see* Levine and others (1942), Proshansky and Murphy (1942).

MURRAY, H. A., and others (1938) *Explorations in personality.* New York, Oxford Univ. Press, xiv, 761 pp.—*263*

NEWCOMB, H., *see* Muenzinger and Newcomb (1935, 1936).

NEWMAN, E. B. (1939) Forgetting of meaningful material during sleep and waking. *Amer. J. Psychol.*, 52, 65-71.—*164, 170, 208*

NISSEN, H. W., *see* Cowles and Nissen (1937).

NOWLIS, H. H. (1941) The influence of success and failure on the resumption of an interrupted task. *J. exp. Psychol.*, 28, 304-325. —*229*

NYSWANDER, D. B., *see* Stone and Nyswander (1927).

OLSON, W. C., and DAVIS, S. I. (1941) The adaptation of instruction in reading to the growth of children. *Educ. Meth.*, 20, 71-79.—*259*

ORR, D. W., and WINDLE, W. F. (1934) The development of behavior in chick embryos: The appearance of somatic movements. *J. comp. Neurol.*, 60, 271-283.—*246*

OSGOOD, C. E. (1946) Meaningful similarity and interference in learning. *J. exp. Psychol.*, 36, 277-301.—*161, 162, 165*

OVSIANKINA, M. (1928) Die Wiederaufnahme unterbrochener Handlungen. *Pyschol. Forsch.*, 11, 302-379.—*212, 229, 233*

PACHAURI, A. R. (1935) A study of gestalt problems in completed and interrupted tasks. *Brit. J. Psychol.*, 25, 447-457.—*229*

PATTON, E. K. (1933) The problem of insightful behavior. *Psychol. Monogr.*, 44, 98-124.—*260*

PAVLOV, I. P. (1927) *Conditioned reflexes.* (Trans. by G. V. Anrep) London, Oxford Univ. Press, xv, 430 pp.—*15, 55, 76, 112*

PAVLOV, I. P. (1928) *Lectures on conditioned reflexes.* (Trans. by W. H. Gantt) New York, International, 414 pp.—*55*

PEAK, H. (1933) Reflex and voluntary reactions of the eyelid. *J. gen. Psychol.*, 8, 130-156.—*117*

PERIN, C. T. (1942) Behavior potentiality as a joint function of the amount of training and the degree of hunger at the time of extinction. *J. exp. Psychol.*, 30, 93-113.—*115*

PERIN, C. T. (1943*a*) A quantitative investigation of the delay-of-reinforcement gradient. *J. exp. Psychol.*, 32, 37-51.—*93*

PERIN, C. T. (1943*b*) The effect of delayed reinforcement upon the differentiation of bar responses in white rats. *J. exp. Psychol.*, 32, 95-109.—*93, 109*

PERKINS, D. T., *see* Hull and others (1940).

PERKINS, F. T. (1932) Symmetry in visual recall. *Amer. J. Psychol.*, 44, 473-490.—*198, 208*

PERKINS, F. T. (1933) A study of cerebral action currents in the dog under sound stimulation. *Psychol. Monogr.*, 44, 1-29.—*260*

PERKINS, F. T., *see also* Wheeler and Perkins (1932).

PERKINS, F. T., and WHEELER, R. H. (1930) Configurational learning in the goldfish. *Comp. Psychol. Monogr.*, 7, No. 31, 50 pp.—*260*

PERRY, R. B. (1918) Docility and purposiveness. *Psychol. Rev.*, 25, 1-20.—*263*

PETERSON, J. (1922) Learning when frequency and recency factors are negative. *J. exp. Psychol.*, 5, 270-300.—*53*

PILZECKER, A., *see* Müller and Pilzecker (1900).

PORTER, J. M., Jr., *see* Karn and Porter (1946).

POSTMAN, L., and ALPER, T. G. (1946) Retroactive inhibition as a function of temporal point of interpolation. *Amer. J. Psychol.*, 59, 439-449.—*161, 166*

PRATT, C. C. (1936) Review of Koffka's *Principles of gestalt psychology. Amer. J. Psychol.*, 48, 527-531.—*207*

PRATT, C. C., *see also* Boring and others (1945).

PRIOR, G., *see* Irwin and others (1934).

PROSHANSKY, H., and MURPHY, G. (1942) The effects of reward and punishment on perception. *J. Psychol.*, 13, 295-305.—*334*

RAPAPORT, D. (1942) *Emotions and memory.* Baltimore, Williams and Wilkins, ix, 282 pp.—*225*

RAZRAN, G. H. S. (1937) Conditioned responses: a classified bibliography. *Psychol. Bull.*, 34, 191-256.—*359*

RAZRAN, G. H. S. (1938) Transposition of relational responses and generalization of conditioned responses. *Psychol. Rev.*, 45, 532-538.—*85*

RESTORFF, H. VON (1933) Analyse von Vorgängen im Spurenfeld. I. Über die Wirkung von Bereichsbildungen im Spurenfeld. *Psychol. Forsch.*, 18, 299-342.—*44, 170, 208*

RETHLINGSHAFER, D. (1941) Measures of tendency-to-continue. *J. genet. Psychol.*, 59, 109-124; 125-138.—*229*

REYNOLDS, B. (1945*a*) The acquisition of a trace conditioned response as a function of the magnitude of the stimulus trace. *J. exp. Psychol.*, 35, 15-30.—*58*

REYNOLDS, B. (1945*b*) A repetition of the Blodgett experiment on 'Latent learning.' *J. exp. Psychol.*, 35, 504-516.—*285*

RIBBLE, M. A. (1943) *The rights of infants.* New York, Columbia Univ. Press, x, 118 pp.—*121*

RICE, P. B. (1946) The ego and the law of effect. *Psychol. Rev.*, 53, 307-320.—*231*

RICHARDS, I. A. (1943) *Basic English and its uses.* New York, Norton, 114 pp.—*48*

RICHARDS, L., *see* Muenzinger and others (1938).

RITCHIE, B. F. (1944) Hull's treatment of learning. *Psychol. Bull.*, 41, 640-652.—*114*

RITCHIE, B. F. (1947) Studies in spatial learning. III. Two paths to the same location and two paths to different locations. *J. exp. Psychol.*, 37, 25-38.—*293, 355*

RITCHIE, B. F., *see also* Tolman and others (1946*a*, 1946*b*, 1947*a*, 1947*b*).

ROBINSON, E. S. (1920) Some factors determining the degree of retroactive inhibition. *Psychol. Monogr.*, 28, No. 128, 57 pp.—*161*

ROBINSON, E. S. (1927) The 'similarity' factor in retroaction. *Amer. J. Psychol.*, 39, 297-312.—*162, 163*

ROBINSON, E. S. (1930) Review of Köhler's *Gestalt psychology. J. genet. Psychol.*, 37, 431-450.—*208*

ROBINSON, E. S. (1932*a*) *Association theory today.* New York, D. Appleton-Century viii, 142 pp.—*147-150, 165, 175*

ROBINSON, E. S. (1932*b*) *Man as psychology sees him.* New York, Macmillan, 376 pp.—*155, 172*

ROBINSON, E. S. (1935) *Law and the lawyers.* New York, Macmillan, xi, 348 pp.—*172*

ROBINSON, E. S., and BROWN, M. A. (1926) Effect of serial position upon memorization. *Amer. J. Psychol.*, 37, 538-552.—*176*

ROBINSON, E. S., and HERON, W. T. (1922) Results of variations in length of memorized material. *J. exp. Psychol.*, 5, 428-448.—*176*

ROCK, R. T., JR. (1935) The influence upon learning of the quantitative variation of after-effects. *Teach. Coll. Contr. Educ.*, No. 650, xii, 78 pp.—*51*

ROCK, R. T., JR. (1940) Thorndike's contributions to the psychology of learning. *Teach. Coll. Rec.*, 41, 751-761.—*50*

ROCK, R. T., JR., *see also* Thorndike and Rock (1934).

ROSENZWEIG, S. (1933) Preferences in the repetition of successful and unsuccessful activities as a function of age and personality. *J. genet. Psychol.*, 42, 423-441.—*229*

ROSENZWEIG, S., and MASON, G. (1934) An experimental study of memory in relation to the theory of repression. *Brit. J. Psychol.*, 24, 247-265.—*229*

ROSS, R. T., *see* Hull and others (1940).

ROUSE, R. O. (1943) The oscillation function in compound trial-and-error learning. *J. comp. Psychol.*, 35, 177-186—*115*

SANDIFORD, P. (1942) Connectionism: Its origins and major features. *Natl. Soc. Stud. Educ.*, 41st Yearbook, Part II, 97-140.—*50*

SANFORD, R. N. (1936) The effects of abstinence from food upon imaginal processes. *J. Psychol.*, 2, 129-136.—*333*

SANFORD, R. N. (1937) The effects of abstinence from food upon imaginal processes: a further experiment. *J. Psychol.*, 3, 145-159. —*333*

SANFORD, R. N. (1946) Age as a factor in the recall of interrupted tasks. *Psychol. Rev.*, 53, 234-240.—*229*

SCHLOSBERG, H. (1937) The relationship between success and the laws of conditioning. *Psychol. Rev.*, 44, 379-394.—*360*

SCHLOSBERG, H., *see also* Kappauf and Schlosberg (1937).

SCHNEIRLA, T. C., *see* Maier and Schneirla (1935, 1942).

SCHWARZ, G. (1927) Über Rückfälligkeit bei Umgewöhnung. *Psychol. Forsch.*, 9, 86-158.—*233*

SEARS, P. S. (1940) Levels of aspiration in academically successful and unsuccessful children. *J. abnorm. (soc.) Psychol.*, 35, 498-536.—*223, 225*

SEARS, P. S. (1941) Level of aspiration in relation to some variables of personality: clinical studies. *J. soc. Psychol.*, 14, 311-336.—*223, 225*

SEARS, P. S., *see also* Lewin and others (1944).

SEARS, R. R. (1936a) Functional abnormalities of memory with special reference to amnesia. *Psychol. Bull.*, 33, 229-274.—*225*

SEARS, R. R. (1936b) Review of Lewin's *A dynamic theory of personality. Psychol. Bull.*, 33, 548-552.—*232*

SEARS, R. R. (1939) Review of Guthrie's *The psychology of human conflict. Psychol. Bull.*, 36, 829-830.—*75*

SEASHORE, H., and BAVELAS, A. (1941) The functioning of knowledge of results in Thorndike's line-drawing experiment. *Psychol. Rev.*, 48, 155-164.—*31*

SELLS, S. B., *see* Woodworth and Sells (1935).

SETTLAGE, P. H., *see* Harlow and Settlage (1934).

SEWARD, J. P. (1942) An experimental study of Guthrie's theory of reinforcement. *J. exp. Psychol.*, 30, 247-256.—75

SEWARD, J. P. (1947) A theoretical derivation of latent learning. *Psychol. Rev.*, 54, 83-98—288

SHEFFIELD, F. D., *see* Jenkins and Sheffield (1946).

SHERRINGTON, C. S. (1906) *The integrative action of the nervous system.* New Haven, Yale Univ. Press, xvi, 411 pp.—62, 159

SHURRAGER, P. S., and SHURRAGER, H. C. (1946) The rate of learning measured at a single synapse. *J. exp. Psychol.*, 36, 347-354.—334

SINGER, E. A. (1911) Mind as an observable object. *J. Phil. Psychol. sci. Meth.*, 8, 180-186.—53

SKAGGS, E. B. (1925) Further studies in retroactive inhibition. *Psychol. Monogr.*, 34, No. 161, v, 60 pp.—162

SKINNER, B. F. (1931) The concept of the reflex in the description of behavior. *J. gen. Psychol.*, 5, 427-458.—143

SKINNER, B. F. (1932) Drive and reflex strength. *J. gen. Psychol.*, 6, 22-37; 38-48.—145

SKINNER, B. F. (1933) 'Resistance to extinction' in the process of conditioning. *J. gen. Psychol.*, 9, 420-429.—122. 145

SKINNER, B. F. (1935a) The generic nature of the concepts of stimulus and response. *J. gen. Psychol.*, 12, 40-65.—145

SKINNER, B. F. (1935b) Two types of conditioned reflex and a pseudo type. *J. gen. Psychol.*, 12, 66-77.—145

SKINNER, B. F. (1936a) The reinforcing effect of a differentiating stimulus. *J. gen. Psychol.*, 14, 263-278.—145

SKINNER, B. F. (1936b) The effect on the amount of conditioning of an interval of time before reinforcement. *J. gen. Psychol.*, 14, 279-295.—145

SKINNER, B. F. (1936c) The verbal summator and a method for the study of latent speech. *J. Psychol.*, 2, 71-107.—144, 145

SKINNER, B. F. (1937) The distribution of associated words. *Psychol. Rec.*, 1, 71-76.—144

SKINNER, B. F. (1938) *The behavior of organisms.* New York, D. Appleton-Century, ix, 457 pp.—107, 112-132, 135, 143, 145, 348, 354

SKINNER, B. F. (1939) The alliteration in Shakespeare's sonnets: A study in literary behavior. *Psychol. Rec.*, 3, 186-192.—144

SKINNER, B. F. (1941) A quantitative estimate of certain types of sound-patterning in poetry. *Amer. J. Psychol.*, 54, 64-79.—144, 145

SKINNER, B. F. (1944) Review of Hull's *Principles of behavior. Amer. J. Psychol.*, 57, 276-281.—82, 114, 135

SKINNER, B. F. (1945) The operational analysis of psychological terms. *Psychol. Rev.*, 52, 270-277.—144

SKINNER, B. F., *see also* Boring and others (1945) Cook and Skinner (1939), Estes and Skinner (1941), Heron and Skinner (1937, 1940).

SKINNER, B. F., and HERON, W. T. (1937) Effects of caffeine and benzedrine upon conditioning and extinction. *Psychol. Rec.*, 1, 340-346.—*145*

SMITH, M. B., *see* Hilgard and Smith (1942)

SMITH, S., and FITCH, E. E. (1935) Skill and proprioceptor pattern. *J. genet. Psychol.*, 46, 303-310.—*75*

SMITH, S., and GUTHRIE, E. R. (1921) *General psychology in terms of behavior.* New York, Appleton, xii, 270 pp.—*54, 62, 153*

SNODDY, G. S. (1920) An experimental analysis of a case of trial and error learning in the human subject. *Psychol. Monogr.*, 28, No. 124, 78 pp.—*239*

SNODDY, G. S. (1935) *Evidence for two opposed processes in mental growth.* Lancaster, Pa., Science Press, 103 pp.—*255, 260*

SNODDY, G. S. (1945) Evidence for a universal shock factor in learning. *J. exp. Psychol.*, 35, 403-417.—*255, 256*

SNYGG, D. (1936) Mazes in which rats take the longer path to food. *J. Psychol.*, 1, 153-166.—*247, 248, 260*

SNYGG, D. (1941) The need for a phenomenological system of psychology. *Psychol., Rev.*, 48, 404-424.—*360*

SPEMANN, H. (1938) *Embryonic development and induction.* New Haven, Yale Univ. Press, xii, 401 pp.—*235*

SPENCE, K. W. (1936) The nature of discrimination learning in animals. *Psychol. Rev.*, 43, 427-449.—*307, 355*

SPENCE, K. W. (1937) The differential response in animals to stimuli varying within a single dimension. *Psychol. Rev.*, 44, 430-444.—*85, 308, 309, 337, 355, 361*

SPENCE, K. W. (1939) A reply to Dr. Razran on the transposition of response in discrimination experiments. *Psychol. Rev.*, 46, 88-91. —*85*

SPENCE, K. W. (1941) Review of Köhler's *Dynamics in psychology. Psychol. Bull.*, 38, 886-889.—*208*

SPENCE, K. W. (1942*a*) The basis of solution by chimpanzees of the intermediate size problem. *J. exp. Psychol.*, 31, 257-271.—*115*

SPENCE, K. W. (1942*b*) Theoretical interpretations of learning. In F. A. Moss, edit., *Comparative psychology* (Revised edition). New York, Prentice-Hall, 280-329.—*9, 75, 114*

SPENCE, K. W. (1944) The nature of theory construction in contemporary psychology. *Psychol. Rev.*, 51, 47-68.—*91, 95, 360*

SPENCE, K. W. (1945) An experimental test of the continuity and non-continuity theories of discrimination learning. *J. exp. Psychol.*, 35, 253-266.—*309*

SPENCE, K. W. (1947) The role of secondary reinforcement in delayed reward learning. *Psychol. Rev.*, 54, 1-8.—*93, 110, 345*

SPENCE, K. W., *see also* Bergmann and Spence (1941).

SPENCE, K. W., and LIPPITT, R. (1940) 'Latent' learning of a simple maze problem with relevant needs satiated. *Psychol. Bull.*, 37, 429.—*286*

SPENCE, K. W., and LIPPITT, R. (1946) An experimental test of the sign-gestalt theory of trial and error learning. *J. exp. Psychol.*, 36, 491-502.—*286*

SPRAGG, S. D. S., *see* Wolfe and Spragg (1934).

STAUFFACHER, J. C., *see* Bills and Stauffacher (1937).

STEPHENS, J. M. (1934) A change in the interpretation of the law of effect. *Brit. J. Psychol.*, 24, 266-275.—*37, 44*

STEPHENS, J. M. (1941) The influence of symbolic punishment and reward upon strong and upon weak associations. *J. gen. Psychol.*, 25, 177-185.—*39*

STEPHENS, J. M. (1942) Expectancy vs. effect-substitution as a general principle of reinforcement. *Psychol. Rev.*, 49, 102-116.—*298*

STEVENS, S. S. (1939) Psychology and the science of science. *Psychol. Bull.*, 36, 221-263.—*360*

STONE, C. P., and NYSWANDER, D. B. (1927) Reliability of rat learning scores from the multiple-T maze as determined by four different methods. *J. genet. Psychol.*, 34, 497-524.—*283*

STONE, G. R., *see* Melton and Stone (1942).

STRATTON, G. M. (1896) Some preliminary experiments on vision without the inversion of the retinal image. *Psychol. Rev.*, 3, 611-617; 4, 341-360.—*10*

STROUD, J. B. (1932) Effect of complexity of material upon the form of learning curves. *Amer. J. Psychol.*, 44, 721-731.—*176*

SWENSON, E. J. (1941) *Retroactive inhibition: a review of the literature.* Minneapolis, Univ. Minnesota Press, 59 pp.—*161, 166*

SZYMANSKI, J. S. (1918) Versuche über die wirkung der Factoren, die als Antrieb zum Erlernen einer Handlung dienen können. *Pflüg. Arch. ges. Psysiol.*, 171, 374-385.—*271*

TAYLOR, D. W., and WRIGHT, S. T. H. (1947) Distributed practice in verbal learning and the maturation hypothesis. (To appear).—*255*

THORNDIKE, E. L. (1898) Animal intelligence: an experimental study of the associative processes in animals. *Psychol. Rev., Monog. Suppl.*, 2 No. 8, 109 pp.—*2, 19, 20*

THORNDIKE, E. L. (1903) *Educational psychology.* New York, Lemcke and Buechner, vii, 177 pp.—*29*

THORNDIKE, E. L. (1908) The effect of practice in the case of a purely intellectual function. *Amer. J. Psychol.*, 19, 374-384.—*51*

THORNDIKE, E. L. (1910) Practice in the case of addition. *Amer. J. Psychol.*, 21 483-486.—*51*

THORNDIKE, E. L. (1911) *Animal intelligence*. New York, Macmillan, viii, 297 pp.—*20, 50*

THORNDIKE, E. L. (1913*a*) *The original nature of man* (Educational psychology, I.) New York, Teachers College, vii, 327 pp.—*20, 22*

THORNDIKE, E. L. (1913*b*) *The psychology of learning*. (Educational psychology, II.) New York, Teachers College, xi, 452 pp.—*20-29, 49, 50, 150, 280*

THORNDIKE, E. L. (1922) *The psychology of arithmetic*. New York, Macmillan, xvi, 314 pp.—*50*

THORNDIKE, E. L. (1924) Mental discipline in high school studies. *J. educ. Psychol.*, 15, 1-22; 83-98.—*51*

THORNDIKE, E. L. (1927) The influence of primacy. *J. exp. Psychol.*, 10, 18-29.—*51*

THORNDIKE, E. L. (1932*a*) *The fundamentals of learning*. New York, Teachers College, xvii, 638 pp.—*31-33, 35, 50*

THORNDIKE, E. L. (1932*b*) Reward and punishment in animal learning. *Comp. Psychol. Monogr.*, 8, No. 39, 65 pp.—*32, 51*

THORNDIKE, E. L. (1933*a*) A proof of the law of effect. *Science*, 77, 173-175.—*35*

THORNDIKE, E. L. (1933*b*) An experimental study of rewards. *Teach. Coll. Contr. Educ.*, No. 580, 72 pp.—*35, 51*

THORNDIKE, E. L. (1933*c*) A theory of the action of the after-effects of a connection upon it. *Psychol. Rev.*, 40, 434-439.—*34*

THORNDIKE, E. L. (1935) *The psychology of wants, interests and attitudes*, New York, D. Appleton-Century, x, 301 pp.—*27, 31, 33, 35, 50*

THORNDIKE, E. L. (1940) *Human nature and the social order*. New York, Macmillan, xx, 1019 pp.—*31, 50*

THORNDIKE, E. L., and others (1927) *The measurement of intelligence*. New York, Teachers College, xxvi, 616 pp.—*46*

THORNDIKE, E. L., and others (1928) *Adult learning*. New York, Macmillan, x, 335 pp.—*50*

THORNDIKE, E. L., and LORGE, I. (1935) The influence of relevance and belonging. *J. exp. Psychol.*, 18, 574-584.—*51*

THORNDIKE, E. L., and ROCK, R. T., JR. (1934) Learning without awareness of what is being learned or intent to learn it. *J. exp. Psychol.*, 17, 1-19.—*51, 342*

THORNDIKE, E. L., and WOODWORTH, R. S. (1901) The influence of improvement in one mental function upon the efficiency of other functions. *Psychol. Rev.*, 8, 247-261, 384-395, 553-564.—*29*

THUNE, L. E., and UNDERWOOD, B. J. (1943) Retroactive inhibition as a function of degree of interpolated learning. *J. exp. Psychol.*, 32, 185-201.—*161*

THURSTONE, L. L. (1923) The stimulus-response fallacy in psychology. *Psychol. Rev.*, 30, 354-369.—*349*

TILTON, J. W. (1939) The effect of "right" and "wrong" upon the learning of nonsense syllables in multiple choice arrangement. *J. educ. Psychol.*, 30, 95-115.—*37, 44, 45*

TILTON, J. W. (1945) Gradients of effect. *J. genet. Psychol.*, 66, 3-19. —*37, 38, 45*

TINKLEPAUGH, O. L. (1928) An experimental study of representative factors in monkeys. *J. comp. Psychol.*, 8, 197-236.—*266*

TOLMAN, E. C. (1917) Retroactive inhibition as affected by conditions of learning. *Psychol. Monogr.*, 25, No. 107, 50 pp.—*289*

TOLMAN, E. C. (1932*a*) Lewin's concept of vectors. *J. gen. Psychol.*, 7, 3-15.—*290*

TOLMAN, E. C. (1932*b*) *Purposive behavior in animals and men.* New York, D. Appleton-Century, xiv, 463 pp.—*3, 83, 247, 261, 279-281, 292, 345*

TOLMAN, E. C. (1934) Theories of learning. In F. A. Moss, edit., *Comparative psychology*, New York, Prentice-Hall, 367-408.—*9, 282, 293*

TOLMAN, E. C. (1936) Connectionism; wants, interests, and attitudes. *Character & Pers.*, 4, 245-253.—*44, 51*

TOLMAN, E. C. (1937) The acquisition of string-pulling by rats— conditioned response or sign-gestalt? *Psychol. Rev.*, 44, 195-211. —*282*

TOLMAN, E. C. (1938*a*) The determiners of behavior at a choice points. *Psychol. Rev.*, 45, 1-41.—*19, 263, 265, 293, 361*

TOLMAN, E. C. (1938*b*) The law of effect. *Psychol. Rev.*, 45, 165-203. —*282, 298*

TOLMAN, E. C. (1939) Prediction of vicarious trial and error by means of the schematic sowbug. *Psychol. Rev.*, 46, 318-336.—*265, 337*

TOLMAN, E. C. (1941) Discrimination vs. learning and the schematic sowbug. *Psychol. Rev.*, 48, 367-382.—*265, 337, 361*

TOLMAN, E. C. (1942) *Drives toward war.* New York, D. Appleton-Century, xv. 118 pp.—*277, 289, 291, 292*

TOLMAN, E. C. (1945) A stimulus-expectancy need-cathexis psychology. *Science*, 101, 160-166.—*288, 291, 330*

TOLMAN, E. C., *see also* Geier and Tolman (1943) Honzik and Tolman (1936).

TOLMAN, E. C., and BRUNSWIK, E. (1935) The organism and the causal texture of the environment. *Psychol. Rev.*, 42, 43-77.—*261, 272*

TOLMAN, E. C., HALL, C. S., and BRETNALL, E. P. (1932) A disproof of the law of effect and a substitution of the laws of emphasis, motivation and disruption. *J. exp. Psychol.*, 15, 601-614.—*44, 276, 293*

TOLMAN, E. C., and HONZIK, C. H. (1930*a*) "Insight" in rats. *Univ. Calif. Publ. Psychol.*, 4, 215-232.—*269, 270*

TOLMAN, E. C., and HONZIK, C. H. (1930b) Introduction and removal of reward, and maze performance in rats. *Univ. Calif. Publ. Psychol.*, 4, 257-275.—*282, 283*

TOLMAN, E. C., and MINIUM, E. (1942) VTE in rats: overlearning and difficulty of discrimination. *J. comp. Psychol.*, 34, 301-306. —*293*

TOLMAN, E. C., RITCHIE, B. F., and KALISH, D. (1946a) Studies in spatial learning. I. Orientation and the short-cut. *J. exp. Psychol.*, 36, 13-24.—*268, 271, 272, 355*

TOLMAN, E. C., RITCHIE, B. F., and KALISH, D. (1946b) Studies in spatial learning. II. Place learning versus response learning. *J. exp. Psychol.*, 36, 221-229.—*267, 268, 355*

TOLMAN, E. C., RITCHIE, B. F., and KALISH, D. (1947a) Studies in spatial learning. IV. The transfer of place learning to other starting paths. *J. exp. Psychol.*, 37, 39-47.—*293, 355*

TOLMAN, E. C., RITCHIE, B. F., and KALISH, D. (1947b) Studies in spatial learning. V. Response learning vs. place learning by the non-correction method. *J. exp. Psychol.*, 37, 285-292.—*268, 355*

TROWBRIDGE, M. H., and CASON, H. (1932) An experimental study of Thorndike's theory of learning. *J. gen. Psychol.*, 7, 245-258.—*31*

TRYON, R. C. (1940) Studies in individual differences in maze ability. VII. The specific components of maze ability, and a general theory of psychological components. *J. comp. Psychol.*, 30, 283-335.—*330*

UNDERWOOD, B. J. (1945) The effect of successive interpolations on retroactive and proactive inhibition. *Psychol. Monogr.*, 59, No. 273, 33 pp.—*161, 168, 355*

UNDERWOOD, B. J. *see also* Thune and Underwood (1943).

VAN ORMER, E. B. (1932) Retention after intervals of sleep and of waking. *Arch. Psychol.*, N. Y., 21, No. 137, 49 pp.—*164, 176*

VERNON, P. E. (1935-1936) Review of Koffka's *Principles of gestalt psychology. Character & Pers.*, 4, 92-94.—*208*

VOEKS, V. (1945) What fixes the correct response? *Psychol. Rev.*, 52, 49-51.—*75, 110*

VOEKS, V. (1948) Postremity, recency and frequency as bases for prediction in the maze situation. *J. exp. Psychol.* (To appear.)—*75*

VON LACKUM, W. J., *see* Melton and Von Lackum (1941).

WADE, M., *see* Lashley and Wade (1946).

WALLACH, H., and HENLE, M. (1941) An experimental analysis of the law of effect. *J. exp. Psychol.*, 28, 340-349.—*39, 41, 44*

WALLACH, H., and HENLE, M. (1942) A further study of the function of reward. *J. exp. Psychol.*, 30, 147-160.—*41*

WARD, L. B. (1937) Reminiscence and rote learning. *Psychol. Monogr.*, 49, No. 220, v, 64 pp.—*100, 101*

WATERS, R. H. (1928) The influence of tuition on ideational learning. *J. gen. Psychol.*, 1, 534-547.—*176*

WATERS, R. H. (1937) The principle of least effort in learning. *J. gen. Psychol.*, 16, 3-20.—*247*

WATSON, J. B. (1907) Kinesthetic and organic sensations: their role in the reactions of the white rat to the maze. *Psychol. Monogr.*, 8, No. 33, vi, 100 pp.—*58*

WATSON, J. B. (1913) Psychology as the behaviorist views it. *Psychol. Rev.*, 20, 158-177.—*52*

WATSON, J. B. (1914) *Behavior. An introduction to comparative psychology.* New York, Holt, xii, 439 pp.—*53*

WATSON, J. B. (1916) The place of the conditioned reflex in psychology. *Psychol. Rev.*, 23, 89-116.—*54*

WATSON, J. B. (1919) *Psychology from the standpoint of a behaviorist.* Philadelphia, Lippincott, ix, 429 pp.—*54*

WATSON, J. B. (1925) *Behaviorism.* New York, Norton, 251 pp.—*11*

WEAVER, H. B., *see* Irwin and others (1934).

WEISS, A. P. (1929) *A theoretical basis of human behavior* (Revised edition). Columbus, Ohio, R. G. Adams, xvii, 479 pp.—*243*

WEISS, P. (1939) *Principles of development.* New York, Holt, ix, 601 pp.—*235, 236, 245*

WELCH, J. C., *see* Moore and Welch (1940).

WELCH, L. (1945) An examination of Dr. Leeper's review of Hull's *Principles of behavior. J genet. Psychol.*, 67, 3-15.—*114*

WENDT, G. R. (1937) Two and one-half year retention of a conditioned response. *J. gen Psychol.*, 17, 178-180.—*59*

WENTINK, E. (1938) The effects of certain drugs and hormones upon conditioning. *J. exp. Psychol.*, 22, 150-163.—*145*

WERTHEIMER, M. (1912) Experimentelle Studien über das Sehen von Bewegungen. *Z. Psychol.*, 61, 161-265.—*177*

WERTHEIMER, M. (1923) Untersuchungen zur Lehre von der Gestalt, II. *Psychol. Forsch.*, 4, 301-350. [Translated and condensed as "Laws of organization in perceptual forms" in Ellis (1938), pages 71-88]—*183*

WERTHEIMER, M. (1925) Über Schlussprozesse im produktiven Denken. *Drei Abhandlungen zur Gestalttheorie.* Berlin, Erlangen, 164-184. [Translated and condensed as "The syllogism and productive thinking" in Ellis (1938), pages 274-282.]—*208*

WERTHEIMER, M. (1945) *Productive thinking.* New York, Harper, x, 224 pp.—*195-197, 207, 340*

WHEELER, R. H. (1929) *The science of psychology.* New York, Crowell, xvii, 556 pp.—*234, 260*

WHEELER, R. H. (1932) *The laws of human nature.* New York, Appleton, xiv, 235 pp.—*260*

WHEELER, R. H. (1935*a*) Organismic vs. mechanistic logic. *Psychol. Rev.*, 42, 335-353.—*260*

WHEELER, R. H. (1935*b*) A set of postulates for educational theory. I. The background. *J. educ. Res.*, 28, 321-333.—*260*

WHEELER, R. H. (1940) *The science of psychology.* (Second edition) New York, Crowell, xviii, 436 pp.—*234, 238, 241, 246-248, 257, 259, 260*

WHEELER, R. H. (1946) Climate and human behavior. In P. L. Harriman, edit., *Encyclopedia of psychology.* New York, Philosophical Library, 78-86.—*260*

WHEELER, R. H., *see also* Perkins and Wheeler (1930).

WHEELER, R. H., and PERKINS, F. T. (1932) *Principles of mental development.* New York, Crowell, xxvi, 529 pp.—*234, 239, 240, 258, 260*

WHITE, R. K. (1943) The case for the Tolman-Lewin interpretation of learning. Psychol. Rev., 50, 157-186.—*290*

WHITE, R. K., *see also* Lewin and others (1939).

WICKENS, D. D. (1940) Conditioned response data and the holistic point of view. *Psychol. Rev.*, 47, 155-168.—*320, 360*

WINDLE, W. F., *see* Orr and Windle (1934).

WOLFE, J. B. (1934) The effect of delayed reward upon learning in the white rat. *J. comp. Psychol.*, 17 1-21.—*93*

WOLFE, J. B., and SPRAGG, S. D. S. (1934) Some experimental tests of 'reasoning' in white rats. *J. comp. Psychol.*, 18, 455-469.—*312*

WOLFLE, D. L., *see* Gulliksen and Wolfle (1938).

WOLFLE, H. M. (1930) Time factors in conditioning finger-withdrawal. *J. gen. Psychol.*, 4, 372-378.—*92*

WOLFLE, H. M. (1932) Conditioning as a function of the interval between the conditioned and the original stimulus. *J. gen. Psychol.*, 7, 80-103.—*92*

WOOD, A., *see* Muenzinger and Wood (1935).

WOODBURY, C. B. (1943) The learning of stimulus patterns by dogs. *J. comp. Psychol.*, 35, 29-40.—*115*

WOODROW, H. (1939) Review of Lewin's *Conceptual representation and the measurement of psychological forces. Psychometrika*, 4, 175-176.—*232*

WOODROW, H. (1942) The problem of general quantitative laws in psychology. *Psychol. Bull.*, 39, 1-27.—*361*

WOODWORTH, R. S. (1906) Imageless thought. *J. Phil. Psychol. sci. Meth.*, 3, 701-708.—*160*

WOODWORTH, R. S. (1918) *Dynamic psychology.* New York, Columbia Univ. Press, 210 pp.—*62, 153, 159, 175, 231*

WOODWORTH, R. S. (1930) Dynamic psychology. In C. Murchison, edit., *Psychologies of 1930.* Worcester, Mass., Clark Univ. Press, 327-336—*176*

WOODWORTH, R. S. (1931) *Contemporary schools of psychology*
New York, Ronald, vi, 232 pp.—*18*
WOODWORTH, R. S. (1937) Situation- and goal-set. *Amer. J. Psychol.*,
50, 130-140.—*160, 161*
WOODWORTH, R. S. (1938) *Experimental psychology.* New York,
Holt, xi, 889 pp.—*18, 172, 175, 198*
WOODWORTH, R. S. (1943) The adolescence of American psychology.
Psychol. Rev., 50, 10-32.—*174*
WOODWORTH, R. S. (1947) Reinforcement of perception. *Amer. J.
Psychol.*, 60, 119-124.—*337*
WOODWORTH, R. S., *see also* Thorndike and Woodworth (1901).
WOODWORTH, R. S., and SELLS, S. B. (1935) An atmosphere effect in
formal syllogistic reasoning. *J. exp. Psychol.*, 18, 451-460.—*176,
311*
WRIGHT, S. T. H., *see* Taylor and Wright (1947).
WULF, F. (1922) Über die Veränderung von Vorstellungen (Ge-
dächtnis und Gestalt). *Psychol. Forsch.*, 1, 333-373. [Translated
and condensed as "Tendencies in figural variation" in Ellis
(1938), pages 136-148.]—*187, 198, 208*

YACORZYNSKI, G. K., and GUTHRIE, E. R. (1937) A comparative study
of involuntary and voluntary conditioned responses. *J. gen.
Psychol.*, 16, 235-257.—*75*
YERKES, R. M. (1916) The mental life of monkeys and apes: a study
of ideational behavior. *Behav. Monogr.*, 3, No. 12, iv, 145 pp.—*180*
YERKES, R. M. (1927) The mind of a gorilla: I. *Genet. Psychol.
Monogr.*, 2, 1-193.—*190*
YERKES, R. M. (1943) *Chimpanzees: A laboratory colony.* New
Haven, Yale Univ. Press, xv, 321 pp.—*192*
YOUNG, P. T. (1933) Review of Tolman's *Purposive behavior in ani-
mals and men. Amer. J. Psychol.*, 45, 177-178.—*293*

ZEIGARNIK, B. (1927) Das Behalten erledigter und unerledigter Hand-
lungen. *Psychol. Forsch.*, 9, 1-85. [Translated and condensed as
"On finished and unfinished tasks" in Ellis (1938), pages 300-314.]
—*212, 226, 233*
ZENER, K. (1937) The significance of behavior accompanying condi-
tioned salivary secretion for theories of the conditioned response.
Amer. J. Psychol., 50, 384-403.—*295, 324*
ZIPF, G. K. (1935) *The psycho-biology of language.* Boston, Hough-
ton Mifflin, ix, 336 pp.—*144*
ZIRKLE, G. A. (1946a) Success and failure in serial learning. I. The
Thorndike effect. *J. exp. Psychol.*, 36, 230-236.—*41*
ZIRKLE, G. A. (1946b) Success and failure in serial learning. II. Isola-
tion and the Thorndike effect. *J. exp. Psychol.*, 36, 302-315.—*42*
44

SUBJECT INDEX